W9-BTJ-804

Teaching
Foreign-Language
Skills

WILGA M. RIVERS

Teaching Foreign-Language Skills

WINGATE COLLEGE LIBRARY
WINGATE, N. C.

The University of Chicago Press   *Chicago and London*

Standard Book Number: 226–72096–9
Library of Congress Catalog Card Number: 68–26761

The University of Chicago Press, Chicago 60637
The University of Chicago Press, Ltd., London

© 1968 by The University of Chicago. All rights reserved.
Published 1968. Second Impression 1969.
Printed in the United States of America

CONTENTS

v

45923

PREFACE

For Students and Teachers

This book has been written especially for those of you who are preparing to become foreign-language teachers. It will also be useful to practicing teachers who wish to familiarize themselves with contemporary thinking on matters of language and the processes of language learning. Some of you will expect a book of this type to tell you exactly what techniques to use to present any particular aspect of the language you are teaching to students at a certain level. You may be surprised to read instead a theoretical discussion of the linguistic and pedagogical background to the teaching of each language skill. This book is intended to prepare you for a foreign-language teaching career, not for the lessons you may have to give in your first few weeks in the classroom. You will find a great deal of information on specific techniques for classroom teaching, but the desirability of employing these techniques will, in each case, be discussed in the light of what is known of the nature of the skill to be taught.

During your teaching career you will be faced from time to time with changes in emphases and recommendations from various quarters for the adoption of new procedures. Your studies in methodology should give you an understanding of the foundations of foreign-language pedagogy so that you may be able to read and assess intelligently new trends as they develop and be sufficiently flexible to adjust to changing circumstances. You will then be well prepared, when you have had more experience, to think out for yourselves new ways of presenting language material which are consistent with the objectives you have set yourself but which are also valid procedures from a theoretical point of view. It is the opportunity to innovate in this way which will keep your interest in your chosen vocation at a high level.

It is intended that this book be used in association with regular visits to classrooms to watch master teachers coping with the types of problems which are discussed in these pages. These visits will make the discussion of the material in each chapter more real to you and will be a source of ideas on how to approach specific problems which arise from the course of study. Hints of this type have little place in a method textbook, partly because your particular needs in this area are unpredictable, and partly because original ways of presenting some structure or varying the classroom presentation at some specific point are best acquired from discussion with teachers whom you have watched at work. During your student-teacher training you should begin to make notes of ideas of this type, gathered while you have been observing other teachers' classes.

Many of you may wonder why, in the pages of this book, no examples are given in any particular language. There are several reasons for this omission. First of all, the theoretical and practical discussion is intended to guide teachers of many different languages. It would not be feasible to include examples from more than four or five of these languages (and even these would make the book considerably longer), yet the examples given might not be the ones about which you yourself were seeking information. In the Annotated Reading Lists, indications are given of books which supply examples in the languages most commonly taught at secondary level. In your method class the instructor will work with you on the practical application of the ideas expounded to the particular language you will be teaching.

This book is, then, only part of a course in methods of foreign-language teaching. It is intended as a source of ideas for discussion in and out of class, and as a guide to further study for all who read it. The carefully selected readings appended to each chapter are intended to complement the textbook and should not be ignored. Those who wish to study some area of theory in greater detail will find many useful readings listed in the footnotes. Reading and discussion are, of course, not enough. It is the author's earnest hope that these will be followed by enlightened experimentation in the classroom which will lead to an improvement in foreign-language presentation in our secondary schools.

ACKNOWLEDGMENTS

Now that my task is finished, I should like to register here my sincere thanks to Dr. Nicolas Morcovescu for his readiness at all times to discuss problems in linguistics and to give me advice on further reading in this area; and to Mr T. J. Quinn and Mr J. A. Wheeler, both experienced and successful classroom teachers, who have always been most willing to discuss with me the usefulness and validity of various sections of this work as it proceeded. Finally, I should like to thank Mrs Arlette Patron, whose very efficient typing saved me much toil in the final stages.

In a book of this type it is inevitable that the ideas of many other writers in this field will be reflected and developed. Where the derivation of ideas was clear to me, I have included the writings which stimulated my thinking in the Annotated Reading Lists or referred to them in the footnotes. My debt to the authors of the books listed in the Bibliography is, in many cases, equally great. To all these scholars I offer my sincere thanks.

MONASH UNIVERSITY
VICTORIA, AUSTRALIA

1

Objectives and Methods

International understanding, intellectual training, cultural enrichment, interpersonal communication, a feeling for language (his own and those of others): amid a welter of such slogans, the trainee teacher approaches his foreign-language teaching career with some understandable uncertainty. What, he asks himself, is the role of foreign-language instruction in the educational program, and in what way should he present the language to his students to make it most useful?

As a part of his initial training, he is usually sent into several classrooms to see the way experienced teachers are approaching their task. Let us join him in an inconspicuous place at the back of the room.

In Classroom A he takes a seat out of the view of the students and opens his notepad. In the rows before him the students are opening their foreign-language textbooks and preparing for the day's lesson. They are about to begin a new section. Before them on the page is a reading selection with, above it, two or three long columns of new vocabulary items with native-language equivalents. These the students have been asked to learn by heart the night before. As this memorization is a rather boring chore, some of the students are hastily babbling over to themselves some of the words they have not yet learned. The lesson begins with a quick written test of these new words. Students, when asked to give their answers, spell out the foreign-language words letter by letter in their native language, because they feel shy and uncertain about pronouncing them in front of their classmates. The teacher is not very satisfied with the result of this test, but the work for the day must be covered, so he moves on. The students are asked to read out in the foreign language the selection in the book before them. One after another they stumble through the sentences. After a while this reading around the class is omitted because the procedure is too painful for the teacher and too embarrassing for the students. For a few sentences the teacher reads the passage aloud to the class himself. Then the students are asked to look over the rest of the passage silently, because the reading-aloud process seems rather wasteful of class time for the little it achieves.

Then begins the process of translation. One after another students translate the sentences of the passage into their native language, with occasional help from the teacher. Things are progressing well: the teacher can now pass on to what he feels is the real business of the day. On the chalkboard, he sets out what he considers to be a lucid outline of the use of the past tense, examples of which have been artificially and cunningly worked into the reading passage. He warms to his task, explaining in great detail in the native language the traditional rules for the use of this particular tense in all the logically possible situations. Where these explanations involve terminology with which the students are presumed not to be familiar, he takes some time to teach this terminology as it applies to the grammar of the native language and then applies it to the foreign language. The students copy into their books various rules, examples, and what seem to them to be even more numerous exceptions. The teacher asks a few questions. When the students appear to have grasped the point of the grammatical exposition they settle down to spend the rest of the lesson on the not-too-demanding task of writing out paradigms and filling in blanks in grammatical exercises, or they translate from the native language into the foreign language sentences in which the past tense is required. For this latter exercise the students are presented with sentences which have been artificially constructed to include all possible aspects of the rules being studied. Many of these sentences are very unlikely to be of any real value to the students who frequently distort the original meaning as they try to construct their own version of the foreign language. Exercises the students have not finished and the learning of rules and paradigms are assigned for home study, with the extra spice of a few irregular verbs and some more vocabulary items. As our would-be teacher moves on to the next classroom, his mind goes back over what he has just observed. On reflection, it occurs to him that he heard very little of the foreign language during the lesson—a little reading aloud at the beginning of the lesson and a few isolated words and phrases from time to time. Most of what he did hear in the foreign language was halting and badly pronounced. Perhaps time and further knowledge will bring improvement, he says to himself—and wonders.

In Classroom B an energetic teacher comes into the room greeting the class in the foreign language; the students reply in the foreign language and wait expectantly. The teacher continues to talk in the foreign language about objects in the classroom, to ask questions, and to give orders. As the students obey the orders they are given, they tell the class in the foreign language what they have been doing, and the class tells the teacher what has been performed. The lesson then develops around a picture which illustrates an area of vocabulary and certain activities associated with the situation depicted. In this lesson, the picture shows some people shopping. The teacher describes in the foreign language what the students can see in the picture, demonstrating the meaning of new action or relational words by miming until the class looks enlightened. The students repeat the new words and phrases and, in response to questions, try to form their own sentences in the foreign language on the model they have heard. They do this with a greater or lesser degree of accuracy according to the individual. When they appear to have understood and assimilated the area of vocabulary or usage to which they have been introduced and have shown evidence of being able to use it orally, they read a passage of similar content aloud from their books, reading after the teacher at first and then individually. The passage is not translated by the teacher or the students, but the teacher asks questions about it in the foreign language, to which the students reply in the foreign language. Where further difficulties of vocabulary or structure occur these are explained in the foreign language, and students make notes on them, again in the foreign language. The lesson ends with a song in which the students join with gusto. Throughout the lesson there has been a great deal of activity by teacher and students alike. Not surprisingly the teacher, having conducted several lessons of this type during the morning, is very glad to sit down in the staff common room for a quiet cup of coffee with our observer.

On his way to Classroom C our student teacher begins to wonder whether the two teachers he has so far observed can be considered to be engaged in the same activity. There are more surprises in store for him.

Arriving a little late at Classroom C, our observer sees books again in evidence. This time the students are using small readers rather than large textbooks. On looking into the reader which the teacher has given him to peruse, the trainee teacher notices that it contains a continuous reading text of some twenty pages, written in a simple style in the foreign language within the limits of a frequency word-count.[1] As new words occur in the text, they are explained in the foreign language at the foot of the page. The story seems to be interesting and amusing. Since this reader is new to the class, the teacher is endeavoring to interest the students in its contents. With the help of some pictures he describes in simple foreign-language phrases the setting of the story, which is in the country where the language is spoken. He talks very briefly about the main characters, writing their names on the chalkboard. To interest the students still further in the story he reads the first section of it aloud in the foreign language in as interesting a way as possible, with the students following the text in their books. He asks in the native language a few questions about what he has been reading and then tells the students to reread the section silently, looking for answers to certain questions which they were unable to answer. When they have reread this part of the text he asks them more questions, this time in the foreign language; the students find the answers in the text, framing their replies in the foreign language. For the second half of the lesson, the students form working pairs, or choose to work on

1 For a discussion on the establishing of frequency word counts, see M. Halliday, A. McIntosh, and P. Strevens, *The Linguistic Sciences and Language Teaching* (London, 1964), pp. 190–98.

their own, and settle down to read as much of the story as they can during the remainder of the lesson. A quiet murmur is heard throughout the room as the students concentrate on their task. As difficulties arise, they seek the teacher's help. As they reach the end of certain divisions of the reader, they take the book to the teacher, who asks them questions in the native language about what they have just read. Sometimes he gives them a short true-false test in the foreign language to see whether they have understood the details of the story. As the lesson draws to a close, the teacher asks how many pages the various pairs or individuals have read, and congratulates those who have read the most. For home study, the students are asked to write answers in the foreign language to questions on the section they have been reading.

From Classroom D comes the sound of voices. The lesson has already begun. As the observer settles down, he hears the class repeating sentences in the foreign language in chorus, imitating the pronunciation and intonation of the teacher. They are learning the various utterances in a dialogue based on an everyday incident in the life of a student in the country where the language is spoken. A native-language version of the sentences the students are repeating has been pinned to the chalkboard. The students are not looking at this version, but are intent on watching the lip movements and expressions of the teacher. From time to time, however, a student will glance at the native-language sentences as if to refresh his mind on the meaning of what he is saying. The students' textbooks are closed. When a pair of sentences is being repeated well in chorus, the teacher asks halves of the class to repeat this section, one in response to the other. When these smaller groups are repeating well, he asks the students to repeat the sentences by rows. Since the sentences seem now to be well memorized the teacher calls on individuals to repeat the new sentences, sometimes in association with sentences learned the preceding day. If the individuals falter, the teacher returns to interchanges between small groups or reverts to choral repetition until the difficult part has been mastered. After a certain amount of material has been learned in this fashion students act out the conversational interchange in pairs. After the dialogue sentences are well learned, the students open their books and practice reading together after the teacher what they have just been repeating.

The time has now come for closer study of parts of the dialogue sentences, so the teacher moves on to pattern drilling. The class repeats several times after the teacher a pattern sentence containing a structural element which the students will need to be able to use quite flexibly in new utterances. The students then repeat several other sentences of identical structure but with minimal changes of vocabulary. At a word cue from the teacher the class constructs a slightly different sentence on the same structural pattern. At another cue the structure is again produced with a further slight variation of lexical content. Seven or eight changes of this type are effected by the class in chorus as they continue their practice. At one stage the class appears to hesitate and some students look puzzled. At this point the teacher makes a short comment on the sentences being constructed, drawing attention to what they have in common. The practice then continues with greater assurance on the part of the students. When the choral repetition is ringing out clearly and confidently the teacher gives the cues to small groups, and finally to individuals, to make sure that all have assimilated the uses of the structure being drilled. As a consolidating activity, the students are asked to write out the structure drill they have been repeating aloud, adding lexical variants of their own choosing. For home study, the students take away small plastic disks which they will play over to help them memorize thoroughly the dialogue sentences they have been learning; they are also asked to transcribe several times certain words and phrases which present difficulties in writing.

As our observer makes his way back to the teachers' common room, he reflects on what he has seen during the day. Why, he wonders, have all these foreign-language teachers been conducting their lessons so differently when they must surely be moving toward a common goal?

Over coffee he endeavors to find out what the four teachers have been trying to achieve. Teacher A seems a little disconcerted when asked about his long-range objectives in teaching a foreign language. "It is tremendously important that the students know their grammar," he says, "and they'll never pass their examinations if they cannot write a good, accurate translation." Beyond this, he seems to think that the aims of his lessons are self-evident: "They must know their past tense," he adds, in a way which precludes further discussion. Teacher B says: "I want them to be able to speak the language and understand it, and I want them to know something about the people who speak the language. I don't want them to translate. I want them to think in the foreign language as they do in their own, whether they are engaged in conversation, reading, or writing." "But our students will rarely have the opportunity to speak the language," interrupts Teacher C. "When they leave my classes I want them to be able to pick up a book or a magazine in the foreign language and read it without having to stop and translate every phrase or look up every second word in a bilingual dictionary. This is the most important thing for them to learn in the foreign-language class." "I want them to be able to do all these things," says Teacher D. "I want to train them carefully in all the language skills: in listening and speaking as well as in reading and writing. I want to lay solid foundations for these skills by giving them confidence in the active use of the structural patterns of the language. I try to train them in each skill in succession in relation to any section of the work so that what has been learned in one skill area acts as a foundation for learning in the next. . . . And I am most anxious for them to understand the cultural patterns and ways of thinking of the speakers of the language," he adds.

AIMS AND OBJECTIVES

Our observer feels bewildered. He has watched the work of four experienced teachers and he has found that each of these teachers has a different combination and priority of objectives in mind. He has seen widely differing techniques for achieving these objectives even when the objectives as stated seemed to coincide. Where does the trainee teacher begin? At least one fact emerges clearly from the situation described: it is the teacher's objectives which determine the way he approaches the organization of his language lesson.

It is objectives, then, that the trainee teacher must consider first. Many teachers whose classes he will observe have never gone back in their thinking to this foundational stage; their teaching techniques as a result are diverse and imitative. Frequently such teachers teach as they were taught, by teachers who taught as they were taught, and techniques appropriate in another era are perpetuated. From time to time such teachers add a few techniques which they have seen demonstrated or of which they have read, but their approach to their lessons remains fundamentally unchanged. Their students may not find the lessons particularly interesting or exciting, but if they pass examinations of a traditional type their teachers are satisfied. Such teachers continue to conduct their classes as they have always conducted them, unaware of the fact that objectives in foreign-language teaching may be changing around them and that their teaching may have become anachronistic and irrelevant to the young people who pass through their classes. With the passing of time, new situations arise for a nation and its people and these establish priorities of objectives for the foreign-language teacher, who must be continually aware of such changes if his teaching is to be appropriate to the generation of students before him.

It is a useful exercise for teachers or trainee teachers to set down in some order of priority their long-range objectives in the teaching of a foreign language. On analysis, the answers of any substantial group of teachers will usually be seen to fall into six categories. The priorities ascribed to these categories of objectives will vary from country to country and from period to period, but each of the six will appear, either in implicit or in explicit form, among those listed. The six classes of objectives are as follows: to develop the student's intellectual powers through foreign-language study; to increase the student's personal culture through the study of the great literature and philosophy to which it is the key; to increase the student's understanding of how language functions and to bring him, through the study of a foreign language, to a greater awareness of the functioning of his own language; to teach the student to read the foreign language with comprehension so that he may keep abreast of modern writing, research, and information; to bring the student to a greater understanding of people across national barriers by giving him a sympathetic insight into the ways of life and ways of thinking of the people who speak the language he is learning; to provide the student with skills which will enable him to communicate orally, and to some degree in writing, with the speakers of another language and with people of other nationalities who have also learned this language. Each of these objectives has at some time or in some place predominated in the stated aims of foreign-language teaching. ✓

It is not proposed here to set out in detail the history of foreign-language teaching. Teachers should, however, be familiar with the leading personalities and movements which have determined many of the features of the major teaching methods; they will then be able to reexamine the appropriateness of certain techniques in their own situation in full cognizance of the aims of those who first advocated them. The references in the Annotated Reading List at the end of this chapter should be studied with careful attention. From this reading it will be evident that the various foreign-language teaching methods have derived from an educational philosophy or a pedagogical theory which has satisfied certain demands or requirements either of the period in which it has flourished or of the peculiar situation of the people who have adopted it. The first aim listed, the development of the student's intellectual powers, was particularly emphasized at the time when modern language teachers were trying to justify their area of study as of equal value with the study of the classical languages, Greek and Latin. As a result, modern language teaching took on many of the traditional features of the teaching of these languages. Since at this period faculty psychology [2] formed the basis for educational theory, it is not surprising that language teachers justified the inclusion of their subject in the educational system by asserting its value for training in memory and in the application of logical processes. In conformity with this aim, class lessons were devoted to the

2   The mind was considered to have certain faculties (such as those of concentration, reasoning, analyzing, and remembering) which could be better trained through the study of certain subjects than others. Classical studies, philosophy, and mathematics were considered to be particularly appropriate for such mind-training. See R. F. Butts and L. A. Cremin, *A History of Education in American Culture* (New York, 1953), pp. 176–79, and R. S. Woodworth, *Contemporary Schools of Psychology*, rev. ed. (New York, 1948), pp. 12–13.

learning of rules and the presumably logical application of these in the construction of artificial sentences in the foreign language, and there was much memorizing of paradigms and lengthy vocabulary lists. As with the classical languages, the matter of pronunciation was considered of minor concern.

At the period when secondary and university level education were available only to an intellectual and social elite it was feasible to emphasize the learning of a language as the key to the great literature and philosophy of another culture, since the students of advanced modern language courses had already spent a number of years in close study of the language and had studied in some detail the literature and philosophy of their own culture. With the growing availability of advanced study for an ever increasing proportion of the population and the great increase in subjects in the curriculum at secondary and tertiary level, this situation no longer holds. Students today have much less time in which to acquire a knowledge of a foreign language as one small part of their training for some vocation or profession. Many of our advanced language students belong to the first generation of their families to have the opportunity to study at advanced secondary or undergraduate level and do not have the background of literary culture which would make the foreign literature more accessible to them. This aim is, therefore, less appropriate as a principal objective than in an earlier period, although it will always have its place at the advanced level.

As we shall see, the last four of the aims listed above are the most relevant for today's student at the secondary level. In the last few decades there has been an increase in research into language as such, and the interest of many in foreign languages has been stimulated as a result. This research has led to a reexamination of language-teaching methods. With the development of rapid communications and the proliferation of international contacts on the group and individual level has come a realization of the need to be able to communicate readily with people who speak other languages and to be able to understand their ways of thinking and reacting. With rapid advances in all branches of knowledge, it has become imperative for many people to be able to read some of the enormous quantity of information being poured out by printing presses all over the world.

In a present-day foreign-language class all four of these aims will be pursued: teaching more about the nature and functioning of language, teaching students to communicate in a foreign language, developing understanding of the people with whom one wishes to communicate, and teaching students to read all kinds of material fluently in the foreign language. The order of priority assigned to these aims will be determined by geographical situation, national demands, and the interests and aspirations of the type of student being taught. The most appropriate method for the present time will be the one which leads most efficiently to the achievement of all four of these objectives, which closer examination will show to be interdependent. Understanding of the nature of language is basic to a methodology which develops effective communication skills; effective communication is impossible without some understanding of the culture of the speakers of the language; fluency in reading with direct comprehension derives from the ability to think in the language, which is established by prior training in the active communication skills of listening and speaking; for many types of reading material mere comprehension of the printed words is valueless without the ability to interpret what one is reading in the light of cultural patterns and attitudes.

EVALUATING FOREIGN-LANGUAGE TEACHING METHODS

As we read the story of foreign-language teaching over several centuries and analyze the theoretical positions at the base of various approaches, we can distinguish two main streams of thought, each developing an integrated system of techniques devolving from its fundamental premises. For convenience, we shall term representatives of these two groups the formalists and the activists. Obviously many teachers have taken a position between these two, applying formalist techniques for some sections of the work or for some levels of instruction and activist techniques for others. The distinction is, however, a useful one in the consideration of the rationale of various teaching methods.

In the early teaching of the classical languages, these two tendencies may be discerned. When Latin was required for oral communication among scholars and as the medium of instruction it was taught through active use of the language by the student. Gradually a more formalist approach became general, with emphasis on the study of forms and on knowledge of the categories to which they were traditionally assigned. The learning of rules and their application in every detail became the chief occupation of numbers of students, and this approach was adopted by many teachers of modern languages. Voices were continually raised, however, urging the presentation of the language in its most useful form, and the gradual acquisition of language forms through using them frequently in realistic language situations.

Formalists have mostly relied on a deductive form of teaching, moving from the statement of the rule to its application in the example; activists have advocated the apprehension of a generalization by the student himself after he has heard and used certain forms in a number of ways—a process of inductive learning. Formalists with a commendable regard for thoroughness have sometimes become too preoccupied with the pedantic elaboration of fine details of grammar, whereas activists have consistently urged a functional approach to structure whereby the student is first taught what is most useful and most generally applicable, being left to discover at later stages the rare and the exceptional. As a result, formalist teaching has often been based on artificial exercises and led to a stilted use of language, emphasizing the features of the written language used in literary work, whereas activist teaching has sought to familiarize the student first with the forms of language used for general communication in speech and in less formal writing, teaching the more literary forms of the language at an advanced level only. In actual classroom procedures, a strictly formalist approach has favored a passive student situation where the student receives instruction and applies it as directed. On the other hand, to be effective, an activist approach requires ready participation by the student in the learning process in order to develop language skills through active use.

These divergent attitudes toward various aspects of foreign-language teaching have led to a very different order of priorities in the teaching of the four skills, the formalist tending to value highly skill in reading and accurate writing (especially as demonstrated by the ability to translate), the activist laying emphasis on oral understanding and speaking as basic to fluent reading and original writing. Teachers who see their work as essentially a process of instruction tend to adopt the formalist approach; teachers for whom teaching is a process in which student and instructor interact and in which the student learns by discovery and performance tend to favor the activist approach.

Languages have been taught to students down the centuries by a variety of methods, and with a competent teacher the student learns what the teacher feels it is important for him to learn. No matter what method is in vogue or is officially advocated, the individual teacher who is professionally alert will adapt its techniques to his purposes, to his own personality, and to what he feels to be appropriate for the particular class he is teaching, having regard to their age level, their situation, and their educational needs. Any method ceases to be efficient when it is applied inflexibly, according to set procedures, in every situation. As we study the evolution of language-teaching methods we see what is most effective in each method being taken up again at a later date, elaborated and refashioned, so that the best of the past is not lost but serves the purposes of the present.

MAJOR FOREIGN-LANGUAGE TEACHING METHODS

As a prelude to the study of techniques for teaching the various language skills, we shall examine the tenets of the major methods which have held sway in the past century: the grammar-translation method, the direct method, the reading method, and the audio-lingual method.[3]

In evaluating the effectiveness of these methods the trainee teacher should keep certain questions in mind. He should ask

3   The term "fundamental skills" method was suggested by the Modern Language Association of America as an alternative to audio-lingual method and is sometimes used in the literature. See also chapter 2, note 1.

WINGATE COLLEGE LIBRARY
WINGATE, N. C.

himself what are the objectives of the method under discussion and whether these objectives are appropriate for the teaching situation in which he will find himself. He should then consider whether the techniques advocated by the proponents of the method achieve the stated objectives in the most economical way (that is, whether they provide the most direct route to these objectives). Since techniques may be economical in the attainment of objectives but intensely boring, inhibiting, or overdemanding for the students, he should next ask whether these techniques maintain the interest and enthusiasm of the learners, and at what level of instruction. In view of the rapidly expanding body of high school and undergraduate students in our day he will then wish to consider whether these techniques are appropriate for all types of students. Finally, he will keep in mind a question which is often overlooked: whether the demands these techniques make on the teacher are such that he can carry a full day's teaching load. Some methods are excellent for a one-hour demonstration class but demand so much preparation or expenditure of effort by the teacher that they have to be modified in a normal teaching situation.

With these five questions in mind, we shall now consider the objectives and techniques of each of the methods we have listed.

THE GRAMMAR-TRANSLATION METHOD

In Classroom A, we saw a grammar-translation class in action. Such classes will be found in schools all over the world. This method cannot be traced back to the tenets of any particular master teacher, but it is clearly rooted in the formal teaching of Latin and Greek which prevailed in Europe for many centuries. When Latin was no longer learned as a language for communication between scholars, its primacy as a matter for study could not be justified on utilitarian grounds; indeed, utility was considered at that time an inappropriate criterion to be applied to any area of advanced study. The learning of Latin and Greek was then justified as an intellectual discipline: the mind being trained, it was asserted, by logical analysis of the language, much memorization of complicated rules and paradigms, and the application of these in translation exercises. Latin and Greek were further justified as the key to the thought and literature of a great and ancient civilization. The reading and translation of texts was, therefore, of great importance, as were writing exercises in imitation of these texts. Modern languages were accepted as reputable areas of study only after much controversy and opposition from the supporters of classical studies. They had to prove themselves of equal value for the training of the mind and as the key to a great literature and civilization. It was inevitable, then, that modern-language teaching methods should be modeled at this stage on the methods already employed for the teaching of an ancient language no longer in use for communication, the original pronunciation of which was even in doubt.

The classical method has persisted in many areas, despite attempts to introduce methods which may be considered more appropriate to the teaching of a living language, with a contemporary literature, to high school students, whose range of abilities and interests is very wide. This resistance to change in methods may well have been due to the constant publication for school use of textbooks written by scholars not engaged in teaching at secondary level. Prepared in the quietness of a study away from the urgent realities of the classroom, many such textbooks are notable for the meticulous detail of their descriptions of the grammar of the language, based on the traditional categories of Latin and Greek grammar, their preoccupation with written exercises, especially translation exercises, and their lengthy bilingual vocabulary lists. They usually contain long extracts from great writers, chosen for their intellectual content rather than for the standard of difficulty of the language or their intrinsic interest for the adolescent student. These textbooks dominate the work of the teacher who follows this method, his most immediate aim becoming the completion of all the exercises in each lesson and the covering of all the lessons in the book in a given period of time. The teacher who was himself taught by this method and who has not had adequate training in modern-language teaching methodology continues this tradition. New textbooks modeled on the old tend to imitate the grammatical descriptions and exercises of their predecessors with the result that archaic structures and obsolete vocabulary and phrases continue to be taught to successive generations of students. A teacher wishing to use active methods who is forced to use such a textbook tries to introduce some practice in communication into his classes but is frustrated by the academic and unreal forms of language it contains and the enormous range of vocabulary, while his students are bored by the repetitive form of the innumerable written exercises.

This method, then, aims at inculcating an understanding of the grammar of the language, expressed in traditional terms, and at training the student to write the language accurately by regular practice in translating from his native language. It aims at providing the student with a wide literary vocabulary, often of an unnecessarily detailed nature; it aims at training the student to extract the meaning from foreign texts by translation into the native language and, at advanced stages, to appreciate the literary significance and value of what he has been reading. These aims are achieved in the classroom by long and elaborate grammatical explanations and demonstrations in the native language, followed by practice on the part of the student in the writing of paradigms, in the applying of the rules he has learned to the construction of sentences in the foreign language, and in the translation of consecutive passages of prose from the native to the foreign language. Texts in the foreign language are translated into the native language orally and in writing and, ideally, their literary and cultural significance is discussed, although in many classes, because of the limitation in the time available, this is done very perfunctorily, if at all. Students are expected to know the rules for the correct association of sounds with the graphic symbols in the foreign writing system, but are given little opportunity to practice these associations except in occasional reading practice in class and in the writing from dictation of passages which are usually of a literary character. The foreign language is not used in class to any extent, except when stereotyped questions may be asked about the subject matter of a reading passage, and the students answer in the foreign language with sentences drawn directly from the text. Often these questions are given in writing and answered in writing. Students taught by this method are frequently confused when addressed in the foreign language and may be very embarrassed when asked to pronounce anything themselves.

What, then, can be said in favor of this method? Applying our five questions, we find that it sets itself limited objectives, and that its techniques do achieve its objectives where the group of students being taught is highly intellectual and interested in abstract reasoning. Such students try to understand the logic of the grammar as presented; they learn the rules and exceptions and memorize the paradigms and vocabulary lists. They become reasonably adept at taking dictation and translating foreign-language texts into the native language. Their translation of native-language texts into the foreign language may not produce versions which sound natural to a native speaker, but at their best they are accurate, with careful attention to the many rules the students have been taught. The grammar-translation method is not successful, however, with the less intellectual, who muddle through, making many mistakes over and over again and thus building up cumulative habits of inaccuracy which are difficult to eradicate at a more advanced stage. Such students find foreign-language study very tedious and they drop out of the class as soon as this is permitted. The method is not too demanding on the teacher; when he is tired, he can always set the class a written exercise. The techniques described can be used with large groups who listen, copy rules, and write out exercises and correct them from the chalkboard. It is easy to make tests along the lines of the work that has been done in class and to assign grades for these. The teacher does not need to show much imagination in planning his lessons since he usually follows the textbook page by page and exercise by exercise.

The main defects of the method have been pointed out in the process of description. Little stress is laid on accurate pronunciation and intonation; communication skills are neglected; there is a great deal of stress on knowing rules and exceptions, but little training in using the language actively to express one's own meaning, even in writing. In an endeavor to practice the application of rules and the use of exceptional forms, the student is often trained in artificial forms of language, some of which are rare, some old-fashioned, many of little practical use. The language learned is mostly of a literary type, and the vocabulary is detailed and sometimes esoteric. The average student has to work hard at what he considers laborious and monotonous chores—vocabulary learning, translation, and endless written exercises—without much feeling of progress in the mastery of the language and with very little opportunity to express himself through it. His role in the classroom is, for the greater part of the time, a passive one—he absorbs and then reconstitutes what he has absorbed to satisfy his teacher.

DIRECT METHOD

Advocates of active classroom methods continued to make themselves heard in various countries throughout the nineteenth century,[4] and by the end of the century some of them had had considerable influence on foreign-language teachers. These theorists shared a common belief that students learn to understand a language by listening to a great deal of it and that they learn to speak it by speaking it—associating speech with appropriate action. This, they observed, was the way children learned their native language, and this was the way children who had been transferred to a foreign environment acquired a second language apparently without great difficulty. The various "oral" and "natural" methods which developed at this time can be grouped together as forms of the direct method, in that they advocated learning by the direct association of foreign words and phrases with objects and actions, without the use of the native language by teacher or student. Speech preceded reading, but even in reading students were encouraged to forge this direct bond between the printed word and their understanding of it without passing through an intermediate stage of translation into the native language. The ultimate aim was to develop the ability to think in the language, whether conversing, reading, or writing.

This new emphasis on the foreign language as the medium of

4   See P. Hagboldt, "The Teaching of Languages from the Middle Ages to the Present," in M. Newmark, ed., *Twentieth Century Modern Language Teaching* (New York, 1948), pp. 5–9; and E. A. Méras, *A Language Teacher's Guide,* 2d ed. (New York, 1962), pp. 35–45.

instruction in the classroom [5] meant that correct pronunciation became an important consideration. Since the study of phonetics had developed during the second half of the nineteenth century, teachers were able to make use of its findings on the mechanics of sound production and of its newly developed system of notation.[6] Direct-method teachers frequently began a language course with an introductory period during which students were taught the new sound system. Often, for an initial period of several months, the only representation students saw of the sounds they were learning to produce and discriminate was a phonetic notation. In this way they were able to develop correct pronunciation without being influenced by similarities between foreign- and native-language orthography.

A direct-method class provided a clear contrast with the prevailing grammar-translation classes. The course began with the learning of the foreign words and phrases for objects and actions in the classroom. When these could be used readily and appropriately, the learning moved to the common situations and settings of everyday life, the lesson often developing around specially constructed pictures of life in the country where the language was spoken. Where the meaning of words could not be made clear by concrete representation, the teacher resorted to miming, sketches, or explanations in the foreign language but never supplied native-language translations. From the beginning the students were accustomed to hear complete, meaningful sentences which formed part of a simple discourse, often in the form of a question-answer interchange. Grammar was not taught explicitly and deductively as in the grammar-translation class but was learned largely through practice. Students were encouraged to draw their own structural generalizations from what they had been learning by an inductive process. In this way, the study of grammar was kept at a functional level, being confined to those areas which were continually being used in speech. When grammar was taught

5 For an account of advocates of an oral approach to the teaching of foreign languages in the sixteenth, seventeenth, and eighteenth centuries, see Newmark (1948), pp. 2–5.
6 The notation referred to is the International Phonetic Alphabet (I.P.A.) the first version of which was published in 1888.

more systematically, at a later stage, it was taught in the foreign language with the use of foreign-language terminology.

When students were introduced to reading material, they read about things they had already discussed orally, the teacher preparing the students for reading selections by a preceding oral presentation of new words and new situations. Texts were read aloud by teacher and students, and the students were encouraged to seek direct comprehension by inferring meanings of unknown elements from the context rather than by seeking equivalents in a bilingual vocabulary list. Where the meaning could not be discovered in this way the teacher gave explanations in the foreign language. Students were never asked to translate passages into their native language; instead, their apprehension of the meaning was tested by questioning and discussion in the foreign language. They learned to write the language first of all by transcription, then by composing summaries of what they had been reading or simple accounts of what had been discussed. The classroom was continually filled with the sound of the foreign language, and all activity was closely linked with its use in speech and writing.

At its best, the direct method provided an exciting and interesting way of learning the foreign language through activity. It proved to be successful in releasing students from the inhibitions all too often associated with speaking a foreign tongue, particularly at the early stages. Its main defect, however, was that it plunged the student into expressing himself too soon in the foreign language in a relatively unstructured situation, with the result that he tended to develop a glib but inaccurate fluency, clothing native-language structures in foreign vocabulary. It was unrealistic to believe that the conditions of native-language learning could be re-created in the classroom with adolescent students. Unlike the infant learner, the student already possesses well-established native-language speech habits. These will inevitably determine the form in which he expresses himself unless he has been given systematic practice in foreign-language structure, particularly at the points where the foreign language and the native language do not run parallel. In unplanned discourse which arises from a situation created in the classroom, all kinds of structures may be heard or be needed by the speaker. It is very difficult to restrict their occurrence or to ensure that they will recur at regular intervals. In the direct method, there was not sufficient provision for systematic practice of structures in a planned sequence. As a result, students often lacked a clear idea of what they were trying to do and made haphazard progress.

Since students were required at all times to make a direct association between foreign phrase and situation, it was the highly intelligent student with well-developed powers of induction who profited most from the method, which could be very discouraging and bewildering for the less talented. As a result, the members of an average class soon diverged considerably from each other in degree of foreign-language acquisition. The method made great demands on the energy of the teacher. He had of necessity to be fluent in the language, and very resourceful, in order to make meaning clear in a variety of ways without resorting at any time to the use of the native language. The greatest success with this method was achieved in situations where the student could hear and practice the language outside the classroom. For these reasons many teachers who had taught for some time by the direct method began to modify it in a number of ways.

The direct method continues to flourish in its modified form in many areas. To counteract the tendency toward inaccuracy and vagueness, teachers reintroduced some grammatical explanation of a strictly functional kind, given in the native language, while retaining the inductive approach wherever possible. They also added more practice of grammatical structures, sometimes with the use of substitution tables, the forerunner of pattern drills. Where it was difficult to make the meaning of words and phrases clear by sketch or gesture, they would give a short explanation in the native language. They also reintroduced occasional translation of words and phrases as a check on comprehension of precise details in reading. This modified form of the direct method is very similar to what has been called the eclectic method. Eclecticists try to absorb the best techniques of all the well-known language-teaching methods into their classroom procedures, using them for the purposes for which they are most appropriate. The true eclecticist, as distinguished from the drifter who adopts new techniques cumulatively and purposelessly, seeks the balanced development of all four skills at all stages, while retaining the emphasis on an oral presentation first. He adapts his method to the changing objectives of the day and to the types of students who pass through his classes, gradually evolving a method which suits his personality as a teacher. The best type of eclectic teacher is imaginative, energetic, and willing to experiment. As a result his lessons are varied and interesting.

THE READING METHOD

After the publication in 1929 of the Coleman report as part of the *Modern Foreign Language Study* in the United States, it became clear that the majority of American students studied a foreign language for a period of two years only. The report maintained that the only objective which could be considered attainable in such a short period was the development of reading ability. Because teachers in other countries were reexamining their objectives in foreign-language study, this report had considerable influence. As a result of the Coleman recommendations teachers began to seek the most effective ways of developing the reading skill so that the graduate of a language course of limited duration would be capable of independent reading after his formal study of the language had ended. Students were to be trained to read the foreign language with direct apprehension of meaning, without a conscious effort to translate what they were reading. It was felt that facility in reading could not be developed unless the students were trained in correct pronunciation, comprehension of uncomplicated spoken language, and the use of simple speech patterns. The students could then read aloud to help them with comprehension, and "hear" the text mentally as they were reading silently. Writing was to be limited to exercises which would help the student to remember vocabulary and structures essential to the comprehension of the text. The study of grammar was to be specially geared to the needs of the reader, for whom quick recognition of certain verb forms, tenses, negations, and other modifications was important, but for whom active reproduction of such features was unnecessary.

Where the reading method was adopted, the study of the language began with an oral phase. In the first weeks the student was thoroughly initiated into the sound system of the language and became accustomed to listening to and speaking in simple phrases. It was maintained that the auditory image of the language that he was acquiring would assist him later when he turned to the reading of a text. After the introduction of reading there continued to be oral practice in association with the text; this usually took the form of reading aloud by the teacher or a student, and questions and answers on the text. The main part of the course was then divided into intensive and extensive reading. Intensive reading, under the teacher's supervision, was more analytic and was the source of material for grammatical study, for the acquisition of vocabulary, and for training in reading complete sentences for comprehension. The student was not encouraged to translate but was trained to infer the meaning of unknown words from the context or from cognates in his own or other languages. During this intensive reading the teacher was able to check in detail the degree of comprehension achieved by the student. For extensive reading the student read entirely on his own many pages of connected discourse graded to his level of achievement. Special readers were published which conformed to specific levels of word-frequency and idiom counts, and the student was guided by the teacher from level to level as his reading ability developed. In this way he acquired a large passive, or recognition, vocabulary. His comprehension of what he had read was tested by questions on the content of the reading material, not by translation. So that the students might read with greater appreciation of cultural differences, class projects were undertaken on the background of the country where the language was spoken and on the ways of life and customs of the people. These projects often entailed further reading in the foreign language as the student gathered the necessary information.

The reading method increased the ability of the better students to read in the foreign language but was a burden to students who had reading difficulties in their native language. The system of extensive reading gave students the opportunity to progress at their own rate; students within the same class could work with readers at different levels of difficulty. The method also aroused interest in the people who spoke the language, and a curiosity about their way of life.

If not sufficiently controlled, the system of extensive reading led to satisfaction with quantity rather than quality—number of pages read rather than degree of comprehension. Students were frequently content if they could pick out the main line of development of the thought, even if they were unable to answer questions of detail, particularly details dependent on structural elements rather than on lexical items. The system of graded readers, while valuable from the pedagogical point of view, gave a false impression of the level of reading achieved. It is very doubtful whether students of short courses in high schools were ever able to read ungraded material with ease and direct comprehension at the end of the course. As soon as they encountered ungraded material they were forced back into deciphering with the aid of a dictionary, and valuable training in the reading skill was wasted. As a justification for short language courses, the reading aim was thus spurious. Language courses which are not long enough to ensure a reasonable level of language mastery may be justified as providing an educational experience which gives some insight into the ways of thinking of another people and some realization of the problems of communication, but the degree to which language learned during such short courses will prove useful to the student must not be exaggerated.

The reading method for the most part produced students who were unable to comprehend and speak the language beyond the very simplest of exchanges. World War II and the increasingly closer contacts between nations made it apparent that the reading skill alone was not enough as the end product of a foreign-language course. In the next chapter we shall examine in some detail the audio-lingual method which developed in response to new needs.

AREAS OF CONTROVERSY

Can a foreign language be justified as a subject in the high school curriculum?

In the twentieth century there are many demands on the high school curriculum. The rapid development of new fields of knowledge and the overwhelming increase of information in established areas of study require foundational knowledge of many kinds to be imparted at secondary level, yet the number of hours in the school day remains constant. The curriculum must be continually reviewed in the light of present and future needs. Traditional acceptance can no longer justify the inclusion of any one subject in the program. Each must justify its place in the face of the claims made for others.

We may first ask whether foreign languages can be justified on the grounds of utility. Will foreign-language study at high school prove useful to the student after he has left school? In a society where the foreign language taught is either the national language which is not the native language of the student, a second language in widespread use, or the language of a neighboring country with which there is close and constant contact, the answer to this question will be in the affirmative. In societies where this is not the case, it will be very difficult to judge which of a number of languages will be of practical use to any particular student during his lifetime. It is undeniable that knowledge of one or another of the acknowledged languages of international communication can be of use in many careers in trade, commerce, international and national agencies, diplomacy, journalism, certain areas of science and engineering, librarianship, and, of course, teaching. Moving beyond the personal level, however, it is important in the modern age that there should be in most countries a large body of people able to communicate with persons of other nations in their own language. The geographical position, international relations, and cultural associations of the country will determine the appropriate languages to be offered.

To justify the place of foreign languages in the curriculum we need a more cogent argument than that of utility. There are very few subjects taught at high school level which can be irrefutably justified on the grounds of their ultimate usefulness to individual students. We must ask ourselves whether the study of a foreign language has anything to contribute to the total educational experience of the adolescent which such study alone can provide or which such study can provide more effectively than any other subject in the curriculum.

Foreign-language teachers should not underrate the educational value of the learning of a language other than one's own. Apart from the ability to communicate directly with people of other countries (both those who speak the language as natives and the great number who have also learned the language as a foreign language), the experience of learning a language by a conscious process and endeavoring to communicate in it gives students a deeper understanding of the nature and role of language, the forms and nuances of their own language, and the problems of communication. As they penetrate beyond the mere manipulation of language elements to the meanings which native speakers encode in their language they come to understand more intimately the ways of thinking and reacting of persons of another culture. These deeper meanings are often lost or disguised in translation of speech or writing. As students act out the role of the foreigner, trying to use his language as he would use it and see things as he would see them, reading what he would read, they are able to identify with him in a way which is not possible in a course in social studies or comparative literature in translation. This experience opens the door to a deeper understanding of another culture and a wider tolerance of different ideas and patterns of behavior.

Other advantages which devolve from knowledge of a foreign language are more frequently cited: the knowledge of a language provides ready access to its heritage of literature and thought; it introduces the student to an activity which can prove enjoyable and profitable to him in his leisure time (a factor increasing in importance as hours of work decrease in many occupations); it increases his interest in and enjoyment of travel; it enables him to correspond freely with persons in other countries for business or pleasure; it opens up to him sources of information for his occupational or leisure-time interests; properly presented it gives him experience in language learning which will enable him to learn another language more efficiently should this necessity arise in later life.

The arguments in favor of the learning of a foreign language which are set out above are valid only if the language is taught in such a way that these advantages do in fact accrue: if the language is so presented that the student does in fact learn to communicate and to apprehend meaning directly in reading, if he is in fact guided into an understanding of the culture of the speakers of the language, and if he is taught how to learn a language efficiently. In many language classes this is not only not the case, but the students acquire quite erroneous notions of what is involved in an act of communication; they come to look upon the foreign language as a code to be transformed in tedious fashion into their own code; and they see the foreign culture as peculiar, somewhat ridiculous, and obviously inferior to their own. In such cases the foreign language is hard to justify as an essential part of adolescent education.

The educational benefits which have been outlined are not, for the most part, attainable in short foreign-language courses at high school level. If the foreign language is retained in the curriculum, it must be established as a continuing study from the first to the last year of the junior and senior high school program, so that students have sufficient time to acquire some degree of facility in its use beyond the simple interchange of everyday banalities and to become acquainted with important aspects of the culture of which it is a part.

Should the opportunity to study a foreign language be limited to students of proven scholastic ability?

The attitude one takes to this question derives from one's philosophy of education. If the program of education for the individual child is designed from a utilitarian standpoint (that is, in order to provide the student with skills which will enable him to fill a useful role in society), then the study of a foreign language will be limited to those who are most likely to reach the stage of mastery where the foreign language can become an efficient tool in business, in diplomatic relationships, or as a key to sources of information. Since research has shown success in foreign-language study to be related to overall scholastic ability,[7] the study of a language would in this case be limited to an elite group.

If the educational program has as its basic aim providing each student with the opportunity to develop every aspect of his personality and talents to the fullest, then each student should have some experience of the learning of a foreign language. Through acting out the role of a foreigner he may come to realize that all men do not think and act alike and that "difference" does not necessarily mean inferiority or lack of

7 P. Pimsleur, "Testing in Foreign Language Teaching," in A. Valdman, ed., *Trends in Language Teaching* (New York, 1966), pp. 176–77.

moral principle. He should be given an insight into the achievements and problems of another group of people than those of his own society. He should also have the opportunity to examine with closer attention the tool of language which he uses every day, in order to understand more fully its nature and function.

The junior high school curriculum should provide the student with an organized introduction to the many avenues of human knowledge and experience: showing him the possibilities which lie before him, giving him some experience of what these avenues promise, and providing him with some of the elementary skills he will require to enter into these avenues. Since foreign language is one such avenue, all students should have the opportunity to savor what it offers. Taught by active methods, where the language is used and enjoyed and the people who speak the language are sympathetically presented, foreign-language study at the elementary level is accessible to all, although all do not assimilate it to the same degree or at the same pace. Some who do not appear to have outstanding gifts in other areas may find that they have a certain language aptitude and that this study interests them.

After the junior high school stage, the demands of the curriculum and the limitations of the school program will force many students to choose from among the many attractive avenues of study those which they wish to investigate more thoroughly and those for which they have already shown some aptitude. At this stage some will not continue with the foreign language, but they will have had the opportunity to enjoy some of the benefits of such a study. Others, however, will pursue the study further in order to acquire greater mastery and a deeper comprehension, through the language, of the foreign society.

The utilitarian aspect of education should acquire some real importance only at the advanced level of study where students are preparing for a career and must therefore devote their time more exclusively to skills which will serve their future purposes. At this stage some will choose foreign-language study as their main center of interest, while others will continue it in order to possess an auxiliary skill or as a fruitful source of future enjoyment.

APPENDIX

Values of Foreign Language Study

The study of a foreign language, like that of most other basic disciplines, is both a progressive *experience* and a progressive acquisition of a *skill*. At no point can the experience be considered complete, or the skill perfect. Many pupils study a foreign language only two years; longer time is of course needed to approach mastery. At *any* point, however, the progress made in a language, when properly taught, will have positive value and lay a foundation upon which further progress can be built. It is evident therefore that the expectancy of values to be derived from language study must be relative to the amount of time and effort devoted to it.

The study of a foreign language, skillfully taught under proper conditions, provides a *new experience,* progressively enlarging the pupil's horizon through the introduction to a new medium of communication and a new culture pattern, and progressively adding to his sense of pleasurable achievement. This experience involves:

1. The acquisition of a set of *skills*, which can become real mastery for professional use when practiced long enough. The international contacts and responsibilities of the United States make the possession of these skills by more and more Americans a matter of national urgency. These skills include:

a. The increasing ability to *understand* a foreign language when spoken, making possible greater profit and enjoyment in such steadily expanding activities as foreign travel, business abroad. foreign language movies and broadcasts.

b. The increasing ability to *speak* a foreign language in direct communication with people of another culture, either for business or for pleasure.

c. The ability to *read* the foreign language with progressively greater ease and enjoyment, making possible the broadening effects of direct acquaintance with the recorded thoughts of another people, or making possible study for vocational or professional (e.g., scientific or journalistic) purposes.

2. A new understanding of *language,* progressively revealing to the pupil the *structure* of language and giving him a new perspective

From Foreign Language Program Policy of the Modern Language Association of America in *PMLA*, pt. 2, September, 1956 on English, as well as an increased vocabulary and greater effectiveness in expression.

3. A gradually expanding and deepening knowledge of a foreign country—its geography, history, social organization, literature, and culture—and, as a consequence, a better perspective on American culture and a more enlightened Americanism through adjustment to the concept of differences between cultures.

Progress in any one of these experiences is relative to the emphasis given it in the instructional program and to the interests and aptitude of the learner. Language *skills*, like all practical skills, may never be perfected, and may be later forgotten, yet the enlarging and enriching results of the *cultural experience* endure throughout life.

ANNOTATED READING LIST

History of Modern Language Teaching

NEWMARK, M., ed. *Twentieth Century Modern Language Teaching: Sources and Readings.* New York: Philosophical Library, 1948. Pp. 1–86. Articles on leading movements and personalities in modern language teaching from the Middle Ages to the present day.

TITONE, RENZO. *Teaching Foreign Languages: An Historical Sketch.* Washington, D.C.: Georgetown University Press, 1968. Useful summaries of the approach to foreign-language teaching of many leading exponents through the centuries.

Teaching of Specific Languages

MARCKWARDT, ALBERT H. "Teaching English as a Foreign Language: A Survey of the Past Decade." *Linguistic Reporter,* Supplement 19 (October, 1967): 1–8.

WATTS, GEORGE B. "The Teaching of French in the United States: A History." *French Review,* 37, no. 1 (October, 1963): 9–165.

ZEYDEL, EDWIN H. "The Teaching of German in the United States from Colonial Times to the Present." In J. W. CHILDERS, DONALD D. WALSH and G. WINCHESTER STONE, JR., eds. *Reports of Surveys and Studies in the Teaching of Modern Foreign Languages.* New York: Modern Language Association of America, 1961. Pp. 285–308.

PARRY, ALBERT. *America Learns Russian.* Syracuse, N.Y.: Syracuse University Press, 1967.

LEAVITT, STURGIS E. "The Teaching of Spanish in the United States." In J. W. CHILDERS, *Reports,* pp. 309–26.

Methods of Foreign-Language Teaching

Direct Method (with modifications): SWEET, H. *The Practical Study of Languages.* London: Oxford University Press, 1964. Originally London: Dent, 1899. JESPERSEN, OTTO. *How to Teach a Foreign Language.* London: George Allen & Unwin Ltd., 1904. Reset 1961.

Eclectic Method: PALMER, H. E. *The Principles of Language-Study.* London: Oxford University Press, 1964. A reprint of the 1921 text.

Reading Method: WEST, MICHAEL. *Learning to Read a Foreign Language.* London: Longmans, 1941.

Audio-Lingual Method: BROOKS, NELSON. *Language and Language Learning.* New York: Harcourt, Brace & World, 1960.

The Value of Foreign-Language Study

HUEBENER, THEODORE. *Why Johnny Should Learn Foreign Languages.* Philadelphia: Chilton Co., 1961. Pp. 42–79. Practical reasons for learning foreign languages.

2

The Audio-Lingual Method

In the last few years, communication among nations has rapidly increased, with the growing volume of commerce, international radio and television programs, projects of technical assistance, and educational exchanges. Committees and congresses in most unlikely places discuss a multitude of subjects and plan a multitude of enterprises. There is an ever growing need for scholars and technicians to be conversant with research in progress in other countries. As a result of such developments, many people who have hitherto been indifferent have begun to appreciate the value of a thorough knowledge of a language other than their native language. Above all, there has been a worldwide awakening to the importance of being able to speak a foreign language and understand it when spoken by a native speaker, and a growing impatience with methods which teach students to read a foreign language fluently and write it accurately but leave the student helpless before the steady flow of native speech and the rapid fire of discussion. The new emphasis on being able to communicate in a foreign language has led to the coining of the term "aural-oral" for a method which aims at developing listening and speaking skills first, as the foundation on which to build the skills of reading and writing. As "aural-oral" was found to be confusing and difficult to pronounce, Nelson Brooks of Yale University suggested the term "audio-lingual" for this method.[1]

1 See comments in Nelson Brooks, *Language and Language Learning* (New York, 1960), p. 201. Although one publisher (Harcourt, Brace & World, New York, 1961) has used the name "A-LM Audio-Lingual

The designation "audio-lingual" will be used in this chapter, although the term "aural-oral" is still used by some teachers, and by some publishers of materials constructed on similar principles.

The origins of the audio-lingual method may be found in the work of the American structural linguists and cultural anthropologists who were working in the same climate of opinion as the behaviorist psychologists. In the twenties and thirties, the call was sounding for a strictly scientific and objective investigation of human behavior. In linguistics, this took the form of a descriptive approach to the study of language. Structural linguists tried to describe the sound patterns and word combinations of each language as they observed them in a corpus, without attempting to fit them into a preconceived framework based on the structures of Greek and Latin and of the languages derived from them. This descriptive approach was even more appropriate in view of the fact that the early work of these linguistic scientists was for the main part in the area of American Indian languages and other little-known non-European languages.

The descriptive approach led to research into what people really do say in their mother tongue, in contradistinction to what some traditional grammarians maintain they ought to say. (For most of the linguists in this American context the mother tongue was English.) Fries, for instance, examined mechanically recorded conversations and a large number of letters by ordinary people to find what were the characteristics of modern American English.[2] This nonprescriptive attitude toward language caused much heated debate like that which later followed the publication of the Third Edition of Webster's Dictionary. This edition gives place in its columns to the words people use, even though their acceptability may be

---

Materials" as a commercial trade name, the term "audio-lingual" as used in this chapter does not refer to these materials but to a method of teaching foreign languages which has been described in detail in Nelson Brooks's book. Because of some confusion between A-LM and M.L.A., the Modern Language Association of America suggested the term "fundamental skills" method.

2 See H. A. Gleason, Jr., *Linguistics and English Grammar* (New York, 1965), pp. 17–18; and C. C. Fries, *The Structure of English* (New York, 1952), p. 3.

questioned by those who consider themselves guardians of the canons of the language.[3] The structural linguists regarded language as a living, evolving thing, not as a static corpus of forms and expressions.

At this period, much research was being carried out by anthropologists into patterns of human behavior in a culture. To these students of behavior, language appeared as an activity learned in the social life of a people, just as were other culturally determined acts. Language use was a set of habits, established, as later behaviorist research in psychology was to suggest, by reinforcement or reward in the social situation. The native language as learned behavior is acquired by the infant in spoken form first, and this led to the theory that students acquire a foreign language more easily if it is presented in the spoken form before the written form. This notion seemed even more self-evident to the early linguistic scientists because many of the languages they were studying did not exist in written form, or possessed very little literature.

In *The National Interest and Foreign Languages* (pp. 74–75), Parker has listed the ways in which linguistic scientists felt that their conclusions about language could help the foreign-language teacher. They considered that their major contribution would be through a scientific analysis of the language to be taught which would bring out:

a) the system of mutually contrasting basic sounds, or "phonemes," and the conditions under which they appear;

b) the grammar, stated not in traditional terms of Western philosophy but in terms of the system of form classes, inflections, constructions, sentence types, and actually functioning "rules" as determined by analysis of utterances;

c) the contrasts between the learner's mother tongue and the language being learned.

Further help would be given to the foreign-language teacher by the study of the physiology of sound production and by considerations of the nature of language itself, which charac-

---

3 An indication is given, however, of their level of acceptability (e.g., some words are marked "substandard").

teristically exists as a system of spoken communication and only derivatively as a system of written communication.

The application of the principles of the linguistic scientists to the teaching of foreign languages came to the attention of the public in the early years of World War II. The American authorities discovered the degree to which the study of languages had been neglected in the United States when they were faced with a totally inadequate supply of interpreters for communication with their allies and with enemy contacts. In an attempt to rectify this situation as quickly as possible, they called for the help of the American Council of Learned Societies, whose members had already been at work analyzing lesser-known languages and developing intensive language-teaching programs in certain universities.

In this wartime setting, understanding a native speaker and speaking a language with near-native accent were first priorities. With small classes, native informants, explanations of structure by linguistic experts, and long hours of drilling and active practice with graded materials based on this analysis of structure, selected members of the armed forces acquired a high degree of aural-oral skill for the purposes and situations for which it was required.

After the war, foreign-language teachers and educational authorities became interested in techniques developed at this time, and also in those used extensively for teaching English to foreign students studying in the United States.[4] New teaching materials for high school and undergraduate study of the commonly taught languages (Spanish, French, German, and later Russian) were prepared by experienced teachers with the advice of linguistic scientists who had made descriptive analyses of these languages, and these teaching materials were tried out experimentally in schools. After successive revisions, the earliest materials of this type came on the American market in the late fifties.

At about the same time (1958) the American nation's con-

---

4 The most notable research center for methods and materials for teaching English to foreign students in American universities was the English Language Institute of the University of Michigan. See C. C. Fries, *Teaching and Learning English as a Foreign Language* (Ann Arbor, Mich., 1945).

cern about the foreign-language situation in schools found expression in the National Defense Education Act (N.D.E.A.). This act provided funds for research in foreign-language teaching and for intensive training courses for practicing teachers in listening and speaking skills, in the understanding of linguistic principles, and in the use of audio-lingual techniques in high schools, junior high schools, and elementary schools. Efforts have also been made to extend such methodological training to teachers of undergraduates (particularly those concerned with elementary language courses).

Interest in the audio-lingual method now extends to every continent. It has been enthusiastically endorsed by some teachers and accepted with reserve by others, as has happened with all new approaches to foreign-language teaching. Like all living ideas, it is in a process of evolution, and some of the more controversial elements of the first proposals are being modified through the experiences of many teachers and students.

Concurrently with these developments in method came new aids for teaching in the form of magnetic tape and language laboratory equipment, and it was soon found that these were very useful for the teaching of listening and speaking skills. The use of tapes and laboratories should not, however, be presumed to indicate teaching by audio-lingual techniques. A teacher without a tape recorder may teach by a purely audio-lingual method, and a teacher whose method is oriented toward grammar explanations and the writing of exercises may use a laboratory, although usually very ineffectively.

APPLICATION OF LINGUISTIC PRINCIPLES TO FOREIGN-LANGUAGE TEACHING

William Moulton of Princeton University, a linguistic scientist and a foreign-language teacher who has participated in both wartime and N.D.E.A. programs, has summarized the five "slogans of the day" which guided teachers in applying the results of linguistic research to the preparation of teaching materials and to classroom techniques. In *Trends in European and American Linguistics*, he lists them [5] as follows:

Language is speech, not writing.
A language is a set of habits.
Teach the language, not about the language.
A language is what its native speakers say, not what someone thinks they ought to say.
Languages are different.

These slogans will now be examined in detail to see what bearing they have on techniques advocated by the pioneers of the audio-lingual method.

1. *Language is speech, not writing.*

As we normally learn our mother tongue in the spoken form before being introduced to its representation by graphic symbols, and as "speech," or sound communication, is the form in which all natural languages first developed, proponents of the audio-lingual method lay stress on learning to understand and speak at least some of the language before learning to read and write it. This does not mean that the student must know the language thoroughly before learning to read it, but rather that any portion under study should be mastered orally before being introduced in printed or written form. This order of presentation (listening and speaking before reading and writing) has been accompanied by great emphasis on correct articulation and intonation. The early introduction of the graphic form of the language has been regarded as a potential threat to mastery of the sound system and to the development of a near-native accent because the symbols used in writing or printing already have associations with native-language pronunciations. A time lag has been advocated between the introduction of new material orally and its presentation in graphic form.

This emphasis on spoken language has led to a radical

5 "Linguistics and Language Teaching in the United States 1940–1960," in C. Mohrmann, A. Sommerfelt, and J. Whatmough, eds., *Trends in European and American Linguistics, 1930–1960* (Utrecht: Spectrum Publishers, 1961), pp. 86–89.

change in the type of material selected as a basis for teaching in the early stages. Complete utterances are learned from the first lesson and these utterances are expressed in the colloquial forms of speech which would be used in the foreign country by a person of age and situation similar to that of the learner. Such utterances contrast with the stilted, literary style of language often presented in elementary textbooks. The differences between everyday speech and literary language are greater in some languages than in others, but there is always some difference. In the audio-lingual method, students are encouraged to listen to and repeat these utterances at normal native speed with the usual elisions and liaisons of the native speaker.

This first slogan, "Language is speech, not writing," has led many people to believe that the written form of the language is neglected in the audio-lingual method. It becomes quite clear that this is an incorrect assumption when one examines materials prepared for the advanced levels of audio-lingual or aural-oral texts. The order advocated for the learning of the language skills is listening, speaking, reading, writing; each of these is taught in turn and practiced to an advanced level.

2. *A language is a set of habits.*

Just as other social habits are acquired by a child growing up in a particular culture, so is the language of his group. The way in which this slogan has found application in foreign-language teaching techniques has been dependent on the concept of habit formation accepted. Early audio-lingual exponents writing on the acquisition of language habits were strongly influenced by the operant conditioning theories of B. F. Skinner, according to which habits are established when reward or reinforcement follows immediately on the occurrences of an act. According to Skinner, the origin of the act, the understanding of the act by the actor, and his attitude to the act were not factors which could be objectively studied and were therefore not to be taken into account in the consideration of habit formation.

The application of this concept in audio-lingual techniques has taken the form of mimicry-memorization (usually of dialogue material) and pattern drilling (whereby students learn to manipulate structures to a point of automatic response to a language stimulus). When we are using our native language we are not conscious of the structures we are using to convey our meaning. Audio-lingual techniques aim to provide the student with a similarly automatic control of the framework of the foreign language. Unimpeded, then, by attention to forms he can concentrate on the essence of the communication he wishes to convey.

3. *Teach the language and not about the language.*

This slogan reflects the revolt of the audio-lingual teachers against the grammar-translation method, where, in the process of studying the structure of the language, there is much class-room discussion of grammar rules and the exceptions to these rules, followed by written exercises to see if the student has grasped these details, but little practice in the active oral use of the language by the student. For the audio-lingual teacher, grammar is a means to an end. That which is most useful is stressed and is practiced thoroughly. A detailed analysis of structure is regarded as an advanced study, a goal in itself for the linguistically inclined, but not essential for the student whose main aim is to be able to use the language in communication.

4. *A language is what its native speakers say, not what someone thinks they ought to say.*

The expressions students learn from audio-lingual materials are those that they would hear around them in the country where the language is spoken. In too many textbooks of an earlier period the language used was artificially constructed to teach certain points of grammar, or was drawn from literary texts accepted as classics and therefore usually of another era. Such language has proved to be of little practical use in the day-to-day experience of living with people of the foreign country, although it has provided a suitable selection of structures and vocabulary for the reading of their literature.

In audio-lingual materials, the structure in common use is

preferred where there is an alternative. Contemporary colloquial clichés of conversation are taught in the dialogues, even
if these expressions sometimes reflect an evolution which has
not yet been registered in the rules set out in traditional
grammar books. Careful attention is paid, however, to levels of
language, to ensure that the colloquial speech learned is of a
type suitable to the general social level of a student population. Situations in the dialogues are carefully described so that
the student is conscious of the emotional effect of the language
he is using: whether it be formal or informal, respectful or
condescending, friendly or hostile, subservient or gently teasing. At advanced levels attention is also paid to regional
differences of pronunciation and expression.

5. *Languages are different.*

Structural linguists, having rejected the notion of a universal
grammatical system which can serve as a framework for the
organization of the facts of all languages, have analyzed each
language they have described according to its unique interrelationships. Since the major difficulties for the language
learner are to be found at those points where the foreign language differs most radically from the native language, audio-
lingual materials are designed, wherever possible, to present
the problems of a specific foreign language to students who
speak another specific language. The materials emphasize and
give special drilling in the major contrasts between these two
languages. The contrasts are the features which the student has
most difficulty in reproducing automatically when his mind is
on his message. Audio-lingual materials differ, then, from more
traditional grammar-oriented texts in that the presentation of
the grammar is not based on a logical exposition of structure
whereby every aspect of each part of speech is dealt with in
turn. Rather, the most useful structures and those most easily
confused are presented first, with continual drilling and review
to ensure mastery.

Contrary to direct-method practice, in audio-lingual materials versions of the foreign-language dialogues are supplied in
the native language. These translations do not, however, attempt to provide a native-language gloss for each word. Since

"meaning," factual and emotional, of segments of native-language discourse is acquired in situations in the native culture, one-to-one equivalents for words in another language can be very misleading. The native-language versions which accompany the dialogues consist of idiomatic expressions which convey the same idea as the foreign-language expressions, and students are given the opportunity to assimilate the cultural significance of the new expressions by learning to use them in situations similar to those in which they would be used in the foreign culture. Traditional translation exercises are regarded by audio-lingualists as a dangerous occupation in the early stages of learning a foreign language because of the tendency of students to look for exact equivalents of individual words. On the other hand, students may be asked to transpose rapidly short stimulus sentences from the native language to the foreign language in translation drills. In this case the native-language stimulus, a simple, uncomplicated utterance, provides a valuable aid for provoking utterances in the foreign language. Prolonged and detailed translation is kept for advanced stages when it is taught as a skill with its own techniques.

TECHNIQUES OF THE AUDIO-LINGUAL METHOD

Since the audio-lingual method aims at teaching the language skills in the order of listening, speaking, reading, and writing, the emphasis in the early years is on the language as it is spoken in everyday situations, moving at advanced levels to the more literary forms of expression as the last two skills receive increasing emphasis. At no stage, however, are the listening and speaking skills neglected. These are kept at a high level by continual practice.

At the first level of instruction, sometimes longer, learning is based on dialogues containing commonly used everyday expressions and basic structures of high frequency. The vocabulary content is kept to a useful minimum so that the student may concentrate on establishing a solid control of structure. The dialogues are learned by a process of mimicry-memorization. Students learn the dialogue sentences by heart one by one. First they listen carefully to the teacher, or a native model on tape, until they can distinguish the sounds and intonation of the phrase to be learned. Then they repeat the phrase after the model until they are repeating it accurately and fluently. When each student can repeat it acceptably on his own, further phrases are learned. This learning process is at first a group activity. Students repeat the phrase together in chorus, then in smaller and smaller groups (i.e., halves of the class, rows), and finally individually. If a group falters, the class returns to choral repetition; if the individual falters the teacher returns to small-group repetition. This choral repetition becomes dialogue when several phrases are already learned: question and answer are now exchanged by halves of the class, rows, or teacher and class, with frequent reversal of roles so that all students have practice in both asking questions and answering them.

After a dialogue has been learned, adaptations of the dialogue, with a more personal application to the student's own situation, provide further consolidation of learning and give opportunity for more flexible use of the material.

The dialogue sentences being by now very familiar, pattern drills based on the structures in the dialogues usually become the main activity. The various types of pattern drills are discussed in chapter 4 of this book. Some authors of audio-lingual texts prefer to develop drills on structures apart from those in the dialogues, believing that in this way they can provide a more logical development of basic language requirements. They maintain that dialogues should be used solely for familiarizing students with the common expressions that make for a natural conversational interchange in everyday situations, and that artificiality results when dialogues are made to serve the additional purpose of exposition of specific structures which are to be taken up in later parts of the unit. Even where the structures to be drilled are drawn directly from the dialogue material, pattern drills develop the potential of the structures beyond their function in a particular dialogue, giving the students practice in using them in wider contexts.

Pattern drills are practiced orally first, with a classroom technique similar to that for dialogues. Choral repetition is followed by small-group practice and then individual response, with a return to the larger group when the smaller group or the individual falters. When the student has achieved a certain facility in manipulating a particular structure, he is given, in some texts, a generalization about the structural pattern with which he has been working. This generalization sets out in organized form what he has been doing in the drill, rather than acting as a rule telling him what he should do. In some materials, mostly those devised for junior high schools, these generalizations are omitted because it is believed that the very design of the materials will lead to an inductive apprehension of structural relationships which will suffice for the student's needs.

After several sections of the work have been learned entirely orally without recourse to the textbook, the student is systematically introduced to the reading of the printed script. Some languages, like French and Russian, provide particular difficulties at this point, and the sight of familiar, or seemingly familiar, symbols can lead to incorrect pronunciations. To obviate such mistakes, the student first reads what he has memorized and practiced orally in class, and his attention is drawn to the relationships between sounds and symbols. Even after he has been allowed access to the printed page, he is always taught new material orally and given oral practice with the script before he is allowed to work with it on his own. It is not until he has a firm grip of most basic structures that he is permitted to read material which is not an adaptation or recombination of what he has already learned orally.

Writing is at first imitative, consisting of transcriptions of words and dialogue sentences from the book. The student may also be given the opportunity to write out variations of pattern-drill items, just as he has constructed variants orally in class sessions. After he has acquired a small stock of useful expressions and some confidence in manipulating basic structures, he will be encouraged to express himself a little more comprehensively on certain topics by giving oral reports to the class and by writing these down in the form of short compositions. These first efforts at recombining what has been learned in order to make comments of a more personal nature are strictly controlled in content so that the student will not fall into linguistic traps of which he is quite ignorant. The student may be required to answer a series of questions or to follow a basic framework set out in the foreign language. At the elementary level of instruction all oral and written practice of this type is kept rigorously within the limits of what has been learned thoroughly. The emphasis is on structuring the situation so that the student will not make mistakes, or at least will make very few.

At more advanced levels, attention turns more and more to reading materials. Passages of literary quality, carefully chosen for difficulty of language and for the authentic picture they convey of the culture of the people who speak the language, are read in the foreign language. Even at this stage, however, listening and speaking are not neglected; texts being read are discussed orally and sometimes listened to on tape or record. Then written composition provides the student with further opportunity to use the language material he has learned in order to express himself in an individual fashion. When the student has learned to read fluently in the foreign language he is encouraged to embark on wider reading of his own choice.

EVALUATION OF THE AUDIO-LINGUAL METHOD

We shall now assess the strengths and weaknesses of the audio-lingual method by the criteria of the five questions set out in chapter 1.[6]

The objectives of the audio-lingual method are clearly stated to be the development of mastery, at various levels of competency, in all four language skills—beginning with listening and speaking, and using these as a basis for the teaching of reading and writing. Paralleling this linguistic aim is the endeavor to develop understanding of the foreign culture and the foreign people through experience with their language. These aims are undoubtedly appropriate in the present age when ability to use a foreign language actively and to understand people of other cultures is thrust upon us, in no matter what country we live.

By the techniques we have described, audio-lingualists do achieve success in developing comprehension and fluency in

6   The five questions are set out on pp. 13–14 of this book.

speaking the foreign language very early in the student's learning experience, although, as they readily admit, this is within a limited body of language material. From the beginning the student learns segments of language which could be of immediate use for communication in a foreign-language situation, and he is trained to understand and produce foreign-language utterances with recognizable and acceptable sound patterns and at a normal speed of delivery. With much practice in listening he is trained in auditory memory and in making fine discriminations among sounds—both very important factors in successful language learning.

Since audio-lingual teaching materials are more scientifically and systematically designed than most one-author texts, the student spends more time on the features of the foreign language which contrast with those already familiar to him, and less time on areas in which his native-language habits cause a minimum of interference. Structural patterns are more systematically introduced and repracticed than in certain other methods where grammatical features are taught either in a supposedly logical order which has little relation to communication needs, or haphazardly according to the whim of the author or the fortuitous way in which they appear in selected texts. By the techniques of mimicry-memorization and pattern-drilling the student is given very thorough practice in the production and manipulation of structural elements which he must learn to use eventually without conscious attention to their systematic features.

Reading and writing are not neglected. The student is not, however, left to pick up these skills as best he can, using his native language as the basis of all his thinking. Instead, he is trained to build up skill in these areas step by step, capitalizing on his growing knowledge of the structure of the language, until both reading and writing become for him not exercises in transposition from one language to another but activities to be conducted entirely in the foreign language.

Student motivation in audio-lingual classes is, on the whole, high. Students enjoy learning to use a language from the very first days of their introduction to it. Both they and their parents feel that this is "real" language. They experience very early in their studies a satisfying sense of achievement in being able to use what they have learned. The techniques advocated permit of active participation by all students for most of the time, yet in circumstances (e.g., choral and group repetition and drill) which protect them from the embarrassment that students in more traditional classes feel on hearing themselves uttering foreign sounds and phrases before their classmates. The type of repetitious practice advocated is ideally suited for individual work with tape recorders or in a language laboratory, and the teacher is therefore able to pay closer attention to the work of individual students than in some traditional classroom situations and to give them immediate confirmation of success and help with difficulties.

There are, however, certain dangers in this method of teaching which can be avoided if the teacher is aware of them and takes steps to counteract them.

Students trained audio-lingually, in a mechanical way, can progress like well-trained parrots: able to repeat whole utterances perfectly when given a certain stimulus, but uncertain of the meaning of what they are saying and unable to use perfectly memorized materials in contexts other than that in which they have learned them. If this inflexibility is to be avoided, students must be trained from the first lesson to apply what they have memorized, or practiced in drills, in communication situations contrived within the classroom group. This very important question of the passage from repetitive practice to facility in a spontaneous conversational interchange is discussed fully in chapters 7 and 8.

It has been objected that the techniques of memorization and drilling that this method implies can become intensely tedious and boring, causing fatigue and distaste on the part of the student. This is certainly true when audio-lingual techniques are applied rigorously by an unimaginative teacher who is not sensitive to student reaction. A successful application of the audio-lingual method requires inventiveness and resourcefulness on the part of the teacher, who must be continually alert for opportunities to vary the presentation of material and to force the students into interesting and intriguing situations where they will feel a spontaneous desire to express themselves through what they have learned. Methods of varying drills and exercises and putting memorized material to active use are discussed in chapters 4 and 7.

A further common objection to the audio-lingual method is that students are trained to make variations on language patterns by a process of analogy without being given a very clear idea of what they are supposed to be doing in the process. As a result, they do not understand the possibilities and limitations of the operations they are performing and are unable, later, to use these patterns outside the framework of a particular drill. This vagueness and bewilderment can result if students are drilled mechanically in certain structural manipulations without the teacher's satisfying himself that they are aware of the linguistic implications of what they are doing. With a well-structured sequence of dialogues and drills, there will be little need for lengthy explanations of structural relationships. Students will become aware of these through the way in which material is being used in simulated communication. Where these relationships are not clear, the teacher will need to draw the attention of the students to the crucial element in a series of drills so that they may realize the significance of variations they are making and so absorb the structural meaning.

Finally, objections have been raised to the advocated time lag between the presentation of foreign-language material orally and the presentation of the same material in printed or written form. Some audio-lingual experimenters have suggested periods of as long as twenty-four weeks of purely oral work before students see anything in graphic form,[7] although periods of from six to ten weeks are more common. It is believed that this time lag obviates the interference of native-language habits of pronunciation associated with the printed symbols where these are the same for the two languages, and also that it forces the student to concentrate his attention on accurate and thorough learning of the foreign-language material. Some experienced teachers have objected that certain students feel very insecure when they are forced to depend on the ear alone, partly because they find it hard to remember all they hear in a situation where so many of the sound clues are

7 See F. Marty's description of the Middlebury College experiment in *Language Laboratory Learning* (Wellesley, Mass., 1960), p. 75.

unfamiliar to them, and partly because all through school they have been trained to work with books. Such students sometimes develop emotional reactions to aural-oral work which hinder them in the learning of the language. Still other teachers maintain that students from whom all graphic representation of the foreign language is withheld will make their own imperfect notes and thus learn incorrectly;[8] it is therefore better for the students, they consider, to see the correct and accepted version of the written language at an earlier stage and learn to use it as a help to memorization and practice. Students who have immediate access to a graphic representation of what they are learning will often depend on it too much and not give sufficient time to practicing until the work is memorized and internalized. For these reasons the best approach appears to be to present all foreign-language material at first in oral form, especially in the elementary sections of the course; to train students in working with this material orally until they can handle it with ease; then to train them with the script, which they may use as a help to clarification and memorization. Under no circumstances, however, must teacher or student feel that once the material is presented in graphic form the time for practice is over. After the student has received some help and support from the printed version he must be made to practice the use of the material orally until he shows that he has learned it thoroughly.

Whether the audio-lingual method is appropriate for all types of students and for students of all ages is another controversial subject. Experience has shown the method to be very appropriate for younger children, who love to mimic and act out roles and to learn through activity rather than through explanations and the learning of facts. The less gifted student also seems to profit more from this method than from more traditional methods. This type of student finds it hard to cope with the abstractions of the grammar-translation method and is often left behind by students of higher intelligence in the direct method, where he must acquire the meanings of words and the functioning of structural patterns inductively with very few props to help him. In the audio-lingual method he is

8   *Ibid.,* p. 76.

carried along by the work with the group; he learns to mimic, repeat utterances, and manipulate structures with relative ease and feels he is making progress. He enjoys the foreign language while he is with the class, usually dropping out before he falls too far behind to be able to cope with the general activities. Some people have maintained that the audio-lingual method is most helpful for the average and weaker students; they assert that the most gifted become bored long before the other students have had enough repetitive practice to develop firm habits of correct structural associations. Sometimes the more intelligent student becomes impatient if he cannot move on to new material as soon as he has a clear understanding of the principles involved in what he is learning. Such students need more practice than they realize in order to develop habitual responses at the level of the manipulation of structural combinations. The teacher must help them to understand what is involved in real language mastery so that they will see the importance of thorough practice. When they accept the discipline the method implies, they reach heights of achievement which no teacher using traditional methods would expect of students at that stage. Like most other foreign-language teaching methods, however, the audio-lingual method can be applied most appropriately, after the elementary stages, in streamed groups, because students of varying degrees of ability soon separate out widely in the amount of material they have assimilated. With adult students, who need to learn any subject in a shorter period of time than younger students and have developed certain habits of organizing material they are studying, the audio-lingual method is still appropriate if memorization and drilling are accompanied by some explanation of the place of structures being practiced in the system of the language as a whole.

The audio-lingual method makes considerable demands upon the teacher. It demands of him a near-native articulation and intonation if he is to model utterances for the students. (If he is lacking in this area he must learn to use a tape model and work along with the class at making up his deficiencies). The method calls for considerable energy if the teacher is to keep oral practice moving smartly, and imagination and enterprise in using persons and situations in the classroom if foreign-language material is to acquire reality and relevance. It also demands of the teacher careful preparation and organization of material. For these reasons it is difficult for a teacher to teach a number of parallel classes during the day by this method without becoming weary of the material and physically and emotionally exhausted. Teachers who are in this situation may need to introduce reading and writing activities sooner than they might have wished if they are to maintain the same level of energy in classes throughout the day.

The effectiveness of any method in a particular situation is a function of the actual classroom performance of the individual teacher. It does appear, however, that audio-lingual techniques intelligently applied will lead to very thorough learning. Progress through the body of material may be slower than in the past, but there should be no need for the teaching and reteaching in successive years which have long characterized foreign-language classes. The student's understanding of the language will be more systematic and direct, and he will be able to use what he knows for his own purposes, within limitations which he has accepted, long before he could have been expected to do so by more traditional methods. As a result, he should retain his interest in and enthusiasm for foreign-language learning and be willing to continue the study until he has achieved some degree of mastery. Teachers who have become accustomed to piecemeal knowledge, recurrent errors, and an apathetic response from their classes should find this changed situation ample repayment for the time and energy which this type of teaching has demanded of them.

AREAS OF CONTROVERSY

Should foreign-language skills be learned in the order in which the child learns his native language?

The order recommended by audio-lingualists for the learning of foreign-language skills (listening, speaking, reading, writing) is sometimes justified by the argument that it is the order in which the child learns his native language. The situation of the child learning his native language and that of the high school student learning a foreign language are, however, quite dissimilar.[9]

The child is exploring his environment, forming concepts, and acquiring language at the same time. He is surrounded by the speech of his family group for most of his waking hours and soon learns the sound combinations that can get him what he wants and needs. His smallest, most incorrect attempts at imitating this language are rewarded by approval and interest, and gradually he finds himself able to communicate his needs and excitements by this new means. All these factors encourage him to greater efforts at mastery.

The high school student already possesses an effective method of communication. To learn another which does not supply any of his needs, he must limit himself and humiliate himself by his obvious incapacity to express his real meaning. His incorrect efforts often bring more disapproval than a stubborn silence. Sounds which his social group has previously approved are now not good enough. To him all this foreign-language-learning business is a classroom activity which ceases once the bell has announced the end of the hour.

The adolescent student has been trained to study with books and pen. Now he is denied these aids and asked to depend on his auditory memory alone. He is not permitted to make notes as he is accustomed to do, and if he makes them surreptitiously they are frequently misleading. His mind is full of another language the concepts of which do not appear to be adequate for this new language. It is obvious that he has neither the motivation nor the unique situational opportunity of the languageless infant.

This order of learning language skills cannot be justified, then, by such analogy with native-language learning. It is, however, a logical order. Since a language is an arbitrary code associated with the behavior of a certain group of people, it must, if it is to be understood, be pronounced and phrased as this group has habitually pronounced and phrased it. After the student has heard the correct spoken form of the language, he

9 For Lenneberg's view of child language-learning as maturational, see chapter 3.

can attempt to reproduce it himself. Until he has learned the correct pronunciation, he cannot read it as it would be read by a native speaker. Until he has read a script demonstrating the way its native speakers consider it should be written, he cannot attempt to write it himself.

The optimum time interval separating the stages of aural presentation and oral repetition from reading and writing is still a matter for experimentation, and experienced teachers differ in their considered judgment at this point.

Do students trained by the audio-lingual method learn to read and write the language well?

Some teachers have hesitated to adopt the audio-lingual method because they fear it may not train students in all four language skills; others have accused teachers using the method of producing "language illiterates." These teachers are therefore waiting for experimental evidence of the efficacy of the audio-lingual method, before they are willing to adopt it themselves.

Of particular interest is the very thorough, scientifically controlled experiment that was conducted by G. Scherer and his colleagues at the University of Colorado in 1960–62, under contract to the U.S. Office of Education. This investigation is reported in *A Psycholinguistic Experiment in Foreign-language Teaching* (1964).

The study covered all the beginning students of German at the University of Colorado in the fall semester of 1960. These students were carefully observed and tested for a period of two years. About a hundred and fifty students were taught by the audio-lingual method, with laboratory practice. These students did not see any written or printed form of the materials used until the thirteenth week of the course. Their course consisted of dialogue learning and pattern drills. About a hundred and thirty students in the control groups were taught by a more traditional, multiple-approach method in which students were trained in all skills from the beginning, with an emphasis on grammatical analysis. Teachers of both experimental and control groups were well prepared for their teaching assignments by directors enthusiastic about their particular method of teaching.

All groups were given the same tests at the end of each semester, no matter how appropriate or inappropriate these might appear to be. The tests consisted of a speaking test; a listening test; a reading test (German-to-English translation); a writing test (English-to-German translation); reading and writing tests requiring no translation in either direction; and a battery of tests designed to reveal any differences in direct association, motivation, attitudes, and improvement in English listening comprehension. In the second year it became impossible, because of student registration problems, to keep the two groups in separate sections, so all students were taught by an audio-lingual approach but were required to complete a review grammar, for which the control groups were undoubtedly better prepared.

The results of the experiment were as follows:

In *listening comprehension* the experimental group proved superior at the end of the first year, but this superiority had disappeared by the end of the second year.

In *speaking* the experimental group remained superior throughout the experiment.

In *reading* the traditional students proved superior at the end of the first year, but this difference had disappeared by the end of the second year.

In *writing* the traditional students remained superior throughout the experiment.

In *German-to-English translation* the traditional students remained superior throughout the experiment.

In *English-to-German translation* the traditional students were superior at the end of the first year, but this difference had disappeared by the end of the second year.

There was no evidence of any improvement in *English listening comprehension* in either group.

In *assimilation of sentence meaning* and in ability to *think in German* the audio-lingual groups were superior throughout the experiment, and they showed *more desirable attitudes* toward things German and the speaking of German themselves.

They proved to be the equals of the traditional groups in *grammatical proficiency* and *knowledge of vocabulary*, while being slightly superior in the *active use of vocabulary*. A standardized combination score showed no difference in overall proficiency for the two groups.

Examining these results, we can draw the following conclusions:

—Students trained by the audio-lingual method achieve results which are comparable with those achieved by students taught by more traditional methods.

—Students tend to do well in those sections of the work which are emphasized in the teaching method. The audio-lingual students were taught to speak and spoke well. Since they were not taught to translate from German into English, they did not develop this skill. They were, however, superior in grasping sentence meaning and in making direct associations between German symbols and their meanings. The writing of German was not emphasized and so they did not do as well in this area as the students in the control groups. On the other hand, the students in the control groups did not do as well in speaking German, which had not been emphasized, but were superior at writing German and translating from German to English, skills on which they had spent more time than the students in the audio-lingual groups.

—It is interesting to note that the oral practice of dialogue sentences and structures had given the audio-lingual students a good foundation for reading, organized study of grammar in the second year, and English-to-German translation.

—Finally, this study makes it quite clear that the objectives of the course will decide the method to be adopted. If speaking is to be a major objective, then the audio-lingual method is indicated and the experimental evidence suggests that the students will be given a sound foundation for acquiring skill in listening, reading, and English-to-German translation.

On the other hand, if writing German and the ability to translate from German into English are of greater importance as objectives than speaking, then effort should be concentrated on developing these skills specifically, as has been done where more traditional methods have been used.

ANNOTATED READING LIST

BROOKS, N. *Language and Language Learning.* 2d ed. New York: Harcourt, Brace & World, 1964. Indispensable reference for all aspects of audio-lingual teaching.

LADO, R. *Language Teaching, A Scientific Approach.* New York: McGraw-Hill, 1964. A clear exposition of the methodology and techniques of the audio-lingual method.

MOULTON, W. M. "Linguistics and Language Teaching in the United States 1940–1960." In C. MOHRMANN; A. SOMMERFELT; and J. WHATMOUGH, eds. *Trends in European and American Linguistics, 1930–1960.* Utrecht: Spectrum Publishers, 1961. Pp. 82–109. Gives a thorough treatment of the origin and linguistic bases of the audio-lingual method with valuable bibliographic information.

RIVERS, W. M. *The Psychologist and the Foreign-Language Teacher.* Chicago: University of Chicago Press, 1964. Describes the audio-lingual method and analyzes the psychological implications on which it is based. Suggests improvements to teaching techniques.

SCHERER, G., and WERTHEIMER, M. *A Psycholinguistic Experiment in Foreign-language Teaching.* New York: McGraw-Hill, 1964. Describes a very thorough, controlled experiment to determine differences in achievement, over a period of two years, of beginning students of German at the University of Colorado when taught by an audio-lingual method and a multiple-approach method.

3

The Place of Grammar

To many people—former students in our schools—foreign-language learning is essentially a question of grammar. We hear the complaint: "I was never any good at foreign language because I could never remember the grammar." In the description of various methods of teaching foreign languages in chapter 1, some of the disagreement very clearly stemmed from the attitude of the teachers toward grammar. "It is tremendously important that the students know their grammar," said Teacher A, while Teacher D spoke of giving the students "confidence in the active use of the structural patterns of the language,"—surely another way of speaking about grammar. Some teachers, on the other hand, maintain that we can speak and write our native language with ease and assurance "without knowing any grammar" and that no more need be required of the person learning a foreign language. As soon as the fundamental question of the role of grammar is raised in foreign-language-teaching circles, the discussion becomes animated, even heated, and before the discussion has finished some of the participants at least are likely to have taken up rigid and uncompromising positions.

What, then, is grammar? To most people grammar is the rules of a language set out in a terminology which is hard to remember, with many exceptions appended to each rule. Few people stop to think of the origin of these "rules" or of their validity; fewer people ask themselves why there are so many exceptions. Everyone has been taught his grammar rules at school and is convinced that these rules have existed since schools began; they may not be questioned; they tell us what is right and what is wrong in what people write and say. They seem as immutable as the moral code of the community despite the fact that the language we hear and read every day does not conform entirely to the standard established in the rules. It is because of this almost superstitious regard for the "rules of grammar" that scholars who have dared to rewrite the grammar of an established language have been treated as iconoclasts and dangerous heretics. In attempting a new description of the language they have cast doubt on the validity of accepted categories and have proposed new ones; they have rejected time-honored injunctions and prohibitions in order to make the rules more congruent with actual usage and have thus appeared to some to be threatening the very foundations of the established order.[1]

The writing of a grammar is basically an attempt at systematization and codification of a mass of data which may at first sight appear amorphous but within which recurrent regularities can be discerned. The way in which this systematization is approached will depend on the convictions of the grammarian about the nature of language.

In the European tradition, grammatical analyses have come down to us from the scholars of ancient Greece, and the basic divergence in approach which existed among grammarians at that time is still reflected in the differing viewpoints we hear today. For some, language reflects a reality which exists beyond language itself: either categories of logic derived from man's innate neural organization, or relationships observable in the physical world; for others, a language is a purely arbitrary set of associations among which systematic relationships can be discerned and described and for which categories can be established in terms of the unique system of the particular language being studied. For those who hold the first of these views, the categories of grammar are held to be the same for all languages because the external reality they represent is the same for all men; for those holding the second view, each language must be described in terms of its own coherent sys-

1   An example of this emotional reaction can be seen in the title of a book opposing C. C. Fries's approach to English grammar: *Who Killed Grammar?* by H. Warfel (Gainesville, Fla., 1952).

tem. Although the Greeks originally described their language in terms of observed form and function (that is, relationships among elements of the language), they also attached to the formal categories they had established concepts which related this system of classification to the external environment. Later, Greek language description passed, by way of Latin, to other languages, European and non-European, for which this particular description of forms and relationships was no longer valid. As a formal definition of the established categories was now meaningless, it was the conceptual interpretation which was transferred to the new situation. These conceptual interpretations (e.g., nouns as names of people, places, and things) were vague and inexact in their application to the various categories even in the Greek language. Referring as they did to features of an environment familiar to all men, they were, however, readily adopted by grammarians of other languages, who, faced with an obvious discrepancy with the facts, proceeded to tailor the descriptions of their own languages to what they accepted as being categories of universal application.

For some time there has been a revolt against this practice of describing any and every language with the same set of conceptual terms which hinder the precise identification of elements of structure and their interrelationships in a wide variety of language systems. From this ferment have emerged new ways of describing languages. When these methods have been applied to the description of little-known languages which have never before been closely studied they have passed unnoticed except by scholars in the field; applied to languages for which there are well-established and widely accepted grammatical analyses of the traditional kind these innovations have caused considerable bewilderment and have sometimes aroused active resistance.

Further discussion and controversy have been provoked by a shift of emphasis in grammatical study from the structural patterns of written language to those of spoken language. Although some grammarians down the centuries have always maintained that speech is the fundamental model from which written forms have been derived, written language data have been more readily available in a permanent form than records of speech.[2] Written language has therefore been the traditional basis of grammatical study. With the development of recording equipment, modern grammarians have had greater opportunities than their predecessors to examine in depth the characteristics of spoken language. Their analyses of speech data have shown that the accepted patterns for writing a language are not necessarily those which are used in oral communication. Since written language represents for the most part the production of literate and educated persons who edit, and re-edit, their original output it evolves less rapidly than spoken language, conserving many forms which are no longer heard. On the other hand, examination of what people actually say has revealed that many forms which grammarians have declared to be incorrect and unacceptable are current in the everyday speech even of educated persons. Grammars derived from speech data may therefore be expected to diverge to some extent from grammars of written language if they are faithful to the recorded corpus. To many people who have been trained from childhood to believe in a standard of "correct speech" to which nobody conforms in every detail, but which is enshrined in the grammar book, the inclusion in new grammars of the patterns of spoken language has seemed to give these a stamp of official acceptance against which they have revolted. The concept of a grammar as a description of all the observed phenomena rather than as a prescriptive manual to which they can turn for guidance is an idea which they find hard to accept.

Since the time of the Swiss linguistic scientist Ferdinand de Saussure it has become customary to distinguish between two aspects of language: "parole" and "langue." What people say in a language is "parole," and this varies to some extent from individual to individual and from situation to situation. "Parole" is affected by the purposes of the speaker, his emotions at the time when he is expressing himself, the circumstances of the utterance (the speaker may be tired, or preoccupied, or in great haste), and the individual memory span of the speaker (who may begin his utterance in one conventional form and

2   The Sanskrit grammarian Pāṇini, writing between 350 and 250 B.C., discusses speech and pronunciation, presenting the sounds in an involved, but very precise, phonemic system.

finish it in quite another). An individual piece of writing also falls into the category of "parole" and is similarly affected by many contingencies. Because of the variety of factors which may affect the form of a specific utterance or piece of writing, it is difficult to study "parole" systematically. From samples of "parole" (spoken or written) can be abstracted the system of language habits of a whole social group: "the social side of speech, outside the individual who can never create nor modify it by himself"; [3] this is what de Saussure terms "langue." It is this systematic patterning underlying individual utterances which makes it possible for one person to understand or be understood by another. Every native speaker has acquired this language system through his experiences in his cultural group, and the system can be discerned, however imperfectly, in everything he says or writes. Grammar is not a description of "parole" with its infinite, and therefore unpredictable, possibilities of variation, but of the coherent system of patterning in "langue." When we say that a grammar describes spoken forms of speech, it is the abstraction, the average drawn from the individual utterances of many speakers, to which we are referring, and not to particular utterances, which may be "ungrammatical" in that they do not conform in certain details to the language conventions of the group. These individual lapses and idiosyncrasies are different from the "common errors" listed in school textbooks. "Common errors" have a distribution far beyond the individual; they are a part of "langue." Often they provide evidence of evolution in the language. At other times they represent forms and patterns which prescriptive grammarians have outlawed because they did not fit neatly into the system they had elaborated. As living patterns they have flourished despite all efforts through the schools to bring about their extinction. The new grammars attempt to account for phenomena of this type as well as for those already covered in traditional grammars.

There are various ways of approaching the description of a corpus of language data. Some grammarians begin with phonology and move on to morphology and syntax, describing each

---

3   F. de Saussure, *Course in General Linguistics,* trans. W. Baskin (New York, 1959), p. 14.

as a separate system while showing points of interaction among them; others consider these three traditional areas of analysis to be so closely interwoven in the expression of meaning that they must be dealt with as manifestations of one basic structural system which is not apparent in surface phenomena but must be sought by analysis in depth. Interest in language description has been keen during the last few decades with the result that several new approaches to this task have emerged. It is therefore more appropriate at the present time to speak of the various "grammars" of a language rather than of "the grammar." The most well-known grammars at the present time are traditional grammar (the exponents of which continue to refine the categories and rules of their predecessors), immediate-constituent or structural grammar, transformational-generative grammar, and the British system of multi-level language analysis. The approach of traditional grammarians has already been discussed in some detail. The newer approaches to grammar require more explanation and will now be described individually.

Immediate-Constituent or Phrase-Structure Grammar

The approach to grammar associated with the names of such linguistic scientists as Bloomfield, Fries, and Bloch [4] is called immediate-constituent or sometimes phrase-structure grammar. It differs from traditional grammar in its concentration on structural meaning in the sense in which Fries uses this term. For Fries there are three types or "modes" of meaning in language: lexical, structural and social-cultural. [5] Lexical meaning is what we commonly consider the "dictionary meaning" of words and is not regarded as a part of grammar, being an area of study in its own right. Social-cultural meaning refers to the special significance which language elements acquire for persons living in a particular culture and is related to

4 L. Bloomfield, *Language* (New York, 1933); C. C. Fries, *American English Grammar* (New York, 1940); and B. Bloch and G. Trager, *Outline of Linguistic Analysis* (Baltimore, 1942).
5 "Meaning and Linguistic Analysis," in H. B. Allen, ed., *Readings in Applied English Linguistics* (New York, 1964) pp. 107–9, reprinted from *Language*, 30 (January–March, 1954): 57–68.

the values, customs, and interests of the social group; this again is outside the realm of grammar. There remains structural meaning, which is conveyed by the relationships among the elements in an utterance. As Fries expresses it: structural meanings are "specifically signaled by a complex system of contrastive patterns." [6] In traditional grammar, as found in school textbooks, structural meaning has been expressed in conceptual terms which have confused the function of one element in relation to other elements within a segment of discourse with the functioning of these elements in a contextual situation, that is, in the expression of an idea or message. Structural grammar has set out to explain grammatical relationships only in terms of the formal features observable within the language corpus.

In language analysis as practiced by structuralists, structural meaning is established at several levels. Syntactical relationships are identified first (that is, relationships between sections of a sentence, between phrases such as a noun phrase and a verb phrase, or between words within phrases). Larger entities are gradually broken down by a process of binary division into smaller and smaller constituents until ultimate constituents which can undergo no further division are identified. The constituents at a particular level under consideration are called immediate constituents. At the level of the word constituents are grouped into categories according to function, these functional categories being signaled by formal features. Thus word-class membership indicates identity of relationship with other elements in the structure and is not, as in traditional grammar, conceptually based. These functional categories are more rigorously related to the particular system of the language being analyzed than the presumably universal categories of an earlier day. Below the word level, segments of words are identified as morphemes, that is, the smallest elements which convey meaning, and therefore the ultimate constituents in morphology. Since stress and intonation signal relationships between the segments, or constituents, at any one level they are termed suprasegmentals. Phonology is studied separately from morphology and syntax, the stream of sound

6 *Ibid.,* p. 108.

being reduced in a similar fashion to its ultimate constituents the phonemes, which are the smallest elements of sound which convey distinctions in meaning. The hierarchy of binary combinations in phrase structure is usually represented by a tree diagram which clearly indicates the relationships between groupings of constituents at higher and lower levels.

Hockett has queried the possibility of dividing discourse into immediate constituents in an absolute fashion in many language situations because of the existence of processes such as fusion. He suggests an item-and-process theory to account for certain phenomena rather than the item-and-arrangement theory of immediate-constituent grammar.[7] This approach is of considerable interest to foreign-language teachers because it provides for the description of phenomena which are otherwise difficult to categorize.

Structural grammar has had considerable influence on the preparing of materials for foreign-language teaching. The emphasis on structural rather than lexical or situational meaning has been basic to the technique of pattern or structure drill. In pattern drills, certain formal or functional features have been isolated and students have been taught to create new utterances in response to formal cues rather than as an expression of personal meaning.

In this way an attempt has been made to build in systematic habits in the foreign language. Talking about the operation of the foreign language in conceptual terms or in terms applicable to the system of another language has been discouraged. Despite a widespread misconception, this change of approach has not meant the abandonment of grammar but has made the active practice of grammar the core of the language program. A further influence of structural grammar has been the emphasis on the teaching of phonemic distinctions in the sound system of the language, rather than phonetic differences. Suprasegmentals have also been included as essential to meaning.

7   C. F. Hockett, "Two Models of Grammatical Description," *Word*, 10 (1954): 210–31, reprinted in M. Joos, ed., *Readings in Linguistics*, 2d ed. (New York, 1958), pp. 386–99; and "Linguistic Elements and their Relations," *Language*, 37 (1961): 29–53. This viewpoint is discussed in K. L. Pike, *Language in Relation to a Unified Theory of the Structure of Human Behavior*, 2d ed. rev. (The Hague, 1967), pp. 545–55.

Transformational-Generative Grammar

In recent years interest has been growing in transformational-generative grammar. This new approach to grammar, which is due primarily to the research of Harris, Chomsky, and Halle,[8] is still in a process of evolution. Its exponents have concentrated their research in the areas of syntax and phonology, considering that most morphological properties can be more conveniently studied in association with the lexicon. Unlike some immediate-constituent grammarians, transformationalists have seen no need to discard the categories of traditional grammar while recognizing that their boundaries need to be redefined for different languages.

Basic to transformational-generative theory is the distinction between competence and performance.[9] The competence of a speaker-hearer is his intuitive knowledge of the complex system of rules of his language. Evidence of the existence of this underlying competence is provided by his intuitive recognition of the degree of grammaticalness of any utterance in the language and by his ability to produce a grammatical utterance, although he may not in fact always do so. His performance is his own production of utterances in actual situations. As with "parole," performance is very variable and may not conform at all times with the speaker-hearer's competence. Language competence is established in the first place from a study of sentences which are samples of performance, but once

---

8 Z. Harris, "Discourse Analysis," *Language,* 28 (1952): 1–30, and "Co-occurrence and Transformation in Linguistic Structure," *Language,* 33 (1957): 283–340; also M. Halle, "Phonology in a Generative Grammar," *Word,* 18 (1962): 54–72. These three articles are reprinted in J. Fodor and J. Katz, eds., *The Structure of Language* (Englewood Cliffs, N.J., 1964). See also M. Halle, *The Sound Pattern of Russian* (The Hague, 1959); N. Chomsky, *Syntactic Structures* (The Hague, 1957), and *Aspects of the Theory of Syntax* (Cambridge, Mass., 1965). Other writings in this area are: P. Postal, *Constituent Structure, a Study of Contemporary Models of Syntactic Description,* pt. 3 of *IJAL,* 30, no. 1 (Bloomington, Ind., and the Hague, 1964); and J. Katz and P. Postal, *An Integrated Theory of Linguistic Descriptions,* Research Monograph no. 26 (Cambridge, Mass., 1964).

9 See N. Chomsky, *Aspects of the Theory of Syntax* (Cambridge, Mass., 1965) pp. 3–9.

a theory of competence is elaborated it can prove invaluable in the study of the more complex aspects of performance.

According to Chomsky's formulation, the native speaker has internalized a complex "system of rules that relate signals to semantic interpretations of these signals" [10] and which can generate all the grammatical sentences of the language. The speaker-hearer is not conscious of this system; nevertheless, it determines the form of his utterances. The transformational grammarian seeks to ascertain these rules from a study of overt performance. He delves beneath the surface structure of an utterance to the deep structure which has generated this utterance by a series of transformational rules from basic strings of structural formatives which are the product of universal principles of great abstractness. Every utterance can be analyzed through successive transformations (processes such as replacement, addition, deletion, changes of position) until its base structure is revealed. Where base structures are particularly simple we have kernel sentences. The base structures, containing only obligatory transformations such as agreement, conform to the abstract systems of grammatical relations which can be discovered in the deep structures of all languages, and which, according to Chomsky, are not learned by the child in the process of acquiring his native language but correspond to the structure of his innate neural organization. As example of such universals Chomsky cites the subject-predicate relationship, and the noun-verb distinction which appears in all languages even though the boundaries between the two categories may vary. According to Chomsky and Halle, phonological structure is derived by rule from the syntactic structure and is therefore equally derivative from the deep structure of the language, both systems contributing to the semantic interpretation of an utterance. Grammar, then, is a system of transformational and rewrite rules which can predict all possible sentences of the language, but none which the native speaker will consider unacceptable. Generative grammar can deal with ambiguities which surface phrase-structure grammar would not elucidate: it provides a method for un-

10 N. Chomsky, "Topics in the Theory of Generative Grammar," in T. Sebeok, ed., *Current Trends in Linguistics,* vol. 3 (The Hague, 1966), p. 3.

covering the variation in deep structure of two utterances which would appear identical in an immediate-constituent analysis. It can also uncover kernel sentences which have become embedded or nested in other sentences. In these ways it is more powerful than immediate-constituent grammar.

It is what Chomsky has called the "creative aspect of normal language use" [11] which has provided a particular stimulus to the thinking of transformational grammarians: at any moment, a speaker may produce an utterance which has never been heard before in that identical form, and this utterance will be understood by other speakers of his language who have never heard an identical utterance. To Chomsky it is this "stimulus-free and innovative" [12] property of language that has been ignored in modern linguistic theory and which, to his mind, cannot possibly be explained in terms of stimulus-and-response habit formation and generalization. This aspect of language can, however, be explained in terms of an internalized system of rules which can generate an infinite number of grammatical sentences which will be comprehensible and acceptable when uttered with the appropriate lexical elements in a communication situation. If students are to use the foreign language, as they do the native language, for the production of novel utterances which express their personal meaning, teachers must go beyond an earnest attempt to build in language habits and associations. It is the most difficult task of the foreign-language teacher to prepare students for such freedom in language use. Later in this chapter we shall see that teaching with this ultimate aim in view is not incompatible with concentrated training in the formation of language habits, but that the two are complementary.

Chomsky distinguishes between two types of grammars. "A grammar in the traditional view," he says, "is an account of competence. It describes and attempts to account for the ability of a speaker to understand an arbitrary sentence of his language and to produce an appropriate sentence on a given occasion. If it is a pedagogic grammar, it attempts to provide

11 *Ibid.,* p. 4.
12 "Linguistic Theory," in *Language Teaching: Broader Contexts,* Northeast Conference on the Teaching of Foreign Languages, 1966, p. 46 [hereinafter referred to as Northeast Conference (1966)].

the student with this ability; if a linguistic grammar, it aims to discover and exhibit the mechanisms that make this achievement possible." [13] A pedagogic grammar for foreign-language teaching constructed on transformational principles would be designed to establish ability to recognize and produce grammatical sentences in the foreign language: in other words, to build up competence. Acceptable performance is not possible while competence is defective. Practice in performance in the classroom is practice in generating new utterances, not in parroting utterances produced by the teacher. This innovative ability will, according to Chomsky, exist only to the degree that underlying competence exists. The student who has merely constructed utterances according to a pattern set by the teacher without understanding the structural system according to which these utterances are operating may, when left to his own devices, produce utterances based on his competence in his own language or on some vaguely developed system based on erroneous assumptions. It would appear, then, that students must move beyond the stage of producing utterances by analogy with other utterances to the stage where they are constructing utterances in strict conformity with the foreign-language system, but without conscious attention to the rules they are applying. This they can do only in limited areas at first. As their knowledge increases, they can expand their efforts until, at a final stage, they can express themselves freely in a wide variety of structural patterns. How students should be taught in order to bring them to this stage will be discussed at length in later chapters of this book. Chomsky himself does not consider that linguistic theory should determine foreign-language teaching methods. Insights from linguistics, he says quite categorically, must be validated or refuted by the experienced language teacher.[14] Since the analyses of deep structure developed by transformational-generative grammarians can uncover unsuspected relationships and clarify functions in a foreign language, the contribution of this type of grammar to foreign-language teaching will be rather in the area of ensuring better learning materials than in the suggesting of new classroom techniques.

13 Chomsky, *Current Trends in Linguistics,* vol. 3 (1966), p. 3.
14 "Linguistic Theory," in Northeast Conference (1966), p. 45.

British Multilevel Linguistic System

Another theory of grammar of interest to foreign-language teachers is the British system of linguistic description developed by Halliday on the foundational work of Firth.[15] Like the two preceding systems, it is an attempt to establish a linguistic theory of a sufficient degree of abstraction to make it applicable to the description of all languages.

In this system language is studied at three levels: substance (phonological or graphological); form (which relates to the study of grammar and of lexis or vocabulary); and content, or situation-substance.[16] These aspects of language are described as levels because they do not follow one another in sequence but are in operation simultaneously. What concerns us particularly in this chapter is the level of form, "the way in which a language is internally structured to carry contrasts in meaning. The problem is to recognize and account for all those places in the language where there is a possibility of meaningful choice; and to state the range of possibilities at each place."[17] In the study of lexis attention is paid to lexical sets, groups of words which occur in close association or collocation. These are open sets and the range of possible choices is wide. In grammar the range of possibilities is much more circumscribed, and for this reason the theory of grammar is more fully elaborated at the moment than the theory of lexis.

To facilitate the study of grammar (and of phonology also) four theoretical categories are posited: unit, class, structure,

15 See J. R. Firth, *Papers in Linguistics 1934–1951* (London, 1957); and M. Halliday, A. McIntosh, and P. Strevens, *The Linguistic Sciences and Language Teaching* (London, 1964). Later theories, mainly American (e.g. Lamb's stratificational grammar), have not as yet been applied to foreign-language teaching and are not therefore discussed in this chapter. See Sydney M. Lamb, *Outline of Stratificational Grammar* (Washington, D.C., 1966). Tagmemic theory, developed mainly by K. L. Pike, is discussed in chapter 4.

16 J. Catford, in *A Linguistic Theory of Translation* (London, 1965) p. 3, calls substance "medium-substance" and adds the study of "medium-form." He calls the third level "situation-substance" and retains the term "context" or "contextual meaning" for the relationship between grammar/lexis and situation.

17 Halliday, McIntosh, and Strevens (1964), p. 21.

and system. The theory developed for each of these theoretical categories applies to all languages, but descriptive categories of a more detailed nature give instances of these theoretical categories which are appropriate to a given language being described. As a theoretical category, "unit" applies to "any stretch of language that carries grammatical patterns." [18] In English and in certain other languages the theoretical category "unit" has a hierarchical arrangement of instances at five levels (sentence, clause, group, word, morpheme), the instance at the higher level always containing within itself one or more occurrences of the instance at the level immediately below it. In English phonology, the descriptive category units are, in hierarchical order, the tone group, the foot, the syllable, and the phoneme. "Class" refers to any set of items which perform the same function within any unit at a particular level (e.g., in English, "verbal group" within the unit "sentence"; "noun" or "adverb" within the unit "group"). "Structure" refers to the systematic interrelationships between "classes," while "system" refers to restricted groups of items which provide a choice of possibilities for a particular function within a structure (e.g., the closed system in English: this, that, these, those).

The British linguistic theorists lay considerable emphasis on the differences in grammar and lexis in the various "registers" of language; certain types of language are acceptable in the community, even expected, for certain situations and for special purposes. Registers differ according to field of discourse (for instance, the language may be for technical or nontechnical purposes); mode of discourse (there are notable differences in most languages between spoken language and literary text); and style of discourse (this depending on the relationship between the speaker and hearer, colloquial speech differing considerably from formal speech). [19] Persons who are not native speakers of a language can easily cause offence and give wrong impressions by mixing elements from several registers in speech and in writing. Students in foreign-language classes should be made conscious of this problem of registers and taught to recognize differences so that they may not only

18 *Ibid.,* p. 25.
19 The matter of "registers" is discussed in full in Halliday, McIntosh, and Strevens (1964), pp. 87–98.

choose the right register for a particular purpose but be able to keep a section of discourse within the one register.

For the British linguistic scientists meaning is a property of all three levels of language: in other words, all patterning is meaningful. While laying stress on structural or formal meaning, they do not, as do some American structuralists, minimize the importance of contextual meaning. They retain traditional terminology for linguistic categories but reject conceptual definitions of function as being circular and therefore useless for description. Traditional terms are given formal definitions and their boundaries redefined to fit the facts of the particular language being described.

As for methods of foreign-language teaching, the British linguistic scientists consider that these must be worked out by practicing teachers in accordance with pedagogical principles, not by theoreticians of language. They feel, however, that the work of foreign-language teachers is considerably hampered by the bad grammar which underlies the textbooks they are forced to use. "Criticism of the linguistic theory that lies behind such grammars," they say, "can be summarized under five headings: unclear categories, heterogeneous criteria, fictions, conceptual formulations and value judgments. To these could be added two more which lie outside grammar but contribute to the total picture of the languages inaccurate phonetics, and confusion of media." [20] The first contribution, then, of linguistic theorists to foreign-language teaching must be what the linguistic scientists are most qualified to contribute: good descriptions of the foreign language being taught and of the native language of the students, in order to make the transition more effective. Once valid and consistent descriptions are available, teachers with the necessary pedagogical understanding and knowledge of adolescent psychology will be able to write appropriate textbooks. This, it will be remembered, was also the viewpoint of the transformationalists. Teachers must become more critical of the grammatical descriptions in textbooks and choose those which have applied appropriately the best language descriptions which are currently available.

20 *Ibid.*, p. 157.

HOW IS LANGUAGE ACQUIRED?

So far we have talked a great deal about ways of describing languages, and from this discussion it becomes obvious that grammar is the core of language. Without grammar we are left with a few words as labels for features of the physical environment. Our next problem is: how can our students acquire the grammar of a foreign language so that it functions for them as does the grammar of their native language—as a flexible vehicle of meaning which they do not even realize they are using. The place of grammar in language teaching will devolve from the type of study we believe foreign-language learning to be.

The controversy rages whether ability to use a foreign language is a skill or involves the exercise of the intellect. Some people claim that language is a skill to be acquired, as are other skills, mainly by long and intensive practice until the smallest elements can be manipulated in correct sequence without hesitation or reflection; other people consider intellectual training necessary so that students may be able to make correct choices of rules to be put into operation in order to express themselves comprehensibly in the new medium.

In the past emphasis has, on the whole, been placed on the intellectual aspect of language learning, so that there has been in the classroom much talk about the language, close analysis of the language system, and practice in the construction of foreign-language phrases and sentences according to the rules. Communication skills have been developed slowly, if at all. In a revolution of language-teaching methods the major emphasis has swung to the early development of communication skills by teaching students to use the foreign language without a thorough understanding of its systematic operation; this approach has been regarded as consistent with native-language use, where the speaker can handle the language in all its complexity without conscious effort and without being able to verbalize the rules to which his language behavior is conforming. At one extreme we have had students able to repeat rules and paradigms and concoct artificial samples of the foreign language without being able to communicate effectively, either in speech or writing; at the other extreme we have had students who are very fluent in the production of set phrases which they have learned by imitation but who are unable to create at will new utterances to convey their message in the foreign language. Surely competent foreign-language use is something other than either of these.

This fundamental problem of language use as a skill or as rule-governed behavior revives several persistent controversies which we shall discuss to some depth in this and subsequent chapters:

Is foreign-language learning a matter of habit formation or of the inculcation of rules?

Is a foreign language learned most effectively by inductive or by deductive processes, by analogy or by analysis?

Should the foreign-language learning situation be so structured that students are induced into making only the correct response, or does trial-and-error learning have a part to play in foreign-language acquisition?

Does ability to use what one has learned of the foreign language in wider contexts and for new purposes develop as the result of identical-elements transfer, or as the result of a process of transposition wherein the understanding of the functioning of the part in the whole has a vital role? [21]

If we can identify two levels of foreign-language behavior for which our students must be trained: the level of manipulation of language elements which occur in fixed relationships in clearly defined closed systems (that is, relationships which will vary within very narrow limits) ; and a level of expression of personal meaning at which possible variations are infinite, depending on such factors as the type of message to be conveyed, the situation in which the utterance takes place, the relationship between speaker and hearer or hearers, and the degree of intensity with which the message is conveyed—then it is clear that one type of teaching will not be sufficient for the task. A place must be found for both habit formation and the understanding of a complex system with its infinite possibilities of expression. The problem is to define the role of each of these types of learning in the teaching of the foreign language.

21 These controversies are examined in great detail in W. Rivers, *The Psychologist and the Foreign-Language Teacher* (Chicago, 1964), chaps. 5–7, 11.

Basically, the two approaches to foreign-language learning which have been described stem from two theories about how the native language is learned in the first place. The behaviorist theory of stimulus-response learning, particularly as developed in the operant conditioning model of Skinner,[22] considers all learning to be the establishment of habits as the result of reinforcement or reward. According to this theory, the infant acquires native-language habits in the following fashion. At some stage in his random babbling, the infant makes a sound which resembles the appropriate word for some person or object near him. For this he is rewarded by the approving noises or smiles of those about him and so the probability of his emitting the same grouping of sounds in a similar situation is increased. With repeated reinforcement a habit is established and he continues to name this person or object in this way. As he continues to imitate sounds around him more combinations are reinforced. When he names something imperiously, it is brought to him, and so he learns to use words with sentence intention as mands, and later to combine words to convey more complexity of meaning. As he acquires more syntactic and morphological variations he creates new combinations by generalization or analogy, sometimes making mistakes by producing analogies which are not permissible in the language. By a trial-and-error process, in which acceptable utterances are reinforced by comprehension and approval and unacceptable utterances are inhibited by lack of reward, he gradually learns to make finer and finer discriminations until his utterances approximate more and more closely the speech of the community in which he is growing up.

This behaviorist view of native-language learning has been rejected by a number of theorists, notably Chomsky and Lenneberg. These writers maintain that there are certain aspects of native-language learning which make it impossible to accept the habit-formation-by-reinforcement theory.[23] Lenneberg draws attention to the fact that all children, with the rare ex-

---

22 B. F. Skinner, *Verbal Behavior* (New York, 1957).

23 Chomsky, "Linguistic Theory," in Northeast Conference (1966), p. 44; and E. Lenneberg, "The Capacity for Language Acquisition," in Fodor and Katz (1964), pp. 579–603, revised and expanded version of "Language, Evolution and Purposive Behavior" (1960).

ception of children with certain physical disabilities, learn a language to a similar degree of mastery of basic structures, despite great differences in cultural environment and amount of parental attention. All children learn the language of their community at about the same age, irrespective of the degree of structural complexity, and all children pass through the same stages of development in acquiring it. He points out that child language learning does not appear to be a process of pure imitation but seems to involve active selection. Combining of words in meaningful sequences seems to develop at a stage when the infant realizes that sounds and objects or situations have some relationship. The available evidence seems to support the view that this realization is a matter of maturation. Lenneberg considers that speech is a species-specific ability which is peculiar to man. He maintains, with Chomsky, that man has certain innate propensities for acquiring a language, and for acquiring a language with a complicated grammar. He draws attention to the fact that children add endings to nonsense words in a way which they have never heard around them, and that as children master various aspects of syntax they produce utterances they have certainly never heard before. Chomsky, with his interest in the hierarchical operation of syntax, is struck with the way the child seems quite rapidly to internalize a most complicated system of grammar, so that he is able to recognize and produce at will any number of novel utterances. To Chomsky, it is manifestly impossible for the child to acquire this system of grammar by some vague process of imitation and generalization. He is convinced that because the innate logical structure of the child's nervous system conforms with the abstract universal categories and organization underlying his language, the child identifies the basic syntactic system and his mastery of the language develops from this identification, rather than by being built in by sheer repetition and reinforcement. As Lenneberg puts it: "Obviously, children are not given rules they can apply. They are merely exposed to a great number of examples of how the syntax works, and from these examples they completely automatically acquire principles with which new sentences can be formed that will conform to the universally recognized rules of the game. . . . words are neither randomly arranged nor confined to unchangeable, stereotyped sequences. At every stage there is a characteristic structure. . . . The appearance of language may be thought to be due to an innately mapped-in *program* for behavior, the exact realization of the program being dependent upon the peculiarities of the (speech) environment." [24] These two widely divergent views on native-language learning have been espoused on the whole by the proponents of the two main schools of thought on grammar: the structuralists and the transformationalists. The structuralists, in the early stages, took considerable interest in the problems of teaching foreign languages, and, in conformity with the stimulus-response psychology of their day, tended to emphasize the necessity for building in habits in the use of correct structure by mimicry-memorization of whole utterances and by drilling patterns, with minimal variations. A number of them, however, have always advocated careful instruction in the structure of the language to parallel such intensive drilling, particularly with adult students. [25] Those preparing materials for high schools did not feel that this was appropriate for adolescent students and, attempting as they were to make a clear break with past practices, strongly emphasized habit-formation techniques with little or no structural explanation, particularly at the elementary level. Where they admitted structural explanations, they advocated practice to a point of automatic response before explanations were given. Teachers with a brief acquaintance with the linguistic and psychological principles upon which these techniques were founded have sometimes carried this practice to an extreme, in a blind devotion to a new cause, while linguistic scientists, particularly those influenced by transformationalist theory, have questioned this approach to language learning. They

24 Lenneberg (1964), pp. 599–600.
25 C. C. Fries, in *Teaching and Learning English as a Foreign Language* (Ann Arbor, 1945), p. 29, says, "An adult can be helped considerably in building up the necessary habits if the basic matters of this required knowledge are definitely stated in generalizations for his guidance." E. Nida, in *Learning a Foreign Language,* rev. ed. (Ann Arbor, Mich., 1957), p. 41, note 3, says, "The introduction of grammatical explanations makes this system considerably different from and superior to the Berlitz method. . . . For adults, who have been trained by educational maturity to analyze and synthesize, it is a great advantage to have accurate grammatical explanations."

have repeatedly pointed out that language behavior is not just the reeling off of automatic responses to stimuli by a process of association of linguistic elements in correct relationships in a linear sequence, but is rule-governed behavior in which higher-level choices bring lower-level adjustments into play.

A detailed account of the implications for classroom practice of these two positions may make the points at issue a little clearer.

LANGUAGE TEACHING AS THE FORMATION OF LANGUAGE HABITS

The proponents of the habit-formation approach see language as primarily speech and secondarily writing and believe that a surer foundation for all language skills will be laid if new language material is first studied in its oral form. They regard language as a patterning of smaller and larger elements in close functional relationships and maintain that facility in the recognition and use of these patterns is a matter of habits which have been formed as the result of reinforcement in a social situation. They do not advocate the teaching of a language through detailed explanations of the functioning of the language system. They believe that intellectual analysis leads to hesitancy at the point of choice, whereas the fluent speaker of a language, through inbuilt intralanguage associations, produces language elements in correct sequence without the need for reflection and is thus able to concentrate on his message. This automatic production of language response to language stimulus they endeavor to develop through dialogue memorization, the learning of structural patterns, choral and individual oral drill, and practice with minimal variations. Incorrect responses are reduced to a minimum by structuring the situation, through carefully planned drills and exercises, so that the student will produce the right response on most occasions without any hesitation. Since the correct form is always given by the teacher immediately after the student's attempt, the student's correct response is rewarded, or reinforced, by knowledge of the value of his performance, and his incorrect response, if it did occur, is inhibited. In drilling, emphasis on meaning is underplayed in favor of quick response to a language stimulus (e.g., correct answer form to a question form), familiarity with meaning being gradually acquired by frequent association of language elements with particular situations and with other language elements. Rules for language use are not set out explicitly when structural patterns are being practiced, but after the pattern has been learned to a point of automatic production a generalization of what the student has been doing is sometimes given. Generalizations become more comprehensive as the student advances in knowledge of the language and is able to recognize characteristic features of the language structure. In some materials, particularly for younger students, no generalizations are given, and all learning of structure is inductive, with the student assimilating the way language functions through using functioning language. The emphasis, then, is on the apprehension of structural meaning through experience with the patterns and the common expressions of the language. Since it is obvious that students cannot learn all possible language combinations by memorization and drilling in the precise form in which an utterance will be made, opportunity is provided for the students to make new combinations by analogy, using the same structural elements with different lexical items. It is believed that the students, having acquired considerable experience in the automatic association of certain structural elements, will retain this automaticity in constructing further utterances of a similar form.

LANGUAGE TEACHING AS THE ESTABLISHMENT OF RULE-GOVERNED BEHAVIOR

According to this view, language is not only patterned but the patterns are manifestations of a tightly interwoven code of rules which govern the production of acceptable and comprehensible utterances. In speech and writing, higher-level choices must be made which set lower-level patterns in operation. Language behavior is too complicated to be learned purely by imitation and repetition. It would be impossible to learn all the possible sentences of the language in this way because of the strain on the memory, yet dependence on analogy for the construction of new utterances can be as misleading as it is helpful. The student, having an incomplete knowledge of the structure of the language, is unable to determine the limits within which analogy may be applied. Students need a clear picture of what they are trying to do within the system of the new language; that is, they need to understand the possible extensions and limitations of certain interrelationships. Some deductive explanation, some establishing of rules, is necessary. When students understand how the structures they are seeking to control function in relation to other parts of the language system, they will be able to construct new utterances which will be recognized as authentically patterned by native speakers of the language.

This view is a modernized version of the attitude of many foreign-language teachers through the centuries. It has not, on the whole, produced students who can construct at will new utterances without hesitation and reflection. This is because, for the most part, speakers trained in this fashion pause before producing any utterance in order to apply rules, not only at the higher controlling levels but at all the lower levels of interrelated features as well. Because of the number and complexity of the rules they must apply at the same time, their utterances are rarely correctly formed in every detail.

A PLACE FOR BOTH POINTS OF VIEW

There is no reason to believe that the two positions which have just been described are mutually exclusive. Language is a very complex phenomenon, and the way in which we learn to use a foreign language and what is involved in using it freely for our own purposes is far from clear. Many persons down the ages have acquired a fluent grasp of a foreign language by very varied methods, while many others taught by these same methods seem to have been halted in their progress at a certain point and never to have attained fluency of expression in speech or writing. This fact seems to indicate that the methods used have been haphazard and that personal success or failure has been the result of factors other than the techniques used in the classroom.

What appears to have been ignored in teaching is the fact

that certain elements of language remain in fixed relationships in small, closed systems, so that once the system is invoked in a particular way a succession of interrelated formal features appears. Fluent speakers are able to make these interrelated adjustments irrespective of the particular message they wish to produce. The elements which interact in restricted systems may be practiced separately in order to forge strong habitual associations from which the speaker never deviates (this applies to such elements as inflection of person and number, agreements of gender, fixed forms for interrogation or negation, and formal features of tenses). These elements do not require intellectual analysis: they exist, and they must be used in a certain way in certain environments and in no other way.[26] For these features, drill is a very effective technique. They may be inductively learned by the students without more than an occasional word of explanation by the teacher when there is hesitation or bewilderment. In structured classroom practice their use may be extended, by the process of analogy, to other utterances with different combinations of lexical items.

On the other hand, other elements of language, mainly at the level of syntax, involve decisions more intimately connected with the contextual meaning. A decision at this higher level has implications for structure beyond the word or the phrase, often beyond the sentence. A slight variation in the decision will often mean the construction of quite a different message. Elements of this second type usually involve several features in interaction, and therefore a more complicated initial choice which entails further choices of a more limited character. In order to express exactly what one wishes to say, one must view it in relation to the potential of the structural system of the language as a whole. This is the higher-level decision which sets in motion operations at lower levels which are interdependent. The decision to make a particular type of statement about something which has taken place recently involves a choice of register; a choice of degree of intensity; and the use of lexical items in certain syntactical relationships which will

---

26 It is interesting to note that many of these features, particularly the morphological ones, are excluded by Chomsky from his system of rewrite rules and are included in the lexicon as parts of complex symbols. See *Aspects of the Theory of Syntax*, pp. 82–88.

involve the production of certain morphological elements, phonemic distinctions, and stress and intonation patterns. The
interrelationships within the language system which are involved in these higher-level decisions may need to be clarified
in deductive fashion by teacher or textbook. Practice at this
level must be practice with understanding, where the student is
conscious of the implications and ramifications of changes he is
making. This he will best do if the practice involves making
decisions in real communication situations devised in the classroom, rather than in continual drills and exercises. In such
interchanges the feedback from the other participants brings a
realization of the effect of the decision the speaker has made.

There must be, then, a constant interplay in the classroom of
learning by analogy and by analysis, of inductive and deductive processes, according to the nature of the operation the
student is learning. It is evident that higher-level choices cannot be put into operation with ease if facility has not been
developed in the production of the interdependent lower-level
elements, and so learning by induction, drill, and analogy will
be the commonest features of the early stages. Genuine freedom in language use will, however, develop only as the student
gains control of the system as a whole, beyond the mastery of
patterns in isolation.

PRACTICAL APPLICATION TO THE LANGUAGE CLASS

It becomes clear that the second level of language use, which
we have just described, is of a more advanced type than the
first level, requiring as it does sufficient knowledge of the total
possibilities of the language to be able to make higher-level
choices, as well as skill in the manipulation of numerous lower-
level elements in accordance with the higher-level decision.
Too often in the past foreign-language teaching has concentrated on an understanding of the language system as a whole
without providing for the amount of sheer repetitious practice
that the lower-level elements demand. On the other hand, some
modern methods in which only the problems of the early stages
seem to have been considered to any serious extent have
worked out techniques which develop the lower-level manipu-

lative skill but leave the student unpracticed in the making of decisions at the higher level. In the planning of the language course, provision must be made for training at both levels. The stage at which training at the second level, which involves a clear understanding of the functioning of the language system as a whole, should begin will depend on the age and maturity of the student. At the elementary school level, the learning of the language will be largely imitative and manipulative. (According to the studies of Inhelder and Piaget, students at this age are not as yet sufficiently mature to handle "formal operations" of a logical character.) [27] If the Lenneberg hypothesis [28] is valid, however, they will still retain sufficient inductive language-learning ability to be able to make higher-level decisions of an uncomplicated variety in the context of simple classroom activities. At the level of an adult, or undergraduate, elementary foreign-language course, students will be mature enough and have sufficient formal educational experience to undertake a systematic study of the structure of the language after they have acquired a certain skill in manipulating the most frequently recurring formal elements and in expressing their meaning in simple utterances. In this chapter, we shall concentrate on what is appropriate for the junior and senior high school student.

In the initial stages, preferably at junior high school level, grammatical principles will be implicit in language material presented to the student orally. Students will learn complete utterances of high frequency of occurrence, and will have plenty of opportunity to practice variations in structure by oral exercises or by a pattern-drill procedure. (The principles of the pattern-drill procedure and the varieties of drills which are suitable for this level are discussed fully in chapter 4.) Through this oral practice they will learn to recognize structural signals to meaning and learn to produce these appropriately and automatically in response to other structural signals, as we do in communication. The emphasis at this stage will be

27 B. Inhelder and J. Piaget, *The Growth of Logical Thinking from Childhood to Adolescence,* trans. A. Parsons and S. Milgram (New York, 1958).
28 E. Lenneberg: "The Natural History of Language," in F. Smith and G. A. Miller, eds., *The Genesis of Language* (Cambridge, Mass., 1966), pp. 239–40.

on how the language functions at specific points rather than on the relationship of these particular elements to the whole language system. Complete utterances will be the basis for recognition and reproduction exercises, so that students will be building up gradually an image of the language system which will make later instruction in its organization intelligible.

Even at this stage, however, the student should not be required to perform language operations in a void. If he is asked to effect a number of variations on a language pattern, it is in the nature of the learning process that he will either be repeating and varying items mechanically without concentration and without any real learning taking place or he will be organizing the elements of the drill in a way which is meaningful to him in order to help him to remember what he assumes to be the point at issue.[29] This individual organization may well be along the lines of his native-language system, if he knows no other, and can lead to erroneous assumptions which will hinder him in the correct use of the language form he is practicing when he tries to use it for his own purposes. Advocacy of the necessity to drill language structures without any indication to the student of the point at issue has sprung from a strictly behavioristic concept of stimulus-response learning which does not take into account the needs and reactions of the learner. If the drill is to be effective, the student must be aware of the crucial element in the operations he is performing. When drills are based on uncomplicated patterns drawn from material thoroughly learned and practiced in a situation context, students usually establish for themselves what the point at issue is, and little or no explanation is necessary. When the point at issue forms a contrast with native-language usage, or is in any way obscure, the teacher should make sure that the students understand what they are expected to learn by the drill. In practice, then, the structure should be familiar to the students in that it has already appeared several times in work they have been learning; the students should repeat the structure after the teacher a number of times, with simple variations of lexical content, and then be asked to indicate the crucial changes being made and their functions. There should

29 This aspect of learning is discussed at length in Rivers (1964), pp. 120–24.

be no need to insist upon the main point of the drill, but if the students are obviously vague about what they are doing the teacher should make the significance of the variations clear to them in a few simple words. The students should then continue to drill the structure with further variation until they can demonstrate that they are able to use it without hesitation.

When the students have acquired facility in expressing themselves within a limited area of language [30] (after perhaps two years of study at junior high school level, a year of study at senior high school, at least half a year at undergraduate level), they will, with properly planned teaching materials, be familiar with a sufficient number of the structures of the language to benefit from a more systematic study at a formal level. The habit-formation techniques will have given them confidence in the use of many frequently occurring patterns of the language; it will now be the time to systematize and organize what they know so that the interrelationships become apparent. This organization of knowledge will take place gradually over a period of years and will avoid all superfluous and anachronistic detail of the type which was the bane of language students of an earlier period. It will aim at systematizing what the student has already learned to use, and introducing further, more abstract, relationships as the student is able to assimilate and practice them. Well-prepared teaching materials will avoid the situation, so common in the past, where a tremendous amount of detail about the language system is presented to the student in his first year and has to be retaught in the following year, and in successive years, without any clear signs that it has been assimilated even after many representations. This situation is inevitable when much talk about the language, fascinating as it may be, replaces active practice in the use of the language.

Grammatical material must be carefully graded so that the student advances slowly from material thoroughly learned and practiced to more complicated material which involves more conscious choices. This does not mean, as some school grammars have assumed, that students must first be presented with the smallest elements of the language. Patterns of wide ap-

30 For a full discussion of the techniques for helping students to reach this stage in all skill areas, see chapters 6–10.

plicability should be presented in the early stages so that students are soon able to use some of the language in real communication. A strong case can also be made for the early presentation of structures which contrast with those of the native-language system. This approach makes students conscious from the start of the existence of a different way of looking at things; it ensures that those facets of the language which are most difficult for the student, because of the interference of native-language habits, will receive the most practice during the course of the foreign-language program.

At whatever stage a new structure is introduced, it should be presented first in concrete form, in speech or in writing, before it becomes the object of an abstract organization. This practice enables the student to make some inductive systematization of his own, keeping him alert to regularities within variations in living language materials. Grammatical principles should be made explicit only after the student has had some experience of their operation; in this way each structure will be seen to have a place in a functioning system and to have a value only in relation to other elements within the language. Until the student has such a coherent view of structural patterns he will not be able to use the language as the flexible instrument he requires for the expression of the nuances of meaning he has in mind.[31]

AREAS OF CONTROVERSY

Should the foreign language or the native language be used to explain problems of structure?

In an attempt to keep the students thinking and working entirely in the foreign language, direct-method teachers gave all instruction in the language being learned. Everything in the textbook, including directions, was in the foreign language, and grammar books gave structural explanations as well as exercises in the language. To achieve this aim the accepted grammatical terminology of the foreign language was employed.

31 Further elaboration of some of the material in this chapter will be found in a paper by the author included in "Proceedings of the 1967 MLA Convention," *MLJ*, April, 1968.

It is clear from the discussion in this chapter that, after an initial period of familiarization with the most frequently used patterns of the language, it is useful to draw together the students' ideas in a more systematic way, by studying aspects of the language structure in relation to other features. If this study is to be carried through entirely in the foreign language, the students must be taught the terminology which will act as a convenient system of reference for these explanations.

Some terms which describe features found in most languages will be acquired quite readily by the students, to whom the concepts to which they apply are already familiar from their study of the native language. Since each language should be discussed in terms of its own system, there will usually also be a number of terms which apply to features not found in the native language; for these appropriate terminology would have to be learned in association with new concepts, whether explanations were being given in the foreign language or in the native language. For these reasons, the learning of foreign-language terminology does not present an insuperable obstacle.

The question we must ask ourselves is the following: for whom do we consider this systematization of structure the most useful? The more apt of the students, who have gained a firm control of basic structure in the earlier stages of language learning, will follow quite easily discussions about the structure in the foreign language. Their accurate knowledge of the recurring features will help them in this study. These are, however, not the students who are most in need of this systematic instruction in the grammar of the new language; it is the weak students who have not recognized interrelationships for themselves for whom this teaching should be designed. These are the very students who will have difficulty in following abstract explanations in the foreign language. A short elucidation of a grammatical point in the native language will help these students much more than a prolonged attempt to explain and reexplain in the foreign language and will leave more time for practice of the feature under discussion—practice that is essential if such students are to be able to use the structural patterns about which they are learning.

To summarize: with a homogeneous group of gifted students who already have an understanding of fundamental structural relations, discussion of the structural system in the foreign language is an appropriate technique; for students who are finding the language study difficult, explanations in the native language which are brief, coherent, and to the point, followed by active practice of the features under discussion, are more effective.

ANNOTATED READING LIST

NIDA, E. A. *Toward a Science of Translating.* Leiden: E. J. Brill, 1964. Pp. 57–69. Chapter 4, "Linguistic Meaning," contains a lucid discussion of immediate-constituent and transformational-generative grammars.

GLEASON, JR., H. A. *Linguistics and English Grammar.* New York: Holt, Rinehart & Winston, 1965. Chapter 4, "English Grammars," discusses various approaches to grammar.

————. *An Introduction to Descriptive Linguistics.* Rev. ed. New York: Holt, Rinehart & Winston, 1961. Chapter 10, "Immediate Constituents," Chapter 11, "Syntactic Devices," and Chapter 12, "Transformations," give a clear presentation of the descriptive and earlier transformational approaches to grammar

HALLIDAY, M. A. K.; MCINTOSH, A.; and STREVENS, P. *The Linguistic Sciences and Language Teaching.* London: Longmans, 1964. Chapter 1, "Linguistics and Phonetics," and Chapter 2, "Linguistics in the Description of Language," set out the British system of multilevel language analysis; Chapter 6, "The Basic Role of Linguistics and Phonetics," outlines the historical development of the study of grammar and criticizes the grammatical descriptions in language textbooks.

CHOMSKY, N. *Syntactic Structures.* The Hague: Mouton & Co., 1957; and *Aspects of the Theory of Syntax.* Cambridge, Mass.: M.I.T. Press, 1965, set out the transformational-generative view of grammar.

NORTHEAST CONFERENCE ON THE TEACHING OF FOREIGN LANGUAGES, 1966. *Language Teaching: Broader Contexts.* Contains an article by N. Chomsky, "Linguistic Theory" (pp. 43–49), in which he sets out his views on language learning.

SAPORTA, S. "Applied Linguistics and Generative Grammar." In A. VALDMAN, ed., *Trends in Language Teaching*. New York: McGraw-Hill, 1966. Pp. 81–92. Discusses the role of grammar in foreign-language teaching.

ANISFELD, M. "Psycholinguistic Perspectives on Language Learning." In Valdman (1966). Pp. 107–19. Discusses linguistic competence and the psychological processes in language acquisition.

RIVERS, W. M. *The Psychologist and the Foreign-Language Teacher*. Chicago: The University of Chicago Press, 1964. Relevant chapters are: Chapter 6: "Two Levels of Language"; Chapter 8: "Foreign-Language Habits are Formed . . . by giving the Right Response . . ."; Chapter 11: "Analogy Provides a Better Foundation for Foreign-Language Learning than Analysis."

4

Construction of Grammatical
Drills and Exercises

Mention has been made in chapter 3 of the influence of the
psychological theory of B. F. Skinner on foreign-language
teaching techniques. Skinner himself applied his theory, derived from his experiments with rats and pigeons, to a method
of teaching factual material to human subjects. Although he
was not the first person to devise materials for self-instruction,[1] it is from his work that we can date the widespread
interest in programmed instructional materials. His famous
article "The Science of Learning and the Art of Teaching"
(1954) has been studied, quoted, and reprinted constantly.[2] It
should be read as a background to any study of programmed
instruction.

Skinner's principles for changing behavior (reinforcement of
correct responses in a series involving minimal changes) were
already being used extensively by some foreign-language
teachers at this time. They are basic to the pattern practice
techniques which were advocated by leading teachers of Eng-

---

1 Sidney Pressey was experimenting with programs for "teaching machines" as early as 1924. For articles by the leading figures in the
 programming movement, see A. A. Lumsdaine and R. Glaser, eds.,
 Teaching Machines and Programmed Learning (Washington, D.C.,
 1960).
2 *Harvard Educational Review*, 24 (1954): 86–97. This article has been
 reprinted in Lumsdaine and Glaser (1960), pp. 99–113.

lish as a foreign language [3] and which were very much in evidence in many of the wartime foreign-language programs in the United States. The programming movement encouraged the writers of language-teaching materials to examine more closely the sequencing and development of their drills and exercises. Since the theoretical position basic to these types of instructional materials is more fully developed by experimentalists in the area of programmed instruction, we shall deal with this subject first and then apply our findings to a description and evaluation of drills and exercises for classroom and language laboratory use.

The question how students learn is a vital one for all teachers. Much teaching is a diffuse, hit-or-miss procedure because of the unclear notions teachers have on this subject. Increased efficiency must result from scientifically based insight into learning processes. For Skinner, learning is demonstrated by a change in behavior. His operant conditioning experiments have led him to believe that changes in behavior can be induced as follows: a behavioral response is made to occur through control of the environment in which the subject is placed; a reinforcing or rewarding stimulus which follows this response makes the response more likely to recur; if this rewarding state of affairs consistently follows the selected response, the response becomes conditioned as a habit. If the response is undesirable it is left unrewarded and soon becomes extinguished. If the experimenter wishes to induce a certain pattern of behavior, no matter how foreign to the subject, he waits until a response occurs which resembles to some extent the desired behavior. He rewards this response and not others. Methodically he continues to reward responses which approximate more and more closely the desired behavior, not rewarding others, until through a series of "successive approximations" he shapes the behavior to his preconceived pattern. In this fashion, he can induce subjects to make very fine discriminations among similar stimuli, and to follow through a complex series of well-defined responses.

3 See C. C. Fries, *Teaching and Learning English as a Foreign Language* (Ann Arbor, Mich., 1945). Substitution frames were already being advocated by H. E. Palmer in *The Principles of Language Study* (London, 1921), reprinted by Oxford University Press in 1964.

The programming movement has adopted this paradigm of learning and applied it as follows: the programmer draws up very careful specifications of the "terminal behavior" he wishes to induce in the learner; he also analyzes the initial or existent behavior of the learner; he then establishes a program (that is, a sequence of learning steps) by which the learner's responses will be shaped until the desired behavior is demonstrated. This program controls the learning environment of the student. Sometimes it is presented as a programmed textbook, sometimes in some type of teaching machine. In either case, through a series of "frames" which the student must study, the amount of attention he will give to any one element of the sequence and the order in which he will study these elements are under the control of the programmer, who can therefore prescribe as much practice as he considers necessary at any one point. The programmer prompts or provokes responses to the frames. These responses are given immediate reinforcement, in that the student receives confirmation of the acceptability of his response without delay, by seeing or hearing the correct version with which he may compare his own. The aim of the programmer is to present the material for learning in such a sequence and in such easily digested or minimal steps that the student will not make mistakes but, by being constantly reinforced by his success, will develop habitual behavior of the kind desired by the programmer.

There are certain ways in which programmed self-instruction is theoretically (that is, with ideal conditions and first-class programs) superior to the usual classroom instruction. It provides for active participation by the student throughout the learning session; each student is able to make far more individual responses in the lesson period than as a member of a class group. If the student learns what the programmer has intended him to learn, he proceeds to new work; if he has not succeeded in learning it, he remains at the same point in the instructional material until he has had further practice. At times, he may be directed back to earlier material for further study. In this way, programmed materials are considered to be "self-pacing," providing for individual differences in rates of learning which cannot be accommodated in the classroom. With no time limit set for the completion of any section of the program, the faster-learning student is not held back and the slow-learning student is not harassed and bewildered. A program which is seriously planned is revised according to the errors made in trial runs by the students. It is therefore those for whom the program is intended who ultimately determine many aspects of the program sequence, and not some theoretician detached from the learning situation. Programmers emphasize the fact that the program does not replace the classroom teacher. Students left to work on their own for long periods with machines or programmed texts miss the stimulation they receive from their interaction with a person interested in their progress.[4] The program does, however, free the teacher from constant attention to the needs of a large group of students, so that he may give personal attention and tuition to those students who most need his help, at the moment when they need it.

Two types of programs have been advocated for use with teaching machines or programmed textbooks. The first type, the Skinnerian program, is linear in the sense that each student works his way step by step through the whole sequence. In the second type, intrinsic programming as advocated by Crowder,[5] provision is made, by branching techniques, for fast-learning students to skip parts of the program and for slow-learning students to be directed to supplementary sets of frames of a remedial nature.

Linear programs require constructed responses, often the filling in of a blank in a frame. Each correct response prepares the way for the next step in the program, each step being indispensable for the comprehension of the succeeding step. It is this careful arrangement of steps which shapes the student's learning toward the desired terminal outcome. Sometimes responses are imitative or echoic; sometimes they are elicited by the logic of the progression of steps; sometimes they are prompted by the provision of some elements of the required response. Where some parts of the response are supplied, these

4 F. Marty, *Programing a Basic Foreign Language Course* (Hollins College, Va., 1962), pp. 16–17.
5 N. A. Crowder, "On the Differences between Linear and Intrinsic Programming" in A. de Grazia and D. Sohn, eds., *Programs, Teachers, and Machines* (New York, 1964), pp. 77–99.

may be faded out gradually in succeeding frames until the student is able to make the response without prompting.

The aim of a linear program is for the student to pass through it from beginning to end making the minimum of errors that is consistent with occasional inattention and distraction. It is therefore very dependent for its success in promoting learning on the size of step from frame to frame. If the size of the step is very small, an error-free passage is possible for most students; such a program, however, can be very boring and irritating to many students because the answers, being too obvious, do not require alertness and careful thought on their part. In this case the force of confirmation of response is lost because there is no feeling of success in finding the correct answer in this time-wasting way. Step size may also be too great, not only forcing some students into error but discouraging others from pursuing the task to the end; it is at these points that the programmer, in revising his work, must devise intermediate steps to help the students.

Intrinsic programming is characterized by the provision of multiple-choice answers for selection of response. These multiple-choice answers reflect possible errors due to misapprehensions about the learning material. According to his choice of answer, the learner is either directed to new material or branched off into a series of remedial frames which reteach what the student has not understood. (Where a programmed textbook is used, the various segments of the program are "scrambled" so that the student cannot ignore branching directions and proceed with the program; he must know the correct response in order to determine the position in the book of the next section of new material). Intrinsic programming is based on the premise that learning takes place through a trial-and-error process—that students can learn from their mistakes. It is considered by its proponents to be more sensitive to individual differences than linear programming because it provides shorter programs for faster learners and more detailed study or practice for slower learners.

Intrinsic programming has not been used to any great extent for foreign-language teaching. It is generally considered inadvisable for foreign-language students to be presented with incorrect alternatives which they may well "learn" from the program instead of the correct response. Furthermore, in most programs, allowing students to skip sections is a concession to those who easily acquire an intellectual understanding of the logic of a sequence of ideas and do not need repetitious elaboration. Such a procedure is applicable in foreign-language study only if teachers are satisfied for their students to "learn about the language." Those who most quickly attain an understanding of interrelationships in a foreign language often do not appreciate the need to practice what they are learning until they can use basic language elements automatically. Opportunity for these students to skip over too many practice exercises can be detrimental to their progress. Some linear programmers have attempted to make greater provision for individual rate of progress without resorting to intrinsic methods. Carroll [6] has experimented with the introduction into the program of "loops" which enable the students to rework material a number of times, eliminating mistakes on successive passages through the loop. In this way all students are given what seems to the programmer to be sufficient practice, yet provision is made for students who need to do so to repractice the material as often as they wish before proceeding to a new section. The multiple-choice recognition response of intrinsic programming may be useful at a more advanced level in foreign-language study: to test comprehension of material presented aurally or graphically, or to test knowledge of fine distinctions in structural usage. Their value is very doubtful at the stage when the student is learning to use actively the basic structural patterns of the language.

In this book the important question to be asked about programmed instruction is: is it appropriate for the special requirements of foreign-language learning? Returning to the viewpoint developed in chapter 3, we may say that careful programming of the types described is very useful in the development of sound discrimination and production, aural and reading comprehension, skill in the automatic manipulation of language elements in closed systems, and ability to write the language accurately at the nonspontaneous level. For foreign-language learning, the teaching machine or pro-

6 J. B. Carroll, "A Primer of Programmed Instruction in Foreign Language Teaching," *IRAL* I/2 (1963): 129.

grammed textbook must be accompanied by sound and recording facilities. Some visual element (films, filmstrips, slides,
cartoons, or other pictures) can facilitate the learning. There
is, however, the danger that a purely self-instructional foreign-language course will teach very thoroughly the elements
of the language in certain contexts without giving the student
facility and confidence in using these at the level of active
communication. Spolsky, in discussing this type of inflexibility, makes a distinction between "knowing a language" and
"language-like behavior," asserting that being able to recite a
number of sentences in a foreign language is an example of the
latter, while the former "involves the ability to produce an
indefinite number of utterances in response to an indefinite
number of stimuli." [7] Both Marty and Valdman advocate, in
association with periods of self-instruction, sessions in small
groups [8] where students can practice using what they have
learned in actual communication with an instructor and each
other. Such sessions provide an element of public reinforcement which cannot be provided by a machine or a textbook;
the students are able to display what they know and to receive
the reinforcement of comprehension and approval from their
fellows and their teacher. This increases their desire to be
successful in the self-instructional part of the course, thus
encouraging them to persevere despite the difficulties they may
encounter.

One of the major problems in the programming of foreign-
language courses is the elaboration of detailed specifications of
the desired terminal behavior. Since the students will learn
what the program teaches them this preliminary work must be
very well done if the students are to develop all-round skill in
language use. The programmer must decide what type of language mastery he wishes to develop, setting out some practical
and well-defined criteria of attainment; he must establish
what skills are involved in this terminal behavior, and what
elements are essential to the exercise of these skills; and finally
he must establish pedagogically useful groupings for the great

---

7 Bernard Spolsky, "A Psycholinguistic Critique of Programmed
   Foreign Language Instruction," *IRAL* IV/2 (1966): 124.
8 F. Marty (1962), p. 21; and A. Valdman, "Toward Self-Instruction
   in Foreign Language Learning," *IRAL* II/1 (1964): 7.

number of elements thus identified. In order to establish these essential basic elements, he will need to draw on the most thorough linguistic description of the language available to him and, if possible, a contrastive study of the foreign and native languages in order to pinpoint the areas of major interference for the student. Having made this detailed analysis of elements to be learned, he will then need to find the most effective order for introducing them into the program. The choice of order of presentation will reflect his pedagogical orientation and will not necessarily parallel the order of linguistic description; it will also be dependent on the educational level for which the program is being written and the purposes it will serve.

It is clear, then, that programming for self-instruction in foreign languages is a task for a team of experts, not for the individual classroom teacher, who will have neither the basic training, time, nor money to undertake such a project. This discussion of what is involved in a good program will, however, assist the teacher in evaluating programmed courses which he may be considering for use with his classes.

Is the introduction of programmed self-instruction on a wide scale imminent in high schools? Probably not, for a number of reasons. At present there is a paucity of good programs for use in high schools. Some commercially produced courses are little more than the translation to programmed form of material from some traditional textbook. No thorough examination of desirable terminal behavior in view of present-day objectives in foreign-language learning has preceded the programming of these courses, and it is very doubtful whether they provide any more than a skilled teacher who is using the original textbook could provide. They will ensure, perhaps, that the student knows more thoroughly certain facts about the language but will not ensure that he can use it more effectively. One reason why texts programmed in the light of present-day objectives and linguistic knowledge are so rare is that experimentation with programmed courses is long and very costly, requiring much revision after trial use with students. The cost of full courses is likely to remain high until a much greater volume of sales is possible. The use of full programs of self-instruction in foreign languages also involves the provision of recording-playback equipment for each student and, preferably, some portable equipment for home study. Schools will need to be very sure that the programs they are introducing will be much more effective than the present classroom-laboratory teaching in order to justify the expense involved.

The most that many schools can anticipate at present is the possibility of using short self-instructional courses for specific purposes: for teaching certain circumscribed areas of particular difficulty (e.g., the use of a new alphabet) ; the learning of sound discriminations and production in the foreign language; or the learning of certain structural features which are subject to particular interference from native-language habits. Short remedial courses in such areas could prove very useful to the teacher who wishes to provide extra practice for the slow learner, the absentee, or the transfer student. Carefully designed short courses could also be useful for accelerating the learning of gifted students for whom the pace of normal classroom instruction is tedious. If experimentation were to center for some time on such short courses, more schools would be able to profit from what this new approach has to offer.

Without attempting to create a completely self-instructional program, the teacher may learn from a study of programming theory many things which will improve his approach to the organization of his teaching and help him to construct drills and exercises which will promote more efficient learning. If he is attempting to write a short self-instructional program for his own interest, he should keep in mind the following facts:

—Vague definitions of the desired terminal behavior will lead to the creation of a confused and aimless program.

—The student will learn only what the program teaches and will arrive at specific behavior only if the program is designed to lead him to it.

—Optimal step size is usually smaller than the inexperienced programmer realizes. This is the way in which programmed instruction differs from the usual textbook presentation.

—The sequence of a program should not be haphazard; it must follow a very careful development. For this reason programs cannot be written hastily, following a progression the teacher has used in a classroom presentation where he was able to make up for deficiencies by re-presenting material in a new way as soon as it became evident that the students had not understood.

—Immediate confirmation of each step must be built into the program.

—To maintain the interest of the student, the program must provide some challenge which sets the student on his mettle and keeps him alert.

—The student will be encouraged to persevere if the material leads him at certain intervals to subgoals which give him a sense of progress and achievement on the long road to the final goal to which the program is directing him.

While the teacher is waiting for easily available programs, well designed and well constructed, which are appropriate for the level of the students he is teaching, he should concentrate on seeing that the drills and exercises he uses in classroom and laboratory are as well organized and as soundly based in learning theory as the best programmed self-instructional materials.

GRAMMATICAL EXERCISES FOR CLASSROOM AND LABORATORY

By their systematic design, programmed self-instructional texts are in marked contrast to the types of teaching materials used in many of our classrooms. Frequently the class text reflects the way some enthusiastic and successful teacher has organized the language material for his students over a period of some years; close analysis and tabulation of the contents from the linguistic and behavioral points of view will usually reveal undue emphasis at certain points and inexplicable superficiality at others. The basis of choice of material and of sequencing in such texts is empirical rather than deriving from any scientific study of the unique way in which the foreign language is structured, or of the elements of language behavior to be expected of the student at the end of the course. The exercises provided for the student also reflect the teacher-writer's preferences and prejudices. If the author is a talented teacher, the exercises may be interesting and varied, but as a general rule they follow well-defined patterns. There is often a multiplicity of these exercises and it is left to the teacher to decide whether to use them all as they are set out or to present the same material in a different way. Most teachers find it less arduous to take the first course.

Let us look, then, at some of these traditional types of exercises. They usually follow an explanation of a grammatical feature which has been introduced, rather artificially, into a preceding reading passage. In the exercise, the student may be asked to write out paradigms, or to construct forms in the foreign language according to a traditional grammatical description (e.g., he may be asked to "write the 3rd person, plural, future, interrogative, negative" of some verb). He may be asked to change unnaturally complicated sentences from singular to plural, from affirmative to negative, from declarative form to interrogative, or from one tense to another; he may be asked to combine sentences in specific ways, to add some elements to sentences, or to fill in blanks with words which change form according to structural environment. He may be asked to translate involved sentences from the native language to the foreign language, or be required to write answers to questions in order to demonstrate actively his understanding of some grammatical feature, or combination of features. Exercises set out in texts based on modern theories of grammar and language learning may resemble some of these exercises in certain ways, but there will be basic differences in conception and formulation.

In more traditional textbooks exercises will be very varied in lexical content, favoring words which have peculiar spellings or irregularities that the student readily forgets, and will often involve the manipulation at one and the same time of several grammatical features in involved interrelationships. They will often consist of a mixture of foreign-language and native-language forms, the student being asked to find equivalents of the native-language forms to complete the foreign-language utterances. This may appear to be an innocent enough procedure, but used indiscriminately it can give the student the unfortunate impression that there is a one-to-one equivalence between forms in different languages which it is his task to discover. Traditional exercises are nearly always designed to be read, analyzed, and then written, and to be edited and re-edited by the student in his search for an acceptable answer. They will often require the student to work out his own version of the foreign language, which unfortunately may not always coincide with that of a native speaker. They will usually move rather rapidly from the manipulation of one aspect of a grammatical feature to another, trying to include in a short sequence every possible facet of the feature under study; in this way they will be designed to test whether the student has understood the reasoning behind the grammatical explanation which preceded the exercises. If the student's performance has shown that he has not assimilated all that was explained, the teacher will usually expound still further on the grammatical feature, with additional examples of its functioning, and then set more exercises to test the student's intellectual understanding of the point at issue. As soon as an acceptable proportion of the students have been able to complete the exercises more or less correctly, the teacher will move on to the next unit in the book, which will introduce further grammatical features the understanding of which will be tested in the same, rather cursory, fashion. Not surprisingly, the teacher will find after some months, even weeks, that the students' "intellectual understanding" of preceding units has dimmed, or even faded away, and the students themselves will wonder why they continue to misapply rules they thought they knew so well.

Although exercises of the type described have been in use for many years they have not proved outstandingly successful in developing lasting skill in the manipulation of grammatical features. As a result, scholars and teachers have devoted much time and effort to devising more effective ways of ensuring that students will be able to apply readily what they have studied. The new types of exercises are designed to give the students many opportunities for systematic practice of particular features in naturally phrased and easily remembered foreign-language utterances. Lexical items are limited in variety in order to concentrate attention on the grammatical features under study. In this way understanding of structural interrelationships (that is, of structural meaning) grows through use of structure, rather than through intellectual apprehension. Exercises of this type are often called pattern or structure drills. They are based on the assumption, discussed in some detail in chapter 3, that a large part of foreign-language learning, particularly in the earlier years, should be the formation of habits of intralanguage association, so that when the student attempts to express himself in the foreign language he will not have to give careful attention to the functioning of those language elements which vary only within restricted systems. In this chapter, the term "structure" will be reserved for the underlying system of principles which determine the observable interrelationships of language elements. These overt interrelationships will be called "patterns," or "structural patterns." Through practice in the use of these patterns, the student comes to understand the structural system, which he will study comprehensively at a later stage. The term "drill" is preferred to "exercise" because it implies rigorous attention to performance until the activity which is being learned has been brought to a high degree of automatic response.

A pattern is, then, a typical combination of interrelationships. Formed by various arrangements of lexical items, it conveys a meaning beyond the lexical content of these items themselves. To learn to use for his own purposes the meaning conveyed by the pattern (that is, its structural meaning), within the limitations imposed by the context of the utterance, the student must be able to reproduce the pattern without hesitation no matter what lexical items may be involved. In the simplest form of drill, he does this by substituting lexical items within the same pattern framework. Hill has stated that "every occurrence of language is a substitution frame," [9] an assertion that would be challenged by Chomsky.[10] It is true that flexible use of language involves more than lexical substitution, that it involves choice of direction within the system, but this choice, once made, forces the speaker into the use of certain structural patterns. It is within the limited range of permissible variations of each specific pattern that the foreign-language learner must be trained to operate at the elementary level.

9 A. A. Hill, *Introduction to Linguistic Structures* (New York, 1958), p. 5.
10 N. Chomsky in "Linguistic Theory" (Northeast Conference [1966], p. 44) says: "Linguists have had their share in perpetuating the myth that linguistic behavior is 'habitual' and that a fixed stock of 'patterns' is acquired through practice and used as the basis for 'analogy.' These views could be maintained only as long as grammatical description was sufficiently vague and imprecise."

TYPES OF PATTERN DRILLS

Moulton suggests that the three main classes of pattern drills reflect three basic approaches to the analysis of syntax: tagmemics or slot-and-filler theory, the theory of immediate constituents, and transformational grammar.[11] Although the drills may not be derived directly from these three theories they derive from the characteristics of language structure which these theories attempt to elucidate.

In tagmemics, an utterance is regarded as a type of frame consisting of slots into which words which fulfill a similar structural function may be inserted. Once a particular type of frame has been identified as a pattern, students may be drilled in substituting in the slots a variety of fillers, provided that each filler, or lexical variant, falls into the same functional category as the original item for which it is being substituted. In this way students are able to practice the construction of innumerable sentences while retaining the basic structural pattern. This type of drill is appropriate so long as no changes in word order are required when substitutions are made. Sometimes the insertion of a new item in one slot will involve a morphological change for an item in another slot (as with singular-plural, masculine-feminine adjustments in some languages, changes of person in relation to the verb, or adjustments devolving from a change of preposition) ; at other times, substitution in one slot will automatically lead to substitution in another slot in order to maintain some type of grammatical consistency. The purpose of the drill is to concentrate the attention of the student on one structural problem at a time and to provide him with steady practice in handling this problem in various lexical contexts, without requiring him to give conscious attention to the details of the sequence. To

11 W. G. Moulton, "What Is Structural Drill?" in F. W. Gravit and A. Valdman, eds., *Structural Drill and the Language Laboratory* (The Hague, 1963), pp. 11–14. Tagmemic theory is described in Kenneth L. Pike, *Language in Relation to a Unified Theory of the Structure of Human Behavior*, 2d ed. rev. (The Hague, 1967). References for other theories of syntax are given in notes to chapter 4 (the theory of immediate constituents in note 4; transformational grammar in note 8).

ensure this type of practice, care must be taken to keep the number of changes to be made in one operation to a minimum. In some drills, this is achieved by maintaining one section of the original utterance intact, while making consistent changes in a dependent section; Stack calls this a "fixed increment drill." In order to keep the student working entirely in the foreign language, cue words or expressions in the language are given to trigger the desired change in the next step of the drill; these cues may indicate the word to be substituted, or they may form a question which forces out an answer containing the desired formal change.

The preoccupation of the theory of immediate constituents with the hierarchical nature of language structure is reflected in expansion, contraction, and combination drills; these drills give practice in varying syntactic patterns. Students are shown how to expand, contract, or combine sentences in specific ways and are then given practice in these operations with attention to any resulting modifications. Even before the development of the theory of syntax as a series of transformations from basic kernel sentences, foreign-language teachers recognized the value of asking students to transform sentence patterns from declarative to interrogative, from positive to negative, from active to passive, from past to present or future, and so on. Directed dialogue is a form of transformation drill, as is much of the traditional question-answer practice. Transformations can often be cued by a single word which sets the tone for a different syntactical pattern, by the asking of a question, or even by the supplying of an answer for which a question must be created. More detailed descriptions of the different types of pattern drills will be found in the references in the Annotated Reading List at the end of this chapter.

CHARACTERISTICS OF A GOOD PATTERN DRILL

With the emergence of a certain vogue for pattern drilling, accelerated by the need for suitable taped materials for use in language laboratories, many commercial publishers have hastily reset exercises in existing textbooks in some kind of pattern drill form. Similarly, authors with little training in the technique have tried their hand at the new form of exercise. As a result, teachers have found that these inexpertly created drills were either very difficult and frustrating for their classes or else so simple that students were bored by the lack of challenge. It is important that teachers know the principles of construction of drills and have the experience of trying to construct a series of drills themselves, in order to be able to recognize well-designed drills when choosing textbooks or tapes for their classes.

The following observations may serve as an evaluative checklist.

1. A drill series is designed for *teaching* the manipulation of grammatical structures, *not for testing* what the student already knows. The series should, therefore, provide considerable practice in the use of each element before moving on to the presentation of another.

2. Each drill should be concerned with *one specific structural pattern*. The student is thus able to concentrate on one foreign-language problem at a time, usually a pattern which contrasts with his native-language habits. The novice drill-constructor will need to pay very careful attention as he develops each drill or he will find that, unwittingly, he has allowed a feature of another pattern to creep into the sequence.

3. The structural feature to be drilled will have been *encountered already* by the student in recent study material: in a dialogue he has memorized, or in a reading passage or conversation with which he has been working.

4. The pattern will be drilled consistently through a series of *six or eight cue-response items* in order to give the student time to assimilate the pattern, or the pattern change, before he is asked to make more complicated variations.

5. *Changes* made between one cue-response item and the next will be *minimal*, involving usually one lexical change with, at most, an associated adjustment (or short series of interrelated adjustments) of a formal nature. As the student moves into the next drill in a series, the pattern will be varied to a minor degree. This is in accordance with the principle of programmed instruction: that the sequence should be so designed that the student will produce the right response on practically every occasion.

6. Each item in the series will be *short,* so that the student

will have no difficulty keeping it in his mind as he tries to construct a variant according to the cue given.

7. Each item will be a *complete utterance* of a type which could conceivably occur in a conversational interchange. In this way the student will be acquiring intralanguage associations in useful segments of language.

8. The drill will be designed in such a way that the cue will provoke *only the desired response* and not other feasible responses. Since the response is to be followed by immediate confirmation (in the form of the correct response, given for purposes of comparison and imitation by the teacher or the voice on the tape) there must be *no ambiguity*. Any cause for hesitation can only be bewildering to the student, interrupting the smooth flow of the drill exercise.

9. In a structural pattern drill, variety of *vocabulary will be kept to a minimum*. Only very familiar words will be used, so that the student's attention is not distracted from the structural feature which he is learning to manipulate. (Vocabulary itself may be the subject of a drill, in which case the student will be learning associations of lexical sets).

10. Both cue and response items will usually be *in the foreign language*. With a certain amount of ingenuity and imagination it is possible to construct cues which will provoke most of the structural features which need to be drilled. Where this is not possible, a translation drill will be used. A translation drill differs from the traditional translation exercise in that it conforms to all the preceding recommendations.

11. Drills will be *conducted orally* until the students are responding readily and accurately to the cues. For variety they may be used as reading or writing exercises, but not to the exclusion of oral practice. They are designed primarily for training with ear and tongue, and not merely for visual scanning.

12. Drills will *not be purely imitative,* although some imitative drills are necessary when students are being familiarized with a pattern. After an initial repetition drill, drills should be designed to require thought on the part of the student, but only at the point of teaching; in other words, extraneous complications should be eliminated.

13. Drills will be *varied* in type to alleviate the boredom engendered by one type of activity.
14. The teaching phase of a series of drills will be followed by a *testing phase.* This may be accomplished by re-presenting in random order material which has been drilled in a programmed sequence in order to see whether students can still produce the required response on hearing the cue.

    Alternatively, a logical progression of drills may work up to a testing drill where multiple substitutions require the student's full concentration and distract his attention from the grammatical feature he has been practicing. If the student is still able to manipulate accurately and effortlessly the feature he has been practicing, while concentrating his attention on other elements of the utterance, he may be presumed to have acquired a firm control over it.
15. Some provision will be made for the student to *apply what he has learned* in the drill series in a structured communication situation, that is, in directed dialogue, by questions and answers within the class group, in some form of game, or in short, oral reports.

CLASSROOM PRESENTATION OF PATTERN DRILLS

As with every other teaching procedure, pattern drilling may be performed well or it may be performed badly. The fact that the drilling is ineffective is not always apparent to the inexperienced observer. An energetic teacher who is not very sensitive to student reaction may conduct a series of drills at a smart tempo, receiving a prompt response from students right through to the end of the series without being conscious of the fact that the students' minds are not on their task and that they are merely parroting what has been suggested to them by the programming of the exercise. The students from such a class are at a loss when asked to apply what they have been learning because they do not have a clear concept of the meaning of what they have been repeating, nor of the significance of structural changes they have been making. The following suggestions for the stages of presentation of a series of drills are designed to avoid such a situation.

First, the student should encounter a certain structural pattern several times in authentic stretches of foreign-language discourse (that is, in context: in dialogue, reading passage, or conversation). In this way he will be able to observe its relationship to other structural elements in the language system. Before he is asked to produce the pattern himself, he should hear it a certain number of times, so that he is able to recognize it aurally. If the pattern is embedded in a dialogue, he will be hearing it repeatedly as he endeavors to memorize the dialogue. At this initial stage, he is becoming familiar with the pattern, not with some rule about the pattern, and he begins the process of assimilating it as a whole.

As the drill period begins, he is presented aurally with several examples of the pattern grouped together in a repetition drill. As he repeats these, he will begin to discern a certain consistency of structure in the various utterances. In this repetition series only a limited number of well-known lexical items will occur, so that the student's attention is not distracted from the pattern he is to learn to use. Each item in the series is presented to him, and he is asked to repeat it, at a normal speed of production and with a natural intonation. This does not mean that the speech must be rapid; it may be at a moderate speed of delivery but it must not be distorted in a way which would strike a native speaker as unnatural. At this point, the student's responses are imitative; he is not asked to produce anything which has not first been modeled by the teacher or a model voice on tape.

At the next stage, the student is asked to reproduce the pattern with some difference in lexical content in response to a cue, receiving confirmation of the acceptability of his response as he compares it with the correct version supplied by the teacher or the tape. As the student works through this drill, with its variations of the basic pattern, he begins to recognize the regularity underlying the changes, and because of his natural tendency to organize what he wishes to remember he starts to evolve for himself a generalization which will account for the consistency he has observed. If the drill is well planned and the feature of grammatical structure uncomplicated, the generalizations of most of the students will be valid. Some form of native-language interference or some unexpected feature of the pattern may, however, cause the student to draw the wrong conclusion and this will prevent him from learning to use the pattern effectively.

At this stage, then, the teacher will observe the students' responses carefully. If he senses that the students are a little uncertain of the crucial feature of the pattern they are varying, he will make a brief comment to elucidate the point at issue. This will not be a detailed, deductive exposition of structural relationships; such explanations will come at a more advanced stage when students have sufficient acquaintance with the structure of the language to be able to appreciate these interrelationships. All that is required at this point is a few words to guide the students to a correct interpretation of what they are trying to do. When it is clear that the students understand what is involved, they will continue to practice the pattern with further variations, thus constructing new utterances by analogy with preceding utterances.

When the teacher judges by the alert and ready response of the class that the pattern has been assimilated, he will engage the students in a mixed drill, or a multiple-substitution drill, to see whether the response is still prompt and accurate when the student is not guided to the correct answer by the logic of the programming. He will not, however, consider the pattern to be thoroughly learned until he sees that the students are able to use it in the wider context of conversational interchanges in the classroom. If this evidence is not forthcoming, he will provide further practice with the pattern in a subsequent lesson. Even when the pattern appears to be thoroughly assimilated the teacher will give the students further practice with it before many lessons have passed so that the newly formed habits will be maintained. This later practice may again be oral, or the drill may provide material for a reading exercise. If it is used as a writing exercise, the students should be encouraged to continue the series with sentences of their own creation.

Pattern drills are essentially oral practice in the manipulation of grammatical features. They should, for the most part, be conducted without the visual support of a script, so that students may concentrate their attention on active formulation of utterances. This does not preclude a brief glance at the drill in the textbook early in the session, to help fix certain features in the minds of the students, always provided that the students then close their books and strive for automaticity of response without any further support from the text. If students are allowed to follow drills in their books throughout the drill session, they will feel they know the work before they have really assimilated it: having made a mental note of what is involved for future reference, they may become bored with what seems to be overinsistence on such a simple feature. The teacher's difficulties will be increased, too, in that it is often difficult to gauge whether students working with a text need more practice for satisfactory assimilation of the pattern.

Methods of conducting drills so that each student has the maximum opportunity for participation and the teacher the maximum opportunity for finding out what each student knows have been described in detail in chapter 2.

There is a danger with pattern drilling that a zealous but unimaginative teacher, believing that the more students repeat patterns the sooner they will be able to speak the language spontaneously, will keep the students at useful but dull drills for far too long. Such drilling becomes very boring and tedious to students, who may either seek escape in absent-minded vocal participation or grow to loathe the foreign-language lesson. Too much intensive drilling of a structural pattern to a point of automatic response can develop in the student an inflexibility which prevents him from producing the practiced pattern in an appropriate context which is not identical with the drill cue.

This danger can be avoided if the teacher considers carefully ways of ensuring the necessary amount of repetition and response to cues without always following the same drill procedure. The introduction of the drill material may be so designed as to provide practice in aural recognition and comprehension. The desired variations of the patterns may be cued by the presentation of pictures or objects as a change from aural cues; this demands constant attention from the students and is an antidote to absent-minded participation. A cue which leads to a humorous or unexpected response relaxes the students and renews their interest in the activity, keeping them alert to what is coming next. Group and row participation in drills can be given a competitive element which retains the attention of the students. Many drills may be given the appearance of a game, or of elementary communication, by provoking the students into asking the teacher a series of questions in response to cues, or into making a series of comments about the teacher's activities and interests, or those of other students.

Certainly game techniques should be employed to provoke the students into using patterns in natural situations after a period of intensive drilling. With a little thought, the teacher will find that many well-known parlor and television games, and children's guessing and repetition games, are easily converted into extensions of pattern drills. The more simple and familiar the game the better, because complicated new games demand so much concentration from the students that they distract their attention from the language forms they are supposed to be using. The more the student is interested in an activity in the foreign language, the more he feels the desire to communicate in the language, and this is the first and most vital step in learning to use language forms spontaneously.

Although this chapter has concentrated on structural pattern drills, it must be borne in mind that drill techniques are also appropriate for learning the sound system of the language, increasing knowledge of vocabulary items and their appropriate use in context, and improving skill in writing. Drills, carefully programmed, are a valuable technique for training at the lower level of manipulation of language elements; they concentrate attention on specific points of difficulty until these are mastered. They are, however, merely a step on the way, as we shall see in chapters 6 and 7. The ultimate aim is liberated, spontaneous use of the language, which involves the integration in complicated ways of the separate elements which have been drilled. Perfection at the pattern-drill level, no matter how impressive to the observer, cannot be an end in itself. It is a fruitless activity unless care is taken to see that the skill gained by such training is further extended until the student is capable of autonomous expression.

ANNOTATED READING LIST

Programmed Instruction

CARROLL, J. B. "A Primer of Programmed Instruction in Foreign Language Teaching." *IRAL* 1/2 (1963): 115–41. A thorough study of the principles and practical requirements of programming for foreign-language study. Selected bibliography on programmed instruction. Essential reading.

VALDMAN, A. "Programmed Instruction and Foreign Language Teaching." In A. VALDMAN, ed. *Trends in Language Teaching.* New York: McGraw-Hill, 1966. Pp. 133–58. Shows how the theory of programming works in practice with examples from programs for French, English, and Italian.

NORTHEAST CONFERENCE (1962). "A New Look at Learning." In W. F. BOTTIGLIA, ed. *Current Issues in Language Teaching.* Pp. 19–60. Practical problems of programming are discussed, with examples in Latin and Spanish. Outlines ways in which principles of programming can be applied by teachers who are not using teaching machines or programmed textbooks.

MARTY, F. *Programing a Basic Foreign Language Course.* Hollins College, Va., 1962. A wealth of practical information for any teacher attempting to prepare programs. Specifies terminal behavior for a programmed course in French.

Pattern Drills

STACK, E. M. *The Language Laboratory and Modern Language Teaching.* Rev. ed. New York: Oxford University Press, 1966. Pp. 83–144. The chapters on "Audiolingual Exercises" and "Pattern Drills" should be very carefully studied. Examples of suggested forms of drills and exercises are given in English, French, German, Italian, Russian, and Spanish.

Contrastive Structure Series. CHARLES A. FERGUSON, General Editor. Chicago: University of Chicago Press. This series is a guide to areas of major difficulty for students working with these pairs of languages.

KUFNER, H. L. *The Grammatical Structures of English and German.* 1962.

AGARD, F. B. and DI PIETRO, R. J. *The Grammatical Structures of English and Italian.* 1965.

STOCKWELL, R. P.; BOWEN, J. D.; and MARTIN, JOHN W. *The Grammatical Structures of English and Spanish.* 1965.

RIVERS, W. M. *The Psychologist and the Foreign-Language Teacher.* Chicago: University of Chicago Press, 1964. Chapter 8, "The Right Response," and Chapter 13, "Practical Recommendations" (pp. 149–54). These chapters discuss problems of classroom and laboratory presentation of pattern drills.

Le français dans le monde 41 (juin 1966), Numéro Spécial sur les Exercices Structuraux.

5

Teaching Sounds

GENERAL PROBLEMS

We have all had the experience when listening to a foreigner speaking our language of having great difficulty in understanding what he is trying to say, not because of his lack of knowledge of vocabulary and language structure but because the sounds he produced seemed peculiar and the voice rose and fell in unexpected places. Even immigrants who have lived in the country for twenty years may have a "foreign accent" which makes them difficult to understand. Since language is a means of communication, it is not enough for our students to learn words, phrases, grammatical features, if they will not be able to produce these in a way which makes their utterance comprehensible to a native speaker of the language.

This matter of the acquisition of a near-native articulation and intonation by the students poses one of the most difficult problems for teachers of certain languages. The problem is of greater or less importance according to the degree of difference and the nature of the differences between the sound systems of the native and the foreign language. Some oriental languages provide obvious difficulties because of the system of tones to which speakers of many other languages are not accustomed. Similarly, speakers of tone languages experience difficulty in learning correct production of nontonal languages. Even with European languages pronunciation problems may be greater

Some sections of this chapter appeared in a different version in "Teaching Sounds," *French Review,* 40, no 6 (May, 1967): 802–9.

than students realize. English and French, for instance, have phonological systems which show extreme differences, and speakers of either of these languages have considerable difficulty in speaking the language of the other without a marked "foreign accent." Before the teacher can overcome these inherent difficulties with any degree of efficiency, he must have a clear understanding of the nature of the problem.

The extensive study linguists in the present century have made of many languages has made it abundantly clear that each has a sound system in which all the elements are interrelated, and that it is very rare indeed to find two languages with identical sound systems. Since these differences in sound systems have a physiological basis, for example variations in the position of the speech organs or in breath control, the teacher must understand the physical aspects of sound production. He will not necessarily teach these to the student, but this knowledge will give him a basis for identifying the physical reasons for inaccurate approximations of foreign-language sounds, enabling him to give precise instructions which will help the student to correct his faulty production.

Sounds are differentiated by their timbre (which is caused by the different degrees of resonance resulting from the shape and size of the cavities, or resonating chambers, formed in the mouth and nose), and by variations in the frequency and amplitude of the waves on which they are carried (these variations creating differences in pitch and loudness). The study of the fine distinctions in pitch, loudness, timbre, and duration of sounds of different languages and dialects constitutes the field of acoustic phonetics. Articulatory phonetics studies such aspects as the opening and closing of the vocal cords and of the nasal passage, and the varying positions of the tongue and lips which alter the shape and size of the resonating chambers in the mouth and determine the differences in vowel sounds, at times impeding the free flow of air from the lungs to form consonants. The subject matter of acoustic phonetics is very technical and needs to be interpreted for the classroom teacher. Every foreign-language teacher should, however, understand the principles of articulatory phonetics as they apply both to his own language and to the language he is teaching, so that he may be able to explain to his students the particular difficulties of the transition from one language to the other. Contrastive studies of the phonology of various languages have appeared, and teachers should study publications of this nature as an essential part of their professional preparation. Some available studies are indicated in the Annotated Reading List.

A "foreign accent" is inevitable if students attempt to produce the sounds of a new language while keeping their mouths shaped and their tongues placed as for similar sounds in their native language. The position of the tongue (against the teeth, the gums, or the palate) ; the height of the highest part of the tongue (front or back of the tongue high, mid, or low in the mouth) ; the lips rounded or unrounded—all these elements combine to alter the shape of the front and back resonating chambers in the mouth and thus alter the timbre of the sound produced. The ways in which the airflow is impeded (by tongue tip raised and pressed against the gums, for instance, or tongue tip turned down and pressed against the teeth; by lips held closed and released suddenly; or by air accumulated before release and released slowly) result in distinctly different consonantal sounds. The vocal cords enter into play and by allowing air to pass freely at times may add another dimension to the consonant sound. The airflow for the vowel or for the consonant may pass through the mouth only or through the mouth and the nasal cavities, the result being a distinct difference in timbre. Since so many elements are involved, the number of possibilities is enormous. A given sound can be reproduced accurately only by a similar conjunction of these various elements. Unless the teacher understands how the student is using his speech organs in producing a native-language sound and what he should be doing to reproduce the foreign-language sound acceptably he cannot help the student beyond a certain stage of earnest but inaccurate imitation.

Each language has its characteristic and interrelated mouth positions. Teachers often concentrate on teaching mouth positions for those sounds which do not exist in the native language, while allowing students to produce native-language near-equivalents for the rest. This produces the undesirable situation where a student has to make, in midword, mouth adjustments which are almost impossible physically or at least difficult and awkward, thus deforming the neighboring sounds which would otherwise have been correctly articulated. The student must be made aware of the overall pattern of the integrated phonological system of the new language and of the fact that incorrectly articulated consonants will affect the production of vowels, as vowels will affect consonants. This adopting of a new system of articulatory positions requires steady practice and muscle training, so that the student develops not only an auditory but also a kinesthetic image of the correct sound and develops facility in transferring impulses from brain to correct speech muscles.

As well as articulatory differences among sounds, the foreign-language teacher should understand the concept of a phoneme. A phoneme is the smallest element of sound in a language which is recognized by a native speaker as making a difference to meaning. Each vowel or consonant in the sound system of a language can be produced in a number of slightly varying forms, within a certain band of tolerance, before it ceases to be intelligible to another native speaker in its normal context of accompanying sounds. These slightly varying forms are called allophones of the phoneme. Differences of this kind are phonetic and may be indicative of the social level of the speaker, of some group membership, or of a personal idiosyncrasy. What seems to be a very small phonetic difference may, while being merely allophonic in one language, signal a distinct difference of meaning in some other language. The difference between [f] and [v] does not result from a change in position of tongue and lips, but is purely a matter of voicing (the opening of the vocal cords), yet for a speaker of English this distinction is very important because it brings about a change in meaning (e.g., from "fear" to "veer"; from "feel" to "veal"). In a language where such a change in voicing does not alter the meaning, the difference between [f] and [v] will continue to be a phonetic difference but will not constitute a phonemic difference. A study of the phonemic system of the language to be taught will enable the teacher to emphasize those phonetic differences which will determine whether what the student says is intelligible or unintelligible to a native speaker.

Understanding of phonemic distinctions becomes most important at those points where the phonemic systems of the native language and the foreign language do not coincide. Students listening to a foreign language in the early stages will "hear" the phonemes of their own language, that is, they will automatically classify new sounds as variants of familiar native-language phonemes. Students in whose language the distinction between /ü/ and /u/ [1] does not determine differences of meaning will not at first notice this distinction. It is at such points of divergence that students will have to be taught by aural discrimination exercises to "hear" differences of which they have never before been conscious. Until they can perceive these differences readily they will have great difficulty in producing acceptable imitations of these sounds.

Frequently neglected by foreign-language teachers are the indispensable elements of syllabification (internal juncture), stress, and intonation (variations in pitch). In a situation where we do not hear clearly in the native language it is these features that assist us in piecing together the import of what we have heard. We have all had the experience of completely misinterpreting the utterance of a foreigner who stressed the wrong syllables in our own language and retained his native-language intonation. Stress and intonation may also change considerably the emotional impact of what we hear and make the subtle difference between a polite request and a brusque demand. With incorrect intonation a question in some languages may be interpreted as a statement of fact, with resultant breakdown in communication. The teacher should, therefore, emphasize these elements from the beginning, making clear their important role in comprehensible speech and watching carefully to see that students develop and retain acceptable habits in these areas as well as in the correct production of sounds. Unfortunately, it is often in the area of stress and intonation that the foreign-language teacher who is not a native speaker has the most difficulty himself. It is essential, therefore, that he work consciously at keeping his control of these aspects of the language at a high level, through deliberate study of stress and intonation patterns; through constant ear-training by listening to recordings, radio, and films; and

---

1   In I.P.A. notation this distinction will be inscribed [y] and [u].

by as frequent association as possible with native speakers. He must keep in mind, however, that even native speakers who have been away from their native land for a considerable period cease to provide a reliable intonation model.

Unless tapes or records of the production of native speakers are being used extensively, the student cannot advance in articulation and intonation beyond the stage which his teacher has reached. As the student imitates, the teacher will hear his own weaknesses chorused back at him in all their undisguised inaccuracy, frequently exaggerated at the most difficult point. Continually hearing inaccurate approximations in the classroom will make the teacher less conscious of his own defects and his accent will inevitably deteriorate over a period of years. It is essential, then, that the teacher work at the improvement of his own pronunciation. This is not as difficult now as it used to be because there are available to the teacher tapes and records of native speech with which he himself can practice very profitably even if he does not wish to use them in class. It must be emphasized, however, that in areas where students cannot readily meet native speakers of the language or travel to a country where the language is spoken, tapes and records should be incorporated in the work of the class as often as possible so that students may imitate authentic speech, rather than even a good approximation of it. There are always students who, given such opportunities, can readily acquire a more nearly native pronunciation than that of the nonnative teacher.

INTRODUCING THE PHONOLOGY OF THE FOREIGN LANGUAGE

The student's first contact with the sound patterns of the foreign language he is to learn will most probably be at elementary school level, junior high school level, or senior high school level. The differences in age and maturity at these three levels will involve different techniques and varying emphases.

The younger the child the more he enjoys sheer mimicry and the more frequently he may be engaged in activities which are largely repetitive. The older student likes to understand what he is doing and why. The younger child is less self-conscious about making strange sounds and behaving in ways which are different from those of his fellows and of the community around him. He is still living in a child world. The adolescent is striving to make himself acceptable in an adult world and wishes to behave in a way which distinguishes him from "silly children."

At elementary and junior high school level, the sound patterns of the language should be taught in the context of language material being repeated and memorized. The student should repeat after the teacher the various sounds he encounters in their context. The material for these early lessons should not be artificially constructed to include only certain sounds and not others. The material should consist of utterances selected because they are natural and usable. Although the teacher will choose only certain specific sounds for closer attention and practice during a particular lesson, the student's ear will at the same time gradually become accustomed to the whole phonological system with its distinctive articulatory features and its stress and intonation patterns. He will be making his first faltering efforts at producing sounds which the teacher will not be taking up individually until later, but these he will be slowly acquiring in their normal context and interrelationships.

Even elementary and junior high school students will identify the sounds of the foreign language as variants of familiar native-language phonemes. It will be necessary to instruct the children briefly and succinctly in correct articulation and to insist on repetition of phrases and sentences until this correct articulation becomes habitual. In this way the whole phonological system of the language will be covered as part of an ongoing learning process, rather than as a separate activity only relevant during "pronunciation practice."

It is at this stage that choral repetition is of great value. It gives each student ample opportunity to practice making sounds, thus giving him essential exercise in new muscle movements and time to develop an auditory memory of the sound patterns. In choral practice, shy children are hidden in the crowd and acquire confidence in articulating the foreign sounds, and children with less aptitude for faithful imitation are carried along and must articulate faster than they would on their own. Students who acquire a foreign-language pronunciation rapidly are given ample opportunity for expression and are imitating the correct model at all times, whereas in a one-by-one classroom situation these students often have very few opportunities to practice aloud and are condemned to long periods of listening to the incorrect efforts of their less gifted fellows.

Even at the preadolescent stage, however, children possess powers of mimicry to a greater or less degree, and their imitation of sounds may be startlingly inaccurate. If the teacher listens only to chorus repetition he may be under the illusion that all is well; the inevitable errors of a number of the children (confusion of vowel sounds, incorrect articulation of consonants) will be masked by the torrent of sound. If the teacher is fortunate enough to have regular access to a language laboratory, for short periods at frequent intervals at this age, his students will have the advantages of choral repetition (maximum opportunity for individual imitation of a correct model, protection from the embarrassment of recitation before critical peers, the onmoving lesson which draws from the student a faster participation), yet the teacher will be able to hear and analyze individual difficulties, giving help where needed without interrupting the work of others who do not have the same difficulties.

For students beginning a foreign language at senior high school level, or even later, the introductory lessons may well include some direct instruction in the differences between the phonological systems of the native language and of the foreign language. This may be in ten-minute stretches at the beginning of successive lessons, as long as such theoretical instruction is always accompanied by the learning of some authentic language material. In this way, the students feel they are really getting to grips with the language from the beginning, while having the opportunity to apply what they have just learned about sounds in a practical context.

If correct articulation, stress, and intonation are to become habitual, students must not be allowed to pronounce or read on their own, or act out, anything which has not been carefully practiced orally with the teacher or a model. If the teacher takes the easy way of allowing the students to work for long periods from their books when their acquisition of the sound system is still at a delicate and uncertain stage he will be repaid by hearing a rapid deterioration in articulation and intonation as students try to produce sounds which seem to match the familiar and the unfamiliar combinations of graphic symbols before their eyes. Native-language sounds will creep back in, and remedial practice will have to be instituted. Students allowed to write and present their own little dialogues without careful drilling will also revert rapidly to native-language speech habits.

In order to overcome the natural tendency of the student to "hear" in the categories made familiar by the native language, the teacher will need to give aural-discrimination exercises in which near-equivalents in the native and in the foreign language are clearly demonstrated and in which near-equivalents in the foreign language are distinctly differentiated. Drill in aural discrimination is best accomplished by the use of minimal pairs, words which differ only in pronunciation of the sounds being practiced. (Examples of minimal pairs for aural discrimination of English sounds would be "sheep, ship" or "fat, vat"; and in French "rue, roue"). If words are contrasted in which vowels or consonants are in different environments, consonant anticipation and assimilation may come into play and make it more difficult to demonstrate the essential differences. Nor should a sound be practiced in isolation, since acoustically it then differs from the way in which it is perceived in association with other sounds.

After some practice with aural discrimination of minimal pairs, students should have the opportunity to produce a specific sound themselves, first in simple phrases and then in longer sentences. These sentences should be naturally phrased utterances which the student might well encounter in conversation in the foreign language. Teaching the student to say artificially constructed tongue-twisters in which a particular sound is repeated a number of times may have its place as an amusing diversion, relaxing the tension of concentrated learning, but as a teaching device it carries no guarantee that skill acquired in such manipulations will transfer to a real communication situation. For such transfer to take place, practice must involve useful phrases which the student is likely to use on some future occasion. After the student has practiced a sound in longer utterances, the teacher should listen attentively to his rendering of it in the normal language work of the day. If the student still retains the correct articulation while concentrating on other aspects of the language, then it is clear that he needs no further drilling in the production of the sound as an artificial exercise.

Where a teacher takes over an advanced class which has been poorly trained in pronunciation, he may need to give instruction and practice, in the sequence outlined, as a regular feature of the lessons for some time. In this case, aural discrimination of correctly and incorrectly articulated sounds will need to precede direct practice because the students will have developed the habit of identifying what they are saying with what they are hearing, and they will at first think correct pronunciation of foreign-language speech artificial and amusing.

Where spelling complications do not make it inadvisable (that is, where a certain grouping of letters always represents a certain sound) dictation can be a useful technique for verifying whether students have learned to make certain discriminations among sounds. The material dictated must be essentially a recombination of what has already been used orally and for reading practice, except at advanced levels where the dictation serves a triple purpose: as an exercise in aural comprehension and discrimination, as a test of the student's knowledge of combinations of letters which traditionally represent specific sounds, and as a test of his knowledge of structural elements, particularly those of a morphological nature. If the dictation is to be used solely as a check on aural discrimination it must be very carefully constructed so as to exclude other complications.

Not to be overlooked as a device for pronunciation practice is the learning by heart of rhymes and poems. These must be carefully chosen so that the vocabulary, thought content, and structures are appropriate to the level which the students have reached. Rhymes and poems for early stages should preferably be narrative or descriptive, with short lines, uncomplicated ideas, and a certain amount of repetition. For younger children, many nursery rhymes and counting rhymes are suitable.

Counting rhymes are frequently nonsensical, in a whimsical way, with a certain charm because of their rhythm, vowel music, or alliteration. Because of their lack of meaning, they lend themselves readily to repetition purely for pronunciation purposes. Rhymes and poems learned by heart can be repeated in chorus or by individuals many times over, becoming more attractive with familiarity, whereas dialogue sentences or prose passages repeated as frequently would have long since become tedious and boring.

Some sounds are more easily produced by a foreigner on a musical scale; this applies particularly to vowel sounds, which because of the way they are formed can vary in pitch. Frequent singing of simple songs can establish good production habits with these sounds so long as slurring is immediately checked and attention is paid to clear articulation. Many folk songs have repetitive choruses which provide excellent practice in the production of basic vowels.

The development of good pronunciation is undoubtedly an area in which the tape recorder and the language laboratory can play a very effective role. The tape can provide an authentic model for imitation, an untiring and unvarying model which is clearly heard by every student. It enables students far from the country where the language is spoken to saturate themselves, if they so desire, in the phonological atmosphere of the language. With full recording-playback facilities, the student is able to compare his production with that of the unchanging model and rerecord until he is satisfied with his approximation of each utterance. Just as obviously, the laboratory can confirm the student in bad habits practiced with great zeal and earnestness, and a student who is not properly prepared by his teacher may listen to his poor efforts with considerable satisfaction. If the laboratory is to be effective in the developing of acceptable articulation and intonation, the way in which it is to be used must be carefully studied. Students must be given instruction and practice under supervision in the difficult task of detecting their own weaknesses, and also in methods of remedying the weaknesses of which they become aware. This is a task which requires a certain maturity. Younger students cannot be left to work unmonitored in the laboratory, although older students may be encouraged to use it on a library basis.

Monitoring students in a laboratory is not an easy task. The student interrupted too frequently or for too long finds it difficult to take up the thread of his work. The monitor has only a brief interval in which to assess the major weaknesses to which he wishes to draw the student's attention. At some stage a tape should be made of each student's oral production as he reads a text constructed to contain the major pronunciation difficulties which the student will encounter in the foreign language. Each student's pronunciation should then be analyzed and his strengths and weaknesses noted on a Pronunciation Checklist. As he monitors, the teacher should have this list before him so that he can concentrate on the improvement of the areas of weakness of a particular student and consult notes on what he has drawn to this student's attention during previous sessions. Such a list will enable him to give useful advice in a precise and succinct fashion which makes the interruption as short and as immediately useful as possible. If the student has a similar checklist he can mark his weaknesses as they are drawn to his notice and thus work more purposefully toward improvement.

Even in schools where no laboratory is available, the teacher should have a checklist of particular problems of pronunciation against which he can note each student's progress. The teacher can keep such a checklist in his textbook and mark down his observations about particular students at odd moments during oral and reading lessons. A systematic approach to pronunciation problems will achieve much more satisfactory results than a hit-or-miss assessment based on the most glaring mistake that strikes the teacher's ear in one particular lesson.

Testing of pronunciation has been made considerably easier by the advent of the tape recorder. Judging the level of acceptability of a student's pronunciation as he reads or recites is a chancy process which must be considered highly unreliable. When a tape is made of each student's production, the teacher is able not only to listen several times to one section before making up his mind on the grading but also to listen again to the work of other students and make immediate cross-comparisons of level of proficiency. When grading pronunciation, the teacher should follow a set marking scheme where points are allotted for particular features (e.g., for grouping of words; particular difficulties of vowel or consonant; word linking or division; syllabification, stress, and intonation; and the general fluency and comprehensibility of the rendition). A methodical tabulation of this type will make the final grade an expression of something concrete, thus minimizing the subjective element which inevitably enters into the assessing of the degree of approximation of one sound to another.

PHYSICAL AND PSYCHOLOGICAL PROBLEMS OF TEACHING SOUNDS

In the foreign-language class where oral work plays a prominent role, certain problems of a physical or emotional character are encountered: problems of a kind which do not assume the same importance in the teaching of book-oriented subjects. The teacher must be conscious of the bases of these problems and alert to detect when poor performance has causes other than inattention, poor study habits, or lack of interest in the subject.

Occasionally the teacher will find in his class a student, often eager and attentive, who seems quite unable to reproduce sounds with any degree of accuracy and has difficulty with any form of aural comprehension. As time passes, this student develops an emotional block with respect to all oral work, is embarrassed when asked to participate orally, and is nervous and tense when dictation or testing of oral work takes place. A quiet conference with such a student frequently reveals that he has some difficulty in distinguishing between different vowel sounds (which have distinctive qualities of pitch and timbre) and in retaining patterns of intonation (this requiring a similar ability to that of retaining a musical phrase). Such a student may be to some degree tone-deaf or deficient in tonal memory.[2]

2 Recent experiments concerning the value of tests of ability to distinguish musical elements such as pitch, loudness, rhythm, time, timbre, and tonal memory in the prediction of the degree of success in

Students with difficulties of this type are capable of achieving great fluency and accuracy in reading and writing the language, and a thorough knowledge of structure. They feel relaxed in such activities. They may also learn to express themselves fluently in the language, with perhaps some faulty articulation and intonation. They should be encouraged, when listening to foreign-language utterances, to relax and concentrate on interpreting from the elements they do distinguish the full import of the utterance. All languages are redundant, in that more elements are included in the utterance than are essential to comprehension. It is for this reason that we are able to follow dialogue across a crowded room, over a noisy telephone line, or from the worn soundtrack of an old film. Experimentation has shown that speech can suffer all kinds of distortion before it becomes unintelligible, and students in this situation must learn to piece together the message from the limited spectrum of sound they are receiving. They can be helped with problems of intonation or with tone patterns by the use of visual outlines. Properly guided, students with hearing difficulties which are not physically extreme can, with practice, become reasonably proficient, with occasional lapses, in the interchange of conversation.

Unless the teacher is conscious of the problem facing the student who has difficulty in relying on his ear, he may become tense and anxious himself as he attempts to "reach" the student. This tension compounds the tension the student is already experiencing and causes a feeling of panic in which the student ceases to hear anything distinctly in a blur of sound. This stage is detectable in dictation particularly: the student

---

foreign-language learning have shown tests of tonal memory to have some predictive value. The comments in this section apply to the occasional student with real deficiencies in some of these areas, and not to the majority of our students who have normal capacities to varying degrees of adequacy in this regard. For reports of experiments, see: P. Pimsleur, L. Mosberg, and A. Morrison, "Student Factors in Foreign Language Learning" (section on Pitch Discrimination), *Modern Language Journal*, 46, no. 4 (April, 1962): 163–64; R. Leutenegger and T. Mueller, "Auditory Factors and the Acquisition of French Language Mastery," *MLJ*, 48, no. 3 (March, 1964): 141–46; and R. Leutenegger, T. Mueller, and I. Wershow, "Auditory Factors in Foreign Language Acquisition," *MLJ*, 49, no. 1 (January, 1965): 22–31.

suddenly begins to leave large blanks and puts down a series of completely incoherent phrases in between. The harder he tries, the more tense he becomes and the less he can hear. The only remedy for this situation is for both teacher and student to relax completely. The student may be asked, for instance, to stop taking dictation for several lines, and then to begin again. Above all, he must not be made to feel that this test or exercise is a vital factor in success or failure.

Teaching students to pronounce strange sounds is easier with younger children. Children of elementary school age love making strange noises, mimicking other people, using secret code languages among their friends. They delight in the unusual sound combinations and rhythms of nonsense and counting rhymes and invent strange inversions of people's names. Most elementary pupils, then, are uninhibited in the imitating of foreign-language sounds, although even at this stage they mimic with varying degrees of accuracy according to their natural talents.

Even at junior high school age mimicking of sounds causes little embarrassment if the teacher and students have a friendly and sympathetic relationship. If the teacher, however, seems odd and peculiar to children of this age they will mimic ironically and be unwilling to identify themselves with him to the degree of taking on his way of speaking.

In midadolescence, students are much more self-conscious. Boys are very conscious of voice changes and are sometimes loth to draw attention to their voices by active participation in oral work, particularly in coeducational classes. Both boys and girls of this age hate to make fools of themselves in front of their peers, and this is what they may feel they are doing when making sounds which are not customary in their native language. This natural reluctance and inhibition can be overcome by a friendly, sympathetic classroom atmosphere, where the teacher takes care to see that no student, however poor his production, is ever embarrassed in front of the other students. At this stage, choral repetition provides a screen against undue personal attention, and the language laboratory booth provides isolation where the student may feel free to come out clearly and distinctly with strange sounds until, by sheer familiarity, he comes to feel they are natural and acceptable. Lengthy comment on personal efforts at pronunciation is best given, at this age, in a private conference out of class, or worked into general explanation and practice for the whole class. Unless the class as a whole is made to feel at home in the acquiring of an authentic accent, it may become the accepted thing among the group to retain a native-language pronunciation as a sign of solidarity.

It is partly because of the peculiar psychological and emotional problems posed by adolescent development that the trend more recently has been to introduce students to a foreign language at a preadolescent or early adolescent stage, so that they may become accustomed to foreign sounds and ways of expression before the period of greater self-consciousness. In the fun of hearing and using the language freely in group activities, the child has a happy experience of taking on foreign ways and foreign speech which creates a positive attitude toward further language learning. At whatever level the language study is begun, a class which has been accustomed to hearing and using the language continually from the very first lesson, within a limited amount of material which the student can handle with confidence, will pass through the adolescent stage without suffering to any serious extent from inhibitions and anxieties about oral work.

Many teachers are baffled by the "plateau" in learning to make correct sounds which students seem to reach after some months of foreign-language work: they have assumed the correct articulatory positions for some of the more difficult sounds but still retain a foreign accent. This plateau is a commonly observed feature in learning curves. Students should be discouraged from accepting this level of achievement as the limit of their learning capacity in pronunciation. Psychologists have shown that two things can set a learning curve on an upward trend again: a new method of attack or increased incentive.[3] With this in mind, an imaginative teacher should be able to introduce some new method of attack at this stage to promote greater effort in improving pronunciation. A competition to see

3 See R. S. Woodworth and H. Schlosberg, *Experimental Psychology*, rev. ed. (New York, 1954), p. 538.

which student can learn to recite a simple poem most accepta-bly, or which group of students can present a short dialogue to the rest of the class with articulation and intonation which most resemble those of the native speakers on the tape, or an opportunity not previously provided to record their voices on tape—new approaches such as these should stimulate new in-terest and renewed effort.

An even more discouraging situation frequently presents itself in the second or third year of study. Students who have acquired an acceptable, even creditable, pronunciation often show a distinct deterioration. The students are surrounded by a native-language atmosphere and the better students are con-tinually hearing poor pronunciation from their classmates or even, in some cases, from the poorly prepared teacher. There are several explanations for such deterioration: first, there may be a lack of vigilance on the part of the teacher, who is preoccupied with the problems of new work and new skills to be developed; second, perhaps a diminishing percentage of time is being spent on aural-oral activities, with the result that the student no longer hears authentic native speech with the same frequency; and third, it is possible that no credit is now being given for oral production, since more and more of the quizzes and tests have become wholly written in form. The student will soon follow the teacher's lead in his assessment of the relative importance of the various sections of the work.

The remedy, then, lies in rectifying each of these deficien-cies. Regular oral practice, in laboratory or classroom, is essen-tial at all stages if the gains of the early months are to be consolidated and retained. The more frequently advanced stu-dents can listen to native speech the more attuned will their ears become to the precise qualities of authentic articulation and intonation. At advanced stages students can still profit from regular reading practice from a well-known script where full attention is being paid to pronunciation. If the text chosen is too literary in style, the practice will hardly lead to transfer in a conversational context. A text containing conversation with some narrative is a better choice. To ensure the retention of an acceptable pronunciation, the teacher must continue to turn an attentive ear to the way students are speaking during class discussions and continue to evaluate their level of articulation and intonation at regular intervals, as part of their overall grade, throughout the foreign language course.

Should students be given practice in all the elements of the phonological system as an introduction to the course?

Some language teachers and some textbooks allot several weeks to a complete study of the sound system of the language at the beginning of the foreign-language course, on the assumption that the first words and phrases the students will learn will contain so many different sounds that students will inevitably practice errors if they have not been well prepared beforehand.

A phonological introduction of this type is too abstract for children of elementary school age, for whom the foreign-language lessons should be lively and exciting with much mimicry and active use of the language. Young children will learn sounds as they are mimicking phrases and singing songs, with an incidental articulatory explanation where needed and occasional drilling in areas of special difficulty. At junior high school age a long phonological introduction can also be frustrating. The students are eager to come to grips with the learning of the foreign language, which means to them being able to say something as the speaker of this other language would say it. This initial eagerness can be easily blunted if the experience of saying something meaningful in the foreign language is postponed for several weeks while the students practice sounds which, out of the context of communication, seem pointless and funny.

At senior high school level, a short phonological introduction may serve to make the student aware of the particular problems he will be encountering, and this applies to adult beginners also. Even at a more mature level, however, a thorough treatment of sounds isolated from acts of communication will suffer from apparent irrelevance. Much of what will be brought forward and practiced will not receive, at this initial stage, the attention it would receive later—after the student has become conscious of its importance in understanding and producing utterances.

Should a phonetic or phonemic script be used in teaching pronunciation?

Some methodologists advocate the teaching of the phonology of the language with the aid of a phonetic script (usually the symbols of the International Phonetic Alphabet or I.P.A.) or a phonemic script (several systems of phonemic symbols are in use). Phonetic symbols are usually printed in square brackets (for example, [e]), and phonemic symbols between slanted lines (for example, /e/). Each phonetic symbol represents a precise sound, and advocates of the I.P.A. notation maintain that such symbols become a guide to exact pronunciation for the student. They have the added value that, once learned, they serve as a guide to the pronunciation of other foreign languages. This advantage is more illusory than real, since sounds in two languages may differ only to a slight degree (thus making the use of different phonetic symbols pointless), yet differ sufficiently to make it imperative for the student to learn this slight difference if he wishes to acquire a near-native accent. Phonemic symbols indicate the sounds, within a certain band of tolerance, which are essential to comprehension of meaning in a particular language. Since the phonemic system of one language does not coincide with that of another, the set of symbols of one language will not act as a guide to the learner of another language. Some supporters of the phonemic system use I.P.A. symbols between slanted lines for the phonemes of a language where these are close to the type sounds of the I.P.A. system; others use symbols which are closer to the orthographic conventions of the language being studied. As yet there is no one accepted system for phonemic notation.

We shall not in this discussion consider the relative value of the use of phonetic as opposed to phonemic symbols, but concentrate on the question: should a system of notation of sounds different from, but more consistent than, the conventional spelling system of a language be taught to the students of a foreign language as an aid to the development of correct pronunciation? This problem will not be relevant to the teaching of languages where the orthographic system and the phonological system are consistently related, with one symbol or group of symbols always representing one sound or phonemic distinction. In some languages, however, it is an extremely important consideration either because of the chaotic illogicality of the spelling system (as in some aspects of English) or because one sound may be rendered by as many as five different letters or combinations of letters (as in French).

Once again, it will be necessary to distinguish clearly the level of study at which students are beginning the foreign language. At the elementary school level, the learning of a phonetic or phonemic notation before learning the orthographic system of the language would be confusing. Students at this stage of their education are still consolidating their reading, writing, and spelling skills in their native language. For this reason, among others, there should be little reading and writing, except of what is well known orally, and work in the foreign language should be largely oral and active. At junior and senior high school level, phonetic or phonemic symbols have sometimes been taught in the past in association with introductory lessons on the phonological system of the language. After students had been drilled very thoroughly in the production of certain sounds, phonetic symbols were used for purposes of refinement and explanation. It is undeniable that when they have been made available to the students in this way phonetic symbols have proved to be very useful in helping students to pronounce words which are spelled in an unexpected fashion. Some teachers have found, however, that phonetic or phonemic spellings learned thoroughly in the introductory stages remain with the student as a constant source of interference when he begins to use the traditional spelling system, and they doubt the value of setting up two distinctly different symbolic systems for the same words and phrases, particularly for the adolescent age group. For this reason, and because students easily forget the sound-symbol associations of the phonetic or phonemic system when they are not being actively drilled in them, some teachers feel that the time spent in learning the phonetic or phonemic system sufficiently well for it to be useful might be better spent in drilling the student in the correct pronunciation of the sounds, and in the association of each sound with the various spelling equivalents in the traditional writing system.

At junior and senior high school level, students with no previous experience of a foreign language may not see the relevance of a special system of notation for sounds at first. The phonetic or phonemic notation can be introduced at a later stage when a plateau is reached or a deterioration in pronunciation is threatening to develop. At this stage it may arouse a fresh interest in sounds and provide a new method of attack for an old problem which will push the learning curve up for a further period. It can then be used at more advanced levels as a system of reference for remedial work in pronunciation and for help with exceptional spellings.

Adult students may find a phonetic or phonemic notation helpful after some initial experience with the language because it renders them independent of their teacher and enables them to push ahead in individual study without learning all kinds of erroneous pronunciations which will have to be corrected at a later date.

Is a near-native pronunciation desirable for, or attainable by, the majority of foreign-language students?

There was a period when an English gentleman learning French prided himself on not stooping to adopt the effeminate and obviously degenerate way of speaking of the French. Since he always insisted that any individual worthy of his attention should speak to him in English anyway, it was of no importance that he could not understand or make himself understood in French.

This attitude to the tongue of the foreigner is now a thing of the past in most countries. Except in certain special cases, where a reading knowledge of the language is required without there being any probability of the learner's ever meeting a person who speaks the language, languages are now taught for oral communication as well as for reading and writing.

Communication is a two-way process. A student who has

acquired a native-language approximation to foreign-language sounds will inevitably be disconcerted when he hears a native speaking. He himself may or may not be understood, depending on how much experience the native speaker has had with foreigners with this particular variety of accent. If the student asks a question he will usually not understand the answer. If he is asked a question by a native speaker he will not be able to reply because he will not understand what is required of him. If communication skills are an objective of the language course, then true communication beyond the confines of the classroom must be the ultimate aim. This involves the acquisition of an accent in which the phonemic distinctions are respected and the stress and intonation patterns make the meaning clear.

Because of differences in ability to mimic, and lack of opportunity to hear native speech frequently, many students may be hindered in their efforts to develop a near-native accent. Most students can, however, develop an accent which is acceptable to a native speaker and learn to recognize phonemic distinctions so that they can comprehend what a native speaker is saying. Whether they do in fact acquire these skills is dependent on the teacher's understanding of the bases of speech production, on his careful and conscientious drilling of those areas where the native language and the foreign language most distinctly diverge, and on the frequent use of tapes recorded by native speakers when the teacher himself does not have near-native facility with the language.

ANNOTATED READING LIST

POLITZER, R. *Teaching French: An Introduction to Applied Linguistics*. Boston: Ginn & Co., 1960. Chapter 5 gives a clear outline of the material of articulatory phonetics, useful to teachers of any language. Chapter 6 has valuable material on teaching French pronunciation. Similar chapters are found in the following:

POLITZER, R. *Teaching German: A Linguistic Orientation*. Waltham, Mass.: Blaisdell, 1968.

POLITZER, R. and STAUBACH, C. *Teaching Spanish: A Linguistic Orientation*. Boston: Ginn & Co., 1961.

GLEASON, JR., H. A. *An Introduction to Descriptive Linguistics. Revised edition.* New York: Holt, Rinehart & Winston, 1961. Articulatory features in general are fully described, with particular reference to English. There is a chapter on acoustic phonetics.

PRATOR, JR., C. H. *Manual of American English Pronunciation.* rev. ed. New York: Holt, Rinehart & Winston, 1957.

The D. C. Heath series. S. BELASCO, General Editor. Boston, 1961:

VALDMAN, A. *Applied Linguistics: French.*
MARCHAND, J. *Applied Linguistics: German.*
D. CARDENAS, *Applied Linguistics: Spanish.*
MAGNER, T. *Applied Linguistics: Russian.*
HALL, R. *Applied Linguistics: Italian.*

Each book in the series gives a detailed account of the phonology of the language concerned.

DELATTRE, P. *Principes de phonétique française à l'usage des etudiants anglo-américains.* Middlebury College, Vt., 1951.

Contrastive Structure Series. CHARLES A. FERGUSON, General Editor. Chicago: University of Chicago Press:

MOULTON, W. G. *The Sounds of English and German.* 1962.
AGARD, F. B., and DI PIETRO, R. J. *The Sounds of English and Italian.* 1965.
STOCKWELL, R. P., and BOWEN, J. D. *The Sounds of English and Spanish.* 1965.

6

Listening Comprehension

Teaching language as communication has become an accepted aim of the foreign-language teacher throughout the world. To most this has come to mean that we must teach our students to speak the language with some fluency and authentic idiom. What has been less emphasized, however, is that communication is a process involving at least two people. Speaking does not of itself constitute communication unless what is said is comprehended by another person. The greatest difficulty for a traveller in a foreign country is not primarily that he cannot make himself understood; this he can frequently do by gesture, by writing, or by pointing to something written in a bilingual book of phrases. His first difficulty, and one that leads to considerable emotional tension and embarrassment, is that he cannot understand what is being said to him and around him. Even if the native speaker enunciates his words slowly and distinctly elements of stress, intonation, and word grouping (often exaggerated in an earnest attempt at clarity) add to the confusion of the inexperienced foreigner. As a result there is no communication and the traveller's speaking skills cannot be exercised to great advantage. His enjoyment of and participation in community life and thought are further curtailed by his inability to comprehend announcements, broadcasts, lectures, plays, and films.

Teaching the comprehension of spoken language is therefore of primary importance if the communication aim is to be

Some sections of this chapter appeared in a different version in "Listening Comprehension," *MLJ*, 50, no 4 (April, 1966): 196–204.

achieved. A long-neglected area, listening comprehension has its peculiar problems which arise from the fleeting, immaterial nature of spoken utterances.

THEORETICAL CONCEPTS BASIC TO LISTENING COMPREHENSION

In chapter 5, we have already discussed the special problems of discrimination of sounds, stress, and intonation, but these are only a few of the elements involved in understanding what is being said to us.

Of great value to foreign-language teachers interested in teaching listening comprehension is the extensive research which has been carried out in recent years by communications engineers concerned with the maximum efficiency of telephonic and telegraphic equipment. Research engineers have given considerable thought and study to the nature of the message to be communicated, the particular qualities of the channel by which it passes from emitter to receiver, and the state in which it is received and interpreted by the listener.[1] The foreign-language teacher who understands their theoretical formulations and terminology can extract many seminal lines of thought from their observations.

The speech emitted by the communicator, which contains the message, has phonic patterning distinctive for each language. This conventional patterning limits the possible sequences of sounds for that particular language and determines their frequency of occurrence. As the child learns his native language he comes to expect certain patterns of sound and not others. He is therefore disconcerted by the sound sequences of a foreign language until he has had sufficient experience with them to build up a frame of expectations. This process requires long practice and familiarity. The phonic patterning of a language has not only acceptable sound sequences but anticipated degrees of loudness, levels of pitch, and lengths of pause. With experience the child learns to recognize groupings of these features as clues to meaning. Unexpected variations are clues to emotional states and to attitudes to the message or to the

1   See diagram in chapter 7.

receiver. Some sequences recur with great frequency, and in certain contexts alternatives are inconceivable. Such items are considered to contain little "information," in the technical sense of that term. "Information" in this sense does not refer to meaning but to the range of possible alternative items which could occur in a certain position in speech. As Weaver has put it, "the word information in communication theory relates not so much to what you *do* say, as to what you *could* say. That is, information is a measure of one's freedom of choice when one selects a message." [2] The concept of information in terms of probabilities is mathematical but the basic idea is useful for extrapolation to comprehension situations. If in a given situation any other word would be most unlikely, the word used may be said to give little information; if the range of possibilities is great, then the use of one particular word conveys a great deal of information. If I hold a book in my hand and state, "This is a book," the word conveys little information. Possibilities have been reduced by visual and situational clues which help to delimit the alternatives. On the other hand, if I say of someone who is not present, "He is reading," the word "reading" conveys much information because of the great number of words which could easily have occurred in that situation. In our own language, we have learned to recognize a number of factors which reduce the possibility of occurrence of any one linguistic item—elements such as syntactic relationships, sequences of words and combinations of sounds of high frequency, clichés, and conversational tags and formulas. The effect of these factors in reducing the amount of information conveyed in any one utterance is of great importance because the human organism has a limited capacity for reception of information. When someone is conveying to us a message which is not entirely expected or obvious, we often say: "Wait a minute! Not so fast!" or "Say that again!" These expressions make it clear that we can absorb only a certain amount of information at a time.

In order to reduce to manageable proportions the amount of information in any one sound sequence each language has developed a certain amount of redundancy. It has been esti-

2   C. Shannon and W. Weaver, *The Mathematical Theory of Communication* (Urbana, Ill., 1959), p. 100.

mated, for instance, that the English language is fifty per cent redundant.[3] Were this redundancy eliminated, the human organism could not absorb information at the rate at which it would be emitted in normal speech. Redundancy in languages is to be found in elements of sound and in morphological and syntactical formations which reinforce each other in the conveying of meaning. A French sentence may begin with "est-ce que," which signals a question for which the response will normally be "Oui" or "Non." At the same time the voice will continue to rise in pitch until the end of the sentence, this being also an indication that a question of this type is being asked. The listener who was not attending to the first words of the sentence will be guided by the rising intonation. Both of these features are conveying the same element of meaning and there is, therefore, redundancy.

It is redundancy in language which helps us to piece together the information we hear. Even in communication in our native language we do not hear clearly everything that is said to us, nor do we pay full attention to every element of each utterance. In a language we are learning as foreigners our perceptual difficulties are compounded by many items which we do not recognize or with which we are as yet unfamiliar. Artificially constructed messages, such as those frequently devised for use in foreign-language classes, often unwittingly reduce the amount of redundancy supplied by a speaker in a normal situation. In this way the perception of the foreign-language message is made more difficult even for a person familiar with the language clues.

Over and above the clues provided by sound sequences, we convey further elements of meaning by body movements, facial expressions, and slight changes in breathing, length of pauses, and degrees of emphasis. These elements, usually classed as kinesics and paralanguage, vary from language community to language community, and even within language communities at various levels of intercourse. No full comprehension of oral communication is complete without taking these aspects into consideration as further delimitations of the message. In the classroom, or laboratory, these elements may

3   *Ibid.*, p. 104.

be supplied by a visual accompaniment to an oral tape (a film or filmstrip, preferably the former) so that the student can watch the expressions and gestures of the speakers as an aid to meaning. Such films are a help only if they are of a level acceptable to the student; badly produced, they merely create the impression that the speakers of the language whose ways of behavior are so different from those of the student are rather ridiculous, quaint, or inferior.[4]

The problems of the message itself, then, may be studied in terms of the amount of information it conveys and the rate at which this information is encoded. Further problems arise, however, in the transmission of the message from communicator to receiver. If the message is transmitted with an accompaniment of irrelevant sound, or "noise," some of the message may not be received by the listener. In a language laboratory which is not carefully designed or properly serviced, audial quality may deteriorate. As a result the student has problems of discrimination of sounds, and the message he receives is defective, with certain clues (particularly phonemic distinctions) reduced. A similar difficulty is sometimes experienced in some sections of a classroom which is acoustically faulty. This imperfect reception of audial clues has the same effect as increase of information content. Even when the message is received clearly, unfamiliar elements of it may be perceived in much the same way as noise, so that some parts of the message will be lost in the process of transmission to the receiver. The language learner is then faced with several problems: the identification of patterns and their combinations in the somewhat mutilated message which he has received, the reconstruction of the defective sections according to probabilities of occurrence, and the organization of these patterns in a meaningful way. The organization which results will depend on his previous experience with words, syntactical groupings, situational context, and the cultural elements reflected in the foreign-language usage. His degree of familiarity with these elements will determine what he selects from the stream of sound, which is providing information at a rate which makes it impossible for him to assimilate it totally.

[4] The use of audio-visual materials is discussed at length in chapter 7.

Probabilities of occurrence of certain sequences of sounds are built up through experience with a language. These probabilities determine what we hear; that is, we tend to hear what we expect to hear. A nonconventional, and therefore improbable, sequence of sounds will at first be interpreted as a familiar, or probable, sequence and in this way acquire intelligibility. Psychologists have found that if a nonconventional sequence of sounds is presented to a listener just below the threshold of audibility he will organize it into a conventional sequence; in other words, a series of meaningless syllables with sentence intonation will be interpreted as an intelligible sentence. When a foreign language is being learned many sequences of sounds have low probability of occurrence for the inexperienced listener, and will therefore be misinterpreted, while others which he has never before encountered provide an accompaniment of "noise." His ability to distinguish sequences which are slightly familiar from the unfamiliar may also be affected by the emotional stress and anxiety which not infrequently accompany aural comprehension experiences in a foreign language. Certain students become very tense when expected to depend on the ear alone. As a result of this emotional tension what they are hearing comes to them as an auditory blur and they become panicky. The panic decreases their ability to discriminate sounds and word groupings.

STAGES OF DEVELOPMENT OF LISTENING COMPREHENSION

The student learning a foreign language passes through several stages in the comprehension of speech. On first contact, the foreign language utterances strike his ears as a stream of undifferentiated noises. As he listens, he gradually perceives some order in the noise: a regularity in the rise and fall of the voice and in the breath groups. As he learns some of the arbitrary associations of the particular language (i.e., vocabulary, verb groups, simple expressions) he begins to distinguish the phonic and syntactic patterning: the recurring elements which give form to segments of speech. This is not yet comprehension which requires selection from the stream of speech of what is crucial for the particular situation in which the utterance is heard. The student next passes through a stage when he recognizes familiar elements in the mass of speech but is unable to recognize the interrelationships within the whole stream of sound; this again is not full comprehension. He feels rather like a man walking in a fog which clears in patches and floats back to obscure other points. It is only with much practice that he can pass beyond this stage. As he hears much foreign-language speech, he eventually acquires facility in recognizing the crucial elements which determine the message. At this more advanced stage, he may recognize the essentials of the message, but not be able to remember what he has recognized. This is because he is unable to concentrate his attention on the crucial elements of the message long enough to rehearse them subvocally before moving on with the continuing voice. All his attention is taken up with recognition. In comprehension of native speech he anticipates certain sequences of low information content, which in his previous experiences with the language had occurred in similar contexts, and his full attention is given to the high information items. While the foreign language is still unfamiliar territory there are few low information items which may be anticipated, and accordingly occupy little of his attention. Furthermore, anticipation based on experience with the native language (as with homonyms and structures which appear to parallel those of his own language) may be extremely misleading. Because of the high rate of information contained in sound sequences with which he is not very familiar, he has not sufficient capacity left for retention.

Broadbent of the Applied Psychology Research Unit of the Medical Research Council at Cambridge, England, has developed from the study of a great deal of experimental data a very interesting theory of memory and retention.[5] Consideration of certain aspects of this theory will help us to understand the processes involved when a student is trying to follow listening comprehension exercises. Broadbent maintains that the human organism has a limited capacity for absorbing information (in the sense in which we have been using it in this chapter). Since irrelevant items place an extra load on the sys-

5 D. E. Broadbent, *Perception and Communication* (London and New York, 1958).

tem, information is at first filtered by the perceptual processes according to characteristics which events have in common. This filtered information is then absorbed into the immediate memory, which is a short-term storage mechanism. Information is easily lost from this short-term store if it is not recirculated through the perceptual processes at regular intervals. (Here we may think of the way we repeat a telephone number over to ourselves on the way from the phone book to the dial). Only selected items of information pass from this short-term store to long-term storage in the memory. Since the perceptual system has a limited capacity for absorbing information, when the perceptual processes are bombarded with items in quick succession the immediate memory cannot recirculate what it is retaining, and these items are lost.

Comprehension of speech requires the retaining of information from a whole sequence of sounds, not just from the last sound heard. As a result, when material is unfamiliar, the inexperienced student has a high-information content to absorb from each sound sequence. After a while he is unable to retain the relevant elements from preceding sequences, through recirculation, and still absorb more information from the succeeding sequences. This stage, when the student understands everything as he hears it but is unable to remember what he understood, must be recognized as a legitimate and inevitable phase of the learning process. The student, too, must understand that this is a common experience in language learning, and not be alarmed at what he may feel is a personal failure of memory.

TEACHING LISTENING COMPREHENSION

Before the teacher can devise a sequence of activities which will train students in listening comprehension, he must understand the nature of the skill he is setting out to develop. Listening to a foreign language may be analyzed as involving two levels of activity, both of which must be taught. We shall call these the recognition level and the selection level.

The first level, the recognition level, involves the identification of words and phrases in their structural interrelationships, of time sequences, logical and modifying terms, and of phrases which are redundant interpolations adding nothing to the development of the line of thought. For the student unaccustomed to listening to the foreign language this process of identification completely occupies his perceptual processes so that no retention material can recirculate. It is only after the recognition of these general features has become automatic that the student can be expected to reproduce or respond to what he has heard in a long sequence.

At the second level, the level of selection, the listener is drawing out from the communication those elements which seem to express the purposes of the speaker or those which suit his own purposes. This he can do at first only with short utterances. Extracting relevant facts from a communication occupies some of the capacity of the organism and he also has to hold some of these facts in his immediate memory in order to relate them to other facts. This act of suspended judgment temporarily reduces his capacity for taking in more information. With a long sequence, what are to him still high-information items are emitted in quick succession and he has not sufficient capacity to absorb them. As a result some of them pass unregistered and he misses the point of what he has heard. Alternatively, having misinterpreted some high-information items near the beginning of the sequence he wrongly anticipates the intent of the message, selects accordingly, and does not absorb other elements which were important to the purposes of the speaker. As his familiarity with the language increases through the teaching he is receiving in all skill areas, these difficulties will be reduced and he will be able to follow and retain longer and longer sequences. To be able to listen eventually with ease to the foreign language in normal situations, the student needs thorough training at the recognition level and much practice in selecting from the stream of sound specific details of the message.

Training at the recognition level must begin from the first lesson. This does not mean the presentation of much ungraded and ill-designed aural material in the hope that something will happen. There was a period when teachers were urged to surround their students from the very beginning with a veritable mist of foreign-language speech, thus re-creating in the classroom, so it was believed, the situation in which students would find themselves if suddenly transported to the country where the language is spoken. It is true that, when plunged completely into the foreign-language atmosphere, people do learn to interpret the sounds they are hearing, but to varying degrees of accuracy. One fact which is conveniently overlooked is that many immigrants in a new land are unable, after many years of residence, to interpret more than the simple interchanges of daily life. Some do go beyond the comprehension of banalities but certainly not without effort on their part. When we take into consideration the number of hours during which the average immigrant listens to the new language before he understands it to any degree of effectiveness we appear justified in assuming that he is not learning aural comprehension in the most economical and efficient way. In the considerably fewer hours at the disposal of the teacher in the classroom, methods must be adopted which will lead more directly to the objective, developing the greatest degree of skill that is possible in the time available.

For a method to be economical as well as efficient it must take into account all the skill elements which should be developed. As we have seen, in a listening situation the student must be so familiar with the components of a stream of speech that he can react quickly to some of them and pass rapidly over others which are redundant or irrelevant to his immediate purpose. He must be able to recognize without effort sound patterns (sound discriminations affecting meaning, intonation patterns, significant levels of pitch, word groupings), grammatical sequences and tenses, modifiers and function words, clichés, expletives or hesitation expressions which can be ignored as irrelevant to the message, levels of discourse (colloquial or formal), emotional overtones (excited, disappointed, peremptory, cautious, angry utterances), as well as regional, social, or dialectal variations. As these aspects of speech become familiar to the student his expectation of their occurrence in certain contexts rises and their information content is, as a consequence, lessened. As the human organism is able to absorb only a certain amount of information at one time, this familiarity, by decreasing the information content, increases the number of items with which the student can cope in one utterance. Systematically prepared listening-comprehension materials will provide training, in a steady progression, for all the areas listed, not leaving essential learning to chance. If suitable materials are not available, the teacher will choose, adapt, and refashion those which are obtainable, or prepare his own, with these basic requirements in mind.

The first step in training in listening comprehension is well provided for in dialogue learning. The student is continually hearing the material he is learning repeated by the model, by other students, and by himself. In this way, he forms an auditory image of these short utterances so that he is able to recognize them without analysis. The danger in this situation is that such recognition may remain only at the acoustic level, the student not being more than dimly aware of the meaning of what he is saying. To ensure that the phrases he is learning will be useful also at the selective level, frequent opportunity must be provided for their application to communication situations within the class group, where actual degree of comprehension can be clearly demonstrated by an appropriate response, either physical or oral. This response, if oral, should as a general rule be in the foreign language. If the student is habitually asked to demonstrate his comprehension by translation into his native language a further danger develops. He will acquire the habit of analyzing the elements of every utterance for comparison with what seem to be the most nearly appropriate categories of his native language and he will not learn to perceive short utterances and segments of longer utterances as meaningful in themselves. He will also not develop facility in listening to and registering an ongoing stream of sound for retention. With each utterance he will be busy decomposing the first segment he has heard in order to retain a native-language version of it, when his attention should have been fully engaged in forming an auditory image of the second segment and in selecting from it the elements relating it to the first.

In the early stages, the teacher should concentrate on teaching the immediate apprehension of a segment of sound, not on long-term retention of it: that is, on recognition, not on total or delayed recall. The student, for instance, may not be able to recall a sequence of utterances in a dialogue but may yet be able to respond promptly and appropriately to any one item in the dialogue. He will not be capable of total recall until the material has been overlearned, and a strong frame of expectations has been built up in the language. It is debatable whether time should be wasted on bringing a long series of dialogue sentences to this pitch of overlearning, as the value of the dialogue lies in the usefulness of the individual utterances, not in any intrinsic value in the devised sequence.

The potentialities of a dialogue for improving listening comprehension have not been fully exploited until the student is hearing recombinations of the material in the current and earlier dialogues, particularly in the context of actual situations, as in dramatizations acted out by groups of students or in actual conversational interchanges among students. The sense of reality can also be created by filmed situations where these recombinations are appropriate. In classes where dialogues are not being used, the language material of the current and preceding lessons should be similarly exploited in recombinations in a situational context. Reading extracts should contain a considerable amount of conversation, and from these the students should be encouraged to prepare and act short sketches which are essentially recombinations of words and phrases from the lessons which have been studied, and which their fellow students recognize with ease. The listener cannot concentrate his attention on every constituent of an utterance with the same intensity. The familiar expressions in the recombinations form a matrix from which he selects certain elements which are interrelated from segment to segment and which outline the developing pattern of the ideas which he is pursuing. If the student is confused by an effort to comprehend every element as he hears it, thus concentrating his attention fully on every constituent, he will not perceive these interrelationships and what he has not perceived he will not retain. It is in listening comprehension particularly that the teacher can easily underestimate the difficulties of the student. To the teacher the comprehension of elementary material is immediate and effortless. He must try to see the processes involved from the student's point of view and provide plenty of practice in hearing well-rehearsed material while requiring the abstraction from it of different lines of thought.

Recombinations of listening-comprehension material can,

with a little ingenuity, be included in games requiring a physical or oral response. Often these can take the form of guessing games. Games imaginatively devised give the students comprehension practice in a situation where interest is heightened by the competitive element and their attention is distracted from the skill being practiced. If comprehension is thus demonstrated in a real situation where it is an instrument rather than an objective the teacher will have tangible evidence that the students have passed beyond the recognition stage to that of selection. A few minutes of listening-comprehension games at regular intervals, usually at the end of class lessons, will enable the teacher to reintroduce systematically material which is not currently being actively practiced. In this way, retention of material from earlier lessons will be constantly reinforced by active recapitulation without tedium.

It is only at an advanced stage, where so many more features of the language are familiar, that the teacher may begin to allow the student to listen to material unrelated to what he has been studying, in which he must deduce meanings from context in a very rapid mental process of association. This process is possible only when the effort involved in retention has been considerably reduced by almost automatic recognition of language patterns. At this stage the teacher may seize the opportunity from time to time to enliven the lesson by recounting in the foreign language some amusing incident which has occurred during the day, or by providing some anecdotal background to a subject under discussion. When the teacher uses the foreign language as he would use the native language, the students begin to look upon it as a normal instrument for communication.

When the student has acquired confidence in listening to ungraded material much practice may be given in individual situations: in a language laboratory, in listening booths established in the library, in a listening room equipped with a tape recorder or a record player. At this stage direct listening practice can be divorced from a conversational situation. Material for listening may be drawn from literature being studied and may provide a basis for oral reports in class. Practice in listening may be given by taped lectures on informational subjects, sustained scenes from plays, or readings from poetry and prose. Students may attempt to follow radio broadcasts or the sound track of a commercial film or documentary. They may relax with a program of popular songs.

Groups of schools in the same supervision area should cooperate in the production of material for listening comprehension, freely exchanging tapes which they have had the opportunity to make. One school may be able to tape an interview or conversation with a native speaker who has visited them. This material should be immediately circulated to other schools in the district. In areas where contact with native speakers is rare no opportunity should be lost of building up through cooperative action a supply of semi-informal material in the foreign language. In this way students will have the opportunity to hear a variety of voices of differing quality, and accents representative of several regions and educational backgrounds.

DESIGNING OF EXERCISES FOR LISTENING COMPREHENSION

No language skill should be taught in isolation. Listening-comprehension activities should be related to and spring naturally from material being studied as oral practice or for reading; it can also provide a stimulus for writing activities. Listening comprehension should also be tested at all stages along with the other areas of language study. Exercises should be developed for all four stages in the learning of this skill: identification; identification and selection without retention (that is, listening for pleasure with no questions to be answered); identification and guided selection with short-term retention (where students are given some prior indication of what they are to listen for); and identification and selection with long-term retention. While new material is forming the basis for identification practice, more familiar material is being used for practice in identification and selection without retention, and even more familiar material for identification and selection with retention. Suitable exercises for all four stages will, therefore, be presented regularly at all levels. All material used for listening comprehension, even in the earliest lessons, should be authentic, that is, it should consist of utterances with a high probability of occurrence. Teaching students to comprehend artificial language combinations which would rarely be heard from a native speaker is a waste of time and energy, and can only confuse the student when he is later confronted with natural speech.

Each of the stages outlined above will now be discussed in detail and a list of suggested activities for each stage at elementary, intermediate, and advanced levels will be given. Many of the activities suggested may also serve as testing devices.

Stage 1: Identification

Students need practice in discrimination of sounds and in the elements of meaning conveyed by stress, pitch, and intonation. For the designing of exercises for this purpose, see chapter 5.

Dialogue learning is particularly appropriate to this stage. Dialogues written in authentic speech forms with a normal amount of redundancy and heard and repeated at an accepted conversational speed provide practice in aural identification of common word groupings, phonological and structural patterns, clichés of everyday speech. Students may listen to dialogues they have already learned given at a rapid conversational speed for sheer practice in identification.

Stage 2: Identification and Selection without Retention

At this stage the student listens to a connected sequence with a development of thought which he tries to follow. The student and the teacher are satisfied if he has followed the passage as delivered without worrying about ability to recount or discuss what he has heard. The most suitable materials for this stage are simple plays or sketches depicting normal situations in which the characters use the common, repetitive speech of conversation. The parts should be read with normal everyday diction, not the artificial diction employed on the stage. Also suitable are dramatic readings, by several participants, of stories with a considerable amount of conversation. At a more advanced stage students may listen to group conversations where two or three native speakers with easily identifiable differences of voice discuss a subject of interest to the student. In the excitement of the discussion the speech will be slightly slurred, but this will be compensated for by the hesitations, interruptions, and repetitions characteristic of natural speech. Conversations and discussions of this type may be taped and used over and over again. Simulated telephone conversations, with clear distinctions of voice, are also worthwhile, for they give practice in listening to slightly distorted speech with no visual clues to counteract the effect of the distortion.

At this stage, in laboratory work, the same tape should be repeated several times (in the same session or in successive sessions) to give the students further practice with the same material.

Stage 3: Identification and Guided Selection with Short-Term Retention

Material similar to that for Stage 2 may be used, with clearly distinctive voices and lively themes. At this stage the student is given some questions beforehand, not a great number, and he listens for the answers which he marks on a question sheet as he hears them, or, at a more advanced stage, after he has listened to the whole passage. The passage should be repeated so that the student may have further practice in listening and selecting, and may have an opportunity to verify his answers.

Stage 4: Identification, Selection, and Long-Term Retention

This is the final stage. Here the student is encouraged to listen freely to all kinds of material. He may listen to literary extracts, plays, poems, and lectures on literary or cultural subjects related to his work, or he may listen to all kinds of aural material (news bulletins, discussions on subjects of topical interest, plays, songs, film scenarios) for his own pleasure. At this stage he should have practice in listening to regional accents and to all types of voices. After a period of listening, the student is expected to be able to talk or write about what he has heard.

Summary of Possible Activities for Four Stages of Listening Comprehension

ELEMENTARY LEVEL

A *Identification:*
1. Sound and short-phrase discrimination.
2. Listening to dialogues already learned.
3. Identification of phrases and statements from reading material studied.
4. Games involving identification of words and phrases heard.

B *Identification and Selection without Retention:*
5. Listening to variations of dialogues already learned (these to be spoken at normal speed).
6. Listening to the retelling with variations of reading material already studied (at a normal speed of delivery).

C *Identification and Guided Selection with Short-Term Retention:*
7. True-False questions are supplied on a sheet in front of the student who listens to variations of dialogues or reading material studied.
8. Multiple-choice answers to questions given orally (on the same material as in 7). These answers are before the student as he listens.
9. Questions are supplied beforehand, the student works out the answers as he listens (answers to be given in the native language).

D *Identification, Selection, and Long-Term Retention:*
10. Similar activities to 7, 8, and 9, but the student is expected to answer questions which are provided for him on paper or asked orally *after* he has listened.

INTERMEDIATE LEVEL

A *Identification:*
1. More advanced work in 1, 2, 3, and 4 (elementary level).

B *Identification and Selection without Retention:*
2. More advanced work in 5 and 6 (elementary level).
3. The teacher gives a short account of an amusing incident which occurred on his way to school or to the classroom.
4. The teacher begins the lesson with some interesting background facts or news items, or the students tell prepared news items (without referring to a script).
5. The teacher and/or a group of students give dramatic readings of stories which contain a great deal of conversation. The other students listen with books closed.
6. Listening to group conversations prepared by two or three students.

C *Identification and Guided Selection with Short-Term Retention:*
7. More advanced work on 7, 8, and 9 (elementary level).
8. Listening to carefully graded foreign-language films specially prepared for teaching purposes.
9. The students guess the name of a person or place described by the teacher or by another student.
10. Completion of sentences given orally (definitions; supplying such supplementary information as time, season, or occupation). The answers are chosen from a multiple-choice list supplied to the student, or are given orally.

D *Identification, Selection, and Long-Term Retention:*
11. Similar activities to 10 (elementary level), but the student is now expected to be able to tell in his own words in the foreign language what he has heard. (This leads to oral composition and written composition.)

ADVANCED LEVEL

A *Identification:*
1. Aural discrimination of slight distinctions in sound which

alter the meaning of sentences (e.g., negations, inversions, tense distinctions).

B   *Identification and Selection without Retention:*
2.   More advanced work on 6 (elementary level).
3.   More advanced work on 3, 4, 5, and 6 (intermediate level).
4.   The students listen with books closed while the teacher reads expressively the complete story they have already studied in sections.
5.   Listening to simulated telephone conversations between two students (prepared).
6.   Students (and teacher) prepare accounts of amusing incidents (the students do not read from a script).
7.   Groups of students prepare classroom sessions of well-known television games or competitions.
8.   Listening to records of poems and plays already studied.

C   *Identification and Guided Selection with Short-Term Retention:*
9.   More advanced work on 7, 8, and 9 (elementary level), and 8 and 9 (intermediate level).
10.   Sentence completion at the end of longer and longer sequences, with choice of answer from multiple-choice items (students must explain circumstances, reasons, or situation).
11.   Answering in the native language simple questions on longer sequences (at times associated with composition by requiring answers in the foreign language).
12.   Link with dictation: The teacher prepares a sequence of dictations on subjects of cultural interest. To prepare for the dictation, the teacher gives an account in the foreign language of personalities and background, with pictures, and discussion, and then dictates a relevant passage.

D   *Identification, Selection, and Long-Term Retention:*
13.   Longer passages (anecdotes, short stories, informational material) are read and the students answer questions. Suggested order of development:
   a)   students are required to answer true-false questions on a list supplied beforehand;

b) students select answers from multiple-choice items which have been supplied beforehand;
c) as for (a) or (b) but question papers are supplied after the second reading;
d) answers in the native language to questions in the foreign language;
e) finally, questions in the foreign language to be answered in the foreign language (thus leading to composition practice).

14. As much of each lesson as possible is given in the foreign language to provide continual practice in listening.

15. Ten-minute lecturettes on authors, poets, famous people, with practice in note-taking.

16. The students listen to recordings of plays, poems, or speeches.

17. The students are encouraged to attend foreign-language films when these are screened commercially, and to listen to popular songs.

18. Activities of the foreign-language club, and interschool social evenings with programs of items in the foreign language presented by different schools.

At each level, specially prepared and graded foreign-language films supply practice in identification, selection, and retention as students relate what they have heard to what follows.

Presentation of Listening-Comprehension Exercises

Certain procedural features of the presentation of listening-comprehension exercises have been the subject of experimental study. Physical aspects of the classroom or laboratory presentation, such as speed of utterance, length of segments, length of pauses, and the acoustics of the room, should be carefully studied by the teacher because of their decisive effect on the value of the exercise.

All utterances for listening comprehension should be delivered at normal *speed* from the earliest lessons. Normal speed does not mean rapid native speech, but a speed of delivery which would not appear to a native speaker to be unduly labored—a speed which retains normal word groupings, elisions, liaisons, consonant assimilations, natural rhythm, and intonation. Utterances which are delivered at an unnaturally slow pace are inevitably distorted and the auditory images stored by the student will not be immediately useful when he hears a natural form of speech. It may be argued that in a foreign-language situation the native speaker will, on request, speak very slowly, but in so doing he exaggerates what to the listener are already confusing liaisons, elisions, and phonemic distinctions of his language or tries to incorporate into it, in an unsystematic fashion, what he believes to be the distinctive characteristics of the language of his interlocutor. This labored delivery, running contrary to the expectations of the foreigner, is often as difficult for him to interpret as undistorted speech at normal speed. Even in the very early stages familiar material can be understood when spoken at normal speed. It is obvious that difficulties will arise when unfamiliar material is included, thus increasing rapidly the amount of information to be assimilated. At more advanced stages, when unfamiliar words and phrases are intentionally included in comprehension exercises, they should be embedded in so much easily recognizable material that the student is able to concentrate on comparing the new elements with the surrounding context and deducing their meaning in this way. These new elements are also more easily assimilated at this stage because their characteristic phonological and structural patterning is recognized by the trained ear of the student.

The length of the segments emitted in each breath group and the *length of the pauses* between the segments are of more importance than the actual speed of delivery within the segments. The amount of information in a segment increases rapidly with the length of the segment, a greater number of words allowing for a greater number of alternatives. The longer the segment the greater is the strain on the auditory memory. During the pause between segments, the organism can rehearse what it has heard, thus strengthening the memory trace. Research has shown that the auditory memory span for foreign-language material is considerably less than for native-language material, probably on a ratio of nine words to fifteen.[6] With segments of from eight to ten words (less in the early stages) the mind can recirculate the material during the pause, relating it to what preceded and anticipating to some extent what will follow. Such pauses are supplied in natural speech by hesitations, a certain amount of hemming and hawing, some restating, and by certain conventional expressions contributing nothing to the meaning of the utterance but having a high frequency of occurrence which reflects their usefulness in extending the pauses in a normal utterance. Since artificially prepared material usually omits these common features of natural utterances it tends to deliver information at a much higher rate than normal speech. A slight lengthening of the pauses will supply the extra time which the organism requires to absorb the information presented to it, without adding a time element not available in normal conversation.

For the same reason, listening-comprehension exercises should contain a certain amount of repetitious material. This may take the form, for example, of explanations or descriptions in slightly different versions. Such repetition is another characteristic of normal speech. In conversation and other forms of extempore speech there is redundancy of content as well as linguistic redundancy. It is because redundancy of content has been eliminated that following a close-knit discourse or the reading of a well-written paper, even in the native language, requires a concentrated effort on the part of the listener. This fact is often overlooked with the result that listening-comprehension materials in the foreign language may contain features which make them even more difficult to follow than similar material in the very familiar native language.

Teachers should be aware of certain emotional problems which may arise in connection with listening-comprehension exercises. Natural trepidation on the part of normal students not accustomed to paying close attention to aural messages can be overcome by the early introduction of much practice in listening to a limited amount of linguistic material. Considerable difficulty is experienced, however, by students trained to study the language through written texts when they are suddenly confronted with listening comprehension material of a

6 R. Lado, "Memory Span as a Factor in Second Language Learning," *IRAL*, III/2 (1965): 127.

similar standard of difficulty to that which they are accustomed to study at their leisure in graphic form. The emotional tension associated with this experience is frequently compounded by the near approach of some examination for which this type of activity is preparing the students.

Above all, it must be clearly borne in mind by teacher and student alike that listening comprehension is not a skill which can be mastered once and for all and then ignored while other skills are developed. There must be regular practice with increasingly difficult material. This practice must, however, be regularly spaced over the language-learning period and not massed urgently in great blocks at some moment preceding an examination. Facility in understanding what one hears increases with growing familiarity with the vocabulary and structures of the language. Systematically developed, listening comprehension can provide one of the most enjoyable activities associated with the language program and one which the student continues to enjoy after he has left the classroom.

ANNOTATED READING LIST

MILLER, G. A. *Language and Communication.* New York: McGraw-Hill, 1951. Chapters 1–5 explain the acoustic characteristics of speech, the concept of information as applied to a message, and the conditions of emission and reception of a message.

RIVERS, W. M. *The Psychologist and the Foreign-Language Teacher.* Chicago: The University of Chicago Press, 1964. Chapter 5 discusses the psychological problems involved in hearing a foreign language.

7

The Speaking Skill: Learning the Fundamentals

Let us first examine the following model of a communication system, which derives from the work of Shannon and Weaver.[1] Although originally used as a basis for the study of problems of telegraphic communication, it provides many interesting insights into interpersonal communication through speech.

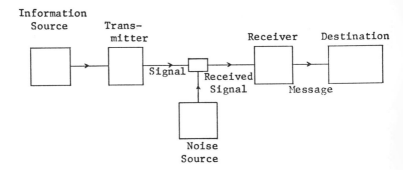

In this model, an information source emits a message which is encoded for transmission as a signal. This signal passes through a channel to a receiver which decodes the message for use at its destination. Paralleling this telegraphic model, Carroll supplies an organismic communication model:[2]

1 From W. Weaver, "Recent Contributions to the Mathematical Theory of Communication," in C. E. Shannon and W. Weaver, *The Mathematical Theory of Communication* (Urbana, Ill., 1959), p. 98.
2 J. B. Carroll, *The Study of Language* (Cambridge, Mass., 1953), p. 88.

Intentive behavior of speaker		Encoding behavior of speaker		Message		Decoding behavior of hearer		Interpretive behavior of hearer
	$\rightarrow$		$\rightarrow$	Message	$\rightarrow$		$\rightarrow$	

In chapter 6 (Listening Comprehension) we have discussed the characteristics of a message, the passage of a message through a channel and the problem of "noise," the reception of the message, and its decoding by the receiver (that is, the right-hand side of each of these models). In discussing the development of the speaking skill, we are concerned with the selection of the message to be sent and the encoding of the message for transmission (that is, the intentive and encoding behavior of the speaker).

The teaching of foreign languages has traditionally concentrated on making the student aware of certain aspects of the code (vocabulary of the foreign language, phonological and morphological features, syntactical rules) without providing adequate practice in the selection of a message and in the process of encoding it for transmission. As a result, after years of study, students have known a great deal about a foreign language without being able to use it to express their intentions. The code has usually been studied in its written manifestation since, before the era of the record player and the tape recorder, this was the most convenient form in which it could be dissected, the parts examined in detail, and interrelationships established. Because of its enduring nature, the written code had also acquired a certain prestige as the standard against which the spoken code should be measured and evaluated; it was, therefore, considered to represent the "correct" form of the code. This written code, once learned, has not proved to be of great use for oral communication, being too elaborate, too cumbersome, and too intellectually demanding because it is less redundant than the spoken code. Aspects of the spoken code which are not noted in the written code have not been taught beyond a very superficial level, for example, the prosodic features of pitch, intonation, and duration; the expressive features of tone of voice, gesture, and facial expression; the phonic features of assimilation and juncture, and sandhi variations (liaisons, elisions), yet all of these play a part in conveying the full import of a spoken message. In this chapter, and the succeeding one, we shall see that an act of speech involves more than knowledge of the code. It involves the selection of integrated patterns of elements of the code for the expression of an intention, and the assembling of the necessary features without undue hesitation (this is the process of encoding). In this chapter, we shall deal specifically with training in encoding (assembling the fundamentals or required features in intricate patterns which are essential for accurate representation of the message) ; in chapter 8, we shall discuss techniques for giving the student practice in selection of the forms of message he wishes to use for particular purposes.

The teaching of the speaking skill is more demanding on the teacher than the teaching of any other language skill. For this reason, many teachers give up the attempt to teach it and concentrate on what they call a more "intellectual" approach to language teaching (the deciphering of the written code and discussion of its features, or the discussion of the content of foreign-language texts). Other teachers persuade themselves that if they speak the foreign language exclusively in the classroom the students will, at some time, begin to speak it fluently too; this they justify by the argument that the students now have the opportunity to learn the foreign language "as the child learns his native language." This reasoning ignores the fact that little children learn to speak their language by continual prattling (frequently using incorrect forms) for most of their waking hours, that they are continually being spoken to and encouraged in their efforts to imitate speech, and that their efforts at producing comprehensible speech enable them to gain things for which they feel a great need (physical satisfactions or mother's attention and proud praise). Students in a foreign-language class will not learn to speak fluently merely by hearing speech, although this is important in familiarizing them with the acceptable forms of the code. The teacher will need to give the students many opportunities to practice the speaking skill; he will need to use his imagination in devising situations which provoke the student to the use of the language in the expression of his own meaning, within the limits of what he has been learning.

The active practice of speech cannot be left to a "later

stage," as some teachers think, when the students presumably "know the language" from the dissection and reassembling of the written script. By this time, many students have developed certain inhibitions about making strange sounds in public and find it difficult to express themselves orally in the polished forms of the literary code they have been taught. Students should be given the opportunity, throughout their years of study, to develop greater and greater skill in encoding their thoughts in ever more complicated patterns of the foreign speech, and in consolidating the muscular control involved in the new speech habits. If each of our students were able to practice these new speech habits throughout the day, as the child does with his native language, our problems would be lessened. Since they practice for perhaps an hour or, in a particularly favorable situation, for one and a half hours or two hours a day, their native speech habits easily reassert themselves when they try to express their message in the foreign language. The prolonged training they require in working with the code must not be delayed. For these reasons, speaking the language should be a natural activity from the first foreign-language lesson.

The early introduction of the speaking of the language is also important for reasons of motivation. Students come to the study of a foreign language in high school with the strong conviction that "language" means "something spoken." They are often discouraged and lose interest when they find that foreign-language study is just like other school subjects: "learning a whole lot of stuff from a book," and that being able to speak the language is some far-distant goal, attainable only after years of uninteresting and uninspiring labor. Pimsleur, in his study of underachievers in foreign-language study,[3] found them anxious to speak the language. They considered it "fun" and felt it to be "important." The child who comes home from his first lesson able to say something useful in the foreign language, no matter how simple it may be, feels a great sense of satisfaction and his attitude toward language learning becomes much more favorable. He is also encouraged in this

3 P. Pimsleur, D. M. Sundland, and R. D. McIntyre, *Under-Achievement in Foreign Language Learning,* Final Report (Columbus, Ohio, 1963), p. 24.

attitude by family and community approval of this evidence of his nascent skill.

To teach the speaking skill it is necessary to have a clear understanding of the processes involved in speech. Through speech, man expresses his emotions, communicates his intentions, reacts to other persons and situations, influences other human beings. At a subvocal level speech enables him to examine and rearrange impressions and associations so that he sees new relationships and evolves new purposes. Spoken language is, then, a tool for man. In the teaching of the speaking skill, we are engaged in two processes: forging an instrument and giving the student guided practice in its use. The student already knows how to use a similar instrument, his native language; finding at first that the new instrument is cumbersome and frustrating, he tends to slip back, where possible, to the use of the instrument to which he is accustomed.

The teaching of the speaking skill, then, involves two levels of activity. The forging of the instrument requires much practice in the arbitrary associations of the new language: lexical items, morphological and syntactical patterns, sentence types. At this level the student is asked merely to manipulate the elements of the foreign-language code, so that he can express a number of possible meanings arbitrarily imposed upon him by the exercise or the teacher. When he has acquired facility in these mechanical associations, he needs practice in setting in motion a number of interacting systems of a hierarchical nature. Speaking to express a personal intention is not a sequential or linear process, one item generating the next throughout the utterance; rather is it a hierarchical process. The intention demands a certain overall construction or sentence type (an exclamation, a statement, a question) alluding to the past, the present, or the future, to the existent or the nonexistent, in absolute or modified form. The speaker selects the general construction of the utterance and, according to his purposes, combinations of segments within it. This he does at lightning speed. He may even pause in the middle of an utterance and reframe it—as we do when we begin a statement and change it in mid-utterance into a question.

The student who is to speak a language so as to express his personal meaning needs much practice in this process of generating new sentences to suit his purposes. In authentic communication the process is not always an initiatory one. The form of the utterance a person is generating has frequently been determined for him by some utterance which he has just perceived and to which he is reacting. Typically this occurs when one is answering a question. As well as sentence type, the speaker must choose the style of language in which he is going to express himself; this is sometimes called the register or level of discourse. In *The Five Clocks,*[4] Joos discusses at length what is involved in the choice from among five styles of English speech: intimate, casual, consultative, formal, and frozen. Similar styles can be established for other languages. Once a choice of style has been made certain subordinate choices of lexical sets and structural patterns will follow. Even apart from the question of style, the emotional or evaluative tone of the utterance will impose further limitations. Finally, the speaker has to articulate the whole utterance by muscle movements which will enable the listener to get the full import of the message. These muscle movements determine not only the segmental phonemes of the utterance and the suprasegmentals, but also such expressive elements as pauses, lengthening, voice quavers, loudness, and facial expression. In a language with which we are familiar all these elements are so integrated that selection at one level sets the appropriate operation in action for selection at the next level. It is this smooth integration of processes which the student of a foreign language has to learn by assiduous practice.

FORGING OF THE INSTRUMENT

At this first level of activity the aim of the teacher is to build in language habits by well-designed practice, so that at a more advanced stage the student can concentrate on what he wants to say and not on the mechanical aspects of how to say it acceptably in the foreign language. As we have seen, in chapter 3, language has structural meaning as well as lexical meaning; that is to say, the interrelationships between words and parts

4 M. Joos, *The Five Clocks* (Bloomington, Ind., 1962).

of words have a big part to play in conveying the message. The associations, juxtapositions, and oppositions that contribute to structural meaning vary considerably from language to language. If a student is not to slip back into native-language habits when expressing his personal meaning, the elements which convey structural meaning in the foreign language must spring automatically into place as required. Lexical items of the foreign language inserted into the structural patterns of the native language will inevitably lead to ambiguity and misunderstanding, while uncertainty as to associations of elements in structural patterns will inhibit the flow of speech. Phonological, morphological, and syntactical habits of the foreign language must be practiced and practiced to a point of overlearning if they are to become part of the student's permanent repertoire so that he is able to use them at any moment without conscious effort. As outlined in chapters 3 and 4, they should be practiced in a situation such as pattern drill where the structuring of the exercise calls forth the correct response, and where immediate confirmation of the correctness of the response is given by the teacher or model. In this way, the student will have the opportunity of practicing these unvarying associations to a point of habitually correct performance.

Building in language habits is a time-consuming activity which must occupy a considerable amount of the class time in the early stages. Teachers to whom these habits have become second nature often weary of directing such training, or presume that students who have had certain structural relationships explained to them will be able to use them when required. Because of the cumulative memory teachers tend to build up over successive years of teaching the same material at the same level, it is easy for them to forget that the practice they remember having directed is not the practice this particular class has been given. Involuntarily they sometimes reduce the amount of time given to intensive practice below the level the students require if they are to gain control of a new structural pattern. A tape recorder, used judiciously as part of the classroom lesson, can help the teacher who has a number of parallel classes at the same level to overcome this natural reluctance to continue drilling at length the same material. Unless students have been given some understanding of the processes of language learning, they may look upon much-needed repetitive practice as futile. They are accustomed in other lessons to understanding principles and memorizing some facts related to these principles, and then moving on to new areas. The teacher should make it clear to them that everything they learn in the language classroom needs to be retained and to be readily available, that the learning of a language is a cumulative process, and that active use of the language will come only from assiduous practice to a point of mastery of each element learned.

Although such steady practice in the forging of the instrument is essential it will not achieve its purpose unless the student is made aware of the pertinence of what he is practicing to situations beyond the classroom. He must be given the opportunity to apply what he has learned in an act of communication provoked among members of the class group. We cannot wait until the student has a sure grasp of all the structures of the language before giving him practice in communication. If he is to do more than glibly reel off mechanical sequences he must be trained continually in using these sequences to generate new utterances in a situational context.

In chapter 4, various types of pattern drills suitable for intensive practice in the use of elements of structure and in structural transformations are discussed. For fluent oral communication, practice is also essential in patterns of intonation. These may be acquired more or less automatically in dialogue learning or in imitation of the speech of the instructor. They will be retained for a longer period, despite the constant influence of native-language habits, if the patterns of the foreign-language intonation are brought to conscious awareness and frequently practiced in the context of appropriate utterances.

Frequently neglected in the endeavor to build in facility in the handling of grammatical features is practice in selection of overall sentence patterns. Such selection should be developed in oral practice where students create new utterances of a particular form by supplying lexical items which suit their purposes and imaginings. Students may be encouraged to vie with each other in the production of affirmative and negative statements, questions, conditional utterances: in the excitement of the contest they forget that this is another practice in structure. Also valuable for the development of fluency in speaking is practice in expanding sentence frames with dependent phrases which elaborate the message: this also can be a competitive or chaining activity within the class group. Students will accept much more repetitive practice if it takes the form of an amusing, even exciting, occupation. Exercises of this type must be practiced orally, without the support of a written script, if students are to become confident in oral manipulation, and to feel that this skill is an important part of language learning. If the teacher feels the need for some visual representation during the preliminary establishment of the frames to be used, he may employ vanishing techniques on the chalkboard, gradually eliminating elements of the visual support until students can work without it.

Overlearning of certain morphological and syntactical elements has been advocated as relieving the student of hesitations and anxieties about forms when he is expressing his message. Teachers frequently try to provide for such overlearning through unimaginative, repetitious activity which causes fatigue and distaste on the part of the student. Thorough practice is necessary for the forging of the instrument, but students can have sufficient practice without this impression of repetition if variety of approach is constantly considered, and the same activity is presented in slightly different forms.

Even with variety of presentation, drilling can become automatic, mechanical manipulation in which meaning is irrelevant. At this stage it ceases to achieve its end. The learning of syntactical and morphological associations which vary within limited systems can be practiced in drills which are also designed to develop skill in expressing individual meaning. Too much overlearning without conscious awareness of what one is trying to say leads to fixation of responses and, as a result, lack of flexibility in using them in a variety of situations or in employing synonymous phrases or parallel constructions where these are appropriate. Students frequently show great adeptness in producing in drills all the forms of a certain verb, even making rapid transformations from one to the other, while being completely at a loss when required to use this verb in a communication situation; they have been practicing oral manipulation of sound combinations without thinking of meaning or appropriate context. A class consists of individuals who have gradually been welded into a group with some knowledge of each other's activities, and some interest in each other's affairs. It is feasible, then, for the teacher to continue giving practice in certain aspects of the language by encouraging active communication among the students. This must be the ultimate aim of any drill session and no structural element may be considered to have been learned satisfactorily until the student shows confidence in using it in a natural way to communicate with another individual.

THE USE OF DIALOGUES AND DRAMATIZATIONS

Many a student well trained in the manipulation of language structures has found himself completely at a loss in conducting a conversation with a native speaker of the language because the books from which he (and his teacher before him) learned the language forms failed to emphasize the characteristic features of everyday spoken language and persistently used archaic or pedantic turns of phrase. Such a student may be perfectly at home with the language of an ode or a classical play, yet find his ears assailed by unfamiliar phrases as soon as he hears two native speakers in discussion. He may be able to talk fluently about peasants and palaces, carriages and wooden ploughs, but be quite unable to ask for air to be put in the tires of his car or the price of a new film for his camera. Vocabulary items are, of course, easily acquired when needed, but the advanced student is most disconcerted when the structure of informal speech does not parallel the meticulous requirements of the literary style, as happens in so many languages. The familiar compliment paid to the language learner: "You speak the language better than we do" may be taken to mean: "You express yourself in a formal idiom which no native speaker would ever use." The student does not learn to speak a language fluently by continual practice in question and answer on a literary text—a very common procedure in foreign-language classes. This technique has its place in the discussion of ideas at an advanced level, but does not provide adequate preparation for informal conversation.

Conversational speech is characterized by the frequent repetition of well-worn expressions (clichés), by tags and formulas now empty of precise denotation, by expletives and exclamations which give the speaker time to reorganize his thoughts and select the form in which he wishes to express them, by pauses and changes in structure as an utterance proceeds. Were these omitted, speech would proceed much more rapidly, and it would be beyond the capacity of the listener-speaker to assimilate much quick-fire conversation. We have only to listen carefully to our friends gossiping over their morning coffee to realize how frequently the same hackneyed phrases and exclamations recur.

Recognition of these features of informal communication has been the basis for the advocacy of *dialogue learning* as a technique for elementary classes. Teachers who have taken over an advanced class which has not had teaching in the oral skill have also found that dialogue learning helps students to acquire rapidly those frequently recurring phrases which make for ease of communication—greetings; expressions of impatience, dismay, or surprise; conventional expressions of agreement and polite disagreement; common forms of question and noncommittal answer; expletives and exclamations which give the speaker time to search for the correct form to express his meaning.

In a dialogue, expertly written, the informal language is learned in an immediately useful form: a form which the student can practice by turning to his neighbor, or apply in contacts outside the classroom. Everything in the dialogue is meaningful and relevant to the situations of his everyday life. The clichés of the language are embedded in typical acts of communication instead of being learned artificially as isolated phrases or sentences. The student learns to return conventional expression for conventional expression as automatically and naturally as he manipulates structures. Most important of all, he learns to speak in the first and second persons whereas in discussion of literary texts he is nearly always using the third person. He learns to ask questions as well as answer them, to speak in short sentences, to reply in incomplete sentences which do not repeat all the elements of the question, to make short rejoinders. He practices the rhythm, the intonation, the liaisons and elisions, the assimilations of the spoken language, and learns to understand and reproduce these at a normal speed of utterance. All the elements of the sound system recur in their natural context and are practiced without being artificially isolated and distorted. The grammatical structures he has drilled, or will drill, separately are practiced in a natural matrix of meaning. Structures he will not meet in a formal way until some time later may be introduced and learned in utterances without his being unduly disconcerted.

Apart from the linguistic value of teaching contemporary speech in an immediately usable form, dialogue learning has definite pedagogical advantages, especially at junior high school level when many students are having their first experience of the study of a foreign language. At this age students like to act out roles, and some of the embarrassment of making strange sounds is eliminated as students take on the personalities of people who speak the language in everyday situations. A set of sentences or a prose reading becomes very boring if students are asked to repeat or read it over and over again, whereas a role in a miniature drama will be acted out by the same or different students many times with a conscious effort at improvement. Different groups of students will vie with each other to produce the best reenactment of the scene, enabling the class to listen again and again to the same phrases without tedium. Students will delight in learning roles by heart. They will set about assiduously writing variations of the basic situation using the now-familiar phrases. Some books provide a number of variations of scene based on a restricted set of phrases, and these variants can be studied as fresh material until the basic sentences are thoroughly assimilated. A dialogue lends itself ideally to chorus repetition with sections of the class taking roles and responding to each other's cues.

In classes where dialogue learning is not part of the method used, an introductory textbook should be chosen in which the early lessons consist of much repetitious conversational material which can be dramatized in the classroom. The material should be acted out by the students, not just read by different students as they remain in their places. The very act of doing what the characters are depicted as doing, while saying what they are reported to have said, gives deeper meaning to the foreign-language words and phrases so that they are more easily recalled in situations where they are appropriate. As with dialogue material, students can write short dramatizations, using the language material they have learned to create variations of situations for their favorite characters.

The interest of the students is more readily aroused if situations in dialogues and material for dramatization involve persons of a similar age to that of the students; they should be engaged in activities appropriate to their age group in the natural setting of life in the country where the language is spoken. Behavior as well as language should be authentic and contemporary, so that the students can feel identity with the characters and be willing to enter into the roles they are enacting.

Writers of dialogues or informal introductory material for language learning should take care to make quite clear the situational context (the place, the time of day, the type of activity involved), the relationships among the characters (approximate age, sex, occupations, authority patterns), and the emotional overtone of their conversation (friendly, formal, hostile, teasing, reprimanding). All of these factors have an important bearing on the level of language used and the choice of vocabulary. They must be clearly appreciated by the student if he is later to use appropriately for his own purposes the forms of language he is learning. Care should also be taken to reintroduce familiar words and phrases as memory aids in later stretches of dialogue. Dialogue sentences are most difficult to learn when pronunciation difficulties, unfamiliar words, and structural novelties are concentrated at about the same point. Any two of these coinciding will cause problems for the student. One of the marks of well-written dialogues is the scattering of these three in any sentences which students are to memorize and assimilate.

Certain effective techniques have been evolved for the teaching of dialogues.[5] The dialogue is first presented in the

5   The techniques described in this section are set out in considerable detail in Patricia O'Connor, *Modern Foreign Languages in High School: Pre-Reading Instruction* (Washington, D.C., 1960).

native language, with visual aids such as flash cards or stick figures drawn on the chalkboard; this sets the students thinking along the right lines. During the memorization which is to follow, a native-language version of the dialogue is available to the students, either in their textbooks or posted for them to see. This native-language version should be in contemporary language the students would use, rather than presenting a stilted attempt at equivalence for the words in the foreign language. Sometimes the dialogue may be acted out in the first place in the native language to instill the meaning of the little scene in the minds of the students for the later interpretation of the foreign-language sound sequences.

The dialogue is next presented in the foreign language several times with the same visual aids, so that the situation becomes quite clear to the students. Now comes the task of memorization of the dialogue sentences. A well-written dialogue falls into short, self-contained segments, usually of three or four utterances. Each of these utterances is to be memorized by the students, by mimicking the teacher, until a point of accurate reproduction is attained. One small segment usually provides sufficient memorization material for one lesson. Each utterance is presented orally by the teacher, who repeats it several times clearly and distinctly at a normal conversational speed, and with correct intonation, usually from different parts of the room. This is the recognition stage, when students concentrate on distinguishing the patterning in the stream of sound. After the students have had the opportunity of hearing the sentence several times, they are invited to imitate what they have heard. Ideally, each utterance in the dialogue should be short, since otherwise students have difficulty in remembering all the sounds in the correct order; when repeating an utterance they tend to omit a few sounds here and there, thus robbing it of meaning and acquiring bad habits of articulation.

As students imitate the teacher's rendering of the utterance they try to memorize it. Some teachers employ at this stage a technique called "the backward buildup": the sentence is divided into meaningful segments (two, three, or four, depending on the structure of the utterance). The students repeat the last segment several times with correct end-of-phrase intonation, then they repeat the second-last segment with the last segment, and finally they repeat the whole sentence. This technique is justified by its advocates on several grounds: as the student memorizes, he moves in repetition from the unfamiliar to the familiar and, for this reason, he does not falter before he reaches the end of the phrase; since each practice carries the student through to the end of the utterance, the appropriate intonation pattern is retained throughout. Some teachers object to the backward buildup, maintaining that the student is not practicing language at each step in an immediately usable form, since he will later need to repeat it from beginning to end, and not with final segments isolated; since he has practiced the last segment most frequently, it is this segment which he will recall most vividly, yet this is not the segment he will need in order to produce the utterance promptly when required. These teachers also point out that the forward movement of an utterance provides cues for succeeding features, and for this reason the backward buildup is not the most effective form of memorization. These objections can be met if the utterance is broken into segments which would still be meaningful in another context, and if the complete utterance is well practiced in its normal sequence after the early processes of memorization.

The memorization of the dialogue proceeds from choral repetition by the whole class, to group repetition (by halves of the class and then by rows) as described in chapter 2. If the smaller groups falter, the teacher returns to large group and full choral repetition, testing progress in memorization by a return to small-group repetition. As the small groups become more accurate and ready in response, the teacher calls on individuals to recite. It is at this point that the teacher discovers the real stage of memorization which has been reached by the majority of the students, since chorus repetition disguises many weaknesses and inaccuracies in the undifferentiated torrent of sound. When several individuals falter, as they will at first, the teacher returns to group repetition, drilling the weaknesses which have been uncovered; the process continues in this way until the majority of the students in the class can demonstrate a near-perfect knowledge of the utterance being memorized. At this stage, the teacher takes up the next utterance, teaching it in a similar fashion and linking it frequently in repetition with the preceding utterance.

If this learning work is not to be mere parroting, the teacher must make sure at frequent intervals that the students are well aware of the meaning of what they are saying. This becomes easier when several utterances have been memorized, because the learning procedure can now include an interchange of question and answer or statement and rejoinder. This interchange takes place at first between teacher and class, then between large groups, between small groups, and finally between individuals. The teacher takes care to see that roles are frequently reversed, so that all sections of the class have the opportunity to ask the question as well as answer it, to make the statement as well as the rejoinder. As soon as a segment of dialogue is learned well enough, students are given the opportunity to use it in near-spontaneous situations where they enter into a conversational interchange with a classmate. This interchange can take place as "directed dialogue" where the teacher suggests to a student that he should ask his classmate a particular question, and suggests to the classmate that he should respond in a particular fashion. Directions for this type of exchange should sometimes be given in the native language to ensure that students are fully aware of the meaning of the interchange that is taking place. When the directions are given in the foreign language, students will need practice in the technique of directed dialogue before they are able to listen to a direction in one person of the verb and, turning to their classmate, use another person of the verb. They are being asked to perform a transformation which is particularly difficult in languages where the verbal inflection changes from person to person.

When students have acquired a considerable number of basic utterances they may enjoy "chain dialogue." In this procedure, one student asks his neighbor a question, his neighbor replies and then immediately asks a question of the next student in the row. This activity gives students an opportunity to practice sentences from a number of dialogues in a relaxing, and slightly competitive, atmosphere similar to that of a game. When one chain peters out, another may be started in a different part of the class. If conducted at a smart pace, with frequent changes of direction, chain dialogue can provide valuable practice without boredom.

Dialogue sentences will soon be forgotten, and their usefulness will prove to be very limited, unless opportunity is taken to reintroduce and practice frequently utterances from earlier lessons. Students will readily reproduce these utterances with ones they are currently learning if some of the procedures just outlined are adopted. They will take pleasure in showing how many expressions they can use if given opportunities to do so in contrived situations where students try to communicate spontaneously with each other. The memorized sentences will also provide material for the drilling of structural features and combinations and, at a later date, for oral reports in class and for practice in reading and writing. Techniques for developing these skills are outlined in chapters 9 and 10.

The teacher must look upon the utterances in dialogues as foundational sentence types and gradually train the students to use them, with variations, for more and more situations outside those of the dialogue sequence. The teacher who is satisfied with glib repetition of sentences, with fine accuracy and an apparent apprehension of appropriateness of context, may well experience considerable disappointment after some months. Students who, to his delight, have performed very well in class exercises may prove to be quite incapable of putting the knowledge they have acquired to use in actual comprehension and communication, divorced from the contrived sequence in which the utterances were learned. Mere learning of dialogue sentences can never be an aim in itself. As a technique, it is justified only when it provides the student with a ready supply of language elements for use in communication.

THE AUDIO-VISUAL APPROACH

Some teachers firmly advocate the use of some form of visual aid in the teaching of speaking, especially in the early stages. Where the visual element is accompanied by recorded voices, the term "audio-visual" has come to be used. "Audio-visual" is not synonymous with "audio-lingual," as some people have presumed. The term "audio-lingual" applies to a particular teaching method with a clearly elaborated theoretical basis and an accepted set of techniques. The term "audio-visual." on the other hand, cannot be identified with one specific method. Some audio-visual materials are constructed according to the principles of the audio-lingual method, adding a further sensory element to the learning situation, but still employing the recognized techniques; other materials are derived from the direct method; still others bear no relationship to either method. Each set of materials which is labelled audio-visual should be examined carefully to see on what method it is based, and whether this method is the most efficient for the development of the speaking skill, in view of the discussion earlier in this chapter.

In its simplest form the audio-visual approach has been employed for many years in classrooms where objects, pictures, actions, and gestures have been systematically used with aural-oral work to elucidate meaning. This practice has always been an essential element in direct method teaching. With the easy availability in recent years of filmstrips, slides, films, and tapes it has been possible to expand this aspect of the direct method, while reducing the strain on the teacher.

Advocates of an audio-visual approach put forward several reasons for considering the visual element essential to the efficient learning of listening and speaking. It is believed that the picture associated with the recorded voice eliminates the need to use the native language, because a direct bond is established for the student between the meaning, as demonstrated in the image, and the foreign-language utterance. The intention is to train the student to think in the foreign language, without recourse to his native tongue, from the first lessons. The need for a script is eliminated, because the spoken words become associated, not only with preceding and succeeding utterances, but also with the picture stimulus, so that it is possible later to eliminate the recorded voice and to use the picture series to evoke the sequence of utterances. In this way the strain on the auditory memory is less than with a purely aural presentation with oral practice. With the elimination of the script certain problems of native-language interference in pronunciation, arising from similarities in appearance of words, do not arise.

Student motivation is also considered to be a strong factor in favor of the audio-visual approach. The modern child is accustomed to looking and listening for long periods. With well-drawn pictures he finds language classes interesting and enjoyable. When he sees the situations in which the phrases he is memorizing are appropriate, he feels he is learning something which is useful and practical. As he associates phrases with people and incidents in the pictures, rather than learning them as abstractions, he sees how these utterances serve real purposes. He feels a more immediate involvement than when he learns from a printed script because he sees the people about whom he is talking, he can address utterances to them, and he can hear replies to his utterances from the recorded voice.

The picture, with accompanying voice, has a greater sensory impact than lines on a printed page, or even than that of the voice alone. The student can see not only situations, but also gestures and expressions which have an essential role in the clarification of elements of meaning conveyed by intonation and tone of voice. Through his observation of personal relationships, the student also acquires some understanding of the register or level of language for which particular utterances are appropriate.[6] The attention of the students is kept focused on the picture, so that all the members of the class are concentrating on the same thing at the same time. This centering of attention is particularly helpful for weaker students who, in a reading-writing or even in a purely aural-oral situation, frequently find their minds wandering to other things than the point on which the teacher is concentrating.

With all the advantages outlined, the audio-visual approach maintains the specific advantages of aural-oral work. The students hear the foreign language continually and speak it often. They hear foreign-language sounds from the first lesson in meaningful sequences with the appropriate intonation patterns, and, concentrating as they are on situation and meaning, they begin to pronounce and speak without self-consciousness.

Audio-visual materials which are available commercially fall into three categories. In the first group, there are traditional materials, oriented toward the teaching of grammar and the understanding of the written form of the language. In these cases, the publishers have decided that the issuing of audio-

6 Registers are discussed in some detail in chapter 3.

visual aids (film strips, pictures, tapes) will make texts already in circulation more attractive to present-day teachers, particularly where the teacher is expected to use a language laboratory or other equipment. The supplementary audio-visual aids supplied may make such a course more entertaining for some students, but a text which has not been designed explicitly for developing the speaking skill cannot be expected to be much more effective in this area because of the fortuitous addition of some pictures and tapes.

The second group may be called "bandwagon" materials. These have usually been put together rather hastily by a teacher, or teachers, with some experience of teaching with other methods, at the request of a publisher who wanted to capitalize on a growing interest in audio-visual materials. On examination, it will usually be found that these materials have not been systematically designed for exploiting to the full the potentialities of the audio-visual elements, nor for developing effectively the communication skills. Since such materials are usually empirical in their approach to the basic problems of foreign-language acquisition, they may prove to be successful in some ways and very unsatisfactory in others.

The most effective audio-visual materials will be those which have been constructed by a team of experts with linguistic and pedagogical experience, who have thought out the problems of developing skill in understanding and speaking a foreign language, and the unique contribution to be made by the visual image and accompanying recorded voices. Materials of this type will follow a graded sequence, and the picture and the tape will be fully integrated with the learning material in the text, in such a way that the contribution of the one consolidates that of the other. The tape and the image will both be carefully designed for progressively building in habits of sound sequences, structural patterns, and common situational utterances before texts for reading and writing are introduced.

Integrated audio-visual materials may again be of two types. Those of the first type are developed along direct-method lines, with the image extending the environment of the classroom. In these materials, the audio-visual aids provide a stimulus for continual hearing and speaking of the language, but they are not always based on a systematic plan for the progressive acquisition of structural control. They may begin with a dialogue for memorization, but, after the learning of the dialogue, they will often concentrate on the development of fluent use of many types of utterances which give practice in the use of various parts of speech rather than of structural patterns. The second type of integrated audio-visual materials is based on audio-lingual principles and uses the image to facilitate not only dialogue memorization but the drilling of fundamental structural patterns.

There is a rather clearly established pattern for the conduct of an audio-visual lesson. A series of pictures, with accompanying recorded voices, is shown several times to give students the opportunity to absorb image and sound and associate the two. During this period students attempt to deduce the meaning of what they are hearing. The recorded voices speak in complete utterances, not in isolated words. In an alternative procedure, a native-language version is presented on the first showing of the pictures, and the foreign-language version a little later when the students have shown that they understand the theme of the recorded dialogue.

Memorization of utterances now begins. Students repeat after the recorded voice while watching the image. The teacher may point to sections of the picture in order to make the meaning of certain words and groups of words clear. After the utterances on several frames (making a meaningful sequence) have been memorized, the students are tested by being asked to respond to alternate frames in response to the voice, and finally to respond to the visual images only. At this stage, the roles in the dialogue may be taken by parts of the class. If the students falter in their reproduction of the dialogue, the teacher returns to the memorization phase. After the students have shown their command of the initial learning material of the unit, they are asked to demonstrate their understanding and control of it by using utterances in contrived communication situations within the class group. (At this stage, many of the techniques already discussed in this chapter are employed.)

Since the situations depicted are intentionally of a type which the students themselves might experience, the language learned in this way is found to be immediately useful in these early attempts at personal communication. It is at this point that any misconceptions the students may have acquired about the actual meaning of what they have been learning become apparent. When the students are working with pictures continually before them, it is sometimes difficult for the teacher to be sure that they are not merely producing responses which they have associated with a certain visual stimulus without really being aware of the meaning of what they are saying. It is particularly difficult to tell whether the students have assimilated the exact nuance of meaning at those points where the situation in the image would allow of several closely related responses. When the student is endeavoring to communicate with another person, or make a meaningful response to what the other person has said to him, he is forced to establish for himself a clear interpretation of each group of language sounds and the teacher has the opportunity to direct and guide him where his interpretation is faulty.

Immediate application is not the final learning stage with audio-visual materials. Even strongly associated aural and visual impressions weaken when the student leaves the classroom. This is especially true of the student with a poor auditory memory. In the method as described, he does not have access to a script to refresh his memory when he is trying to rehearse to himself what he has been learning.[7] For these reasons, material must be reintroduced and repracticed regularly until it is obvious that the students have assimilated it completely.

There are other factors of importance in evaluating audiovisual materials, apart from the principles basic to their design. The quality of the visual image and the quality of production of the recorded voices will make considerable difference to the efficiency of the learning. If the quality of either of these essential components is inferior in materials being examined, it is better to look further for materials for class use.

In evaluating the acceptability of the visual accompaniment

7 The question of the value of withholding the script of what is being learned orally, especially in the early stages, is discussed at some length in Rivers (1964), chapter 10.

in courses for school use, the teacher must not neglect to examine carefully the degree to which the images convey the actual message contained in the foreign-language utterances. In most audio-visual materials sketches are used rather than photographs; in drawing a sketch, the artist can pay particular attention to the production of a clear outline which does not contain any details likely to distract the attention of the learner from the meaning of the utterance it is to illustrate and elucidate. Each picture must demonstrate the meaning of an utterance in an unambiguous way. Sometimes the artist attempts to do this by using certain symbols. He may use an interrogation mark to show that a question is being asked, or that the speaker is puzzled, or he may use an exclamation mark to indicate an expression of astonishment; facial expressions depicted will help the student to interpret the symbols. The artist may place a balloon over the head of a person in the picture in order to show what he is dreaming or thinking. A symbolic representation may be devised to make apparent the sequence of events in time. Since the impact of the visual image is strong, it is essential that the meaning the student absorbs from the image be the one which was intended by the writer of the materials. This is not always the case. Teachers should remember that with audio-visual materials wrong impressions are all the more difficult to eradicate because of this greater sensory impact.

The picture must also be pleasant in line and coloring, with details which will not make it appear old-fashioned with the passage of time; ultrafashionable hemlines, haircuts, and vehicles are traps in this regard. Care must also be taken not to make the pictures too obviously humorous, since jokes wear very thin after their initial presentation. Unintentional humor in the drawings can also make the pictures seem ridiculous and unworthy of the student's close attention. Materials designed to accompany the learning of common situational phrases often contain cultural elements which introduce the student to the ways of behavior and the social attitudes of the people who speak the language. Care must be taken in this regard to see that, in an attempt at simplicity, the picture does not tend toward caricature, thus reinforcing stereotypes of the foreign people which the students may already hold or arousing new prejudices.

Audio-visual materials have, in the past, mainly concentrated on the establishing of basic structural and lexical knowledge. This is partly because of the limitations of the medium. It is difficult to convey by image and voice alone certain relations of opposition, concession, condition, and the like. It is sometimes not easy to make the use of certain function words clear through illustration. The range of language patterns which may be communicated effectively by means of an image is to some extent restricted, although the degree of restriction may vary from language to language. For these reasons, certain language elements of high frequency may have to be omitted in the early stages. With the introduction of reading, some of these problems are resolved, as students study the recurrence of more abstract elements in a number of contexts.

Sometimes the visual accompaniment is a film of the situation. Here students can identify with the persons depicted, in a living experience in the foreign culture, and hear and observe the total response, with facial expressions, gestures, hesitations, and pauses. This type of presentation is useful for classroom teaching so long as the film is not so cluttered with background material of cultural interest (places, ways of dressing and reacting, the objects associated with daily life) that the actual dialogue is of no more than secondary interest to the student. Films which give vivid pictures of the life of the people and the places where they live are valuable at a more advanced level, where they provide much useful information as a background to reading and as a basis for oral discussion.

Mention has been made of the importance of the audial quality of the accompanying tapes. A checklist of desirable features to look for when choosing tapes is included in chapter 13. In addition to these features, tapes to accompany filmstrips or slides should contain signals to indicate to the teacher when he should turn to the next frame, so that there may be no confusion during a class lesson. Pauses should be carefully planned so that neither teacher nor class is misled into believing that the utterance associated with a particular frame has been completed, when only half of it has been given. The most useful materials are those in which the tape is synchronized with the projector, so that a new frame is introduced automatically at the right moment.

Audio-visual materials have many advantages, but it is also important to recognize certain potential disadvantages. Materials and equipment may prove to be costly. Teachers need training in the use of the necessary equipment and, when equipment is not synchronized, in the smooth passage from the operation of one piece of equipment to another. Where the teacher is not proficient in such operations disrupting breakdowns may occur, and projectors and recorders may demand of the teacher an undue expenditure of time and effort which will reduce the value of the learning experience presented to the class. Where a school is unable to spend money freely, available projectors and recorders must serve a number of purposes, often having to be booked well in advance and transported from classroom to classroom. This can become even more of a problem when parallel classes, and classes at more than one level, are wishing to use audio-visual materials as part of their normal program. If audio-visual materials are adopted as the basis of instruction, the foreign-language teachers must take steps to ensure that at least one set of equipment is available for their exclusive use, housed, if possible, in a foreign-language room in which foreign-language classes will be regularly scheduled.

In schools with well-equipped laboratories, the actual presentation of audio-visual material is somewhat simplified, provided that the screen is so placed as to be clearly visible to all students. In some more elaborate installations, the visual material is projected by closed circuit television onto individual screens in the booths, the students then working with individual recorders. In the latter case each student may feel more immediately involved with the situation.

The laboratory may be useful during the memorization and formal practice stages with audio-visual courses, particularly at senior high school and undergraduate level. It is not suitable for the initial presentation of material and for group practice, nor for extension of what has been learned to attempts at real communication. The students are hampered by the unnatural environment and are unable to develop a feeling for group relationships which facilitates such communication. Many of the activities which make foreign-language learning exciting and interesting for younger students, or for beginners at any level, are of necessity excluded from lessons in a room where students are isolated in individual booths. Teachers must resist pressures from colleagues or the administration which would force them into occupying the laboratory for lessons for which it is inappropriate.

All audio-visual lessons must be carefully planned to ensure that the additional sensory elements are exploited to the full. Of themselves, however, equipment and well-designed materials will not ensure effective foreign-language lessons. Of much more importance is the imagination and energy of the teacher who is using the materials so that there is variety and interesting classroom activity, the visual element being considered an aid in the learning process and not an end in itself. The success of the audio-visual course will be seen in the ability of students to use what they have been learning in close association with the visual image when they are in less restricted situations which are similar linguistically but detached from the original stimulus.

AREAS OF CONTROVERSY

Is dialogue learning too mechanical, leading only to parrot-learning of phrases which the student cannot apply in other situations?

This common criticism of dialogue learning is certainly applicable when its techniques are employed without clear understanding of the reasons why dialogues are being used and what this type of learning is expected to achieve. Students will learn phrases by heart and recite them with acceptable articulation and intonation, without any clear idea of what they are saying, and as readily forget them while they embark on the learning of a new series. In these circumstances dialogue learning is a piecemeal, time-consuming, futile activity. If the method is to achieve its objective of enabling students to use freely the most common forms of expression of the language to convey their own meaning, the students must be continually kept aware of the import of what they are repeating. It is sometimes the most impressive dialogue-learning lessons, where memorization proceeds smartly under the direction of a competent drillmaster, which are the least effective. Students are allowed to sink into a repetition mood where prompt echoing is all that is required of them. This they can do without great effort, while their minds are elsewhere. A few keen students set the pace for the rest. It is often after a lesson of this type that the most disappointing results are seen at the stage of individual exchange.

An examination of the techniques of dialogue presentation employed in such cases usually reveals little attention to meaning during the memorization phase. Since many of the students have been learning only sequences of sound combinations, it is not possible for them to put these to use outside the dialogue framework. To avoid such a situation, care must be taken to ensure that students have a clear idea of what the dialogue is about before they begin to memorize it. This can be achieved, as has been suggested in this chapter, by a native-language presentation of the dialogue with situational props to make it more vivid. If the same situational props and visual aids are used for the foreign-language presentation of the dialogue, students will associate the new phrases with the meaning sequence they apprehended in the native-language version. (In an audio-visual presentation, a group of frames or scenes forming a coherent segment should be projected several times at the beginning so that the student may become aware of the import of the individual utterances.) To ensure that students are continually aware of the meaning of successive utterances, the teacher may refer from time to time to a native-language version discreetly posted so that it can be seen by all the members of the class. Occasionally he may check whether the members of the class realize which part of the conversational interchange they are practicing, and, when the utterances are clearly segmented, the meaning of particular segments within an utterance. Where some segments are familiar from earlier memorization, these should be used as a guide to the meaning of the whole utterance. This does not mean that teachers should give word-for-word translations of what is being learned, nor that they should require students continually to translate what they are repeating. For a certain period students may not be conscious of the specific meaning of every element in an utterance (this will come later with wider knowledge), but they will understand the overall meaning of the utterance and its function in communication. Finally, as soon as a useful section of the dialogue is well known, students must be encouraged to use it in actual situations involving communication of meaning to another person.

Further flexibility in the use of set phrases will be developed if drills are evolved from the dialogue material. In these drills, students will be required to use variations of the phrases learned (substituting a different vocabulary content within a set framework or using set phrases with variation of person of the verb or with changes from singular to plural). These variations should introduce new lexical elements which will make the phrases more applicable in conversational exchanges within the classroom. Memory for the phrases learned in dialogues will be consolidated if these phrases are continually reintroduced in later lessons and not allowed to slip into disuse like so much useless impedimenta.

Is the dialogue method or the direct method preferable as an introduction to foreign-language study?

To some teachers dialogue learning seems to be too mechanical, and they fail to see what advantage it has over a direct-method approach of oral learning of phrases, with variations, connected with the activities of the classroom. This direct-method type of learning is active and vocal. The students hear the foreign language all the time and endeavor to use it from the beginning in a context where it has meaning. Several objections are raised by the supporters of the dialogue method to the direct-method approach. The first objection is that the classroom situation is too limited. With dialogues the students move in imagination and dramatized activity out of the confines of pen and paper and chalkboard into situations similar to those they will meet on leaving the classroom. The foreign language, then, is less of a "school" matter and is seen as appropriate to many aspects of social life. The second objection is that in a natural development of discussion around activities and incidents in the classroom it is difficult to keep the language used by the teacher within the confines of a limited number of structures. The variety of the phrases which spring naturally to the lips of the fluent teacher (and the direct-method teacher needs to be fluent in the language) becomes confusing for the student. With a variety of phrases and alternatives at his disposal the student does not practice any of them thoroughly. In order to encourage the efforts of the student, the teacher refrains from correcting him every time he makes a mistake. As a result the student is uninhibited in his flow of language, chatting away glibly in happy ignorance of his inaccuracy. With the dialogue method the teacher and students keep within materials which have been carefully prepared linguistically with a view to promoting a steady growth in control of language structure, and from which confusing alternatives have been eliminated. The less fluent teacher can work within such material and learn with the students. The students practice thoroughly everything they are learning, hearing the correct version from the teacher or tape model, and practicing afresh when they make mistakes. The transition to reading is effected more easily than with the direct method because the structuring of the materials makes it clear which structures should appear first in reading matter. The limitations on the amount of language material contained in the dialogues also makes transition to writing more feasible than in the more amorphous situation of the direct method.

Should dialogues to be learned be designed so as to provide the first introduction of structures to be drilled?

It has been customary in introductory textbooks for passages for reading to contain examples of the grammatical structures to be studied in that particular unit. In most textbooks which begin with dialogues for memorization the same practice is followed, so that the students have a certain familiarity with a grammatical pattern before practicing its use and studying the circumstances of its occurrence. Some writers of textbooks, however, have decided against this common practice. They feel that it requires the adoption of one of two positions, both of which are unsatisfactory. The writer may, on the one hand, distort the natural development of a dialogue in order to introduce all the structural examples he wishes the students to encounter in preparation for their grammatical study. On the other hand, he may allow the dialogue situations to dictate the order in which grammatical structures are to be studied and produce a haphazard, piecemeal sequence of topics in which the students cannot recognize functional relationships.

Some textbook writers, like Fernand Marty, use dialogues purely for rapid teaching of conversational phrases. Marty maintains that the principal value of dialogues is motivational: they give the students an early sense of achievement and great satisfaction in being able to express themselves fluently and acceptably in everyday situations. Side by side with the course in dialogues he advocates a systematic study of the structure of the language, organized in a logical progression.[8]

It may be argued that this controversy can be reduced to the question: for what age group are these materials being written? Late-adolescent and adult students have been trained to seek order in their studies and may feel the need for materials which clearly serve specific purposes. On the other hand, junior high school students need integrated materials which can act as a basis for a variety of activities interwoven into the one lesson. Since students who are beginning the study of the foreign language in early adolescence have perhaps six years or more in which to master the basic structural patterns, it is debatable whether certain structures should be taught first because they seem to have a logical priority in a complete description of the language. The material to be taught first should be chosen for frequency of use and for its adaptability to active classroom practice. Certain persons of the verb may be of more interest in such a situation than others; certain tenses or aspects may be indispensable for communication, despite the fact that they have been traditionally reserved for

8 F. Marty, *Linguistics Applied to the Beginning French Course* (Roanoke, Va., 1963), p. vi.

teaching later in the course. Distortion of dialogues may be avoided by teaching the most immediately useful aspects of a grammatical feature without trying to include every possible example of its use in the dialogue, or even in the unit. At a later stage, when students have acquired a considerable knowledge of the features of the language and are more mature, areas of grammatical interest may be studied in detail as part of a systematic presentation of the structure of the language.

ANNOTATED READING LIST

CARROLL, J. B. *Language and Thought*. Englewood Cliffs, N.J.: Prentice-Hall, 1964. Chapters 1, 2, and 4 give a concise picture of the nature and function of language and the production and understanding of speech.

POLITZER, R. L. *Foreign Language Learning*. Englewood Cliffs, N.J.: Prentice-Hall, 1965. Chapter 14 discusses the importance of quick recognition of structural signals and the processes involved in constructing novel utterances. Examples used are from English, French, German, and Spanish.

O'CONNOR, P. *Modern Foreign Languages in High School: Pre-reading Instruction*. Washington, D.C.: U.S. Office of Education, 1960. Pages 18–31 describe in great detail techniques for teaching by dialogue memorization.

8

The Speaking Skill: Spontaneous Expression

The forging of the instrument is not enough to prepare the student for acts of communication in the foreign language; he now needs guided practice in its use. He has some knowledge of the code, but he has to develop facility and fluency in encoding his own meaning. The ideal way for him to develop the speaking skill to the fullest is to go and live among the people who speak the language; he is then forced to use what he knows to supply his physical and emotional needs. For the average student this is not possible, nor can he, for the most part, have frequent contact with native speakers of the language in his own country. We can, however, impart to him in the classroom basic attitudes and foundational skills upon which he can build rapidly when the opportunity for real communication presents itself. He will be greatly hindered in his progress, and may even retain a permanent disability in communication, if the teaching he has received has forced him into a translating frame of mind where he seeks one-to-one equivalences between the foreign language and his native language, or if he has been overtrained to the point of inflexibility in the use of language patterns, with a corresponding neglect of practice in using them to express his own purposes. If the teacher is to facilitate rather than impede the student's progress in communication he must take account of the nature of the skill being developed and the psychological factors which are involved.

189

THE ACT OF COMMUNICATION

We have already discussed the hierarchical nature of speech, and the fact that the form of an utterance is dependent on the communication situation.[1] In an act of communication we are influenced by environmental cues as well as by our own intentions. We have certain expectations as to the response of the person to whom we are addressing the message, some of these expectations being culturally based, and we frame our message and select the linguistic elements to express it so as to arouse in the receiver the meaning we are trying to convey. Thus we express the same message with different elements if we are addressing it to a child, an intimate friend, a person in authority, or a stranger. If we know that the receiver is sympathetic to the message, we select different items from those we would select if the receiver were hostile or needed to be persuaded. We are not conveying to the receiver a meaning clothed in words, but by our words we are arousing within the receiver associations which will form his interpretation of the intention of the message. If we do not choose our words carefully, and if our expectations as to the reaction of the receiver have been ill-founded, the message decoded may be quite different from the message we intended to convey. This is a frequent occurrence in native-language communication. If there are two receivers of the message, they may decode two different messages from the same signal. Misinterpretation is even more likely to occur when the speaker is using a foreign language for communication with a native speaker, because the cultural associations of the linguistic items, and the accompanying prosodic, paralinguistic, and kinesic elements (intonation, tone of voice, facial movements, gestures), may be quite different for emitter and receiver. By the combination of elements in the utterance we convey our attitude to the basic message (whether we are simply giving information, for instance, or being humorous, ironical, disapproving, and so on). Feedback from the listener (facial expressions, tension, interruptions) gives us indications of the meaning he is extracting, and as a result we may adapt

1   Chapter 7, pp. 162–63.

the message in midutterance (we may change the form of the basic framework; we may expand, omit sections, repeat, emphasize, or modify) in order to arouse the kind of reaction we are seeking. As the emitters of a message we may be reacting to a previous message; in this case, the form and choice of items in our intended message may be to a large extent predetermined, but, again, we adjust and readjust according to the reaction of the listener. Nida maintains that the receiver is often encoding parallel messages as he listens; he is choosing from alternatives the meaning the emitter is trying to convey. This, Nida says, is shown by the fact that when the emitter pauses, the receiver often supplies what he considers to be the appropriate word.[2] Sometimes his choice is accepted by the speaker, sometimes it is rejected, showing in the latter case that the meanings being aroused in the receiver are not those that the emitter intended. These difficulties are compounded when either emitter or receiver (or both) is using a foreign language.

Every act of communication does not involve a rapid-fire exchange. There are hesitations, cliché expressions which fill in pauses, much repetition, and frequent indefiniteness as the emitter seeks the most suitable combination of elements to express his meaning. The foreign-language student who has learned to respond promptly and automatically with substitutions and transformations in pattern drills and oral exercises now has to develop skill in the recombination of elements into novel utterances, each unique in its final form, and each purposeful in its construction. By demanding completely accurate grammatical forms and sentence structure and thoroughly appropriate choice of lexical items, the foreign-language teacher is often demanding of the student a higher level of expression than that of which he is capable in his native language.

According to Skinner, verbal behavior is dependent on reinforcement from another organism;[3] in other words, as utterances are received and bring a response the probability of their recurrence is increased. Learned phrases repeated after a model or reinforced by teacher approval in a drill are likely to

2 E. A. Nida, *Toward a Science of Translating* (Leiden, 1964), pp. 122–23.
3 B. F. Skinner, *Verbal Behavior* (New York, 1957), p. 2.

recur in a drill. When, in an act of communication, they elicit the desired response from another person, they become pertinent to real-life situations and are liable to be emitted in similar circumstances, when there is a similar co-occurrence of environmental cues. In the give-and-take of conversation, many learned structures and phrases prove to be appropriate and responses containing these structures are strengthened, so that they become more readily available for future use. Ability to converse in a foreign language is developed by frequent practice in conversing in that language.

PSYCHOLOGICAL FACTORS IN COMMUNICATION

Certain psychological factors which enter into interpersonal communication are highly relevant to the process of developing conversational abilities in the foreign language within the artificial limits of the classroom. Spontaneous verbal expression is not solely the product of knowledge of and skill in using a language code. It implies that the student has something to communicate. The silent student in the classroom often has "nothing to say" at that moment. The teacher may have chosen a topic which is uncongenial to him or about which he knows very little, and as a result he has nothing to express, whether in the native language or the foreign language.

As well as having something to say, the student must have the desire to communicate this message to some person or group of persons. If the student has an unsympathetic relationship with his teacher, or does not feel at home with his classmates, he may well feel that what he would like to say can be of little interest to them, or would not be appreciated by them. On the other hand, he may be very conscious of his limitations in the foreign language and feel that, by expressing himself in it, he is laying himself open to censure or ridicule. For these reasons, again, he remains silent.

Since conversation is essentially interaction between persons, comprehension plays a role, as well as skill in expression. The student may have acquired skill in expressing himself in the new language code, but have had little practice in understanding the language when spoken at a normal speed of delivery in a conversational situation. He therefore makes a noncommittal acknowledgment of the fact that he has been addressed; he has not comprehended sufficient elements in the message to be able to make a further contribution to the discussion, or to be stimulated into a meaningful rejoinder. The conversational gambit lapses, and in a classroom situation the teacher finds himself obliged to initiate another possible chain of interaction along new lines. Students need much practice in listening to the language before attempting sustained conversation. They also need practice in seizing on the elements of a preceding utterance which will provide them with the breathing space necessary for the formulation of their own contribution to a continuing verbal exchange.

In a class group, the teacher must be alert to recognize personality factors which are affecting participation in foreign-language discussion. Some students are talkative, others are shy or taciturn. These characteristics affect student performance in the oral part of the lesson. Nida noted among missionaries that the talkative extrovert learned the language faster than the quiet, studious person.[4] Some students are, by nature, cautious or meticulously careful; still others are unduly sensitive, and therefore easily embarrassed or upset if found to be in error or not understood. Students in each of these categories often prefer to say nothing rather than run the risk of expressing themselves incorrectly.

In attempting to use the foreign language to express their own thoughts, students find themselves in an abnormally constricting situation where their choice of expression is severely limited. At the age at which many of our students are studying a foreign language they are accustomed to being able to demonstrate orally the maturity of their thought and the breadth of their knowledge. Finding themselves now limited to expressing themselves in childishly simple language, they feel frustrated and exasperated. The teacher must be aware of this psychological factor and conscious of his own advantage of expression in the new medium. He needs to show great restraint in his own contributions to the conversation or discussion, patience with the students' attempts to use the new tool,

4 E. A. Nida, *Learning a Foreign Language,* rev. ed. (New York, 1957) p. 26.

and respect for the fact that, although they are limited in their powers of expression, they are not really the immature persons this limitation might make them appear to be. Before a very advanced stage has been reached, the teacher must not ask the student to express in the foreign language ideas and concepts for which he cannot possibly know the accepted forms of expression and which he cannot discuss with any degree of refinement within the narrow confines of his foreign-language knowledge.

Psychological experiment has shown that people are more likely to continue a conversation when other people agree than when they disagree.[5] In many societies, cultural patterns have conditioned people to keep their ideas to themselves when the expression of them may cause unpleasantness and embarrassment for themselves or for the people with whom they are conversing. The student who is continually corrected by the teacher for every little slip he makes will withdraw from the unequal contest. Students' mistakes must be corrected if improvement is to be made, but when the student is attempting to encode his thoughts at conversational speed he should be interrupted as little as possible. Instead, the teacher should unobtrusively note one or two recurring errors of pronunciation or structure which would impede communication or be unacceptable to a native speaker, and bring these to the attention of the whole class for practice a little later on.

In view of the emotional and personality factors which are involved in a verbal interchange, spontaneous expression in the foreign language can be developed only in a relaxed and friendly atmosphere where students feel at ease with the teacher and with each other. Topics for discussion must be such that the student has something to say, or can make some contribution which will stimulate others to add information or to disagree. The teacher himself must adopt an encouraging rather than a correcting attitude; he must direct the interchanges in such a way that all students are involved at some time, as far as their personalities will permit, while he himself resists the temptation to dominate the discussion.

5   W. S. Verplanck, *Journal of Abnormal Social Psychology,* 51 (1955): pp. 668–79, quoted in J. B. Carroll, *Language and Thought* (New York, 1964), p. 46.

IN THE EARLY STAGES

It is generally admitted that the early stages of foreign-language learning must be largely taken up with the thorough drilling of language forms and sequences, so that intraverbal associations are developed and the student learns to produce correct forms of utterance without concentrating on putting the elements together. In the drills, language elements are learned in their normal sequence in useful utterances and practice is provided in the rapid construction of sentence types through transformation drills. As oral responses are elicited by a carefully programmed series of cues, the teacher tries to maintain a brisk tempo, so that students will learn to produce language patterns as wholes and not as laborious constructions from basic elements. This type of brisk drill can become an end in itself and both class and teacher will then be satisfied with the glib production of correct responses in practiced sequences. This type of result can be produced without a great deal of effort and concentration on the part of the students. As a result some critics of methods of oral drill have maintained that students trained in this fashion are unable to conduct even a simple conversation in the foreign language and are quite at a loss to understand phrases which are not heard in the exact form in which they were practiced. The teacher must be continually alert to the danger of developing mechanical responses without the students' being aware of the purpose and function of particular classroom drills. Theories of transfer of learning suggest that mechanical practice makes a certain skill readily available when an identical situation demands its exercise. Situations do arise where language responses are appropriate in the identical form in which they have been practiced in drills, but such occurrences are adventitious. If learning is to transfer to wider contexts the student must be conscious of the interrelationships within the structure being practiced, and of the parts of the pattern that may be manipulated (transformed, substituted, expanded) to achieve specific purposes. If the student is to acquire facility in adapting learned and drilled patterns to his own purposes in spontaneous expression, he must participate in these drills with understanding and awareness of the crucial element in the pattern which undergoes modification as the drills proceed. In this way he will be more likely to realize where this element may be appropriately inserted and know how to adapt it to the expression of his own purposes.[6]

Awareness of the intention of a drill is only one step towards facility in spontaneous expression. The next, most important, step is the opportunity for the student to demonstrate that he can use the structure he has been manipulating in an actual situation where he is engaged in communication with another person. The teacher must exercise his ingenuity to create in the classroom situations of the type the students would encounter in real life outside the classroom: opportunities to ask each other questions about subjects in which they can be presumed to take an interest, to recount to each other facts and incidents of home and school life, or to comment on and tease their fellow students about current happenings. Some may question whether situations structured in the classroom can be considered real and actual. To the student who spends a large part of his waking hours in school they are as real as any other of his day's experiences, and he is communicating with individuals with whom he communicates normally in out-of-class activities. Where suitable dialogues have been learned, students will have vocabulary and expressions at their command for the discussion of simple relationships, personal interests, and everyday activities.

The student, in the early stages, cannot move directly from drill to spontaneous expression without running the risk of native-language interference and the consequent utilization of structures based on the syntax and morphology to which he is accustomed. The transition must be more gradual: moving from grammatical drill to directed communication which the teacher can control and correct. In this type of guided activity the teacher outlines to the student the content of a question he is to ask a classmate (e.g., "Ask John: Did you go to bed early last night?") and then directs the form of reply to be given by the classmate (e.g., "Reply to Peter: No, I didn't go to bed early last night"). The directions may sometimes be given in

6 Theories of transfer are discussed at length in Rivers (1964), pp. 121–29.

the native language in the exact form the utterance should take to ensure that the student understands what he is saying. They may then be given in indirect form in the foreign language to force the student into framing his own utterance appropriately (e.g., "Ask John if he went to bed early last night," or "Tell Peter what time you went to bed last night"). From directed utterance, the lesson should proceed to some structured situation where the student uses the language formation being practiced in some kind of conversational interchange, with lexical content, as distinct from structural frame, chosen by himself. This structured situation may involve questions and answers where members of the class ask each other questions related to their personal lives. If these questions involve some humor and good-natured teasing, they become less artificial so that students concentrate on meaning rather than mere form of utterance. Students may recount events or incidents; they may give short commentaries on pictures or objects, or descriptions of persons and objects which involve the guessing of identity, or of some other element such as occupation or function. A game or competition may be introduced which forces students into producing the desired structure at frequent intervals. The element of competition and the excitement in a game force out oral expression so that students forget their inhibitions about making mistakes and being embarrassed in front of their fellows. The trainee teacher should begin to make a collection of such games and competitions, noting beside each one the structural pattern and vocabulary area which the students would be practicing during this activity.[7]

As the student's knowledge of the language increases he can begin to give short oral reports to the class. These will at first be guided by a simple outline which will keep him from trying to make his way too soon in the uncharted areas of the language. By the time he begins to develop his own subject without an outline, his whole experience in the language class should have impressed upon him the importance of limiting

---

7   See M. Eriksson, I. Forest, and R. Mulhauser, *Foreign Languages in the Elementary School* (Englewood Cliffs, N.J., 1964), Appendix I, "Games, Activities, and Songs," for ideas on how to adapt well-known games for use in the classroom.

himself severely to expressions and structures which he knows
well and can handle confidently. This is an orientation which
the teacher must continually foster so that every attempt the
student makes at using the language for his own purposes will
be a further occasion for consolidation of basic knowledge and
for confident variation within accepted boundaries. The student may tell in his own words the essence of what he has
heard in a listening-comprehension exercise or what he has
read in a foreign-language text. This will not be mere repetition if he is forced to reconstruct the material in a different
person or tense. He can attempt to tell a story to the class as
he would tell it to a very young child. This is a very useful
exercise because it forces the student to keep to simple vocabulary and simple structure, instead of trying to put into the
foreign language the type of expression and complication of
structure he would be using in telling a story in his native
language. In all such oral work students should be taught that
whenever they are at a loss to express themselves in the foreign
language they should consciously simplify what they want to
say, reducing it to basic patterns with which they are familiar.
If they adopt this as a method of approach, they will gain
more rapidly in confidence and fluency.

ADVANCED STAGE

It is as students move into the advanced stage of learning the
foreign language that many teachers give up regular training
in the speaking skill. The class becomes absorbed in reading
and writing, with attempts at discussion of subjects of which
the students often have little previous knowledge. The student,
with still-fragile speaking habits, is often pushed prematurely
into a situation where he is expected to discuss in the foreign
language literary concepts and problems for which he does not
know the accepted terminology and turns of expression and for
which, very often, he has had no adequate literary training
even in his native language. As a result a pall of silence falls
over what has been in previous years an eager and vocal group.
The teacher, in desperation, proceeds to lecture in the foreign
language, feeling that in this way he is achieving the aims of

his advanced course. Maintaining and developing fluency in spontaneous expression at an advanced level is certainly a demanding task, and many teachers give up the struggle, completely baffled as to how to proceed. Certain guiding principles may help the teacher to see how to plan his work so that further training in this important skill is not neglected.

Not to be underestimated in the development of facility in expressing one's meaning in the foreign language is the role of listening. In a foreign country, the student would hear the language spoken around him continually. Expressions, rhythms, phonological patterns: all strike his ear and impress themselves upon his memory. Without conscious effort he imitates and frames his utterances on the basis of what he has heard. Slowly and surely he advances to the stage where he speaks like those around him. This constant hearing of the language throughout the day is missing in the school environment. Without this opportunity to pattern his utterances continually on an authentic model the student begins to flounder, his dearly won control of structure and conventional expression being too frail to resist the growing pressure of native-language interference as he tries to express himself in a more mature fashion. He must be given opportunities for careful and attentive listening to foreign-language material at frequent intervals, either in a laboratory, or with a tape recorder or record player. Suitable types of listening materials for advanced levels have been listed in chapter 6. Carroll points out that "normal speech involves a perceptual self-monitoring process." [8] If the student has a distinct auditory image of what his speech should sound like, he will be able to listen to his own speech more critically, with a greater possibility of adjusting it gradually to the model of native speech to which he listens frequently.

Also useful in developing the mechanics of fluent speech is frequent repetition, after a model, of conversational utterances of some complexity. Students who do not have ready access to a laboratory or tape recorder can gain great benefit from frequently reading aloud conversational material (e.g., dialogue from modern novels or plays). These utterances may be

8 J. B. Carroll, *Language and Thought* (New York, 1964), pp. 45–46.

practiced after the teacher, then read aloud at home until the phrases trip off the tongue without effort. Repeating and reading aloud help develop those intraverbal associations which are so necessary for rapid production of speech in the foreign language. In the native language these associations are developed in the almost continuous verbal activity of everyday living, and lack of such well-established associations in the foreign language causes a certain hesitancy in articulating the next word in a group of words. Repeating and reading aloud also give practice in the mechanics of pronunciation in larger contexts. The student can concentrate on smooth transition from sound to sound and from word to word, according to the conventions of rapid speech in the foreign language; he can also concentrate on reproducing appropriate intonation patterns; and all of these phonological features can be practiced without the added labor of selecting the most appropriate expressions to clothe his own ideas. Later, when he is trying to express himself, he will be able to reproduce these practiced sound sequences without conscious effort, and give his full attention to the process of selection.

In the early stages, most conversational practice has been related to work learned recently. At the advanced level, conversation calls into play a multiplicity of structures and lexical items which have been learned over a period of years. The student must select from this stored knowledge the lexical items, accepted phrases, and structures most appropriate to the expression of his meaning. Skill in rapid selection can be developed only by much practice in retrieving learned items, in their complicated interrelationships, from the memory store. This practice in selection is facilitated if the student can converse on subjects where ideas spring readily to his mind. If he is forced into a position where the development of ideas is the all-important factor, much of his attention will be given to this process and he will fall back into native-language habits of expression because they are less demanding. For sheer practice in selection, the student should be given the opportunity to chatter on subjects of his own choice, where the production of ideas is effortless and most of his attention is on the process of selection. Students who continue their studies to a high level will have abundant opportunity to talk in the foreign language about advanced ideas in their later studies. Some will immediately ask: are we not to challenge our students intellectually? We are challenging them intellectually by demanding of them fluent expression of their ideas in another language; it is clear that we cannot develop one skill well by demanding that the students perform some other complicated operation at the same time.

Practice in the selection of appropriate language elements will involve a certain amount of experimentation and trial-and-error learning. Students should be encouraged, at the advanced level, to try out new combinations of elements to create novel utterances. This is what the advanced student would do were he to find himself in a foreign country. He would make every effort to express his meaning by all kinds of recombinations of the language elements at his disposal. The more daring he is in such linguistic innovation, the more rapidly he progresses. In the classroom the student has the advantage of a mentor who will guide him in distinguishing acceptable from unacceptable recombinations. In this process he will make mistakes, but, being rewarded by approval and commendation when his innovations are acceptable and not rewarded when they are unacceptable, he will gradually eliminate the unrewarded attempts from his repertoire. As a result his language behavior will gradually approximate more and more closely that of a native speaker. Such trial-and-error behavior is inadvisable when the student is forging the tool of the language code but is very valuable when he is learning to use the tool and experimenting to find new ways of making it express his intentions.

As the student becomes more and more independent of his teacher he should be encouraged to practice talking to himself and thinking in the foreign language as often as possible: describing to himself the things he sees on the way to school, recounting to himself what he has done during the day or what he intends to do. In this way he will give himself some of the practice he would have in the foreign country, because much of what passes for communication in everyday life is merely egocentric monologue.

As we discuss the other language skills it will become more and more apparent that the learning of one skill is intimately interwoven with the learning of each of the other skills. We have already shown this to be so for listening and speaking. Let it be emphasized immediately that growing facility in speaking will also owe much to increasing ability in fluent reading and to the active application of language knowledge in writing. As students read widely, their vocabulary and their understanding of cultural concepts will be greatly developed, so that the knowledge available to them for selection as a basis of spoken expression will also be enlarged. Wide reading and practice in putting some of the material read into a simple written form will deepen the impression of many language items and make them more readily available, when appropriate, in oral expression. To capitalize on the contribution of other skill areas, the teacher should promote active class discussion of what has been heard and read, and require short oral reports of reading done out of class.

CONVERSATION GROUPS AND FOREIGN-LANGUAGE CLUBS

More intensive practice in the art of conversation can be provided, at the advanced level, in small groups meeting together at regular intervals. We may hope that the students will seize opportunities out of class to practice unstructured communication together, and the most enthusiastic certainly will, but there is a valid place for such practice in a situation where the teacher can help and guide. If the school has a language laboratory, scheduling difficulties for such a project are fewer. Half the class (advanced classes are not as yet prohibitively large) may be sent to the language laboratory for individual practice in listening, without books, to records of plays, stories, and poems studied in class or read out of class, in making notes of news broadcasts taped from foreign-language radio programs, in listening to the sound track of a film which has been shown in class or club, or for remedial exercises in pronunciation. If no laboratory is available, much of this listening practice can be provided by a tape recorder in the classroom. The other half of the class will then remain with the teacher, preferably in an informal setting, for practice in free oral expression.

Conversation groups of this kind require careful preparation and special techniques. They cannot be expected to produce good results if the teacher vaguely hopes that the mood of the group will carry all the participants forward in a steady flow of chatter. This may happen on the first occasion, but limitations of vocabulary and paucity of ideas soon make the sessions repetitive and tedious. The teacher must plan a careful series of conversation topics covering a wide field. These may be considered conversation areas in a very broad and flexible sense, and each should be announced in advance. Some teachers like to issue, several days beforehand, sheets of relevant vocabulary for preparation. Lists of words in the foreign language which the students may find in their foreign-language dictionaries are sufficient. If short films on aspects of life in the foreign country are at the teacher's disposal, these may serve to stimulate conversation and will determine the conversation area for the week. The topic chosen is then taken as a wide, elastic area within which all may range, and the students are expected to come prepared with ideas within that area which they will introduce into the conversation either as questions, illustrations, or provocative statements. On one such occasion, for instance, the topic may be announced as the *sea*. For that day any conversational gambit which relates to the sea is permissible: days at the seaside, fishing, sea travel, underwater diving, wrecks, pirates, the life of a sailor, sea tales, sea monsters, films or books about the sea, and so on. The topic itself is merely a focus to give the conversation direction and to provide some community of ideas. The course the conversation takes is spontaneous and not guided by the teacher, who does, however, redirect it or inject it with new interest when it seems to be flagging. Topics of similarly wide scope which spring to mind are: the country, love and marriage, national holidays, sports, travel, leisure-time occupations, favorite authors or films, vacations, home life, school as I would like it to be, if I were President, city life, careers, the things that irritate me most. The imaginative teacher will soon have a list long enough to cover the necessary number of sessions.

Once a conversation group becomes a place for giving oral reports, it ceases to achieve its purpose, since most of the students settle back happily to become listeners, and no longer participate vocally. Just as the setting should be informal and the group small (eight students as a maximum, but preferably six), so should the atmosphere be one of relaxed camaraderie where students feel free to tease each other and the teacher, and are thus eager to hear what is said, to interrupt, and to question. The students should be encouraged to come to the group with the firm intention of making and taking opportunities to make their voices heard.

The role of the teacher in such a group requires alertness and self-discipline. He must not talk too much himself, resisting any temptation to use the session as a forum for giving a lecture in the foreign language. He must watch to see that two or three people do not do all the talking. If such a situation arises, he must be ready to step in and tactfully swing the conversation to another student by asking a question related to what has just been said, particularly watching for opportunities to launch the shy or taciturn. He must have at ready command a few relevant and provocative questions to throw into the ring when conversation is beginning to lose pace, always remembering the stimulating effect of hearing the teacher produce the unexpected.

To what degree should the teacher correct inaccurate speech during such sessions? It is obvious that continual interruption to correct every mistake will discourage, frustrate, and inhibit the students, so that they lose their train of thought and cease to speak freely, yet such a conversation session should be an occasion for improvement. The teacher should listen carefully for consistent inaccuracies, rather than slips of the tongue. A small checklist against which he notes the initials of the student consistently making some structural mistake can be an unobtrusive aid. A correction which he feels must be made immediately can be interjected in a low tone, so that the student speaking picks it up quickly and inserts it into the flow of his speech. If the group as a whole needs some quick reminder, a short comment may be made during a suitable pause in the conversation without inhibiting the spontaneous flow. Otherwise, a few minutes may be reserved at the end of the session for individual or small group conferences on serious mistakes made consistently, while more advanced members of the group talk among themselves under the leadership of one of the more fluent students.

Speaking ability can also be developed in the foreign-language club, where students are forced into an effort at communication in an informal atmosphere. As in the foreign country, a spirit of linguistic innovation and enterprise, within the acknowledged limitations of the standard of language they have reached, can provide students with much practice in selection and variation of structures and vocabulary learned in the classroom. Yet in the atmosphere of the club this seems to be fun, not just so much more classwork. The program of the club should be designed not so much with a teaching aim as with the intention of creating a setting where the students are engaged in activities they would normally enjoy in the native language: preparing one-act plays and skits, organizing competitions and games, seeing films, taking part in mock television programs or panel discussions, singing songs, engaging in informal conversation over coffee cups, meeting native speakers of the language, celebrating festival days of the foreign country.

Although the activities of the club have, basically, a teaching aim, they should be such that the students will enjoy themselves while absorbing some of the spirit and culture of the country where the language is spoken. Songs should be modern in harmony, rhythm, and theme, or folk songs which still appeal musically to the young people of today. Art songs of a more serious nature may be excellent for those who have a developed taste for music, but the foreign-language club should be a place of enjoyment for all, irrespective of tastes, so that the language will be readily practiced. In club sessions, the foreign-language teacher must use all his wiles to make the practicing of the language attractive and not dilute his efforts with other, sometimes conflicting, aims. Plays, for instance, should be presented for fun, with foreign-language fluency of paramount importance, rather than perfection of costuming and stage presentation. In this way, three or four one-act plays can be learned and rehearsed, and more people involved in the acting, in the same period of time which would be required for the thorough staging of one such play. For a successful club from the point of view of foreign-language use, variety and informality should be the keynote through all the year's activities.

If we wish our students to speak with ease in the foreign language we must ensure that they are given ample practice, at all levels, in expressing themselves in situations as close to spontaneous expression as possible. Preoccupation with other aspects of the work must not be allowed to whittle away the time spent in this activity. Nor must the teacher allow himself to become discouraged at the slow rate of development of real facility and fluency. He must recognize the fact that individual students will reach varying levels of self-expression in the foreign language. Students have achieved greater and less degrees of fluency in their native language. Some have wide-ranging vocabularies and a sure choice of felicitous expression; others express themselves badly with much repetition and many trite and well-worn clichés; still others are at a loss for words when asked to explain or describe something out of the usual run of their daily experience. In the native language, some speak rapidly, others very slowly and deliberately. Teachers are by their very choice of profession an articulate group. Without realizing it they often expect of students a greater degree of control of the foreign language than these same students show in their native language; they may even expect more consummate expression than some native speakers display in a natural situation. By their methods of testing, too, teachers often reward the imaginative and the extrovert, under the illusion that they are rewarding fluency of expression in the foreign language. (The whole matter of testing oral production is a difficult problem which will be discussed in chapter 12). Teachers of advanced high school students must keep these factors of individual differences in mind and encourage each student to participate as his personality allows. Then, and only then, will he have a class where the atmosphere lends itself to spontaneous expression and interest in communication.

AREAS OF CONTROVERSY

Is speaking a foreign language a skill worth cultivating when students meet few native speakers and live far from the land where the language is spoken?

Teachers who make this objection usually round it off by adding: If we teach the student to read and write the language well and to understand the grammar, he will learn to speak it quickly enough when he is in a situation where the speaking of the language is important for him.

This type of reasoning ignores pedagogically sound reasons for teaching the speaking skill. One of these has already been discussed: students (and their parents) feel that learning a language is something to do with speaking; they expect to learn to speak it, and early introduction to the aural-oral skills increases their interest in and enthusiasm for foreign-language learning. Besides this, listening and speaking are basic to some of the most interesting and exciting activities in the language classroom. Dull indeed would many lessons be without them. Nor must we forget that we are teaching a generation which spends more of its leisure time before a television set than in reading books. To such students the approach by oral learning seems more natural than to the students of a generation ago.

These motivational factors apart, there are other valid reasons for an aural-oral approach to language learning. When we read and when we write, we call upon what we know of the language orally. In reading, we recognize, behind the script, the oral equivalent, supplying as we read many elements of intonation and vocal emphasis which are not in the printed text. We read more fluently because we are able to recognize whole phrases which we could say aloud. For the student with a poor oral knowledge of the foreign language, most reading is mere deciphering: a painful word-by-word process from which he finds it hard to draw a sequence of meaning until he is able to say over to himself what he thinks it means in his native language. In writing, we put in graphic form what we would say; even at a refined level we repeat phrases over to see which sounds best before making a choice. This the student cannot do if he has been taught only to write things down in the foreign language, not to say them. His efforts at composition become exercises in concoction where he pieces language elements together and rearranges them according to rules he has learned.

Oral exercises permit of much longer and more sustained practice than written exercises, in a situation where the teacher has immediate and direct access to the work of each student and is able to correct and guide it. The vividness of oral practice reinforces the visual impression, while supplying an aural-oral impression which increases retention.

Finally, many people who have learned a foreign language only through reading and writing are severely inhibited when the opportunity arises to practice speaking it. They are uncertain of pronunciation and intonation; at the first signs of incomprehension they withdraw in embarrassment. They are unfamiliar with many of the commonest phrases they hear around them and begin to feel insecure in the knowledge they do have. Once they have overcome their reticence and have found they can understand and be understood, they progress, but the initial stage is often too painful for them and they do not persist. If as young students they had been forced to use the language frequently in front of others in a friendly atmosphere, they would have lost many of their inhibitions early and been eager, rather than reluctant, to try out their skill in a real situation.

Students who have been taught all through their foreign-language studies to understand and speak the language will not only profit in this area but will have a much firmer control of the language for reading and writing as well.

Is the acquisition of an extensive vocabulary one of the most important aspects of foreign-language learning if one is to speak fluently?

In some teaching methods great store is set by the learning of many foreign-language words. Textbooks begin each lesson with lengthy bilingual vocabulary lists, and students learn these lists by heart night after night. In an audio-lingual approach vocabulary learning is given a minor role until the student has a sure control of the basic structural patterns and is able to express himself freely within a limited area of language.

There are various reasons for this reduced emphasis on vocabulary learning. The number of words one can learn in a foreign language is seemingly endless, and it is difficult to know exactly which word one will need next—it may well be a word of very low frequency. Without knowing the circumstances in which our students are likely to use the language, it is difficult to decide which vocabulary areas will ultimately be the most useful for them.[9] Many common objects, whose foreign names the students soon learn, are very rarely talked about in normal conversation. Vocabulary for any specific subject of interest is soon acquired when circumstances demand it.

Excessive vocabulary learning gives students the impression that the most important thing about learning a language is the accumulating of foreign words as equivalents for concepts which they can already express in their native language. They often fail to realize that meaning is expressed in groups of words and in combinations of language segments, and that the meaning of an individual word is usually difficult to determine when it is separated from a context of other words and phrases. Such an attitude can be very deleterious to effective language use.

Once students have acquired a small basic vocabulary, this can be used for giving practice in structural manipulation which is fundamental to any form of communication—in speech or writing. Because the same well-known lexical items are used in drills, students are able to concentrate on the structural elements without distraction. When a structural pattern has been learned well, further useful vocabulary can be included in the drills to draw the student's attention from the feature being practiced. In this way it becomes clear whether the students can now use the structure they have been practicing in an accurate but effortless way.

Hesitancy in speaking a language, or in reading or writing it for that matter, is frequently a question of slow vocabulary recall. This is inevitable when the student has been asked to learn an indigestible number of items. In an audio-lingual approach, where everything is learned thoroughly by being used in aural-oral practice, then in reading, and then in writing, the vocabulary which is learned is not allowed to fall into disuse, but remains readily available for recall. New vocabu-

9   Constructors of frequency counts soon discover the degree to which the use of concrete nouns in particular is a function of the situation in which an utterance takes place. As a result what would normally be regarded as common concrete nouns may be rated as of very low frequency or may not appear at all in a particular corpus of utterances under examination. See Halliday, McIntosh, and Strevens (1964), p. 194.

lary is practiced in vocabulary drills where students learn the structural and lexical context in which the word is used. In this way they use each new word a number of times in probable utterances and assimilate its meaning through use.

Even in the native language, the child acquires vocabulary slowly at first, but makes the maximum use of each item for his purposes. During this early period his passive vocabulary increases through much listening; then, later, when he has a control of certain basic structural patterns, his vocabulary increases by leaps and bounds.[10] The student in the classroom does not have the same opportunity to acquire a wide vocabulary through constant listening; for him this phase comes when he moves into wider reading. The more he reads the more his passive, or recognition, knowledge of vocabulary is increased. A part of this becomes active as he uses it in speech and writing. Just as in the native language, he must never expect to be able to use actively, without hesitation, all the words and expressions he can recognize in his reading. The paucity of his active vocabulary will hinder him in the expression of his meaning only if he continually attempts to express himself beyond the level of his mastery of the foreign language. He must realize that, mature as he is, he is a child in his knowledge of the foreign language. He must try to simplify what he wishes to say, trying to express his meaning as a child would express it—with correct use of uncomplicated structural patterns and a basic general-purpose vocabulary. This attitude will help him through the period when his vocabulary is very limited. As he comes to know many more words and expressions, he will, however, be fitting them into appropriate and correctly combined structural patterns, instead of stringing them together in the hope that they will make a comprehensible sentence.

Can a teacher who is not fluent himself in the foreign language teach the speaking skill?

Despite the fears of many teachers who learned the language by a grammar-translation method with little oral work, it is possible for a teacher who is not a fluent speaker of the

10 G. A. Miller, *Language and Communication* (New York, 1951), pp. 148–54.

language to teach the speaking skill by an audio-lingual approach. It is much more difficult with a direct-method approach where the teacher must keep talking continually and use much ingenuity to ensure that he is understood.

In an audio-lingual, or structural, approach the teacher is expected to keep strictly within the limits of the material the students are learning, drilling it thoroughly and allowing the students to hear and use it as often as time will allow. The teacher who is lacking in confidence can use a tape recorder in the classroom to give the students the opportunity to imitate an authentic accent, and he himself will learn with the students by continually hearing the correct sounds from the model. The audio-lingual method discourages the teacher from doing all the talking in the foreign language himself; he is expected, rather, to use class time for maximum opportunities of participation by all the members of his class. As a result, his deficiencies will not show up very much in the classroom if he has prepared each section of work well, working with the tape recorder at home before presenting any material to his class.

A teacher who is in this position should heed the following advice.

—He will need to pay very careful attention as he compares his own articulation and intonation with that of the tape model. If he has been badly trained, he will have acquired certain inaccuracies and incorrect muscular habits of which he will very probably not be conscious, and which will be hard to eradicate. He may find it helpful to seek the criticism of another teacher as he tries to detect these weaknesses. Once they are identified, he must practice to improve them, both at home and in class. If these weaknesses are very important phonemically, he should warn the class that where there is a discrepancy between what he says and what they hear on the tape, they should be guided by the tape. Above all, he should not be too proud to admit his faults if he finds students have imitated one of his weaknesses, but be ready to correct the class and himself and work with them for the elimination of the inaccuracy.

—He should watch for inhibitions on his part about speaking the language. Such an inhibition will express itself in his taking refuge in the use of the native language when he should be giving the students steady practice in listening to and repeating the foreign language. As a result, his students will later be as unwilling as he to speak the language.

—He should use techniques which encourage the students to use the foreign language as much as possible, so that they will not be dependent on his oral contribution. For variety, he can use the better students to lead drills and dialogue practice, especially if these students have acquired, from imitation of the tape, a better pronunciation than his own.

—He will need to be patient and persevering in improving his own oral skills. He should practice talking to himself; listen to foreign-language tapes, records, and films; and attend inservice training schools and workshops, or meetings of cultural societies.

With the right attitude toward his problem, such a teacher should be able to correct the situation as time goes on without too much inconvenience to his first aural-oral classes. His later classes will profit, as he himself will, from the improvement in his language skills.

ANNOTATED READING LIST

NIDA, E. A. *Toward a Science of Translating.* Leiden: Brill, 1964. Chapter 6, "Dynamic Dimension in Communication," sets out very clearly what is involved in an act of communication.

NORTHEAST CONFERENCE (1968). *Foreign Language Learning: Research and Development,* edited by T. E. BIRD. Report of Working Committee III, "Liberated Expression" (pp. 77–118), discusses the process of passing from controlled responses through constructed responses to free responses, appropriate techniques to assist this process, and the problems of the "semantic component."

MODERN LANGUAGE ASSOCIATION OF AMERICA. *Reports of Surveys and Studies in the Teaching of Modern Foreign Languages.* New York: Modern Language Association, 1962. Section 15, "Good Teaching Practices" by L. Brisley *et al.,* describes a number of classroom activities which are useful in developing the speaking skill (pp. 225–29).

RIVERS, W. M. *The Psychologist and the Foreign-Language Teacher.* Chicago: University of Chicago Press, 1964. Chapter 8 discusses the processes involved in learning to select the appropriate response from a repertoire of learned responses.

9

The Reading Skill

Great stress has so far been laid on the listening and speaking skills. This insistence has been necessary to redress an imbalance in emphasis which many teachers, because of their bookish interests and traditional training, have tended to perpetuate. Recent intensive discussion of ways of developing the listening and speaking skills from the beginning stages of foreign-language study has sometimes given the erroneous impression that advocates of active oral methods neglect the reading skill. As a result, foreign-language teachers are sometimes accused of wishing to produce "language illiterates." Gloomy prophets predict that future graduates of foreign-language classes will be fluent chatterboxes who are able to produce rapid-fire utterances in a foreign language but have nothing worthwhile to say, because they have never been given the opportunity to share the thinking of the great minds of another culture, and so to widen the horizons of their knowledge and understanding. This unfortunate and unfounded impression stems from the fact that many new techniques must of necessity be described as they would apply to elementary or intermediate level foreign-language classes. This does not mean that later teaching must follow exactly the same pattern. The emphasis on early teaching is, however, relevant to the work of the more advanced students in that the ability of a student ultimately to think in a foreign language and understand it without mental translation, in both oral and graphic form, is largely the result of the way in which he has been taught to approach his language study in the early stages.

A study of recent writings in foreign-language methodology will show that no leader in this area advocates the neglect of reading, while the most recent textbooks all provide a great deal of carefully selected reading matter for the advanced classes. The difference lies in the approach to reading. Instead of observing that all high school students can read in the native language and presuming that they can therefore be expected to read in the foreign language without much help, the modern methodologist tries to understand the processes involved in the reading of a written text, especially a text in a foreign language. He then sets out to plan learning experiences which will enable the students to develop habits of reading which will lead them to direct comprehension of the text, without resort to translation into their native language. He realizes that if this aim is to be achieved progress must be slow and steady and the teaching of the skill continuous, with nothing left to chance development.

Justification for an emphasis on the development of the reading skill is not hard to find. In many countries foreign languages are learned by numbers of students who will never have the opportunity of conversing with a native speaker, but who will have access to the literature and periodicals, or scientific and technical journals written in that language. Many will need these publications to assist them with further studies or in their work; others will wish to enjoy them in their leisure time. The reading skill, once developed, is the one which can be most easily maintained at a high level by the student himself without further help from his teacher. Through its exercise he can increase his knowledge and understanding of the culture of the speakers of the language, their ways of thinking, and their contributions to many fields of artistic and intellectual endeavor. To imagine that all students who have learned a foreign language at school will do this, however, is a blissful illusion. Unless the student has been taught during his course to read the foreign language fluently, without deciphering it word by word, and to approach a book or magazine article independently with confidence, it is unlikely that he will be attracted to this type of activity after he has completed his studies; rather, the little knowledge he has acquired will gradually be forgotten, as will so much else that he has studied at school. As with the other areas of language use, reading with direct comprehension and with fluency is a skill which must be taught in progressive stages, and practiced regularly with carefully graded materials.

Before considering efficient approaches to the teaching of reading, it is essential to distinguish clearly two activities which go by this name, but which must not for that reason be confused with each other. A student may be considered to be "reading" when he stands up in class and enunciates in the conventional way the sounds which are symbolized by the printed or written marks on the script in his hand. This he may do in a way which is acceptable and comprehensible to a native speaker, without drawing meaning from what he is reading. This activity is one aspect of reading for which the student must be trained, but it is not the final goal in the foreign-language classroom. He must also be taught to derive meaning from the word combinations in the text and to do this in a consecutive fashion at a reasonable speed, without necessarily vocalizing what he is reading. He has learned to do this in his own language, but he is now faced with a different language code and one with which he is far from familiar.

In reading, then, the student is "developing a *considerable range of habitual responses* to a specific set of patterns of graphic shapes." [1] When learning to read his native language he has acquired essential space and direction habits: he can recognize the shapes of letters in his native-language alphabet and has become skilled at reading these in the direction his language prescribes. He has also learned to recognize certain patterns of arrangement (such as paragraph divisions) and is familiar with the punctuation marks and their function. When he comes to read in the foreign language, then, he already understands what the process of reading signifies. He is alert to the fact that reading involves recognition of certain patterns of symbols and that these represent particular sounds which form words he may use, or may hear spoken. He has also come to recognize with ease particular words which clarify the function of other words close to them, and words which indicate logical relationships among segments of sentences or sections of dis-

1 C. C. Fries, *Linguistics and Reading* (New York, 1963), p. 121.

course. He has also been trained in rapid identification of word groups which have a meaning transcending the meaning of the individual units of which they are composed. This means that he has learned to extract from the printed patterns three levels of meaning: lexical meaning (the semantic content of the words and expressions), structural or grammatical meaning (deriving from interrelationships among words, or parts of words, or from the order of words), and social-cultural meaning (the evaluation which people of his own culture attach to the words and groups of words he is reading).[2]

If the foreign language employs the same alphabet as the student's native language and is a cognate language (as is the case with English and French, or English and German), his well-practiced reading habits may hinder him considerably in extracting from the foreign-language text these three levels of meaning. He will see familiar combinations of letters which signal distinctively different sounds. He will recognize some combinations of letters, identical with those of his native language, which signal different lexical or social-cultural meanings. He will, at times, encounter a word order which has a different structural or grammatical meaning from that which his native language has taught him to expect.

The foreign-language teacher often assumes that because his students have already acquired reading skill in their native language reading in the foreign language should not be difficult for them. It should now be clear that the main element transferred from the student's training in native-language reading is a certain comprehension of what reading is about and a certain awareness of the importance of letter and word combinations. Very little else is of great help to him. Unlike the child learning to read his native language, the student is not recognizing symbols for words and expressions with which he already has considerable acquaintance. If he is forced to read in the foreign language too early in the course, he finds himself adrift in a flood of words and expressions he has never before encountered; with a similar alphabet he is impeded by interference from well-established native-language habits; structural clues are all awry. Forced to decipher with the aid of a dictionary,

2   *Ibid.,* pp. 104–12.

he transfers native-language pronunciations to the foreign-language text, attaches inaccurate lexical meanings to units, and is misled in interpretation by his previous cultural experience.

Some teachers will argue that plenty of experience with a considerable quantity of reading material is essential from an early stage of language learning, in order to expand the student's knowledge of the language. This will give him, they maintain, experience with a much wider range of expressions and structures than he could gain from listening and speaking, which are limited to his time in laboratory or classroom. Let us examine, at this point, one of the practices commonly observed in foreign-language classes where the students spend much of their time reading. We may question whether real knowledge of the language, beyond casual acquaintance with some isolated elements of it, is attained by the following procedure which is common among students: the student deciphers a part of the text with the help of a bilingual dictionary or word list; he hurriedly writes a native-language near-equivalent above each unfamiliar word in the text and rushes on to find out further trivial details of a banal story (as often as not artificially constructed to include certain grammatical forms). If the student does pause to reread, he skips through a hotchpotch of text, with his eye leaping from foreign words to interlinear native-language glosses. This is certainly not reading in the second sense of the term. It is doubtful whether it is even an educative experience which can be defended in the face of pressures on school time.

The preceding discussion has brought out the dangers of allowing students to range too widely in reading material before being thoroughly trained in the reading skill. It was not intended to argue for the exclusion of reading from the foreign-language program. The question now arises: How soon should training in reading begin in the foreign-language course? In our chapters on the Speaking Skill (chapters 7 and 8), we have emphasized the importance of aural-oral learning in the beginning stages of the course, whether by audio-lingual methods of dialogue memorization and pattern drilling or by the direct or situational methods of oral discussion in the context of the classroom. Some methodologists, in their anxiety to establish good habits of pronunciation and intonation untainted by native-language habits, have advocated a purely oral period of learning of considerable length (some weeks or even months) before students are allowed to see a printed or written representation of what they are learning. A long oral training of this kind has been shown to result in most commendable progress in near-native articulation and intonation.[3] Some experienced teachers, however, have found that, even after a very long period of aural-oral training, deterioration in the newly established habits of sound production can set in as soon as students are presented with a script with symbols similar to those of their native language.[4]

A prolonged time lag between the introduction to the language orally and the presentation of what has been learned in graphic form can cause other problems. Students deprived of any visual support tend to make surreptitious notes of what they think they are hearing, in a form which is phonetically inaccurate. It is difficult for them later to correct the mistakes which they have been learning according to their own system. To relieve their anxieties about the accuracy of what they remember of their class work, parents and friends write down for them what they seem to be repeating, or provide them with old-fashioned elementary textbooks in which they seek out the spelling of what they presume they have been learning. Some students with poor auditory memory become overanxious when they are expected to retain everything they hear without the established associations and structural clues on which they are accustomed to rely in the native language. As a result they develop a psychological block against foreign-language learning and try to drop the subject. Even students who enjoy the purely oral period find it hard to practice out of class unless take-home disks or tapes are provided, and so hours of valuable practice are denied them. Finally, where the students have no script of any type, neither reading nor writing exercises are available to provide variety of activity during the classroom lesson and to give the overburdened teacher some relief from the strain of directing oral practice.

3   D. Muller, "The Effect upon Pronunciation and Intonation of Early Exposure to the Written Word," *MLJ,* 49, no. 7 (November, 1965): 411.

4   F. Marty, *Language Laboratory Learning* (Wellesley, Mass., 1960), pp. 75–76.

These practical objections to a prolonged period of purely oral work would suggest that a compromise might be reached which would allow the introduction of training in reading fairly early in the foreign-language course, without sacrificing the undoubted benefits of sustained oral training. The principle to be established in the minds of both teacher and students is that in the early stages new foreign-language material must be learned orally to establish good habits of sound production and to train the student to depend on his ear. The introduction to the foreign language will, then, be entirely oral: for two weeks, four weeks, even six weeks, depending on the age and maturity of the students and the experience and confidence of the teacher. After a careful and systematic introduction of the written script, all new work will still be presented in its oral form first. The graphic form of the new work will be used as a support, after the preliminary oral practice: for consolidation through home learning and private study, for clarification of certain problems, and for some reading and writing practice. The bulk of the class time will still be devoted to aural-oral practice. This early period with a script will be used for training in reading directly in the foreign language without translation. The printed script will represent material which has been learned orally, and the symbols will be continually associated with the oral version. The students will listen or repeat after a model as they read, so that they will, from the beginning, associate correct pronunciation with the sound-symbol combinations in print, and superimpose elements such as stress, pitch, and intonation which the printed script does not indicate.

If both teacher and students remain conscious of the possibility of interference from native-language habits which are associated with the familiar script, and of the constant danger of deterioration of pronunciation with decrease in vigilance, the script will prove to be a help and not a hindrance. Teachers must realize that it is easy to presume the student knows a section of foreign-language work thoroughly because he is able to read and discuss it with the book before him. Such false confidence can lead to a reduction in the amount of practice provided in the active use of language forms. The script is a prop which the student must learn to do without. He must be continually forced into using material he has read in the book in an active interchange of communication while his book remains closed. Only in this way can he prove to himself and to his teacher that he has mastered a particular section of the work sufficiently to need no further practice.

To summarize: the student who is being trained in the use of a printed script from an early stage of foreign-language learning must be made aware of the danger of falling into native-language habits of pronunciation, intonation, and interpretation. He must never be allowed to read alone a script which he has not learned orally first or else heard a number of times, which he has not repeated orally after the teacher or, if he is reading silently, which he is not hearing simultaneously read by a model.

The introduction of reading permits the introduction of carefully controlled writing exercises. These two reinforce each other and consolidate the aural-oral learning. The teaching of the four skills concurrently, with greatest emphasis on practice in listening and speaking in the early stages, provides for greater variety of classroom activity for both teacher and student and enables the teacher to move freely through the complete sequence: from listening to speaking, to reading, to writing, at all stages of the program.

Reading is sometimes referred to as a passive skill, but if we examine the abilities to be developed for fluent direct reading with comprehension of meaning we shall see that the reader is far from passive during this activity. He must be able to recognize sound patterns represented by the graphic symbols and identify their combinations as language units already learned. He must be able to recognize structural clues: the indicators of word classes and of persons and tenses of the verb; the words which introduce phrases and clauses and the particular modifications of meaning they indicate; the adverbs and adverbial expressions which limit the action in time, place, and manner; and the indicators of interrogation and negation. He must be able to distinguish with ease word groupings and their relationships with other word groupings. As he takes in these various clues at a glance he must be able to anticipate what probably follows while holding in his immediate memory inconclusive elements from what precedes. All of this activity is recognition of the language code in its graphic form. These reactions must be trained to such a degree that they occur almost automatically. The mind is then free to assimilate the message being communicated by the interrelationships in the coding, and to deduce from the context the meaning of un-familiar elements through their relationship to the whole message. This process is a most difficult one for the foreign-language student. It is made even more difficult when he is pre-sented with reading material containing many items with which he is not very familiar in their oral form. The first step to fluent reading is the oral mastery of language forms which the student subsequently learns to recognize in the printed script.

In many schools reading of foreign-language texts, in and out of class, has been the main feature of language classes for years, yet, with rare exceptions, direct and fluent independent reading on the part of the students does not seem to have been the ultimate product. What is needed is a carefully designed program of developmental stages,[5] at each of which the student is trained in certain aspects of reading so that he gradually acquires sufficient skill to be able to continue on his own, without returning to laborious deciphering. If the student is to be given thorough training in a progressive acquisition of skill, reading material for each stage must be selected with the aims of that particular stage of mind. Six stages will be described in detail. Students will need to pass through each stage in succes-sion; jumping a stage will lead to regression rather than to accelerated progress.

STAGE ONE OF READING TRAINING

The first stage in learning to read the foreign language has been carefully studied by the proponents of the audio-lingual method. They propose the memorizing of basic dialogue sen-tences, followed by practice in reading these memorized sen-tences in graphic form. This reading should at first be choral,

5 See G. A. Scherer, "Programming Second Language Reading," in G. Mathieu, ed., *Advances in the Teaching of Modern Languages,* vol. 2 (London, 1966), originally published 1964.

the class reading after the teacher or model; then comes unison reading in smaller groups (the group memory helping the individual student to avoid the pitfalls of unfamiliar sound-spelling combinations). After a successful period of unison reading, individuals may be called upon to read. As with small children learning to read their native language, it is essential with the reading of memorized material to ensure that the student is actually reading from the text, and not merely repeating the sentences by heart upon recognition of initial words or phrases. The teacher may ascertain whether students are reading, rather than reciting, by pointing to particular words on a chart of dialogue sentences and calling upon individuals to read them.

The student must become familiar at this first stage with the conventional representation of the phonemes of the foreign language in graphic form. Where a completely unfamiliar script is involved, some teachers prefer to use a romanized script at first so that students will not be deprived of a visual prop during the period of establishing a basic foreign-language repertoire. The unfamiliar script is introduced later when students are able to recognize with reasonable ease the phrases it represents. Where the script differs only in the use of a limited number of symbols, or where there is a one-to-one equivalence between phoneme and symbol, there is no need to delay its introduction any longer than for a familiar script.

Some methodologists advocate direct teaching of sound-symbol relationships quite early in the study of the foreign language. Explanations of the relationships are followed by reading and writing drills on specific sound-spelling combinations. Spot dictation is also useful; in this procedure the teacher reads a short sentence to the class, asking the students to write down a particular word in the sentence which exemplifies the rule under study. For a systematic study of sound-symbol relationships it is sometimes necessary to introduce into the spelling drills words which have not yet been encountered in oral work. Where the relationship constitutes a simple, one-to-one equivalence, the occasional introduction of a new word is not unduly demanding for the student, as most of the material in the drills and exercises is very familiar to him. In languages where the sound-spelling relationship is a complicated one (with perhaps as many as four or five possible spellings for one phoneme) a thoroughly systematic study can be time-consuming and confusing. The learning of all the possible relationships may appear to the student an abstract task unrelated to the more serious business of the learning of living and usable language. With older students such a study may be accepted as an orderly approach to an inescapable problem, but younger students of junior high school age can well learn these relationships incidentally and inductively as part of the ongoing language program.

If the problem is to be approached inductively, students will be oriented from their first contact with the text to observe sound-spelling relationships, watching particularly for variations from the anticipated pattern, and listening for mistakes in interpretation on the part of their fellows. As these variations and slips are noted, the basic relationships between sound and symbol can be briefly analyzed and identified. When a number of words of similar sound have been learned, these may be studied in close association by writing on the board some of the sentences in which they have occurred. The students themselves will supply the sentences, continuing until they feel the list is representative of the various spellings they have encountered for a particular sound. After the different spellings have been highlighted in this way, the students may practice reading these sentences with careful attention to the correct pronunciation of the sound under study. Students may then copy the sentences into their books, adding to the list as more examples accumulate. At intervals students may be asked to reread their lists with the new examples which have been added to them. As time goes on it will be found that all the important sound-symbol combinations have gradually been studied, but in order of frequency of occurrence rather than in some artificial, albeit systematic, fashion. As students read their lists aloud, each sound-symbol training session becomes also a review of pronunciation.

STAGE TWO OF READING TRAINING

At the second stage the students read memorized material in rearrangements and recombinations. The students may read pattern drills which have been developed from dialogue material, or recombination narratives and conversations. At this stage a limited number of new lexical items and some slight adaptations of structure may be introduced to give the students elementary practice in deduction of meaning from context. Where the students have been encouraged to write their own recombinations, keeping strictly within the limits of what they have learned thoroughly, the corrected scripts may be distributed to provide practice in reading for other members of the class. Since these recombination passages are being used as training material for the establishing of efficient reading habits, unfamiliar words or spelling combinations which will cause difficulty will be carefully prepared beforehand, either directly preceding the reading practice or by inclusion in the work of a preceding lesson. The passages will then be read or dramatized for the class by the teacher or by a tape model, and the students will read them after the teacher or model several times to ensure that they will not make mistakes when left to read on their own. The recombination passages will then be discussed orally, the teacher asking questions which the students do not see, or which they can later read in their books. After this oral discussion of subject matter, the students will reread the passage as correctly and expressively as they can. Since the aim at this stage is to ensure correct production of sounds to correspond with the written script, such passages will not be assigned for home- or private-study reading, or for individual reading or dramatization in the classroom, until they have been thoroughly prepared under the teacher's guidance.

At this stage the student must be taught to read in word groups. Fundamentally this means thinking in word groups. The student must be trained to look ahead and recognize sections of the thought as it develops (what Nida has called "meaningful mouthfuls" [6]). In a dialogue approach, this orientation will be developed with the learning of word groups or phrases as wholes in the mimicry-memorization work. In a text where dialogues are not used, the teacher will train the students to repeat the text after him in coherent word groups. In all oral drill in the classroom, whether pronunciation or pat-

6   E. A. Nida, *Toward a Science of Translating* (Leiden, 1964), p. 128.

tern practice, the teacher must take care to see that the students are, on all occasions, repeating meaningful segments. Where a backward-buildup technique is employed (as described in chapter 7), this principle must also be observed. When, later, in the recombination passages, the student encounters these same constructions in a new guise (with variation in lexical content and in perhaps a different position in the sentence), he must be encouraged to read them as groups of words which have an essential relationship and whose juxtaposition represents a single thought.

In native-language reading fluent readers look ahead to the next word group and relate it to what preceded before reading it aloud. This determines the stress and intonation patterns they will use. It is more difficult to do this with a foreign-language text unless the material of which it is composed is very familiar. Students therefore need much practice in reading in "meaningful mouthfuls," never producing orally a new segment until they have identified the word grouping to which it belongs. With recombination conversations or dialogues, a moment to set the scene—to outline briefly the general development of thought or action—will help the student, when reading, to anticipate what probably follows, and so to identify more confidently the next word group. Careful attention to this particular problem from the beginning of reading training is essential if habits which are basic to fluent reading are to be established.

Where the teacher is using a text which has not been constructed on audio-lingual principles, he will prepare the students carefully before expecting them to read passages in the book. He will first give adequate oral practice in the use of vocabulary items and structures before students meet these in the text; he will then ensure that students have a great deal of practice in reading after him or after a model before they essay the reading on their own. He will see that the students have some idea of what they are going to read about, so that they may be helped in anticipation of meaning. Finally he will see that, from the beginning, students are thoroughly trained to read only in word groups and to identify a whole group before they begin to articulate it.

At the second stage, as in the first stage, we are building in habits which are going to determine the approach of our students to foreign-language reading for many years to come. Sometimes there is a tendency to underestimate the amount of training in reading the students need. We do not read fluently what we cannot say aloud with ease. Students should be given the opportunity for frequent reading aloud of very familiar material: earlier dialogues, conversations, and reading passages. This is the type of practice they had in their native language during years of elementary school study. If students are encouraged to compete in groups in acting out conversations and dramatizing reading passages, they will happily read and reread the same material many times, striving to bring out the meaning for their classmates, without experiencing any boredom or tedium.

The problem of choosing a suitable textbook is discussed in chapter 14. If the text in use does not provide recombinations of familiar material or repetitive matter for reading practice in the early stages it should be changed, unless the teacher is prepared to write such recombinations himself for distribution to his class. Without training at this second stage, students will be rushed into attempting to read material which they cannot hope to recognize as a symbolization of something they have learned orally, and they will be well on the way to becoming decipherers, not readers. In their anxiety to hasten the day when their students can read on their own, well-meaning teachers often destroy the developing direct-reading habits of their better students by putting into their hands supplementary readers, simple enough in content, but containing different vocabulary, structure, and even tense forms, from those which the students have learned and practiced in class. Students should not be presented with reading material which is other than a clever recombination of known elements, with a few easily identifiable novelties, until the teacher is reasonably confident that their knowledge of the language is sufficient for them to read most of it without recourse to a dictionary.

STAGE THREE OF READING TRAINING

At the third stage the student may be introduced to more sustained reading under the guidance of the teacher. He is now being trained by the teacher to do without the teacher. While the class program of instruction in new areas of structure, vocabulary, and common expressions continues, the student will be introduced to the pleasure of reading simple narrative and conversational material which develops an uncomplicated but entertaining theme. Materials of this type, written for the most part by native speakers,[7] should be within the limits of vocabulary and structure already learned by the students, except for the gradual introduction of a limited number of unfamiliar lexical items, the meanings of which may reasonably be inferred from illustrations and context. These new items should be repeated often enough throughout the text for them to be assimilated by the reader.[8] Since the memory span for foreign-language material is shorter than for native-language material, the segments which students will be expected to hold in their immediate memory in order to follow the text easily should be somewhat shorter than in the native language. Because these reading materials will be used for practice in effortless direct reading, the degree of difficulty of the foreign-language expression should always be less than that of work being studied currently in the class textbook. If fluency in reading is to be the aim, the action described should be easy to follow without the student's being required to retain a great deal of detail in his mind as he proceeds.

There is some controversy among textbook writers whether simple reading matter of the kind appropriate to this stage should be written around familiar situations in the native culture or placed in the background of the foreign culture. If situations common to young people in both cultures are chosen, with a background of foreign ways and places, the material will be of greater interest to the student despite its simplicity. It will also provide an early introduction to the foreign culture, enabling the student to identify himself with people of his

7 When simple texts are written by nonnative authors, the material should always be checked by a native speaker for authentic expression. Many published texts show all too clearly that this simple precaution has not been taken. As a result, expressions no longer used in the country where the language is spoken continue to be learned by successive generations of language learners.

8 The subject of density of new words in graded or programmed reading material is discussed fully in Northeast Conference (1963), pp. 30–32.

own age and interests in the country where the language is spoken.

At the third stage the student needs practice in quick recognition of structural clues. As he tries to read in word groups without translation, he must develop the art of distinguishing immediately signs of tense, affirmation, negation, question, and exclamation; words which modify the meanings of other words; relationships of time and cause and effect; and conditional statements.

The student should not yet be left to read on his own. His habits of direct reading are still fragile, and as soon as he finds the material difficult he will certainly revert to deciphering and translation. He will, therefore, continue working with the help of the teacher. On the other hand, materials for this stage should be designed specifically for the development of efficient reading habits. They should not be used for grammatical instruction or for any form of intensive language study which will rob them of all interest; they should be kept for amusement and enjoyment. They will be read by students and teacher together in class. Sometimes the teacher will begin with a short preparation of the general vocabulary or background area, or with an introduction to the story in the native language to excite the interest of the students in what follows. Sometimes part of the story will be read in unison by the class after the teacher; sometimes sections will be read silently while students look for answers to questions on matters of fact; sometimes roles will be read by students, with a narrator for intervening description or explanation, or parts of the story will be dramatized by students in front of the class. After class treatment of the material, students will be in a position to reread it as a whole with confidence. For this final exercise, three techniques are suggested: the class may reread the complete story silently as the teacher reads it aloud; the class may listen, with books closed, to a rereading of the story by the teacher; or the students may be encouraged to reread the story silently in a certain space of time to encourage them to concentrate on the flow of the narrative.

Many modern textbooks supply extra reading material of this type within their pages or in supplementary readers constructed for use with the textbook. Where this is not the case, the teacher will need to search for easy readers within a similar frequency word count to that used by the textbook writer. The development of good reading habits is dependent on the teacher's prescribing only readers which are simple enough in expression for the student to follow them without too much thought and effort. Unless such material can be found it is preferable to keep the student at Stage Two for a longer period for consolidation of reading habits rather than to force him prematurely into reading material beyond his stage of development.

STAGE FOUR OF READING TRAINING

At the fourth stage the student's reading activities may be classed as intensive and extensive: intensive reading being related to further progress in language learning under the teacher's guidance, extensive reading developing at the student's own pace according to his individual ability. Intensive reading, at this stage, will still provide a basis for elucidation of difficulties of structure, and for the extension of areas of vocabulary. It will also provide material for developing greater control of language in speech and writing. Students will study short stories and extracts from novels, chosen for the standard of difficulty of language and for the interest they hold for young people still at school. Since this reading matter will be studied in considerable detail, it will not serve as the ideal vehicle for further practice in direct reading. This purpose will be served by the material chosen for extensive reading.

Material for extensive reading will be selected at a lower standard of difficulty than that for intensive reading. Where frequency word counts are available for the language being learned, extensive readers will conform to a lower level of the word count than the readers for intensive study. The purpose of the extensive reading program will be to train the student to read directly and fluently in the foreign language for his own enjoyment, without the aid of the teacher. Structures in the text will be already familiar to him, and new vocabulary will be introduced slowly in such a way that its meaning can be deduced from the context or quickly ascertained. The student will be encouraged to make intelligent guesses at the meaning of unfamiliar items. For this reason, extensive readers will not contain end-vocabularies with glosses in the native language. Some words may be explained in the foreign language in footnotes, and a monolingual foreign-language dictionary will be available on the teacher's table for consultation. This will discourage the students from seeking native-language equivalents for every unfamiliar element they encounter. The material for extensive reading will consist of authentic short stories and plays with certain adaptations of vocabulary and structure to bring them within the level of difficulty required, or of short stories and plays specially written for the purpose.

For the development of fluent reading, the student must be encouraged to read a great deal. This will only be possible if the subject matter of readers is of real interest to him and suitable for his age level. It must approximate as closely as possible the type of material the student would be interested in reading in his mother tongue. If he is at the age when adventure and excitement are important to him in his native-language reading, then he must find these elements in his foreign-language reading. The background should be of the culture of the foreign country with emphasis on present-day living; if the exotic and outlandish are stressed, the student will be unduly puzzled and bewildered by the behavior of the characters about whom he is reading and his ability to deduce meaning from context will be impeded. His mind must be kept leaping ahead and anticipating (as in native-language reading) so that he is distracted from the fact that he is reading in a foreign language, and finds he has been reading directly without having been conscious of it. The style of writing must be such that there is considerable repetition without monotony, and novelties of vocabulary, where these do occur, must not coincide with difficulties of structure. Readers chosen must be attractive in appearance with clear print, and the stories must divide naturally into sections which are not too long, so that the student has a sense of achievement as he reaches the end of a new section. These factors of physical arrangement of material may seem trivial, but they have a psychological importance in increasing the student's enjoyment in reading which must not be underestimated.

The student is now learning to read without the teacher's continual support and help. The teacher's role at this point is to interest the student in the reading matter and to be available for help and consultation. He may choose to introduce a particular story in class: preparing some difficulties, arousing interest in the subject matter, reading the first section with the students, and then allowing them to continue on their own at their own pace. He may allow them to read together in pairs, carefully matched for reading ability. He should certainly allow them to murmur to themselves as they read, since this helps some of the students in the recognition of what they are reading. Sometimes he will set questions beforehand for which they should find answers in the text. At other times, they will come to him as they finish a section to do a quick true-false or multiple-choice test to show that they have understood the script before them. These tests should be based on the important lines of development in the reading material, not on finicking details which test accuracy of memory rather than comprehension. As students show by their comprehension that they have successfully read a particular text they may be encouraged to move on to another, or to do supplementary reading in magazines and newspapers specially written for students of the language. These are freely available for some languages. Where they are not available, teachers' associations should work for their establishment. In some languages, magazines of this type are available at several levels of difficulty. Each student should be encouraged to read at the level at which he can do so with ease and with uninhibited enjoyment. If he or his teacher is overambitious in this regard, his steady acquisition of reading skill will be greatly hindered and he will become satisfied with deciphering for meaning.

Some teachers become concerned because their students, when reading in this way, are not conscious at all times of the exact meaning of every item in each sentence. They forget that such close attention to detail is not necessarily a feature of native-language reading when a person is reading for his own pleasure and not seeking for accurate and detailed information. Children, especially, gain much practice in reading in the native language with books containing many words and expressions with which they are not familiar and which they do not stop to identify precisely. By encountering these words in varying contexts on a number of occasions they do, however, come to class them sufficiently to feel at home with them when they meet them again, and eventually they are able to use them actively with a precise denotation. If students are being encouraged to develop habits of fluent reading in the foreign language a certain vagueness of this sort with some words must be accepted as part of the procedure. Under no circumstances must students be expected to stop whenever they meet a new or rather unfamiliar word and insert a native-language gloss between the lines; this habit must be consistently discouraged if they are to learn to think in the foreign language. On the other hand, students may be encouraged to increase their vocabulary by keeping individual notebooks in which they copy words they wish to remember. These should always be copied down in complete phrases or sentences, so that the students are continually reminded of the context in which these words would be appropriately used. This practice will be more frequently associated with the language-learning activities of intensive reading, but students may be encouraged, after completing an extensive reading assignment, to note down certain new words and expressions which they have marked in their books as being of greater frequency or of particular interest.

STAGE FIVE OF READING TRAINING

At Stage Four we have begun to wean the student from dependence on the teacher in the area of reading. At Stage Five, we expect this independence to be established, but we are more conscious than the student himself that he has been nurtured on artificial food and that he is not yet strong enough to eat of any meat that comes his way. For intensive and extensive reading, he will now be introduced to foreign-language material which has not been adapted in any way to make it more accessible to him. At most it will have undergone some judicious cutting, to eliminate sections of excessively difficult vocabulary or complicated structure. As at Stage Four, the principle will be respected that material selected for intensive reading (that is, as a basis for extension of active knowledge of the language) will be of a greater degree of difficulty than that recommended to the students for fluent reading at an individual pace for their own pleasure.

Intensive reading material will be the basis for a great part of the classroom activity. It will not only be read but discussed in detail in the foreign language, sometimes analyzed, and used as a basis for writing exercises. At this stage, some teachers fall into the monotonous pattern of setting a section of reading material for homework preparation every night; they then begin the lesson each day by asking students to translate what they have prepared, sentence by sentence, around the class. This becomes a tedious chore, completed in a purposeless way, and soon destroys any pleasure in the reading assignment. Teachers must work continually for variety of presentation in the classroom. Sometimes sections of intensive reading material may be set for preparation beforehand; sometimes they may be read by the students together in class while the subject is fresh and interesting. In either case, students must be trained to read whole sections for meaning before attempting to extract the details. In any well-knit writing, details cannot be extracted in linear fashion, and persons most fluent in a foreign language are often at a loss to find exact native-language equivalents for phrases until they have assimilated the meaning of a whole portion of the text. When students do need further help in ascertaining meaning, they should be trained to consult a monolingual foreign-language dictionary, so that they may find what the word really means to a native speaker, instead of being satisfied with the loose fit of a native-language gloss.

The ability of the students to talk and write in the foreign language about the material chosen for intensive reading will be very dependent on the teacher's choice of texts. If the material for study is distinctly harder than that at the fourth stage, if the vocabulary is complicated and esoteric with too many new items per page, if the subject matter is too abstract or highly descriptive, students will feel swamped, and will lose confidence in their ability to read a text directly without the support of the teacher or a dictionary.

This is not yet the stage for selecting texts because of their

historical significance in the development of the foreign literature. While the student is still at high school, the main purpose
of his reading assignments is the consolidation of his language
skills. At a later stage, when their specific areas of interest
have crystallized, some will wish to make a specialized study
of the foreign literature. At high school, the language class
should still contain those whose interests are primarily scientific, sociological, political, or artistic as well as those who are
interested in literature for its own sake. The literature chosen
for intensive study, then, should be predominantly contemporary, or at least twentieth-century in flavor. (This permits the
use of some writers of the nineteenth century whose attitudes
and language do not set a barrier between them and the
modern reader.) The material selected should parallel the type
of material the advanced high school student would enjoy in
his native language: short stories, short novels, plays, poems
where the theme is not too much obscured by experiments with
language, articles on scientific discoveries, artistic achievements, and aspects of contemporary community life in the
country where the language is spoken. Apart from their intrinsic interest for the twentieth-century adolescent, texts of this
nature will keep him in touch with contemporary turns of
speech and will consolidate the work of earlier years in preparing him to understand and be understood in a conversation
with a native speaker. It will be soon enough for him, when he
specializes at a higher level, to read the great works of the
seventeenth and eighteenth century. Indeed, if he has already
had a scrappy and superficial introduction to them at too early
a stage, his interest in them may well be dulled when he is
confronted with them again at a more appropriate level. If we
provide texts with outmoded vocabulary and syntax as the
basic element of the student's diet, we cannot blame him if he
assimilates these elements and speaks to us, and writes for us,
in the noble and outworn phrases of a former day.

One of the aims of the earlier stages of foreign-language
study has been to give the students insight, through their
language experiences, into the cultural attitudes and behavior
patterns of another people.[9] Many students begin their for-

9 For a full discussion of this subject, see chapter 11 on "Cultural
Understanding."

eign-language study with deep-rooted prejudices against the foreign people, based on derogatory stereotypes current in the community. If we choose, at this consolidating stage, material for study which is not contemporary, or at least reasonably close in ways of thinking to the twentieth century, if we choose material which is distinctively provincial, atypical, or subtly satirical, without making clear that these texts are of special historical, anthropological, or sociological significance, we will confirm the students in these stereotypes. Instead of developing a growing sympathy with his contemporaries and peers in another culture, the student will inevitably feel condescension and even contempt for people who seem to him so peculiar, even ridiculous, and obviously ill-adapted to the pressures and demands of our age.[10] Information about the foreign culture and its historical background can be imparted by the social studies or history teacher. Only in the foreign-language class can the student have an experience of the foreign culture by actually participating in an integral part of it, as he does when he reads directly in the language as a native speaker would do. This he can do with greater comprehension if he is brought into contact with that part of it which represents the spirit of his own century. Modern authors who are reflecting the strains and conflicts of our complex age will stimulate his thinking and make him eager to continue his reading beyond the minimum demands of his school program.

This emphasis on contemporary material of varied origins applies even more particularly to the student's extensive reading. The library should be well stocked with reading material, carefully selected for standard of difficulty but varied in subject matter. The teacher should now be able to recommend to each student extensive reading material which corresponds to his individual tastes and interests. Some students may pick up a novel or play of which they have heard, or which has recently been made into a film; others may be encouraged to undertake a course of reading in the foreign language related to some research topic of personal interest to them or required

10 The studies of W. Lambert and his colleagues at McGill University on the "Roles of Attitudes and Motivation in Second Language Learning" are of interest in this regard. These studies are described in Rivers (1964), pp. 140–42.

for another course. A standard encyclopedia in the foreign language, and some serious magazines, kept on file from year to year, will provide much reference material of this type. In this way, habits of using the language for one's own purposes will be fostered, and continue, we may hope, as a source of pleasure and profit after the students have left the classroom. A student who leaves school without having had the experience of reading on his own and enjoying foreign-language material of his own choice is ill-prepared to do so, without prompting, in later life.

Such reading can be made the basis for oral reports to the rest of the class, or short written compositions in which the student answers some specific questions related to the material in the book and the problems it involves. The class may, on occasions, be divided into groups to read interrelated material. Each group may prepare some part of a project on some aspect of the culture and present a group report to the rest of the class. In this way all the members of the class share in what each group has learned from its reading research. This type of class project gives point and purpose to extensive reading. No matter how the teacher organizes the extensive reading program, he should be careful to keep some record of it for grading purposes, so that the students will feel they are getting some credit for the effort they are making. The student will soon set a low priority for any activity which he feels rates low in importance in the mind of the teacher.

For supplementary reading the library should keep a plentiful supply of foreign-language magazines of a popular and readable type; these should be on display and easily accessible to the student with a few minutes to spare. In such magazines, the student will read about similar matters to those he is encountering in his favorite native-language magazines. Pictures and well-designed advertisements will lead him on to read more foreign-language material than he realizes or had intended.

STAGE SIX

The student leaving high school would, it is to be hoped, be able to move into Stage Six of reading development whether he continued his studies of the foreign language or not. At this stage, he should feel confident enough to pick up a book, magazine, or newspaper and read it for his own pleasure and enlightenment, with only occasional resort to a dictionary. This he will not feel tempted to do if he has not been trained during his foreign-language course to read on his own with ever increasing confidence and direct comprehension.

AREAS OF CONTROVERSY

Is reading literature in the original language in which it was written preferable to reading it in translation?

Many teachers when asked why they believe students should study a foreign language will reply that they wish their students to have the experience of reading the literature of another people in the original: not only the belles-lettres, but newspapers, magazines, and books of general interest. They believe that reading literature in the original language will give their students the opportunity to penetrate, to some extent, the thought processes of another people and, through experience of their ways of expressing themselves, to share some part of the heritage of their culture.

This is a very worthy aim. We may, however, ask ourselves whether this is in fact the experience that most foreign-language students have in the area of reading. In classes where the reading skill is not taught carefully through the various stages of development outlined in this chapter, students are forced too soon into attempting to read advanced foreign-language texts. Even though these books may contain material which should be of interest to the students, it is very frequently expressed in language which they cannot possibly understand without help. The students are thus forced into an activity which can only be for them a dreary task: the laborious deciphering of words and expressions with the help of a dictionary. All their attention is devoted to this time-consuming activity, so that the most they gain from the experience is a certain amount of information of which they retain the minimum that is necessary for the comprehension of the central theme.

If the students' only acquaintance with a foreign literature is acquired in this way, by a wearisome process of word-by-word translation, it is very probable that they would acquire much more appreciation of the literary qualities of a particular work, and much more favorable attitudes to the foreign culture and the ways of thinking of the foreign people, from the reading of a well-written translation, with the teacher at hand to add thoughtful words of explanation and elucidation.

This is not to say that the reading of a translation has as much to give the reader as the reading of a work in its original language form. The original will not, however, give the student more than he will get from a good translation unless he has been trained to read fluently and to assimilate meaning directly from the text, without reverting at every step to his native language. A program such as the one just outlined will make the foreign literature accessible eventually to the student who continues with his study of the language until he has reached Stage Six. He will then profit from his reading of the originals more than from reading translations. In the meantime, as he passes through the various earlier stages, he will find the reading of carefully constructed or graded foreign-language texts a pleasant and rewarding activity: this in itself is important if he is to persist in his efforts toward mastery in this skill area.

ANNOTATED READING LIST

NORTHEAST CONFERENCE (1963). *Language Learning: The Intermediate Phase,* edited by w. f. BOTTIGLIA. Report of Working Committee II, "Reading for Meaning" (pp. 22–60), discusses fully the process of moving from recognition of the graphic equivalent of material thoroughly learned to reading unadapted material for pleasure. Also discusses programming of materials for reading to ensure a progressive development of the skill.

SCHERER, G. A. "Programming Second Language Reading." Chapter 5 of *Advances in the Teaching of Modern Languages,* vol. 2, edited by G. MATHIEU. London: Pergamon Press, 1966. Pp. 108–29. Originally published in the *Teacher's Notebook,* Spring 1964. New York: Harcourt, Brace & World. An important article on the mechanics of programming materials for foreign-language reading. Very useful as a guide to the teacher when choosing reading texts for various levels. Discusses briefly the six stages in the development of the reading skill.

NORTHEAST CONFERENCE (1967). *Foreign Languages: Reading, Literature, and Requirements,* edited by T. E. BIRD. Report of Working Committee I, "The Teaching of Reading" (pp. 7–50), discusses the teaching of new grammar and vocabulary in association with reading materials, and suggests audio-lingual exercises to accompany advanced reading. Discusses also frequency lists for French and German. Report of Working Committee II, "The Times and Places for Literature" (pp. 51–102), discusses the place of literature in the language-learning program.

FRIES, C. C. *Linguistics and Reading.* New York: Holt, Rinehart & Winston, 1963. Chapters 2 and 3 analyze the relationship between language meanings and language signals and discuss the processes involved in the act of reading.

RIVERS, W. M. *The Psychologist and the Foreign-Language Teacher.* Chicago: University of Chicago Press, 1964. Chapter 10 examines the psychological questions involved in withholding the written script in the early stages of foreign-language learning.

MODERN LANGUAGE ASSOCIATION OF AMERICA. *Reports of Surveys and Studies in the Teaching of Modern Foreign Languages.* New York: M.L.A., 1962. Section 15, "Good Teaching Practices" by L. Brisley *et al.* (pp. 232–33), describes a number of techniques for bringing variety into reading lessons in the classroom.

10

The Writing Skill

Writing has for many years, even centuries, occupied a large place in teaching and learning procedures in schools. To be literate has implied the ability to read and write in the native language, and it is these skills which students have practiced in class. This approach to native-language learning has easily transferred to the foreign-language classroom, without too much thought given to its appropriateness or inappropriateness in a situation where the student does not have the spoken form of the language already at his command. Writing exercises keep students busy and out of mischief. They are easy to set; the inexperienced or poorly qualified teacher may take them directly from the textbook, with which a key to acceptable answers is usually provided; they may often be corrected as a group procedure in the classroom; and they yield a wide spread of evaluative grades for entry in the teacher's records. With so much writing in foreign-language classes over so many years, one would expect to find that this is the skill for which effective methods have long since been evolved and with which the students have the most success. Unfortunately, examination papers in composition the world over are, with few exceptions, disappointing, and teachers of advanced courses in colleges and universities continue to deplore the inability of students with four, five, and even six, years of secondary school study of the language behind them to express themselves in a clear, correct, and comprehensible manner in writing. We would do well to examine critically the role of writing in foreign-language learning at high school level, to analyze wha is involved in the process of writing a foreign language, and to trace out the steps by which this skill can be progressively mastered.

Before we consider what is the most reasonable role for writing in the foreign-language program, it is as well to recall two facts often ignored by teachers who, by tradition, tend to expect students to write something out as a demonstration of learning: first, that many highly articulate persons express themselves very inadequately in writing in their native language and, second, that only a minority of the speakers of any language acquire the skill of writing it with any degree of finesse, and then only after years of training in school and practice out of school. The vast majority of students will never be required to write the foreign language for anything but the most straightforward of purposes: in letters, memoranda, perhaps short reports. Only at undergraduate or graduate level will they attempt essays in the foreign language, and even for these their tutors will bless them if they can write accurately and idiomatically, without attempting flights of fancy or a literary style which is beyond their capacity. It is in listening comprehension and reading that students need to reach the highest degree of skill, because in these two areas they will have no control over the complexity of the material they encounter. In speaking and writing, the foreigner rarely achieves the same degree of mastery as a native speaker, even after the experience of residence in the foreign country; he needs to be able to use what he does know accurately and flexibly, making the most of the resources at his command.

This does not mean to say that writing has little to contribute to foreign-language learning. Apart from its intrinsic interest or value, it is an essential classroom activity. As we shall see, it is of considerable importance for consolidating learning in the other skill areas, it provides a welcome change of activity, and it will always remain useful, although not indispensable, in the area of testing. It should, however, be considered the handmaid of the other skills and not take precedence as the major skill to be developed.

Traditionally, writing activities in foreign-language classes have taken the form of the writing out of paradigms and grammatical exercises, dictation, translation from native language to foreign language and from foreign language to native language, and imitative and free composition. These exercises have often been the only sections of language study tested in examinations and have therefore become, in the eyes of students and teachers alike, the most important occupations in the foreign-language classroom. The acquiring of a high degree of skill in any of these activities, with the exception of free composition in which few students do reach high standards, can hardly be considered a sufficient aim in itself. It will be readily admitted that the taking of dictation and the writing of grammatical exercises and paradigms are means, rather than ends, and that skill in these intermediate activities does not necessarily reflect ability to comprehend and communicate. Nor can the ubiquitous translation exercises be considered ends in themselves. Few of our students become professional translators, and those who wish to do so would be well advised to pursue specialized courses in the art of translation at a later date. For the rest of our students, continual emphasis on translation inculcates the naïve belief that languages have a basic one-to-one equivalence which they must identify, with the dictionary as their indispensable tool. This attitude of mind, once established, hinders the forging of direct links between meaning and foreign-language expression, a process which is essential for rapid comprehension of oral and written communication, for fluent speaking, and for idiomatic writing. This is not to say that these types of exercises may not have some place in foreign-language teaching, but the value of each must be considered in relation to the whole program of development of the language skills.

Up to this point in our discussion the term "writing" has been used, without definition, to refer to several activities which are obviously quite distinct in the demands they make upon the writer. Before attempting to establish the role of writing in the foreign-language classroom, we must identify clearly these various kinds of writing. In its simplest form writing can be the act of putting down in conventional graphic form something which has been spoken. This act may involve nothing more than the correct association of conventional graphic symbols with sounds which have for the writer no meaning and no significant interrelationships. This form of writing we may call *notation*. This process is sometimes useful

when specific sound-symbol conventions are under consideration, or when the student is being asked to discriminate among
various sounds. If recognizable units of the foreign language
are involved, the process may be called *spelling*. Writing becomes a more complicated process when it involves putting in
graphic form, according to the system accepted by educated
native speakers, combinations of words which might be spoken
in specific circumstances (that is, which convey certain elements of meaning). This is the type of writing which is involved in grammatical exercises, the construction of simple
dialogues, and uncomplicated translation exercises. This activity we may call *writing practice*. In its most highly developed
form, writing refers to the expression of ideas in a consecutive
way, according to the graphic conventions of the language; the
ultimate aim of a writer at this stage is to be able to express
himself in a polished literary form which requires the utilization of a special vocabulary and certain refinements of structure. This we shall call *composition*.

In high school classes, all of these stages of writing have
some place, although most of our students will only approach
composition at an elementary level. With the time at our
disposal we will concentrate on giving them training and practice in writing down what they would say, with some attention
to the differences between the conventions for spoken and
written style. At the more advanced level we will encourage
them to express themselves with some finese in oral discussion
of a more significant subject, and then to write their ideas,
with careful attention to lexical and structural choice.

Skill in writing in an elegant fashion, according to the
canons of an educated elite, is an aim impossible of realization
at the high school stage and demands a mastery of the foreign
language which many high school teachers themselves do not
possess.

The distinctions we have drawn among types of writing
activities reflect the four major areas of learning involved in
the writing process. The student must learn the graphic system
of the foreign language; he must learn to spell according to the
conventions of the language; he must learn to control the
structure of the language so that what he writes is comprehensible to his reader; and he must learn to select from among
possible combinations of words and phrases those which will

convey, the nuances he has in mind in the register which is most appropriate. The first three of these processes must be learned so thoroughly that they no longer require the concentrated attention of the writer, who may then give his mind to the process of selection among possible combinations.

Writing is not, then, a skill which can be learned in isolation. In the apprentice stage of writing, which will last for a considerable time, what the student must learn, apart from the peculiar difficulties of spelling or script, is a counterpart of what he has to learn for the mastery of listening comprehension, speaking, and reading, with the activity of writing helping to consolidate learning in these areas. Writing gives the student practice in manipulating structural variants, adding the reinforcement of the kinesthetic image to the auditory and visual. It is recognized by reading experts as a desirable complementary activity to reading. By drawing attention to the form of words and phrases writing helps the student to distinguish one from the other and to build up a memory of the graphic forms and their associations which facilitates the reading process.[1] In its more advanced form of composition, it is itself dependent on progress in the other skills. Accurate and idiomatic writing is quite different from the mere piecing together of language elements in some artificial patchwork which would never be encountered outside the classroom. Only by hearing and reading a great deal of the language as it is spoken and written by native speakers can the foreigner acquire that feeling for the appropriate use of language forms and combinations which is basic to expressive writing. What he is unable to say over to himself, he will be unlikely to write with ease, and until he has read a great deal he will not be familiar with the way native speakers express themselves, for all kinds of purposes, in writing.

It is obvious, then, that the most effective writing practice, and the most generally useful, will have a close connection with what is being practiced in relation to other skills. Writing practice will at first be a service activity, consolidat-

---

1   See W. S. Gray, *The Teaching of Reading and Writing,* Monographs on Fundamental Education 10 (Paris: UNESCO, 1956); discussed in *Aspects of Reading in the Primary School,* a Review of Research by E. M. Bannan *et al.* (Melbourne, Australia: Australian Council for Educational Research, 1964), p. 50.

ing work in the other areas; yet, while the student is using it to reinforce other learning, he will be mastering the technical details of the art. The higher levels of composition will be possible only when the student has attained a high degree of mastery of the other skills. It will be well for the teacher to keep in mind that some will never reach a high standard in composition in the foreign language, just as they have not attained it in the native language. These students should not be driven into a state of frustration by examinations heavily weighted in favor of the writing skill when it is obvious that they have achieved a satisfactory mastery of the skills of listening comprehension, speaking, and reading.

Many writing weaknesses in advanced classes can be traced back to lack of systematic training during the earlier stages of the foreign-language course. Often students in elementary classes are encouraged to try their hand at creative writing in the foreign language for fun, while the teacher turns a blind eye to the monstrosities they perpetrate. Students develop the habit of attempting to express themselves in strange words, often sought out in an inept way in a dictionary, before they have any satisfactory control of language structure. Believing that they are writing acceptably, they contrive expressions on the pattern of native-language forms, happily constructing hybrid phrases without realizing that they are quite incomprehensible in the context of the foreign language. To be able to write in the foreign language the student must be trained systematically through five stages of development: copying, reproduction, recombination, guided writing, and composition. These stages will overlap, practice of the activities of the previous stages continuing as more complicated work is introduced.

COPYING

The first stage, copying (sometimes called transcription), is often despised by foreign-language teachers as an unworthy and unchallenging occupation for adolescent students. This attitude is unfortunate and ignores the fact that there are many aspects of another language which are very strange to the student and with which he needs to familiarize himself very thoroughly if he is to write the language confidently. Where there is a new script to be learned this attitude is not so prevalent, because the necessity for accurate copying for purposes of recognition and reproduction is too obvious to be ignored. Where the script is the same as in the native language, and where there are many similarities between the two languages, careful copying helps to overcome the interference of native-language habits by focusing the student's attention on the differences. The work set for copying should consist of sections of work already learned orally and read with the teacher. As the student is copying, he should repeat to himself what he is writing. In this way he deepens the impression in his mind of the sounds the symbols represent, and he has further repetition practice of basic dialogue or pattern sentences. After he has had some practice in copying accurately, with correct diacritical and punctuation marks, he may continue to copy as an aid to memorization. At this stage, he repeats a sentence to himself as he copies it, and then tries to say it over to himself two or three times without referring to the script.

In languages where sound-symbol combinations are particularly complicated, copying activities may be continued side by side with more advanced writing practice. Students who have made lists of sentences containing different spellings of the same sounds may copy these lists several times, concentrating on the variations in spelling. If they are assigned lists of words to be learned because of peculiarities of orthography, they may be asked to copy the words several times as they are learning them, thus imprinting the graphic outlines more firmly in their minds. In the early stages credit should be given for accuracy in copying in order to encourage students in careful observation of details.

REPRODUCTION

During the second, or reproduction, stage the student will attempt to write, without originality, what he has learned orally and read in his textbook. This he will be able to do all the more successfully if he has been trained in habits of accuracy during the copying stage. If sound writing habits are to be firmly established, the learning situation must be continually structured so that the students will write correctly, not incorrectly. For this reason the student will at first be asked to reproduce without a copy only the sentences and phrases which he has learned to copy. As a first step he will be asked to rewrite immediately each sentence he has copied without reference to his copy or to the original. He will then compare this version with the original for correction. Next he will be asked to write down sentences he has memorized, read, and copied as they are dictated to him. When dictation procedures are employed it is as well for the teacher to realize that he is calling for the exercise of two skills at once: listening comprehension and writing. Since all the skills are finally integrated in language knowledge, this is not necessarily a disadvantage, but the teacher must be aware of the fact that he is requiring more of the student than a simple exercise in writing. Where particular difficulties of spelling are being emphasized, the spot-dictation procedure may be adopted: a complete sentence will be read, but only the word or words which are repeated will be written. Some teachers supply an outline with blanks to avoid confusion in spot-dictation exercises.

At a further stage the teacher will call for the writing of a learned phrase as a response to a question he is asking, or as a description of a picture he is showing. Here he is requiring a clear understanding of meaning, and memory for learned response, as well as ability to distinguish aurally and write accurately. Further practice in reproduction may take the form of the writing of pattern-drill responses of the repetitive type, as a variation from the oral repetition or reading of these. Where audio-lingual texts are not in use, the students will be asked to reproduce, at a cue from the teacher, pattern sentences which have been practiced orally in classroom activities and studied in the textbook. In no circumstances, at this stage, will the writing activity on the part of the student require variation of learned phrases since the emphasis is entirely on accuracy of reproduction.

RECOMBINATION

The third stage is the recombination stage, where the student is required to reproduce learned work with minor adaptations.

This parallels in conception the recombination stage in oral work and reading. It must, however, be continually borne in mind that the work for recombination in writing will always be some distance behind what is being spoken and read. The writing of recombinations of learned sentences requires not only the ability to manipulate grammatical structures, which is basic to the speaking skill, but also a sound knowledge of the intricacies of representing graphically what the student is required only to recognize in reading. More effective results will be achieved in writing exercises if there is a continual integration of practice in all the skills. The student will have already heard, produced orally, and read in his textbook recombinations of the type he will write. Only when the teacher is confident that the student can say over to himself correctly what he is to write will he be asked to make recombinations himself. This is in conformity with the principle already enunciated of structuring the situation so that the student has the greatest possible chance of writing correctly.

At this stage, writing practice may take a number of forms. Students will write out structure drills of various kinds: making substitutions of words and phrases, transforming sentences, expanding them to include further information within the limits of learned phrases, contracting them by substituting pronouns for nouns or single words for groups of words. Many of the drills discussed in chapter 4 can be used in this way. The writing of drills not only gives valuable practice in accurate and correct construction of sentences but consolidates what has been learned orally. It is a useful home study exercise, ensuring that the student gives careful thought to work studied during the day in class. This becomes difficult where the textbook supplies all the responses to the drills. In such a case the teacher will need to construct drill cues of a similar type to give the students home study practice in recombination.

When students have acquired some confidence in writing simple substitutions and transformations, they may be asked to make recombinations around a theme presented to the class in a picture or a series of pictures. These pictures will, of course, represent situations in connection with which the students have learned phrases orally. The recombinations may take the form of variations of memorized dialogues which, after correction, may be acted out in the classroom. At first these recombinations will not involve any new vocabulary. Later they may provide an occasion for some expansion of vocabulary, carefully introduced orally and learned as a group exercise before being used in writing. At no point, however, will a student be required to make a recombination which involves a structural change and new vocabulary at the same time. The simple rule of one thing at a time will decrease the possibility of error and make for more effective learning. To further ensure correctness in writing, recombinations will first be constructed orally in class. Students will not be asked to write such recombinations unsupervised until they have had sufficient practice to ensure success. If written recombinations are kept together in a special section of their workbooks, in a progressive series, the students will take more interest in recording them accurately. If books are taken up and these writing sections checked and graded as part of the regular assessment, the students will be encouraged to take pride in well-written work.

An exercise which combines recombination and reproduction is recombination dictation. Dictations of this type will consist of rearrangements of dialogue sentences, or narratives constructed from the conversational material and pattern sentences. Since dictation involves ability to recognize recombinations aurally and retain them, as well as reproduce them graphically, such dictations must be constructed with great care to see that problems of aural recognition do not coincide with problems of graphic representation. Work to be written from dictation must contain no new elements, that is, no elements which have not already been practiced and learned thoroughly, studied in graphic form, and used in some kind of writing practice. The dictation will then serve as a form of review and the possibility of error will be reduced. The teacher should dictate at a normal speed of utterance, not distorting the phrases and the flow of speech in any way. Segments dictated should consist of meaningful word groups. Each phrase should be repeated clearly only once before students are expected to write it. Since some students become flustered when expected to retain what they have comprehended aurally long enough to write it accurately, students should be trained to repeat aloud what they have heard before attempting to write it from dictation, and then to repeat it over to themselves as they write it. This oral repetition helps them to retain what they have heard long enough for them to write the complete phrase. After they have had time to write the whole phrase, the same segment should be repeated to allow the students an opportunity to check what they have written and correct any inaccuracies. At the end of the dictation of the whole passage, time should be allowed for rechecking of accuracy of writing before the passage is reread a final time, with normal intonation and fluency. This period for checking forces each student to do some thinking for himself before the final reading, and makes him more alert to the sections of the final reading which he most needs to hear again. If the procedure outlined is adopted from the early stages of foreign-language learning, students will be trained to retain whole phrases in their immediate memory, and the dictation practice will be reinforcing the practice in listening comprehension as well as providing practice in accurate writing. As students advance in language learning, phrases dictated will be gradually lengthened, until the students are eventually able to retain complete sentences in their immediate memory and write them down correctly.

GUIDED WRITING

At the fourth stage, guided writing, the student will be given some freedom in the selection of lexical items and structural patterns for his written exercise, but within a framework which restrains him from attempting to compose at a level beyond his state of knowledge. He will begin with outlines which allow for some individuality, but which also help him to keep to what he has learned, and he will gradually move on to composition which is so closely associated with what he has read or heard that he has no choice but to restrict himself to the known. As his control of writing techniques increases he will be ready to move into the fifth stage, composition, where he may attempt to express his personal meaning in acceptable foreign-language expression.

At the guided writing stage the student may begin with

completion exercises where parts of sentences are given and the structural pattern is thus established for him. Each student will, however, be expected to construct an individual answer by his choice of a completion. Some types of drills provide useful guides at this stage. Replacement exercises may be devised in which a section of the sentence can be replaced by a number of different phrases, giving the student the opportunity to express new meanings. Expansion of a simple sentence by the addition of modifying words and phrases, or the inclusion of further information, can give practice in developing meanings within a framework. Along the lines of a substitution drill, the student may take a given sentence and see how many different meanings he can express by lexical changes, within the limits of the structure provided. Another form of outline supplies lexical items in a fixed order which forces the student to use certain grammatical structures. This restricts the semantic area within which the student may express himself but leaves him free to vary such elements as person, tense, and number.

As the student advances in skill, he may be allowed more freedom in his choice of expression. The framework will now come from stories and articles he has been reading. At this stage he will be learning something about the differences between the conventions for spoken and written style. He may answer questions on a text read or heard, the questions requiring more and more individuality of response as his skill in writing increases. He may write summaries of stories he has studied in class, heard in the laboratory, or enjoyed for extensive reading. He may rewrite a story, or a part of a story, from a different angle (this exercise may be designed so as to require a different tense; the story may be rewritten in the first person as told by one of the characters; or one of the characters may give explanations or explain the reactions of others, thus forcing the student into using indirect discourse). A story may be rewritten in dialogue form or a dialogue rewritten as a narration. The setting or main personalities of a story or dialogue may be changed in such a way as to require certain changes in the description, in the action, or in the tone of the conversational interchange. The skeleton of a story or dialogue may be supplied for development by the student, or an outline given for a description or narration based on a picture or a succession of pictures. As a variation of this procedure, a series of questions may be so constructed that the student writes a continuous narrative as he answers them. If pictures are used, the writing activity may be associated with intensive work in vocabulary building. With some imagination, the teacher will not be at a loss for finding ways of guiding the student in elementary composition.

Writing at this stage is still under supervision. The teacher takes care to see that the student does not lapse into the habit of writing native-language versions which he then translates inexpertly into the foreign language. Students work without bilingual dictionaries, endeavoring at every stage to use what they know or what they can learn from the model on which their guided writing is based. As at all stages in the developing of the writing skill, problems which may arise in the exercise are anticipated in oral group work so that students are sure before they proceed what is expected of them; most of their difficulties are thus overcome before they are left to their own resources. Until the students are thoroughly trained to rely on what they have learned, and to restrict themselves to the limits imposed by the outline or the text on which the writing is based, they will not be allowed to do the initial writing for homework. In an unsupervised situation they may only be permitted to rewrite or improve work which has been thoroughly prepared in class. These restrictions are essential if students are to be trained in good writing habits. Left to their own devices too soon, they will rush to the dictionary, attempt a standard of expression beyond their state of knowledge, and ruin the careful network of habits the teacher has been developing.

COMPOSITION

The final stage of composition involves individual selection of vocabulary and structure for the expression of personal meaning. In a foreign language, the student is still not capable of being truly creative in his writing at this level, since he must write as a native speaker would write, without having, as yet, the same mastery of the language in all its flexibility. His knowledge of the foreign language is still very inferior to his knowledge and control of his native language. If he has been carefully trained for a sufficiently long period through the preceding four stages, he will have developed an attitude of mind which will prevent him from committing the worst excesses of clothing native-language expressions and structures in foreign words. If asked to write on subjects which are too general, too philosophical, or too literary, however, he will be frustrated by his desire to write at the standard which is expected of him in native-language composition classes, at a stage when his resources of expression in the foreign language are still extremely limited. The key word for him to keep in the forefront of his thinking in this dilemma is "simplify." He must clothe his thoughts in simple, lucid language which is well within his command. With the systematic training we have advocated, he will not be tempted to write first in his native language and then translate, realizing that this can lead only to stilted foreign-language expression at the best and to absolute incomprehensibility at the worst. Encouraged to use a monolingual dictionary rather than a bilingual dictionary he will be forced to use what he knows, checking on its accuracy and examining the possibilities of suggested alternatives, rather than seeking inexact and misleading equivalents for notions he has not as yet encountered in his experience with the foreign language.

At this stage he will be increasing his understanding of the differences between speaking and writing a foreign language. Apart from conventional differences in style, he will be trying to express himself more concisely, more descriptively, less casually. This will severely test his control of structure and his precise understanding of lexical meaning. The composition stage provides teacher and student with the opportunity to identify persisting areas of misunderstanding on an individual basis, so that remedial practice may be undertaken where necessary.

When students have reached what is considered to be an advanced class the teacher will need to exercise great care to see that they are not plunged abruptly from guided writing into a limitless sea of free expression. The transition has to be gradual. Exercises in composition will at first be closely linked with material being read and discussed; the student will be asked merely to describe, narrate, and explain, or to summarize. As he becomes more accustomed to expressing himself within consciously accepted restrictions, he will be asked to comment on or develop ideas beyond those in the material read. While at high school he will not be expected to imitate styles of great writers but will concentrate on developing for himself a simple, lucid form of expression which would be acceptable to a native speaker. Nor will he be asked to write literary criticism or discuss ideas at a philosophical or sociological level. For these types of exercises he must possess a specialized vocabulary and a training in concepts which the high school teacher cannot aspire to give him, or can give him only at the expense of the further training in language skills to which class time should be devoted at this stage.

Not all students have a ready flow of ideas when asked to write, even in the native language. Composition exercises which are not closely related to intensive reading assignments should be so designed that they do not become tests of originality and invention. Precise descriptions of persons, places, and things provide excellent training in exact expression. The writing of an original dialogue, using the vocabulary area of some recent reading, keeps the student practiced in the style of speech. Further practice in a more casual style of writing is provided by the keeping of a personal diary in the foreign language and by the encouraging of international correspondence on an individual basis. In the latter case, students are appropriately instructed in the accepted formulas for letter writing. Students may have read to them, or be asked to read, parts of stories which they are then required to complete for themselves; in this way, they have already been initiated into the appropriate vocabulary area and level of language before they attempt to write on their own.

Composition exercises may very profitably be linked with assignments for extensive reading. As each book, story, or play is completed, the student is asked to submit, for correction and evaluation, a short composition based on it. This composition may consist of a summary of the contents with a personal commentary, or the narration of some aspect of the story assigned previously by the teacher. Such extensive reading assignments may direct the student to articles of a serious nature in current foreign-language magazines or newspapers. In this case it is better for the teacher to select the article, with due regard to the special interests of the student, to ensure that it is not too difficult in standard of expression and ideas. Otherwise, discouraged students will take little pleasure in what is planned as an interesting activity. Where foreign-language newspapers are freely available, the students may be asked to submit at regular intervals short accounts of items of news from the country where the language is spoken. These reports may also be given orally, thus providing subject matter for class discussion and further exercise in the speaking skill.

In classes where the students have been encouraged to undertake group or individual projects to deepen their understanding of the culture of the people who speak the language (as described in chapter 11), they will have valuable practice in composition as they draw up reports of their research in various areas (geography, history, sociology, art, music, education, political institutions, lives of famous men and women, and so on). For such projects the students should be required to draw their information from foreign-language sources so that they may use authentic forms of expression in their written and oral reports. They should be trained to submit short reports on sections of their research for correction at regular intervals, rather than one long report at the end. The teacher can then guide them in the progressive improvement of their writing efforts. These reports, like those on extensive reading, should also be given orally to the class and used as a basis for further discussion.

CORRECTION OF WRITTEN EXERCISES

Many experienced teachers will say: "This is fine. This is what we aim to do, but is it possible?" The practical problem is that systematic training in writing requires systematic correction of individual scripts if it is to be effective. This can impose an intolerable burden on the most willing teacher. Methods must be evolved which will give the most help to the student while making reasonable demands on the teacher.

Ideally, individual efforts at writing should be read by the teacher as soon as possible after completion, then corrected and sometimes rewritten by the student without delay. A great deal of uncorrected writing is merely a waste of time and energy. It consolidates the student's bad habits, which are very difficult to eradicate at a later date. Short writing assignments, given at frequent intervals and then carefully corrected and discussed, provide the most effective form of practice.

The following suggestions may be useful for the stage when students are launching out into the area of free expression in the foreign language. First, the students should be asked to write only one or two well-planned, carefully written paragraphs until they have acquired some skill in writing. The approximate number of words may even be stated, so that the more enthusiastic will not stretch their concept of a paragraph beyond reasonable limits. The teacher can cope with the correction of one or two paragraphs where complete compositions would take up far too much of his time. Second, from the very early stages of their writing experience students should be rigorously trained to study their own scripts systematically in order to eliminate as many errors as possible before submitting them for the teacher's perusal. Carelessly presented scripts should be refused and given back for rewriting. In this way the teacher will make a considerable saving in correction time, and the student will be given valuable training in habits of accuracy. Third, the teacher should anticipate certain common types of errors, by giving regular practice in class groups in the use of tenses, ways of combining clauses within sentences, and conventional phrases used for making smooth transitions in thought. Fourth, teacher and class should agree on some system of symbols for correction of compositions. Teachers waste much time writing in comments and suggested improvements on composition scripts. The student who peruses these in a cursory fashion gains little from the teacher's laborious effort. Correction time is reduced by underlining errors and using a letter symbol to indicate the type of mistake made, whether lexical, syntactical, morphological, or orthographical, with special attention to errors which would make the composition incomprehensible to a native speaker. The symbols should correspond to precise categories of errors, so that the student realizes quite clearly the type of correction he should make. When this system is used, the teacher returns the scripts to the students in class, allowing sufficient time for individual correction of mistakes under supervision and for discussion of the implications of the commonest faults. If class size permits it students may resubmit corrected versions for further checking. By making the students think through the errors they have made, the teacher will be using the compositions for teaching, and not merely for unsystematic practice or for constant testing. This system of correction also helps the teacher to evaluate the work more quickly and systematically. An overall intuitive grade for written composition can be seriously influenced by neatness and clear writing. The grade should be a composite one, allowing a certain percentage for grammatical accuracy, for lexical choice, for expression of time sequence, for general idiomaticity or feeling for authentic expression, and for arrangement of ideas. Where a symbol system is used, the teacher can more quickly assess the relative degree of error in the different areas. The emphasis given to each area will vary as students acquire more skill, so that at an advanced level ability to communicate ideas without native-language interference in structural and lexical choice will receive considerable weight.

HOW MUCH WRITING?

The listing of so many possible forms of written exercises may confuse the inexperienced teacher, who, having glimpsed the core of the problem (the thorough, graded training required if students are to be able to write well in the foreign language), may feel that writing practice should occupy a large part of the teaching time at his disposal. This would bring us back to the traditional situation of the silent classroom, disturbed only by the busy scribbling of pens on paper. Some people have tried to estimate the percentage of time which should be allotted to the various skills at different levels of instruction. In his first edition (1960) of *Language and Language Learning*, Brooks tried to set down such percentages, allotting 5 per cent of student time to writing at Level I, 10 per cent at Level II, and 20 per cent at Level III. Level IV, we are told, "differs little in general procedure from Level III." [2] It is interesting to note that calculations of this type are omitted from the second edition of the book (1964). Such precision of time allotment can be no more than suggestive.

What is clear is that writing is a skill which must be taught; it cannot develop haphazardly to any degree of usefulness. It is most efficiently acquired when writing practice parallels practice in the other skills. Writing provides an excellent consolidating activity. Through it the teacher can bring welcome variety into classroom work. It is also useful for setting homework exercises and for some of the class tests. It must not, however, be allowed to absorb time which should be devoted to aural-oral training and to further development of the reading skill. If, as has been suggested, it is considered a service activity rather than an end in itself, the teacher will find that the problem "how much writing" soon solves itself. The type of writing in which the students are engaged will become more sophisticated as students acquire greater facility in the exercise of the other skills.

AREAS OF CONTROVERSY

Should an absolute standard of accuracy be required in foreign-language writing exercises?

Accuracy in written exercises becomes a fetish with some teachers, to such an extent that it distorts their assessment of the relative merits of the written assignments of students. Often teachers demand of their students a standard of accuracy in writing which many educated native speakers of the foreign language do not display. Many students who are the pride of their teachers in creative writing classes in their native language are notoriously careless about details of their writing. (It is significant that publishing houses have to em-

2 N. Brooks, *Language and Language Learning* (New York, 1960). pp. 122–32.

ploy copy editors to revise the scripts submitted by some university professors and professional writers.) It is obvious, then, that skill in writing consists of something more than mere accuracy.

If the teacher takes accuracy as his main criterion the following anomalous situation may well arise. Student A writes an excellent composition in the foreign language, one which a native speaker would comprehend and enjoy. It has an idiomatic flavor, the structural patterns are varied, lexical items have been selected with a feeling for nuance of meaning. He is, however, careless. He has misspelled some words and has left out a number of accent marks and inflectional elements which are not pronounced in speech, but which must be added in a written script. In a few cases where there are several possible sound-symbol combinations, he has chosen the wrong one, although it is obvious that he knows how the words are pronounced. In accordance with the teacher's "one mark off for each mistake" system, he receives a very low grade for his composition.

Student B, on the other hand, is meticulous and careful. His composition contains only a few common structural patterns, which he has used over and over again. His lexical range is very small. He has, however, made no mistakes in spelling, in inflections, in diacritical marks, or in punctuation. He is given a high grade for his assignment.

We may now ask: Which of these two compositions showed the greater development of skill in writing? Without doubt, the work of student A, yet this does not show in the evaluation.

The problem is a real one. If the teacher does not insist on accuracy in writing, many students will hand in sloppy, careless work. Doing work of this type will confirm them in bad habits of writing which will be very difficult to eradicate. The teacher who insists on accuracy will at least get an approximation to accuracy from most of his students. He will be training them to be observant of small details of the written system of the language, and he will also be training them to check through their work very carefully to detect their own inaccuracies. At the written practice stage, especially, unless the teacher insists on accuracy he will be unable to judge whether the student has really assimilated the structural features he has been taught or not. For these reasons, insistence on accuracy is important.

On the other hand, sheer accuracy must not be rewarded at the expense of real knowledge of and ability to use the foreign language. The answer to this problem lies in the awarding of a composite grade for compositions. Part of this grade will be given for accuracy of writing (correct grammatical forms, spelling, diacritics, and so on); another part will be allotted for variety of structure; another for lexical choice; another for idiomatic quality (authentic turn of phrase). In this way the inaccurate student will be penalized for his inaccuracy, but given credit for his ability to communicate his ideas in language which a native speaker would use. The accurate student will be rewarded for his accuracy, but not necessarily graded at a high level if he is lacking in wider knowledge and finesse of expression.

ANNOTATED READING LIST

NORTHEAST CONFERENCE (1963). *Language Learning: The Intermediate Phase,* edited by W. BOTTIGLIA. Working Committee Report, "Writing as Expression" (pp. 62–81), gives many ideas on appropriate writing exercises at various levels. Examples are given in French, German, Russian, and Spanish.

THOMPSON, MARY P. "Writing in an Audio-Lingual Modern Foreign Language Program." In *Foreign Languages and the Schools,* edited by M. R. DONOGHUE. Dubuque, Ia.: William Brown Co., 1967. Chapter 7, Section 4. Also in *Readings in Foreign Languages for the Elementary School,* edited by S. LEVENSON and W. KENDRICK. Waltham, Mass.: Blaisdell, 1967. Pp. 214–20. Gives useful suggestions for types of exercises at various stages of development of the writing skill.

11

Cultural Understanding

Prominent among formulations of objectives in foreign-language teaching we usually find some such statement as the following: "to increase international understanding by enabling the student to enter into the life, thought, and literature of people who speak another language." The priority given to this objective may vary from one period to another, but it has long been present in the thinking of foreign-language teachers.

In 1904, in his book *How to Teach a Foreign Language,* we find Jespersen stating that "the highest purpose in the teaching of languages may perhaps be said to be the access to the best thoughts and institutions of a foreign nation, its literature, culture—in short, the spirit of the nation in the widest sense of the word." [1] In 1933, the Secondary Education Board of Milton, Massachusetts, declared that the primary practical value of foreign-language study was "the breaking down of the barriers of provincialism and the building up of the spirit of international understanding and friendliness, leading toward world peace." [2] Such statements can be found in the listing of objectives in many curricula and courses of study throughout the world. In America, the culminating formulation has been the Modern Language Association policy statement, "F. L.'s and International Understanding" [3] which lists three contributions which foreign-language learning can make to the

1 London: Allen & Unwin, Ltd., 1904, quoted from 12th Impression, 1961, p. 9.
2 Extract reprinted in M. Newmark, *Twentieth Century Modern Language Teaching* (New York, 1948), p. 104.
3 *PMLA,* 71, no. 4, pt. 2 (September, 1956): xvi–xvii.

achievement of international understanding and cooperation: "Direct intercultural communication. . . . Experience of a foreign culture. . . . Information about a foreign culture," and adds: "The third contribution of language learning to international understanding would be inefficient, . . . were it not for the two other contributions which it *uniquely* makes."

It may be well to ask ourselves whether such idealistic aims have been realized in practice: whether international understanding, let alone world peace, can be said to have been promoted by the considerable amount of foreign-language teaching in schools around the world. Diligent learning of foreign words and phrases, laborious copying and recitation of irregular verb paradigms, and the earnest deciphering of texts in the foreign language (many of them unauthentic and trivial) can hardly be considered powerful devices for the development of international understanding and goodwill. It may well be maintained that many hours of tedium and limited comprehension in classrooms around the globe have produced a great deal of international misunderstanding. As with all educational undertakings, the objective will not be achieved without a clear analysis of the factors involved in its attainment so that methods may be employed which take these factors into account. Many teachers of foreign languages, with the best will in the world, have received no preparation at all for this aspect of their work.

Some teachers will object that they do not consider their task to be the development of understanding of the attitudes and ways of life of another people, that their sole purpose in the classroom is to teach their students the fundamental structure of another language and to develop skills of comprehension and language use, both in speech and writing. Such teachers prefer to ignore the fact that a language cannot be separated completely from the culture in which it is deeply embedded. Any authentic use of the language, any reading of original texts (as opposed to those fabricated for classroom use), any listening to the utterances of native speakers, will introduce cultural concomitants into the classroom whether the teacher is conscious of them or not. By not acknowledging their presence and not making them explicit the teacher allows misconceptions to develop in the students' minds. Misunderstanding of the culturally-determined bases for the reactions and behavior of the foreign people can develop in the students contempt for and hostility toward the speakers of the language they are learning. Mere fluency in the production of foreign-language utterances without any awareness of their implications or of their appropriate use, the reading of texts without a realization of the underlying values and assumptions —these so-called skills are of factitious usefulness even on a purely practical level, and may well call into question the claim of foreign-language study to a place in a program of liberal education.

It has been stated in the previous paragraph that language is deeply embedded in culture. To some this may seem an incomprehensible observation. They would say that a foreign language is the key to the cultural heritage of another people, and that knowledge of a foreign language enables an individual to increase his personal culture through contact with great minds and the great works of literature. For these people, culture is defined as "that training which tends to develop the higher faculties, the imagination, the sense of beauty and the intellectual comprehension." [4] For a long time a definition of "culture" along these lines has been accepted in most communities, and it has been one of the aims of education to develop a cultured person in this sense of the word. With the rapid increase in anthropological studies, the word "culture" has come to take on a much broader significance. The culture of a people, as the word is used in this chapter, is certainly the result of training, but training in all aspects of shared life in a community. The child growing up in a social group learns ways of doing things, ways of expressing himself, ways of looking at things, what things he should value and what things he should despise or avoid, what is expected of him and what he may expect of others. These attitudes, reactions, and unspoken assumptions become part of his way of life without his being conscious of them. They are expressed in his actions and in his social relationships, in his moral convictions, in attractions and revulsions, in the institutions his social group establishes and

4 From the report of the committee on "Position of Modern Languages in the Educational System in Great Britain" (1928), as quoted in Massachusetts report, 1933, reprinted in Newmark (1948), p. 104.

conserves, and in the art and literature which the members of the group produce. There are variations within the group which express individual preferences or the orientation of some subgroup, and the literature of the group may reflect some of these alternatives or some evolving area of the culture. Despite such variations and deviations clear patterns of behavior and value systems may be discerned which are integral parts of the cultural whole. For depth of cultural understanding it is necessary to see how such patterns function in relation to each other and to appreciate their place in the cultural system.

In a country where there is one predominant culture, students will have grown up to react in certain ways and to value certain things. Their first encounter with a different set of behavior patterns and a different set of values can come as a shock, causing them to consider the speakers of the language they are learning as very peculiar, bad-mannered, rather stupid, or even morally lax. In a society where different forms of address are used according to the social status of the person being addressed, an important preliminary question in a social situation may be "How much do you earn?" In another society such a question may be considered the height of effrontery. Foreigners in English-speaking countries have been known to judge acquaintances as indifferent to their welfare and brusque in personal relations because they have mistaken the customary greeting of "How are you?" for a genuine enquiry about the visitor's state of health; they have then been disconcerted when their English-speaking acquaintances have not waited for a reply to the query. In a society where the individual must never admit that what he is wearing is valuable or in good taste, the reply of "thank you" to a compliment on his personal appearance may be considered an indication of a certain conceit or lack of breeding. In each of the cases cited, the simple remark is only comprehensible within the structure of relationships and social education in the society. In every language, even at the elementary stage of learning, features such as these emerge to puzzle and perturb the monolingual student. Feigenbaum tells of African students learning English who were shocked when, in a dialogue they were reading, a person refused a drink when it was offered a second time. In many societies this would indicate that the visitor had not enjoyed the drink the first time,[5] while in others such a refusal would indicate polite behavior in a formal situation or naturalness in an informal situation.

The native language is learned along with the ways and attitudes of the social group in which one grows up, and these ways and attitudes find expression through the language. In this way the language is an integral part of the functioning social system. The psychologist Osgood has set out a theory of language "meaning" which maintains that the full meaning of a word for an individual is the result of the sum total of experiences which he has had with that word in the cultural environment in which he has grown up.[6] As the members of the group have had similar experiences this meaning is shared by them all, but may differ in certain respects from the meaning the word has for certain other groups. It is because of this interrelationship of language and culture that one-to-one equivalences can rarely be established between words and expressions in two languages, once one has passed beyond the stage of physical identification. Even here there will be divergences, as the speakers of one language will have formed certain categories, according to their environmental needs, which do not correspond with the categories of the other language. As Hjelmslev has said: "Each language lays down its own boundaries within the amorphous 'thought-mass' and stresses different factors in it in different arrangements, puts the centers of gravity in different places and gives them different emphases." [7]

Where words seem to correspond lexically in their denotation, they may well diverge considerably in their connotation, or the emotional associations which they arouse. The word "mother" may have in one culture strong emotional overtones which are incomprehensible in a culture where children are regarded as belonging to the tribe or clan rather than to their individual parents. Cultural patterning may also lead to expectations of different emotional reactions from various sec-

---

5 I. Feigenbaum, "The Cultural Setting of Language Teaching," *English Teaching Forum* 3 no. 4 (Winter, 1965): p. 11.
6 Osgood's theory is described and discussed in detail in Rivers (1964), chap. 12.
7 Louis Hjelmslev, *Prologomena to a Theory of Language,* trans. Francis J. Whitefield (Madison, Wis., 1961), p. 52.

tions of the social group, as in societies where men and women are expected to react differently to the cry: "Spider!" The institutional system may add strong connotational elements to certain words. The word for "communism" should be easily identifiable in a number of languages, yet the full meaning, denotational and connotational, which a speaker wishes to convey may be very poorly represented in translation by the mere insertion of an "equivalent" word. The misunderstanding is compounded when the word is considered in context and the interplay of nuances in the phrase and in the earlier and later parts of the discourse is taken into consideration.

Osgood maintains that a large part of the "meaning" of words as he has measured it by statistical procedures [8] is concerned with value judgments (good-bad, right-wrong, acceptable-unacceptable). As we have seen, such value judgments are acquired in the culture in which the individual has grown up and are accepted unquestioningly by most members of the social group. For real understanding of both spoken and written messages the student must be conscious of the values and attitudes which are basic to the foreign-language discourse. The student who has learned that a new language is not simply a code that he must crack in order to transform it back into the familiar native language has already gained an important insight into the meaning of culture. He will learn by comparison and contrast a great deal about his own culture as he strives to understand the culture of the speakers of the language he is being taught.

APPLICATION TO THE CLASSROOM

This theoretical discussion may seem a long way from the classroom, but it is essential to an analysis of effective language teaching methods and to a choice of suitable texts for study. As we have seen, a method which employs a large part

8 Osgood has developed a psychological instrument, the Semantic Differential, with which he attempts to measure differences among concepts as between individuals and social groups. See C. Osgood, G. Suci, and P. Tannenbaum, *The Measurement of Meaning* (Urbana, Ill., 1957). The Semantic Differential is discussed in Rivers (1964), pp. 134–35.

of the student's time transposing elements as distinctive units from one language code to another destroys the unity of the language expressed in its systematic interrelationships. Where such methods are used texts chosen for study are often artificially constructed on a theme familiar to the students and reflecting their own culture. This severs the language from its source and presents the students with a defective and incomplete picture of its meaning. To the students the language then appears as a somewhat blurred and indistinct version of their own, rather less expressive and lacking in nuance and vitality. This type of teaching and textual study may give practice in manipulation of language elements and call for alertness and memory, but it adds little to a student's education.

Certain objections may also be made at this point to a strictly direct method. In direct-method teaching only the foreign language is used in the classroom, and the meanings of words and phrases are made clear to the student by situation, demonstration, and the use of pictures and objects. Theoretically this implies that we are able to convey meanings to the student by these means. If, as some psychologists maintain, we are merely arousing within our students meanings which may be forming new associations and recombinations,[9] then it becomes evident that the direct-method approach to meaning is valid only insofar as we are interested in our students' acquiring new labels for common objects, actions, and relationships. We are calling up within our students meanings and reactions which are culturally conditioned by all the experiences they have had with what they take to be equivalent situations in the native environment. Because the direct method begins with the familiar environment, where such equivalence is often possible, this tendency on the part of the students is accentuated by confirmation. At a later stage, when the student has learned to communicate to some degree in the foreign language, this weakness may be overcome, but by this time he will have acquired a great number of misconceptions which will have to be corrected. Even the assumption that objects and persons in the familiar environment provide easily interchangeable concepts between languages may be contested.

9 O. H. Mowrer, *Learning Theory and the Symbolic Processes* (New York, 1960), p. 139.

Since the culture of a social group is developed in close relationship with such objects and persons, it is at this point that cultural divergences are often greatest. The word "father" would seem to have a universally transferable meaning, yet it calls up very different images in different cultures. In some, the father is an austere, distant, highly respected authority, in others an indulgent friend who says "yes" when mother says "no." The concept of "friend" is similarly not easily equated between certain languages. Foods, modes of transport, and common household and schoolroom objects may involve the teaching of rare forms which cannot be considered to have, in a language where they are virtually unknown to a great many people, the connotation our students expect. It is well to be aware of this problem of familiar objects, persons, and experiences if we wish our students to acquire from the beginning any authentic cultural understanding.

IMPLICATIONS FOR THE TEACHER

The M.L.A. Seminar Report (1953), "Developing Cultural Understanding through Foreign Language Study," suggests that "the understanding of the culture of a specific country is not, in and by itself, all that the cultural aspect of language study should contribute to a general and liberal education." [10] The authors suggest three ends which should be kept in view: that the student should gain an understanding of the nature of culture, that his culture-bondage should be reduced, and that he should achieve a fuller understanding of his own cultural background.

Most of our students live in a monolingual and monocultural environment. As a result it is inevitable that they are "culture-bound." The M.L.A. Report defines the culture-bound as "a person whose entire view of the world is determined by the value-perspectives he has gained through a single cultural environment—who thus cannot understand or accept the point of view of another individual whose values have been determined by a different culture. . . . He makes premature and inappropriate value judgments. He is limited in his under-

10 *PMLA*, 68, no. 5: 1203.

standing of the world." [11] This description is applicable to many of our students when they are first brought in close contact with another culture through its language. Their reaction may be one of hostility, emotional revulsion to another set of values, condescension, or simply bewilderment. Such attitudes most certainly do not promote international goodwill and the desire for cooperation, yet in many language classes they are permitted to develop and continue. They can be dissipated only by informed understanding of the basic differences between the two cultures. The study of a language should bring home to the students the realization that there are many ways of looking at things, many ways of doing and expressing things, and that differences do not necessarily represent moral issues of right and wrong. In this way students will develop tolerance of other viewpoints and other forms of behavior. As the students realize that their native language is one among many, each perfectly equipped for dealing with all aspects of reality and all the kinds of experiences which present themselves to the speakers of that language, they will develop an orientation toward language as such which will facilitate their learning of a different language system. Finally, through a study of basic differences, they will become conscious of certain aspects of their own culture, certain attitudes culturally acquired, which they had never questioned nor analyzed. This in itself can be a substantial gain from their classroom experience.

What of the teacher himself? What is required of him? Briefly, he must have an informed insight into the culture of his students, and a similar understanding of the culture of which the language he is teaching is a part. Different problems will arise for the teacher instructing students of his own cultural background in a language which is foreign to him from those which face the teacher who is presenting his own language to students of a different cultural background. For purposes of differentiation in the following discussion, the former will be referred to as the foreign-language teacher and the latter as the native speaker.

At a superficial level it may appear that the foreign-

11 *Ibid.*

language teacher has an initial advantage in that he has an intimate knowledge and understanding of the cultural background of his students. It is true that he will not be surprised by their reactions to certain aspects of the foreign culture and can, therefore, anticipate and attenuate these by his method of presentation. Certainly this will be so where there is a contrast of custom or behavior. Since cultural attitudes and values are, however, to a large extent subconscious, he may share many of the prejudices of his students. It is essential that he undertake some objective study of his own culture so that he may be conscious of the bases of the reactions of his students. This will help him to establish areas of contrast and to give his students sympathetic insight into differences in ways of thinking and reacting. His major problem will be his superficial, outsider's understanding of the culture of the people whose language he is teaching. He may not have had the opportunity to live among these people in their own environment, or he may have spent a short period of residence in the foreign country, during which he was struck by a number of picturesque differences in ways of behavior, without penetrating to their meaning in the context of interrelationships and functions in the cultural system. These observations from the street, or even from a few personal contacts, can be very misleading unless the interpretation of what one has experienced is based on a knowledge of traditions, values, symbols, taboos, and the patterned relationships of the society. Since these change more slowly than external forms of behavior, they help the student of culture to interpret current adaptations of the latter.

A greater advantage would appear to be on the side of the native speaker, who knows the history, literature, philosophy, customs, and folkways of his own people. Like the foreign-language teacher, however, the native speaker may not be conscious of the bases of his value judgments and reactions, nor of the significance of the institutions of his culture; he may subscribe to the myths and rationalizations current in his community. Like the foreign-language teacher, he will need to put some careful work into an objective study of these aspects of his culture. Similarly, he will need to study very carefully the culture of his students so that he is able to present aspects of his own culture in a way that is acceptable to them. This bicultural understanding will help him to identify those areas of his own cultural background and environment which will be completely incomprehensible to his students if presented without explanation. He must also be able to identify danger points of misunderstanding where his own culture and that of his students seem to come very close: where the outward manifestation is very similar but the significance diverges considerably.

Above all, it is essential that the teacher's approach to culture, whether he be foreigner or native speaker, should not be a chauvinistic one: he must overcome any temptation to try to prove the superiority of one culture over another. He is not in the classroom to confirm the prejudices of his students nor to attack their deeply held convictions. His aim should not be to win converts to one system or the other. For these reasons, his presentation of cultural material must be objective, analytic, and informative.

It is clear, then, that there is no short cut to good teaching in this area. The teacher who is unable to spend a considerable period of time in the country where the language is spoken (absorbing its atmosphere; living its life; sharing its experiences; and delving into its literary, historical, artistic, and folk heritage) will have to make up for this lack by disciplined reading. He must study carefully what responsible students of the culture have said, weighing differences of interpretation in the light of the status and recognized scholarship of the writers, taking into consideration possible biases emanating from their social class, their political or religious positions, and, in some cases, their propaganda intentions. This study he will supplement with wide reading in literature and attention to modern media of opinion: newspapers, magazines, radio, and television (if emissions from the foreign country are accessible). He will try to see films made in the country, and make contact with native speakers wherever this is possible.

Unfortunately, few of our foreign-language teachers have had adequate training in the past for this important aspect of their work; they must, therefore, take all the more seriously the responsibility to educate themselves in cultural interpretation. Where possible, in-service education and district workshops should be designed to help them in this endeavor. Future teachers of foreign languages should be provided not only with careful training but with guidelines on how to continue their studies in order to keep abreast of the rapid changes in cultural patterns which are taking place in many areas in this century. They should study, travel, discuss. The more informed and discerning the teacher, the more likelihood there is that his students may achieve some measure of international understanding.

CULTURAL UNDERSTANDING IN THE CLASSROOM

The problem now arises: how best can we communicate insight into a foreign culture to the students in our foreign-language classes. In the past this has commonly been attempted by the method of exposition and explanation: teachers have talked at great length about the geographical environment, the historical development, the literary and artistic achievements, the institutions, even the small details of the everyday life of the people who speak the language. At undergraduate level this has taken the form of a "civilization" course, at secondary level of cultural talks, given sometimes as isolated, slightly irrelevant, interpolations in the general language program, at others as part of a carefully planned and graduated series. Such a series has usually begun, at the elementary stage, with discussions of festivals, leisure-time activities, marriage customs and family ceremonies, features of school life, and so on, proceeding at intermediate and senior stages to geographical study, lives of great men, the history of music, painting, dancing, and film, and achievements in science and exploration. These aspects of the culture have sometimes been presented in lecturettes by teacher or students. At other times they have formed the basis of group or individual research projects, written by the students in their native language and copiously illustrated with maps, charts, and pictures.

Several objections have been made to this method of introducing the culture of the foreign people: that it is an activity more appropriate to the social studies lesson; that it consists of the absorption of a number of uninterpreted and often unrelated facts, interesting in themselves, but throwing very little light on basic beliefs, values, and attitudes; and, last, that it takes students away from the basic task of language learning and communication. At its worst this method becomes a cut-and-paste activity, keeping students busy for the class hour; at its best it provides much valuable background information for the real task of penetrating the foreign culture. At the early stages some work of this kind has motivational value, since language learning must of necessity proceed slowly; reading in the native language about another country and another people provides an interesting out-of-class activity at a stage when most of the classwork is oral. At a more advanced stage, when students are able to present material of this type to their fellows in the foreign language, it can provide a basis for discussions at many a meeting of the foreign-language club.

The question arises: Can we take time in the foreign-language class for the teaching of cultural background in this way? There is another approach which does not take time from the essential work of language learning: the insight into culture proceeds at the same time as the language learning—in other words, teaching for cultural understanding is fully integrated with the process of assimilation of language patterns and lexicon. Since language is so closely interwoven with every aspect of culture, this approach is possible, but it can be possible only when the teacher is well informed and alert to cultural differences. Such a teacher will bring an awareness of cultural meaning into every aspect of his teaching and his students will absorb it in many small ways. This awareness becomes a part of every language act in the classroom, as teacher and student alike ask themselves: How do we say it as a native speaker says it? How do we do it as they do it in the foreign country? What is its underlying significance? Through language use, students become conscious of correct levels of discourse and behavior; formulas of politeness and their relation to the temperament and social attitudes of the people; appropriateness of response in specific situations (within certain social groups, among people of certain age groups). Gradually they begin to perceive the expectations within the society and to glimpse the values which are basic to the various forms of behavior. From the beginning, the teacher should orient the thinking of the students so that they will feel curious about such differences and become observant as they listen and read.

This type of perception on the part of the students is cultivated most easily, in the early stages, in the dialogue type of
lesson. The dialogue should be constructed around an experience, compatible with the age and interests of the students,
which will clearly demonstrate behavior culturally appropriate
for speakers of the language. As students memorize the dialogue and act it out, they learn through role playing, as they
did in their own culture in childhood games and experienced
relationships. They have for a short spell the experience of
feeling Japanese or Russian or French, of reacting as a person
of that nationality would react. Such experiences are more
valuable than many lines of comment and explanation. Even
in books which do not begin with dialogues, the early lessons
are frequently written in a dramatic style which lends itself
easily to the reading of roles and then to transformation into
acted dialogue. Students who would feel foolish, in a conventional teacher-student situation, if asked to respond in a foreign way, with an accurate imitation of the sounds of the
foreign language, lose such inhibitions when acting a role. Here
they are identifying with a person of the foreign culture, seeing
things as he would see them, and naming things as he would
name them. This experience is, of course, authentic only insofar as the dialogue material or dramatic readings faithfully
reflect behavior in the foreign culture.

Great care must be taken by the teacher in the selection of
teaching materials. The textbook is basic and will determine
the trend of the instruction despite the best intentions of the
teacher. Some textbooks deliberately begin with dialogues
which reflect common, everyday experiences of the student in
his native culture, on the principle that the student is not
disconcerted because he recognizes behind the strange forms
the familiar situation. Besides neglecting the opportunity of
introducing students to cultural differences in everyday situations, such texts also fail to capitalize on the natural curiosity
of the beginning foreign-language learner about all things foreign, and deprive the class of the excitement that comes with
novelty. Acting out dialogues of this type confirms the impression of many students that the foreign language is the native
language in another dress: an unnecessarily confusing way of
saying what the student can already express satisfactorily in
any case.

Other textbooks begin with dialogues which are described as being "culturally neutral." The term is a specious one. Just as psychologists use ambiguous drawings in order to discern the attitudes and prejudices of the subject, so "culturally neutral" situations must inevitably be interpreted by the student as familiar patterns of his own culture, unless the teacher takes pains to add what is missing by gesture, action, and situational application. At least with "culturally neutral" dialogues there is more possibility of enrichment of the textbook material by the well-informed teacher than with the culturally familiar.

In choosing a textbook, it is as well to examine even apparently authentic dialogue material with the greatest of care. The dialogues may represent an interesting situation or relationship in the foreign culture, but be expressed in language which would never be used in such circumstances or among people of the type depicted.[12] Even if the language is appropriate, the whole situation may be reproduced in such a stilted way that students feel foolish acting it out. Finally, in an attempt to include cultural material, the writer may have overloaded the dialogue to such an extent that it becomes an artificial inventory and quite unusable as a natural interchange. Dialogues should cover major areas of similarity and contrast between the two cultures in as wide a variety of situations as is feasible but without becoming pedantic and unreal.

The classroom teacher will be hampered in his endeavors until textbook writers have become more conscious of the cultural aspect of their task. Already in 1952 Marckwardt was calling for "the construction of materials designed to produce a cultural orientation" which would be based on "a comparison

---

12 Feigenbaum (1965) gives a very striking example of this type of dialogue (p. 12). It is intended as part of a lesson in American English for Frenchmen.

Pierre: Good Sunday, Henry. How are you?

Henry: I am well, thank you. And you?

Pierre: Very well. One told me that your brother passed the examinations for the second part of the baccalaureate degree.

Henry: Yes, it is true. He decided to continue to study for the philosophy degree. We are very happy that he may complete his studies in high school.

Pierre: Will you be with your family at our house for dinner on Tuesday? My mother will prepare snails, brains, and a special stew of hare . . .

of the two national cultures involved, a determination of the principal points of difference between them, and the selection of materials, literary or expository, which will set forth, illustrate, and perhaps account for, the cultural attitudes involved in those points of difference." [13] This necessity becomes even more acute at senior levels when students are devoting a major part of their time to reading. They expect this reading to increase their knowledge and understanding of the foreign people and their unique contribution to world thought and achievement. Teachers will encourage textbook writers whose work reflects an understanding of cultural distinctiveness by choosing texts based on this approach. As more such textbooks appear, the task of orienting the class toward cultural understanding will be facilitated.

After students have learned dialogues thoroughly, it is advocated that they use these freely in communication situations contrived in the classroom. It may well be asked if this does not mean that the students will be associating native-language behavior with foreign-language forms. This will be true to a greater or less extent depending on the orientation the students are receiving throughout their language instruction. If they are encouraged to look upon much of their foreign-language work as role playing, they can carry this into contrived classroom situations, endeavoring by intonation, gesture, content, and reaction to reproduce a foreign-language atmosphere. They will be able to do this more successfully as time goes on and their knowledge of the cultural behavior of the people increases. Fries speaks of the need for foreign-language students to attain "as complete a realization as possible of the common situations in which the language operates for the native speaker," of being interested in "the whole life-experience of the people." [14] This is a demanding task, which should be begun as soon as possible, that is, from the earliest lessons.

A sense of reality can be brought into the classroom by giving the students an opportunity to enjoy certain activities which the native speakers of the language enjoy. It may be

---

13 A. Marckwardt, quoted in "Developing Cultural Understanding through Foreign Language Study," *PMLA*, 68, no. 5: 1198.
14 C. C. Fries, *Teaching and Learning English as a Foreign Language* (Ann Arbor, Mich., 1945), p. 58.

difficult to introduce national sports, national foods (although these can be cooked by the members of the foreign-language club), but it is possible to introduce students to the songs and dances of the country. The types of songs people sing in moments of happiness, in moments of fervor, or in moments of depression reflect the things they prize, the things that amuse them, the things they fear. As with all cultural material, songs must not be added to a class lesson merely as a kind of end-of-the-hour relaxation, although they certainly are appropriate for this. The students must understand on what occasions these songs are sung, whether they are learned at school or at home, or acquired as part of a group heritage in social festivities, and they must learn to sing them as they are sung in the land of their origin. Every foreign-language class should have a repertoire of such songs which the students come to love and sing spontaneously. A splendid opportunity to give students this feeling of participation in the culture is lost when teachers waste precious time teaching the students songs from their own culture which have been translated into the foreign language. A few stilted words and phrases may remain with the student, but nothing else of value. Every culture has a rich repertoire of songs which are authentic, attractive, and a pleasure to sing. It is for the teacher to begin collecting the most suitable of these from his first initiation to teaching, so that he has in his files appropriate songs for all occasions and for all levels of instruction. Singing games and dances which are accompanied by singing are also suitable activities, on certain occasions, for junior high school classes.

The teacher must also collect pictorial material to illustrate his lessons. Suitable pictures with an authentic cultural setting are available from some publishers. Where there is a paucity of such materials, the teacher must begin his own collection from the pages of magazines. Often advertisements in magazines depict natural situations and the activities of people of different ages. In choosing pictures which will be useful for teaching purposes, care must be taken to see that they are not too cluttered with detail. They should be illustrative of one main aspect of cultural behavior which is clearly depicted without caricaturing the life of the people. It is important that pictures used in the early stages should show life as it is lived at the present time, unless it is made clear to the students that for some specific reason they are being shown pictures of life as it was lived in bygone days. Sometimes it is hard for teachers to resist the picturesque element in pictures of people in national costumes which are no longer worn, engaging in activities of a premechanical age. Such pictures can, however, be the source of considerable cultural misunderstanding. The same comments apply to the use of films and filmstrips. Film is a vivid medium of presentation; for this reason, it is all the more imperative that it should not give a distorted picture of the life of the people. It is easy to yield to the temptation to portray the unusual, rather than the typical. Many films, filmstrips, and transparencies have been made for use in schools. Only certain ones of these are suitable for a program where cultural understanding is integrated completely with language learning. (This subject is discussed at greater length in chapter 7.)

Another means of making life in the country where the language is spoken seem real and actual is the keeping of an up-to-date bulletin board in the language classroom. On this board will be affixed news of current events in the country, of new ventures and achievements. Occasionally the teacher will pin up a reproduction of some outstanding work of art. The students will be given an introduction to the humor of the people by the displaying of cartoons and comic strips, carefully chosen to exclude jokes which depend on puns or turns of speech which are not as yet familiar to the students. Proverbs, too, can be posted. Proverbs contain the folk wisdom of a race and are often a significant index of its value system. Advertisements from current magazines can be very entertaining and teach a great deal of useful modern vocabulary, some of which has not yet appeared in published dictionaries. A well-kept bulletin board of this type will provide for much incidental learning while students wait for lessons to begin, or fill in a few moments during a wet lunch hour. It can also provide material for conversation during the lesson: the teacher adding judicious cultural comments on what has been affixed, as the students ask questions.

From time to time native speakers should be invited into the classroom, especially when students have reached the stage of being able to comprehend consecutive speech. A discussion between the classroom teacher and the native speaker can illuminate differences in points of view, and the students can ask questions about things which have puzzled them. If the native speaker is of the same age as the students, they can ask him about the activities and interests of their counterparts in the foreign environment. Every student may have personal contact with a native speaker by means of international correspondence; as soon as students are able to put together a simple written account of their doings they should be encouraged to enter into correspondence with students of their own age in the foreign country. More can be learned about the life of the speakers of the language in this way than from many hours of formal instruction.

Much of the discussion up to this point has of necessity been limited to the earlier stages of language learning—a period in which a cultural orientation is established. The program as it has been described may have struck the reader as being singularly devoid of substantial content. This, however, is only a preparatory period, during which the student is acquiring a basic knowledge of the language which will enable him to read, discuss, and write about what he has been studying. Margaret Mead speaks of the attitude of high school students who say, "Think of spending the whole year and learning nothing else except a bunch of phrases about how to travel." [15] Such an observation would be a serious indictment of a high school foreign-language program. Other critics have accused foreign-language programs which begin with the development of the aural-oral skills of producing language illiterates, or students who can chatter with great fluency but have nothing to chatter about. If foreign languages are to retain a place in general education, it is important that they fulfill a humanistic as well as a practical purpose.

As the student's control of the language increases, most of the content of the course will come from reading, some will come from films, and some from classroom discussion of what has been read and viewed. Serious thought must therefore be given to the type of reading material which is to be presented

---

15 *The Meaning and Role of Culture in Foreign Language Teaching,* Report of Conference at Georgetown University, Washington, D.C., 1961 (mimeographed), p. 13.

to the student. With the cultural objective in mind, the choice seems to many to lie between factual and expository materials throwing light on the system of culture in its various forms of expression, and the traditional selection of texts representing what the speakers of the language consider to be the masterpieces of literary production of their society. If, as Laurence Wylie considers, "we must make the study of values and attitudes our basic concern,"[16] then both types of materials are essential. Students need an understanding of the basic features of the culture in order to understand the literature they read; they need to penetrate beyond surface detail to its inner significance, to the appeal or message it has for those for whom it has been written. A penetration to the level of values must arouse controversy and lead the student to examine more objectively his own value system. This can be of considerable interest at the adolescent stage when students are asking themselves many questions of a philosophical and ethical nature.

If materials about the basic culture and literary materials are to be used side by side, then one must illuminate the other. The suitable textbook will contain, for intermediate stages, cultural information which will lay the foundation for later literary study, while also providing interesting reading for the type of student who is not yet ready for a steady diet of literary works of a standard he is not accustomed to read in his own language. Such cultural material may take the form in the main of articles from recent magazines and books, or of older articles of outstanding value. These reading materials should be supplemented by short stories, poems, and scenes from plays. The literary items will be selected because they are representative of contemporary attitudes and situations, are expressed in twentieth-century language, and develop themes of interest to young adolescents. The writer of the textbook will show by the development of his material that he has established some rational sequence of cultural insights and interrelationships for appropriate levels of instruction, and that the reading material has been selected with a view to clarifying these insights. Materials selected haphazardly and arranged with no consistent development will not serve the purpose of the informed teacher but will merely exasperate

16 *Ibid.,* p. 27.

him. Frequently such poorly selected and badly arranged materials merely confirm the prejudices of the students and reinforce the stereotypes, or facile generalizations, about the speakers of the language which they have already acquired from the less informed members of their community.[17]

At the advanced high school stage the foreign-language class frequently becomes a class in literary history and criticism conducted in a foreign language. This discourages students whose bent does not lie in literature from pursuing the course for the final year. Study of literary movements and the literature of earlier centuries is best kept for students who wish to specialize in foreign literature at undergraduate or graduate level. If cultural understanding is to be realized, the adolescent student must continue to read the thought and invention of his contemporaries, or such classical literature as is timeless in content and easily accessible in language. Even at this advanced level of high school study, teachers will need to ensure that their students realize that what they read in fiction does not necessarily depict in faithful detail the reality of life for every individual in the foreign country. The ordinary life of an average citizen rarely provides the specific elements sought by the writer of a novel, play, or short story. There will be individual variations and, in some cases, deviations from the social pattern, but the general atmosphere and the attitude of the writer himself to his subject will reveal much of interest to the advanced student who has already received a grounding in cultural interpretation.

A program which seeks to develop systematic progress in cultural understanding side by side with growing mastery of the language will ensure that the student is able to communicate with the speakers of the language in the fullest sense of the word. He will learn to recognize what people of different cultures have in common beneath surface variations, while appreciating that their deeply rooted differences of outlook are related to a whole life-pattern which is an essential development from their experiences as a group in a particular environment. The student who has achieved this type of understanding will form a contrast to many in the past who, after years of

17 Rivers (1964), pp. 140–41, discusses this question of stereotypes.

language study, have been able to do no more than clothe their "cultural offensiveness in the best local diction." [18]

Does each language have a world view?

Since linguists have discovered great variations in the ways in which languages codify experience (different ways of looking at time and space, different categories for many types of physical objects and experiences, different ways of grouping people), and anthropologists have described widely differing behavior patterns and attitudes in many cultures, some scholars have hypothesized that the categories of the native language determine the way an individual looks at reality, and that this in turn affects some aspects of his behavior.

This thesis, which can be traced back to Von Humboldt, was strongly held by Sapir who said, in discussing translation: "The environing world which is referred to is the same for either language; the world of points is the same in either frame of reference. But the formal method of approach to the expressed item of experience, as to the given point of space, is so different that the resulting feeling of orientation can be the same neither in the two languages nor in the two frames of reference." [19] In other words, we see the physical world, finally, as our language trains us to see it, and we can only describe it as our language permits us to describe it. In his collected writings, *Language, Thought, and Reality* (1956), Whorf gives a number of examples which he considers support this hypothesis. Whorf draws his illustrations from the language and culture of the Hopi Indians of the Southwest of the United States, which he had studied intensively for some time. He observes, for instance, that the Hopi language does not have forms or expressions for dividing up the stream of time as do European languages. On the other hand, the verb form indicates the validity the speaker intends the statement to have,

18 G. R. Bishop, Jr., ed., *Culture in Language Learning,* Northeast Conference (1960), p. 35.
19 Edward Sapir, *Selected Writings in Language, Culture and Personality,* ed. D. G. Mandelbaum (Berkeley, Calif., 1949), pp. 153–54.

and aspects and modes of the verb show whether the occurrence is momentary, continued, or repeated. Whorf infers from
these facts that the Hopis view the passage of time differently
from people who speak languages which have very complicated
tense systems. He says: "The background linguistic system (in
other words, the grammar) of each language is not merely a
reproducing instrument for voicing ideas but rather is itself the
shaper of ideas, the program and guide for the individual's
mental activity, for his analysis of impressions, for his syn-
thesis of his mental stock in trade." [20] The Hopis, then, according to Whorf, have a distinctive view of the world which is
determined by the language they learn as children.

Sapir and Whorf's viewpoint has been disputed by other
scholars. Some criticize Whorf's exposition as being unsystematic and consider his observations on the Hopi language not
sufficiently inclusive to establish the existence of a world view.
Carroll quotes research which demonstrates that distinctive
features of the Hopi way of looking at things which appear to
spring from the categorization in their language have also been
observed in non-Hopi speakers.[21] When it comes to determining the metaphysical implications of grammatical features,
there can be considerable diversity of interpretation, most of
which may be considered merely personal, that is, a hypothesis
drawn from the data which is then established by examination
of the same data.

One thing would appear to be undeniable: that different
languages establish different categories for various aspects of
reality. These categories develop because the specific categorization is particularly appropriate to the environment, needs,
and development of the people. As an example, we may quote
the many words for different kinds of snow in the Eskimo
language. For Eskimo activities it is of great importance to
identify the type of snow. Learning the categories established
in the language helps an individual to make identifications
which he would not perhaps have made otherwise. The division
of garden plants into "weeds" and "flowers" in English causes

---

20 Benjamin Lee Whorf, *Language, Thought, and Reality, Selected
   Writings of . . .* , ed. J. B. Carroll (Cambridge, Mass., 1956), p. 212.
21 J. B. Carroll, *Language and Thought* (Englewood Cliffs, N.J., 1964),
   p. 109.

a novice gardener to observe differences which might otherwise have escaped his observation because they held no particular significance for him. As a result he "sees" things differently. The student learning a foreign language has to assimilate many new categorizations and codifications if he is to understand and speak the language as its native speakers do. This does not mean that the student's own language would not have been able to establish such distinctions for him. All languages which have been closely studied seem to possess the potentiality for expressing all kinds of ideas and making all kinds of distinctions. For a particular way of looking at things, one language may have a grammatical form which does not exist in another language. The other language may have to use a circumlocution to express the same aspect of reality because, for some reason, the speakers of the language do not feel the need to express this nuance as frequently as the speakers of the first language. The second language does, however, possess sufficient flexibility to meet the situation when it occurs; should the particular concept acquire greater relevance to the life pattern of the speakers of this language new words, or new members of grammatical categories, will be created or borrowed from some other language.

Carroll has set up a modified hypothesis of linguistic relativity which seems to fit the facts more closely than that of Whorf: "Insofar as languages differ in the ways they encode objective experience, language users tend to sort out and distinguish experiences differently according to the categories provided by their respective languages. These cognitions will tend to have certain effects on behavior." [22] This seems to be as far as we can go in the present state of knowledge; it does not go far enough to justify the assertion that each language imposes on its speakers a distinctive world view.

ANNOTATED READING LIST

NORTHEAST CONFERENCE (1960). *Culture in Language Learning*, edited by G. R. BISHOP, JR. New Brunswick, N.J.: Rutgers, The State University, 1960. A thorough discussion of the anthropological

22 J. B. Carroll, "Linguistic Relativity, Contrastive Linguistics, and Language Learning," *IRAL*, I/1 (1963): 12.

concept of culture, language as culture, and the teaching of Western European, Slavic, and Classical cultures.

RIVERS, W. M. *The Psychologist and the Foreign-Language Teacher.* Chicago: University of Chicago Press, 1964. Chapter 12 deals with meaning and its relationship to the culture of the society, the problem of stereotypes, and practical applications to classroom teaching.

The Meaning and Role of Culture in Foreign Language Teaching. Conference Report, mimeographed. Washington, D.C.: Institute of Languages and Linguistics, Georgetown University, 1961. A most useful, all-round study of culture from the anthropological, humanistic, and integrative points of view, with proposed syllabuses for teaching French, German, Russian, and Spanish culture and civilization (bibliographies attached to each section).

BROOKS, NELSON. *Language and Language Learning.* 2d ed. New York: Harcourt, Brace & World, 1964. Chapter 6 sets out the types of questions anthropologists ask about a culture and the types of topics which are useful for studying a foreign culture in the classroom.
———. "Teaching Culture in the Foreign Language Classroom," *FL Annals* 1, no. 3 (March, 1968): 204–17. Distinguishes between "formal" culture and "deep" culture and gives suggestions for dealing with these in the classroom.

"Six Cultures (French, German, Hispanic, Italian, Luso-Brazilian, Russian): Selective and Annotated Bibliographies" by L. WYLIE, E. M. FLEISSNER, J. MARICHAL, D. PITKIN, and E. J. SIMMONS. In J. W. CHILDERS, D. D. WALSH, and G. WINCHESTER STONE, JR. *Reports of Surveys and Studies in the Teaching of Modern Foreign Languages.* New York: M.L.A., 1962. Pp. 253–75.

MODERN LANGUAGE ASSOCIATION. *Selective List of Materials for Use by Teachers of Modern Foreign Languages,* edited by MARY J. OLLMAN. New York: MLA, 1962. Gives bibliographic lists of books for reference for teachers of French, German, Italian, Modern Hebrew, Norwegian, Polish, Portuguese, Russian, Spanish, Swedish. Appendix contains "Six Cultures" (above). Supplements to this list are published from time to time.

OHANNESSIAN, S. *et al.,* eds. *Reference List of Materials for English as a Second Language.* Part 2: Background Materials. Washington, D.C.: Center for Applied Linguistics, 1964.

12

Testing: Principles and Techniques

Strevens considers many conventional tests inappropriate, mysterious, unreal, subjective, and unstructured.[1] Certainly this has been our own impression of many tests we have had to endure. Many teachers continue to set tests of a kind familiar to them without asking themselves the basic questions: What is my purpose in testing these students? What do I expect this test to achieve? What precisely is being tested? Am I really testing what I have taught? By using these techniques am I actually finding out what the student knows? Answering these apparently simple questions involves a fundamental understanding of the principles of testing. We shall therefore examine the implications of each of these questions in turn.

KNOW WHY YOU ARE TESTING

There are many elements of foreign-language study which may be tested. These may be tested at a number of levels and in a variety of ways. The purposes of the test will determine the selection of elements and the way in which they are to be tested. Is the test intended to indicate how well certain material has been taught and assimilated by the students or is it an elimination test to select a few outstanding candidates from a large group of students from different institutions? Is the test to be the determining factor in placing a new student in a class

1 P. D. Strevens, *Papers in Language and Language Teaching* (London, 1965), pp. 89–90.

working at an appropriate level? Is the test being given to select those who will be most efficient as oral interpreters or those who are likely to be successful as translators of articles for scientific journals? In the past, certain kinds of tasks, usually of the translation type, have been set in all foreign-language tests irrespective of the purpose of the test. If tests are to be effective in grouping candidates as required, decisions like those outlined above must be made before the test is designed. We may need to set prognostic tests, proficiency tests, achievement tests, or diagnostic tests. For each there will be a different approach to the construction of test items. We shall consider each of these kinds of tests in turn and discuss appropriate test items for specific purposes.

Frequently, some indication is required as to whether a particular student is likely to do well in foreign-language study. In recent years several language *aptitude tests* have been developed to help identify students who will learn a foreign language with some facility. The authors of these tests insist that they should not be considered at high school level as instruments of exclusion from foreign-language study since all students can profit from some experience in this area. Although progress has been made, these tests have not as yet been perfected as prognostic tests. They do, however, provide a chart of predicted strengths and weaknesses as a guide in the placing of students in streamed groups, where this is the practice. The analysis they provide is useful to the teacher who is trying to help particular students with serious problems in some skill areas, and is a guide in the identification of underachievers in the foreign-language class. Modern language aptitude tests are discussed in detail later in this chapter.

Tests may also be devised to establish the level of *proficiency* which a student has reached. Such tests may be required to determine the level of language skill of student teachers or practicing teachers who have studied at different institutions, or for the placement of students who have studied a foreign language in elementary school in the appropriate high school class or the high school graduate in the most suitable undergraduate course. Proficiency tests will not be related in their design to the actual studies undertaken by the particular persons to whom they will be administered, but rather to the level of skill which is considered desirable in a successful candidate. Such tests differ from tests of *achievement* administered to groups of students from different institutions who are presenting themselves as candidates for a common terminal examination at the end of a certain period of study. These achievement tests are usually based on a published course of study, however sketchy, and students expect to be tested on what they are supposed to have been learning. Such tests have a considerable influence on methods of teaching, since teachers try to ensure that their students are adequately trained in the particular areas which will be tested. Yearly, half-yearly, and quarterly tests in schools are of this type, especially when the same test is given for students of the same level of study who have been taught in different classes by different teachers. These tests often test what the students are presumed to have been learning rather than what they have actually been learning; for this reason they may be faulty as testing instruments for many of those being examined.

For some languages *standardized achievement tests* are available. These tests, constructed by organizations outside the schools, are designed for different levels of achievement. They are very carefully prepared by experts, pretested, and revised where defects have been revealed by item analysis of the results of the pretests. They are then administered each year to large groups of students from different types of schools in different areas. From the scores which are obtained norms are established so that valid cross-comparisons may be made of the achievements of groups of students in the same year and in different years. Parallel series are sometimes available so that comparisons may also be made of level of achievement at different stages of a teaching sequence. Such tests enable a teacher to see how the standards he has set for his own classes compare with those of other teachers.

Tests set by teachers for their own classes, particularly informal tests during the course of the year's work, may have a different purpose. They may be designed to indicate to teacher and student areas of strength and areas of weakness: the results of these tests will show what sections of the work should be retaught or restudied and where further practice is essential, thus giving the teacher a clear indication whether the students are ready to move on to new work. These tests may be called *diagnostic tests*. Diagnostic tests are reduced in usefulness if they are not corrected thoroughly, returned promptly to the students, discussed in class, and rewritten where necessary by the students.

This chapter will concentrate particularly on the last two types of tests discussed: tests of achievement set within the high school for its own pupils, and diagnostic tests prepared by a teacher for his own classes. Aptitude tests will be discussed at the end of the chapter.

When the time for a periodic class test arrives, the teacher may well ask himself why he is giving this test. The immediate answer for many teachers is that such tests are always given, that they are necessary in order to assign the students some grade for the work they have been doing—the administration demands it. With this administrative requirement before them, many teachers with very little training in principles of testing prepare ill-conceived traditional tests which for the most part reveal what the students do not know and what they have not been taught. To many students these tests seem to provide the teacher with an opportunity to trick them in subtle ways and expose their insufficiencies to public view. As a consequence they dread such tests and become tense and overanxious.

Tests should be conceived as teaching devices and, therefore, as a natural step in the educational process. They should serve a twofold instructional purpose, acting as a guide to the student and a guide to the teacher. Each test should help the student by indicating to him the level of achievement he is expected to have reached, the level he has reached, and the discrepancy between the two. In this way he is able to see where he has mastered the material and where he has still some learning to do. Where the student is encouraged by the teacher and by the form of the test to see his performance in this light, he no longer fears the test but is anxious to show how much he knows, to improve on his previous performances, and to do well in comparison with his classmates. A poor performance is then an incentive to him to improve in areas of weakness, instead of being a disgrace and a discouragement. Well-designed tests are also a guide to the teacher, showing him areas in which his teaching has not been effective: areas which the students are finding particularly difficult and those parts of the work for which the students have not been given adequate practice. Each test is not an end in itself, but a means to the ultimate end of effective language mastery. It is one more step forward, to be followed by reteaching and re-learning, with variation from the original presentation to emphasize more adequately the areas of difficulty which have been revealed. Poor results on a test challenge the thoughtful teacher to a reconsideration of his method of presentation of a particular aspect of the work with a view to a more illuminating and efficient presentation on a future occasion.

KNOW WHAT YOU ARE TESTING

One important concept in testing is that of *validity*. A valid test is one which actually tests what the designer of the test intended it to test. Validity in foreign-language tests is not attainable without a great deal of thought and analysis before the test is constructed. Knowledge of a foreign language is a complex of skills of different kinds; each skill has a number of different aspects and is dependent on knowledge of and facility in manipulating a multiplicity of small elements which are closely interrelated in actual language use. Before deciding which skills he wishes to test and which aspects of skills he will emphasize in particular tests, the teacher must first establish the objectives of the course he is teaching. Once the teacher is sure of his objectives, he should carefully analyze the skill areas involved and devise items which test individually the various elements identified in this analysis as well as these elements in natural combinations. This is the first step in ensuring the validity of the test.

Traditional foreign-language tests have tended to test too many elements in interrelationship so that it has been impossible to tell what the result of the test really shows. A test of this type which is frequently given is the *dictation* of a passage in the foreign language for the student to write down accurately in the foreign language. Some teachers have considered this to be a valid test of the student's ability to understand the spoken language. If we examine the dictation test, we see that it does test recognition of elements of the language when spoken. With languages where there is a close relationship between the sound and the spelling systems it is quite possible, however, to write a passage accurately from dictation without paying much attention to the meaning of the elements dictated and to the overall meaning of the passage. Even where there is not this close relationship, students taking dictation are notoriously inattentive to the meaning of what they are writing, and particularly to the relevance of the segments as they write them to the import of the whole passage; in other words, their attention becomes concentrated on segments, despite the exhortations of the teacher. Further, the student may understand perfectly what he has heard but be unable to retain it long enough to write it down in full, for auditory memory is also involved. With languages where many of the morphological elements are not clearly identifiable by sound, the student has to make adjustments to what he is writing which reflect his knowledge of grammatical patterns. Where there are peculiar relationships between the sound and the combinations of symbols he must demonstrate his knowledge in this area. Then he must write down accurately what he has recognized aurally, this being a skill not all students have cultivated. Finally, dictation may be a test of temperament: the nervous or anxious child suffering from emotional blocks and lapses of memory which do not affect the more stolid and self-assured. The dictation mark, then, is a global mark representing many aspects of language study; it cannot be considered a valid test of listening comprehension alone. Because of the complexity of elements involved, dictation is probably best kept as a teaching technique for developing accuracy in the writing of the language and for consolidating knowledge of sound-symbol relationships and of structural elements which have been thoroughly taught. A passage for dictation which has not been very carefully selected or constructed for its relevance to work which has been studied and to the level of achievement reached can prove a waste of time, and an unnecessary irritation to the students, because of the multiple and unrealistic demands it makes upon them. At an advanced level it can be used as part of a group of tests aimed at determining all-round skill in handling the language, but it is doubtful whether it reveals anything which has not already been identified by other tests in a well-designed battery, in which case its contribution to the result may be considered largely redundant.

Reading comprehension is often tested by asking the student to translate a passage from the foreign language into the native language. It is clear that it is necessary to understand the original passage in order to be able to render it into the native language. It is not so clear that ability to give an idiomatic version of the passage in one's native language is a skill related to reading comprehension. It is possible for the student to understand the passage perfectly and yet do very badly on a test of this type because he does not possess the skill of expressing nuances of meaning in his own language. This type of test, then, favors the student who not only understands the foreign language but also has great facility of expression in his own language. It is a valid type of test if we wish to test comprehension of the foreign language, knowledge of areas of contrast between the foreign and native language and between the foreign and native culture, and also felicity of expression in the mother tongue. If we wish to test reading comprehension alone, however, we must devise a different type of test.

Another common type of test of reading comprehension requires the answering in the foreign language of foreign-language questions on a section of prose. On the surface this appears to be a more valid test of reading comprehension than the preceding one. Actually it is even less satisfactory. Unless the test is very carefully designed, it is often possible to answer questions of this type from the text supplied without knowing the meaning of a number of lexical items. X is mentioned in the question: we identify the sentences about X in the passage and are able to answer the question about X (where it is, what happened to it) without knowing what X really is. Since the answers must be in the foreign language, they can often be supplied very accurately by piecing together sections of sentences from the test—an exercise in quick wit and transcription as much as reading comprehension. At their worst, questions in this type of test may refer to isolated sections of the text which can be pinpointed from certain words in the question and do not test comprehension of the passage as a whole. This is particularly the case where proper names, dates, and numerical allusions are involved. Even where the questions are well constructed, the student may understand the text perfectly but get no credit for comprehension because he is very weak in composing sentences accurately in the foreign language. This type of test is very hard to assess because the skills involved cannot be separated in the answers and each given due credit.

In an endeavor to overcome the defects of this type of reading-comprehension test, some examiners set foreign-language questions on the reading passage to be answered in the native language. This reduces the bias in favor of the student who has great facility in expressing himself in his native language, as in the first type of test described, and enables the student who is weak at composing sentences in the foreign language to gain full credit for understanding what he has read. The validity of a reading-comprehension test of this type depends very largely on the construction of the questions. If the questions require answers which may be located in strict sequence through the text, the student is unduly assisted in answering them by being able to identify the sentence in which the next answer will be found. He may be able to answer many questions in isolation in this way, even though he has not understood the development of thought or the real implications of the passage. Sometimes the way the questions are framed enables the quick-witted student to interpret a passage he has not really understood when reading the passage by himself. Finally, despite the good intentions of the teacher the questions may seem ambiguous to the student, who may lose marks for not supplying the answer the teacher expected or for not including all the details the teacher wished him to write down. The student may be asked, for instance, "Did John know the thief was in the house?" The student who answers quite correctly "No" may, under this system, be given one mark out of the four allotted, because the teacher expected him to write, "No,/ he was watching television/ and the noise of the shooting in the Western/ covered the sound of the breaking glass/." The answer "No" may have indicated that the student understood all of these details in the text, but the teacher may be unwilling to give him credit for comprehension because he has not given sufficient evidence of it. This type of test tests reading comprehension. It also tests the ability to interpret the teacher's requirements. To some extent it tests volubility: many people, and often highly intelligent people, do not go into details when answering questions, considering the details self-evident. Finally, it tests docility, full marks going only to the student who understands the passage, knows what the teacher requires, and supplies it in a dutiful fashion.

Reading comprehension, and reading comprehension alone, is more validly tested by selection of the correct answer from multiple-choice items in the foreign language, on a reading passage. In this case the student shows his ability to comprehend not only the reading passage but also the fine distinctions between the choices offered him. He is not asked to demonstrate any other skill at the same time. This type of test, however, must be prepared with great care. The choices of answer to a question must be constructed in such a way that they contain elements from the reading passage arranged so that each provides a plausible answer for students who have misinterpreted the text in different ways; in other words, each must provide a real choice and a cause for hesitation for the student who is not quite sure of the real import of the text. The choices anticipate the errors in comprehension the students will make. On the other hand, there must be no ambiguity from the point of view of the student; the correct answer must be such that it will be chosen without hesitation by the student who has really understood the text. Effective choices of this type are demanding and time-consuming for the classroom teacher to construct. Until he has accumulated, over a number of years, a series of well-constructed questionnaires, or has discovered a commercially produced series of a suitable standard, he would be well advised to intersperse multiple-choice questionnaires with the more easily constructed type, foreign-language questions with native-language answers, always keeping in mind in the preparation of the questions the possible weaknesses outlined above. Teachers working with classes at the same level should exchange personally constructed material to reduce the burden of preparation and to ensure a greater supply of suitable tests. A well-constructed questionnaire may be kept and reused on a number of occasions provided students have not been allowed to take copies from the classroom.

Objections similar to those set out above may be raised to the testing of *listening comprehension* by means of printed questions in the foreign language to be answered in writing in the foreign language. Once again, students may understand perfectly what they hear but be given no credit for it because they have misinterpreted the printed question before them, or because they have not written the answer correctly or accurately in the foreign language. Some teachers who realize that in this type of test they are testing three skills at once (ability to understand the spoken language, ability to comprehend the printed word, and ability to express oneself in the foreign language in writing) try to compensate for this plurality of effort by awarding some marks for evidence of listening comprehension, irrespective of the correctness of the written response, assessing the written expression separately. In this case, the student receives no credit if he understood the spoken word and would have been able to express the answer in writing but misinterpreted the printed question. He also receives no credit for listening comprehension if he expresses himself so awkwardly in writing that his answer is misinterpreted by the examiner. If the student is to be tested for listening comprehension, this skill must be separated out from others and credit given for evidence of listening comprehension alone. At earlier stages this can be done with the use of pictures and objects. Three comments may be made by the teacher about the picture, two of which are not appropriate. The student will then mark A, B, or C on a sheet to show which one he considers to be the appropriate comment. Alternatively, he may hear a remark in the foreign language and be asked to choose from three oral rejoinders the one which would be an appropriate response. With both pictures and oral rejoinders it is important to avoid all ambiguity. At more advanced stages, when students who have acquired some facility in reading the foreign language are asked to listen to more sustained interchanges or longer narratives or descriptions, multiple-choice answers written in uncomplicated language may serve the purpose better than purely oral choices, because of the element of auditory memory involved in holding every-thing in the mind for a comparatively long period.

To sum up, if a test is to be valid in the sense that it is testing what its author wishes it to test, the teacher must proceed through certain stages. He must first decide exactly what he wishes to test. He must then work out how he will test this skill. At this stage he must analyze the type of test he has chosen to see whether it really tests this skill, and what other skills are required of the student while doing the test. After this careful analysis he will be in a position to modify or redesign the test to ensure that mastery of the specific skill he wishes to test can be clearly identified in the mode of answer-ing and that credit can be given for this skill in isolation, quite apart from skill in other areas.

TEST ONE THING AT A TIME

This is a corollary to the principle discussed in the previous section. Just as the teacher needs to identify the specific skill he wishes to test, so he must distinguish carefully the various aspects of that skill and test these one by one, as well as finally testing them as part of an all-round performance.

As an example we may take the testing of *ability to speak* the foreign language. It would seem that this would be validly tested by placing the student in a communication situation and seeing how he behaves. This is traditionally done in the *oral interview* which forms part of foreign-language tests all over the world. It is true that here we are testing the speaking skill. But we are also testing listening comprehension, to some extent self-assurance and composure, and, if the questions at the interview are not very carefully prepared, ability to talk about almost any subject without preparation. Were we to have discussed another subject the responses of the student may well have been of quite a different standard. When we finally allot a global mark for this interview, we have presumably taken into account ability to comprehend the spoken language, ability to frame a ready response, and ability to express this idea intelligibly in the foreign language with correct structure and appropriate lexical items. If we have found the response comprehensible, then we have presumably allotted some part of the mark for acceptable articulation of sounds, for stress, juncture, and intonation, and for intelligent grouping of words according to structural relationships. As very little time has been available for deciding on the mark, we have arrived at some subjective counterbalance of these various elements and we would not be able to say whether all elements were given equal credit, or whether they ought to have been given equal credit. If someone protests that the student's pronunciation was rather defective in certain areas we probably agree without much hesitation to lower the assessment one or two notches; if someone else intervenes with the suggestion that the candidate seemed to understand quite well everything that was said to him we may raise the grade again. Two examiners talking with the same candidate usually produce slightly different, sometimes substantially different, evaluations depending on which aspects of the speaking skill they think are important. The same examiner confronted with the same candidate on some future occasion may estimate his skill in quite a different fashion.

All the elements we have just shown to be implicit in a comprehensible interchange of speech (listening comprehension, acceptable articulation and intonation, intelligent grouping of words according to structural relationships, use of correct morphological and syntactical patterns, and to some extent range and variety of vocabulary) can be examined and evaluated apart from an act of communication, and therefore through tests which allow for a more objective assessment. The student who can perform acceptably in these areas in separate tests should get credit for this knowledge. Whether he can continue to use these elements effectively when he is thinking about what he wants to say will be shown by a communication assessment, which will be a global mark. Since significant speaking is of necessity part of an act of communication with another person it is inevitable that some part of the evaluation of communication skill will be subjective. The counterbalance of an objective score will make for more reliable evaluation in the final grade.

We have discussed possible techniques for testing listening comprehension, and we shall be discussing later in the chapter the testing of correct use of morphological and syntactical patterns and variety and range of vocabulary. We shall concentrate here on acceptable articulation, stress, juncture, and intonation, and intelligent grouping of words according to structural requirements. These elements can be tested by oral *reading* of a passage chosen, or preferably constructed, to cover a range of sound and word combinations wide enough to reveal the student's grasp of the elements involved. The passage should be of a standard appropriate to the level of achievement of the student so that he will not have difficulty in reading it with understanding. It should contain some conversational passages, where the student can demonstrate his knowledge of the intonation patterns of speech, and some narrative. Before the test begins, the examiner will have established the specific elements which he wishes to evaluate. These will be on a chart before him with a five-column scale for evaluation. A five-column scale reduces the difficulty of quick decision. The examiner's pencil hovers over the center column which represents average achievement (neither particularly meritorious nor particularly reprehensible) ; as he listens his pencil drifts to the right to "good" or "very good" or to the left to "poor" or "very bad." In this way he is able to make decisions on a number of elements while the student is reading, without being unduly influenced by the student's nervousness or self-assurance. If required, these value judgments can be assigned numerical equivalents at a later date.

Further checks can be made on the students' conception of the pronunciation of words by objective tests in which they are required to group words according to sound features or to distinguish words which differ in pronunciation from others in a group. *Aural-discrimination* tests reveal which sounds the students are confounding and, therefore, which sounds they are certainly not distinguishing in their own production. Items from tests of these types are described in some of the books in the Reading List at the end of this chapter.

Features of *sound production* can also be evaluated by the teacher at intervals during the year, in the course of class work. Students will be imitating sounds, repeating drills, acting out dialogues, conducting conversational interchanges of a controlled nature, reading aloud from their books. The alert teacher will keep some record of the production of each student. This will provide a fairer picture of his capabilities than an assessment made in an artificial situation when the student may be tense and anxious.

Teachers must not hesitate to evaluate important areas of skill which are difficult to test. Students soon learn to neglect and underestimate the importance of skills of which the teacher does not take account in the final grade. After the student has attained some measure of control of the language, some test of his ability to use it in a natural situation becomes essential. Rather than reject the interview as too difficult to control, the teacher should look for ways of increasing its reliability. One obvious weakness of most oral tests is the unpredictability of the direction the interchange will take, another is the inability of the tense or nervous student to demonstrate his skill. These two problems can be alleviated if certain conversational areas are established within which the interchange will take place. These will be made known to the student in advance. He can then approach the interview with more assurance, particularly if he is permitted to choose the area within which the first few questions and responses will range. This concession puts the student at his ease—a not inconsiderable factor. When the student's confidence is established the examiner can extend the conversation, drawing him out beyond anything he may have prepared or learned by heart.

Even when the teacher believes he is concentrating the student's attention on just one aspect of the work he may be demanding too many decisions at one point. A common type of question in foreign-language tests has been a series of *sentences to translate* from the native language to the foreign language. This apparently innocent device has become the bugbear of many a student. The author of the sentences becomes preoccupied with the most likely points of structural and lexical difficulty for the student and tries to weave four or five of these into one sentence. The result is usually a very stilted and artificial sentence which can be regarded only as a linguistic curiosity. A quick glance at an old textbook for the teaching of German to speakers of English reveals the following sentences for translation: "Steer courageously the ship through the rolling sea," "My brother has something beautiful and I have nothing ugly," "We do not go to the Dutch captain's, we go to the Russian major's," and "It would be necessary for you to dwell on the seashore." It is difficult to conceive of situations where these sentences could prove to be useful utterances, yet in classrooms all over the world teachers continue to concoct such monstrosities because they consider them an effective way to test the student's understanding of grammatical relationships. The teacher setting sentences of this type for a test makes a superficial count of the difficulties he has included, usually four or five to each sentence. He then allots marks accordingly. Closer examination reveals that each sentence requires perhaps ten or twelve decisions on the part of the student. The student may choose the appropriate lexical equivalents, but not make the necessary morphological adjustments to these words; he may choose the right tense for a verb but forget to make some other adjustment which use of this tense entails, or he may forget that this particular verb has some irregularity of form in this particular tense. Having solved several of these problems he may have paid little attention to some special problem of word order, or omitted to use some idiomatic turn of expression. It is not surprising that the student who gives up the unequal struggle and leaves blanks at various points in the sentence is often credited with a higher mark than the student who has tried to solve most of the problems. This type of question is one of the most flagrant examples of tests which test a number of things at the same time and therefore do not provide the student with a fair opportunity to show what he really knows.

The first step in alleviating the pressure on the student is to test vocabulary and grammatical structure separately. Only the most common lexical items which have been used frequently by the student should be employed in tests designed primarily to ascertain knowledge of morphology and syntax. Similarly, tests designed specifically to determine variety and range of vocabulary should not involve at the same time decisions on tenses, grammatical agreement with other words in the sentence (particularly where this involves the use of rare forms), or unusual word order. Where two difficulties which are different in kind coincide only the most alert student may be expected to deal with both effectively. The very fact that students are anxious to do well in a test often hinders them from seeing more than one point at a time. Coincidence of difficulty can mean that the student who knows what he has been taught is graded on the same level with the student who knows only some sections of the work, whereas one of the main aims of testing should be to distinguish clearly between the two.

TEST WHAT YOU HAVE TAUGHT

With a changing emphasis in teaching objectives and methods, there is always the danger that a time lag will develop between teaching and testing. Certain forms of test become so established with the passing of time that teachers who were tested by these methods themselves tend to accept them without reflection as being of unquestionable value. Many teachers do not even pause to analyze what the types of questions they are asking and the types of exercises they are setting are really testing. They are merely dismayed at the results achieved by their students on these tests and complain about deteriorating standards.

At a time when foreign-language teaching was consciously patterned on the teaching of Latin and Greek, emphasis was laid on a thorough analysis of the grammar of the language according to the traditional system, on the learning of rules, and on the developing of skill in applying these rules deductively. The memory was trained, or so it was believed, by the learning of long lists of foreign words with their native-language equivalents and by the reciting of innumerable conjugational and declensional paradigms. It had been considered by teachers of the classics that to be able to translate a passage from the native language into a reasonable approximation of Latin or Greek was a suitable demonstration of the mastery of the skills being sought: the understanding and memorization of rules and their deductive application. The same test of skill was soon applied in modern language classes. In the present period, what is being demanded of foreign-language students by the community which supports their education is the demonstration of their ability to understand, speak, and read the foreign language. Ability to write the language is rarely required of nonnative speakers. It is expected that after a period of study students will be able to understand and say something in the foreign language, and that they will be able to pick up a foreign-language book or newspaper and read it without too much difficulty. Teachers are conscious of these expectations and, for the most part, are trying to satisfy them by making the active communication skills the foundation of their class-room procedures, and by trying to develop in their students the ability to read in the foreign language without having to stop to translate every word.

Despite this change in approach, many tests, particularly those which have become community institutions and serve many schools, have not changed to a marked degree. They remain as they were many years ago. In the schools, teachers tend to construct their class tests on the same lines as these community-wide tests so that their students may be better prepared to face, at a later date, what are considered to be the most important tests of all. As a result, numbers of students are being taught one way and tested in another. For these students it is no longer true that they are being tested on what they have been taught.

One of the traditional ways of testing knowledge of the foreign language which is still encountered quite frequently is the setting of *a passage of prose to be translated* from the native language into the foreign language. This type of test, as we have seen, accorded well with the way in which the classical languages were taught. It is, however, singularly inappropriate for students who have been taught active use of the language without conscious attention to structural manipulations. In accordance with this approach, students are asked to produce language structures as wholes, to work transformations on them and combine them, without building them up element by element on each occasion. Testing time comes and the student is asked to reverse his procedure completely. He is asked to examine a passage of prose in his native language in the utmost detail, to break it down into its smallest elements, to find foreign-language equivalents for those elements, and then to construct from these foreign-language elements an acceptable segment of discourse. Unless he works in this way he has no hope of succeeding in his task, because in any prose passage there are many problems for the translator, some obvious, some not so obvious. Some of these the teacher has consciously included in the test, others he has overlooked in choosing the passage. If the student has not been trained in translation method and in comparative stylistics, what he finally produces cannot be called a translation: it is frequently no more than the reexpression of the forms of his own language with a lexical overlay from the foreign language. If students are to be asked to translate, they should be taught to translate in an efficient manner: a procedure which is possible only when the student has a considerable grasp of the structure and the lexical possibilities of both languages and has been trained to recognize divergence in linguistic features.[2] Translation cannot be considered a comprehensive test in all teaching situations. It is not only not a fair test for students who have been trained from the beginning to seek a direct grasp of structure and meaning in the foreign language, but it forces them into ways of thinking which can only retard their progress to language mastery.

Where the student has been trained from the early stages to produce acceptable foreign-language utterances as equivalents to stimulus utterances in the native language he may be tested in this form in writing. In appearance such a test resembles sentence translation but in principle it is very different. The sentences for which the student is asked to give foreign-language equivalents are uncomplicated. Each contains one language problem only, a problem which is of common occurrence and well known to the student. The vocabulary in which the utterance is phrased does not of itself require special consideration, and the utterance is one which the student would be likely to hear or use. He is asked to express as a whole in the foreign language the meaning of the native language stimulus utterance, not to construct element by element a supposed

---

2 The specific problems of translation are discussed in greater detail in Wilga M. Rivers, "Contrastive Linguistics in Textbook and Classroom," in *Contrastive Linguistics and Its Pedagogical Implications,* Georgetown Monograph Series on Languages and Linguistics, no. 21 (19th Roundtable), edited by James E. Alatis (Washington, D.C., 1968), pp. 151–58.

equivalent. A series of items of this type is a legitimate test of work which has been learned through dialogue memorization, pattern practice, and directed interchange of communication in the classroom. It is not appropriate for a class that has proceeded on strictly direct-method lines, without use of the native language at any time. This type of test can be continued to an advanced level as a test of the mastery of structural patterns. The student should be expected to give equivalents for a large number of utterances in a short time as a test of quick recall. If students are allowed a long period to pore over such sentences they will be tempted to break them into elements in their search for tricks and hidden difficulties.

Another kind of grammatical question which has been common in tests is the *"fill-in-the-blank"* type. Often this type of exercise has appeared in textbooks and in tests as a conglomeration of foreign-language expressions with native-language inserts. It has usually involved little more than the quick recognition of some structural clue in the foreign-language part of the sentence (in most cases in the segments preceding or following the blank). Many of these fill-in items can be completed quite successfully by a quick-witted student who has a minimal knowledge of the structural pattern required and a very vague idea of the meaning of the sentence. This type of exercise is little improved when foreign-language clues are given instead of native-language clues. Many are the students who have learned to make the required adjustments to foreign-language words without bothering to find out their meaning or to examine their relationship to the whole sentence. Sentence-completion items can be of use if the completion required involves a thorough understanding of the whole sentence. In this case clue words embedded in the item have a vital bearing on the correct decision. With this careful kind of construction, the whole item can be kept in the foreign language so that the student is forced to think in wholes, not to concentrate on meaningless segments.

A number of the various types of *pattern drills* can be converted into test items. The student may be asked to make transformations of sentences according to a cue word given. He may be asked to expand, contract, and combine sentences in various ways. He may be required to choose a correct form for a particular situation from a list of alternatives (this type of item being acceptable only if no incorrect forms, only inappropriate ones, are supplied). He may be given an outline to expand which has been structured in such a way that he is forced into using certain patterns and grammatical forms which he has practiced. Only when he has attained a certain authenticity of expression should the student be asked to express himself in the foreign language in perfect freedom. When he has reached this stage in class and has had considerable experience of such writing, a *free composition* may be set as part of a battery of tests in which objective assessment has predominated. At this point the more subjective evaluation of the composition will complement the grade for the more circumscribed items, just as the mark for the oral interview was shown to do in the area of oral production. Ways of making the assessment of free composition more objective have been discussed in chapter 10.

A new emphasis requires a new approach to testing and a search for types of items which test what we are teaching. A great deal of research is at present going into the designing of new types of tests and teachers should keep in touch with these developments through their professional literature. With the principles enunciated in this chapter in mind, they should experiment with new types of test items themselves, endeavoring to cover all the areas of language study which they are emphasizing in their teaching.

In establishing a final grade, the teacher should take care to see that it reflects the emphases of his teaching method. Even care in constructing his tests is not sufficient guarantee that this will be so. Some skill areas require tests which contain many more items than others. Having assessed a series of tests, teachers must take care to see that the system of "adding up marks" has not given a distorted picture of the individual student's achievement. If a vocabulary test contained fifty items, a listening-comprehension test twenty items, and a structure test twenty items, while an oral interview was assessed out of ten possible points, "adding up the marks" will imply that knowing fifty words is five times as important as being able to communicate effectively, and more than twice as important as understanding the spoken language and knowing how to use structural patterns. Knowledge of vocabulary will also have been assessed as an integral part of each of these tests, which again increases its share of the total. At this stage, the teacher must decide what weight to give to each of the sections of work which have been tested. This decision will depend on the percentage of time he has devoted to each of these areas, the objectives of the course, and the stage of learning that has been reached. Weighting corrects the imbalance caused by the number of small items and is a simple arithmetical procedure. Inexperienced teachers sometimes need to learn that the total of marks in a test is not some rigid reflection of reality; it is often a particularly deceptive objectivization of the defects of the test itself. Where the test does not reflect what the teacher knows of the proficiency of the class (that is, if the test items have proved too difficult and confusing for the candidates, or if the test has obviously been too simple) the teacher should make suitable statistical adjustments in his records. These adjustments will not alter the ranking of the candidates but will standardize the whole range of marks, making comparisons with other test entries more realistic. Guidance for this type of statistical treatment of a range of marks is provided in reference books in the Reading List at the end of the chapter.

TEST TO FIND OUT WHAT THE STUDENT KNOWS

At first reading, the heading of this section may appear so self-evident that it does not warrant discussion. This is far from being the case. It expresses an attitude which, unfortunately, is reflected in far too few of the tests which are set, whether for foreign languages or for other subjects of the curriculum. Questions are often framed in such a way that the successful student is the one who is best able to interpret the teacher's intentions. Questions may be so interrelated throughout the test that a mistake early in the series causes a succession of mistakes, and the student loses credit far in excess of what was warranted by the original error. This can be the case particularly in badly constructed listening-comprehension tests and in translation exercises of a consecutive nature. Tests may be so limited in scope that they provide for certain skill areas and leave others unconsidered: this is noticeably the case when all testing is of the reading-writing variety whereas a great deal of the class work has consisted of listening and speaking.

The method of assessing the total for a test may also prevent the teacher from differentiating clearly between those who have learned an acceptable amount and those who have not. A distinct difference in grading is observable between an assessment based on deduction of points for student errors and addition of points for what the student knows. "One mark off for each mistake" deducted from a predetermined total can mean that a student who has tried hard but made a number of mistakes receives less credit than a student who omitted portions of the work here and there and was therefore not in a position to make so many mistakes. If tests are of the objective type, this kind of discrepancy between points deducted and points allotted is not important. It is also less observable where items are not interdependent than in a test which proceeds in a sequential development.

A special problem arises where several classes at the same level are streamed, either according to predicted ability or according to achievement in earlier years. The purpose of the streaming is to enable students to study with other students who work at approximately the same rate. As a result, one or two of the streamed groups will advance more rapidly than the others. This can be a laudable pedagogical arrangement. Unfortunately the good effects of such streaming are obviated when the department or the administration insists on the construction of one test for the assessment of all groups. Possibly the test will be geared to the achievement of the fast-moving group, in which case it is inevitable that the students in the slower-moving groups will perform very badly, their enthusiasm will be dampened, and discouragement will set in. If, on the other hand, the test is geared to the average student it will provide no challenge for the students who have been moving more quickly. In either case, the test will not help the teacher to find out what a large percentage of the students know of the foreign language. There are several possible solutions to this problem. The teacher may set a progressive test with sections which move from the less advanced to the more advanced areas of the work. In this case, the fast-moving group may be required to complete the whole test while the slower-moving groups complete only certain sections. Alternatively, the teacher may set separate tests geared to the level of achievement of the different groups, adding some symbol to the report card to show the standard represented by the test assessment. There is no reason why students should not proceed in this way over a period of years, with differentiated classes taking different lengths of time to reach various specified levels of language mastery.

DESIGNING CLASS TESTS

Every teacher has to undertake the preparation of his own tests at regular intervals. As he prepares the test he should keep in his mind the image of the particular class for which he is constructing the test. This will act as a corrective to a natural tendency for him to compose the test around what he himself knows of the subject. He should design the test with careful attention to what he has taught this particular class: what he has taught the class thoroughly and not what he had intended to teach or what he feels he should have taught. No test will be efficiently constructed if the teacher designing it does not have a clear picture in his mind of what he expects his students to know. He should decide carefully which skills he wishes to test and which are the best ways to ensure that he is really testing these skills and not something else. Some tests are designed to establish the students' grasp of a particular area of the work; some are intended as all-round tests at the end of a unit of study. If the test is a comprehensive one the teacher should examine it carefully to see that it reflects adequately the amount of time he has spent on practice of the various skills, and that the test items for each skill reflect the way in which this skill was presented and practiced in class.

From the practical point of view the teacher should ask himself the following questions:

Are the instructions in the test so clear that no student can possibly misunderstand what he is expected to do? A foreign-language test is designed to find out what the student knows of the foreign language, not whether he is alert, intelligent, or able to read the teacher's mind. Unless the students have been thoroughly drilled in certain instructions in the foreign language, or have every opportunity to ask questions in case of uncertainty, instructions should be given in the native language. A weak or nervous student may misinterpret instructions in the foreign language and be prevented by this error from demonstrating to the teacher what he knows. If the question requires a particular style of answer misunderstanding may be avoided by the giving of a sample question and answer, but care must be taken, in this case, to see that the sample demonstrates only the way the question should be answered without supplying information which will give clues to the correct answers to later questions.

Is there any ambiguity in the test items? The test must be scrutinized very carefully to see that questions will prompt the response that the teacher is looking for and not leave the way open for other responses which will not be acceptable as a demonstration of learning in this particular area. No item should be included which allows of several possible answers unless it is clear to the student that all of these will be acceptable. It is very difficult for the author of a test to detect certain types of ambiguity, because he is conscious of his own intentions in the creation of the items. For this reason, each test should be submitted to one or two colleagues for criticism before being produced in its final form.

Is the test so constructed that the student begins with easier items and proceeds to the more difficult? This is an important psychological principle in testing. If the test is carefully graded in its development the weaker student who does not complete the test will omit only the items on which, in all probability, he would not have been successful. The weaker student often becomes anxious when he feels unable to answer questions satisfactorily. As a result he becomes tense and finds it difficult to answer even the easier questions. In a graded sequence, he does not reach this stage until the later part of the test when he has already moved confidently through the items which the teacher expected him to be able to complete correctly. A graded sequence also enables the teacher to test at several levels when the class consists of students of a wide range of ability, or when the same test is to be used for several classes which have been streamed according to speed of learning.

Do the items test ability to use the language rather than knowledge about the language? The learning of rules or generalizations about language structure and usage does not ensure ability to use the language effectively in speech or writing. Since teachers tend to teach and students tend to study in the way in which a test is framed, items which require students to write about the language rather than to show how it works have a very damaging effect on foreign-language study. If the language is being taught through use, students must not be expected to be able to make formal statements about its structure. Formal descriptions of the way a language functions should be expected only of students who are making advanced studies of the language at university level.

Are the items in the test linguistically useful? Test items should concentrate on what is normal usage, not on unusual forms about which even a native speaker may show hesitation. They should consist of complete utterances, unless there are very valid reasons for using segments of utterances. An "utterance" in this sense does not mean a complete sentence, in the traditional sense of the term, but a linguistic sample which is meaningful when used on its own. Words in isolation can be ambiguous and obscure in meaning and many students have learned to make adjustments to such isolated elements without having any clear idea how they function in a meaningful context. When elements being tested are placed in a linguistically useful utterance the student demonstrates more knowledge than when he is dealing with the same element in isolation, and his feeling for appropriate context is strengthened by this further contact. Items which present the student with a mixture of foreign-language and native-language forms force him into concentrating on disconnected elements of an utterance and hinder him in his efforts to think in the foreign language. Incorrect forms for identification or correction should be avoided: while the student is pondering his answer these incorrect versions are being impressed on his senses and may be learned incidentally, quite contrary to the teacher's intentions.

CONSTRUCTION AND USE OF OBJECTIVE TESTS

Earlier in this chapter it has been pointed out that many aspects of foreign-language learning can be tested by carefully constructed objective tests. They are especially useful when it is considered desirable to test certain aspects of language skills in isolation, as for instance: aural discrimination of sounds, comprehension of spoken speech and of written texts, range of vocabulary, or understanding of the function of elements of grammatical structure. Objective tests may be considered more reliable, in the statistical sense of the word, than more traditional tests in that they would be assessed in an identical fashion even if corrected by several different persons.

Objective tests have several other advantages over tests of a more traditional character. Although they take much longer to prepare, they are more easily and rapidly corrected, and when both preparation and correction time have been taken into account they represent a great saving where large groups of students are involved. They may be machine-corrected if numbers warrant it. If numbers are small, they are quickly corrected by visual scrutiny or with the aid of a cardboard key with holes punched for the appropriate answers. Teachers are thus able to test more frequently without fearing the burden of many hours of laborious correction. With objective tests, more questions can be answered by students in a test period because time is not taken up with a lot of redundant writing, much of which is mere copying from the test paper. Consequently, questions can range over a much greater area of the work studied, giving students more opportunity to show what they have learned than in the hit-or-miss procedure of a few limited questions.

There are several types of objective tests which may be used in foreign-language classes: true-false, multiple-choice, fill-in-the-blank, and matching tests.

True-false tests involve the acceptance or rejection of a

statement or utterance heard or read. They are most useful as tests of listening or reading comprehension, or of knowledge of historical, literary, and cultural facts related to the foreign-language study. Since the choice is a two-way one, the probability of a chance success is much higher than in a multiple-choice test. Even when a third choice, "Don't know," is added, there is little guarantee that students will not prefer to make a guess at the answer. A heavier penalty for a wrong answer than for "Don't know" may discourage this to some extent but makes correction a little more complicated. For these reasons, true-false tests are probably best kept as a method of checking whether students have prepared certain work, or as a guide to the student on his understanding of a text he has been reading on his own. Where a more penetrating discrimination of student achievement is sought, a more elaborate type of test is advisable.

Multiple-choice tests provide answers to questions on, for example, listening- or reading-comprehension material, lexical meanings of words, appropriateness of rejoinder in spoken language. Of the answers supplied only one is appropriate; the others are based on likely errors which the student will be led to make by not discriminating between words of similar sound in listening comprehension, by confusion of vocabulary or misinterpretation of structural relationships in reading comprehension, by not distinguishing between words which are similar in spelling and form in vocabulary tests, or by mis-hearing or misreading the question under consideration. Contrary to the belief of some persons untrained in probability theory, a well-constructed multiple-choice test with a large number of items, each with three or four choices, does not make it easy for students to guess their way through to success. Apart from the restricted statistical probabilities of successful guessing, well-designed choices of answer in a multiple-choice test seem plausible to the student who does not know his work thoroughly and are, therefore, not chosen by the student on a purely chance basis. The arrangement of the appropriate choices on the answer sheet (the choices are usually labelled A, B, C, D) should be randomized, so that students cannot hit upon a pattern of response, however unintentional on the part of the constructor, which will help in guessing. The use of a table of random numbers is useful in establishing the order of placement of the correct choices.

The fill-in-the-blank type of test may be multiple-choice or it may require the student to fill in an appropriate foreign-language word. These tests are very suitable for testing knowledge of grammatical structure, use of tenses, and vocabulary. Care must be taken to ensure that the sentences are quite unambiguous and can be completed appropriately by only one word. Where choices are given, they must all be real possibilities for the student who has not taken account of all the clues in the item, and there must be no possibility of the student arriving at the correct decision by a process of elimination. Write-in completion tests are less objective than multiple-choice completion tests because students may make errors other than those which the teacher has foreseen, and the possibility of ambiguity must be even more rigorously controlled.

Matching tests are commonly used as vocabulary tests. Students are asked to match synonyms, antonyms, names of objects with names of groups or classes of objects, names of objects with occupations, and so on. Tests of this type can also be used for testing knowledge of facts about the foreign culture. It is in matching tests that there is the greatest possibility of reaching correct decisions by a process of elimination. This danger can be avoided by providing unequal lists for the matching process, or by providing several items which may be matched with more than one item, and others which do not match at all.

Objective tests require skill and ingenuity in their construction. With a little imagination and humor, items can be made interesting as well as useful. If students are not allowed to retain their question papers, tests may be reused in successive years, with items improved where experience and item analysis have shown them to be ineffective or defective. In revising a test the teacher should be watchful to eliminate items which basically test the same thing and therefore distort the score. These are not always obvious to the teacher when he is first constructing the test and earnestly seeking valid items. Once an effective test has been produced in certain areas, notably in testing grammatical structure, parallel tests can be created without a great deal of difficulty by converting items from the lexical point of view without altering other relationships. There are many practical hints of this type to be gleaned with regard to the effective construction and revision of objective tests; some of these can be found in the literature on language testing, others will come with experience. If the position of objective tests is to be justified in the foreign-language program, however, it must be remembered that they test only certain aspects of language study (passive knowledge rather than active use) and that they must be combined with other, more subjectively evaluated, tests of language skill to give an all-round picture of the student's achievement.

AREAS OF CONTROVERSY

Is it possible to predict student success in foreign-language study?

Along with growing appreciation in the community of the importance of the learning of foreign languages, and more widespread teaching of languages in the schools, has come an interest in the problems of students who are not successful in the foreign-language course. Research workers have turned their attention to the possibility of predicting student success or failure by analysis of performance on a battery of tests of aptitude for foreign-language learning. Traditionally it has been considered that measures of general intelligence and of achievement in native-language studies were the best predictors of success with a foreign language. Pimsleur has found these to be inferior to other measures.[3] Before any decision can be made about the best predictors we must consider the method by which the foreign language will be taught to the particular students whose success or failure we wish to predict. If the foreign-language course is to be a silent one consisting mainly of reading, translation, and the learning of rules and paradigms different abilities will be called into play than in a course where the foreign language is taught primarily for communication. Most of the recent research has been conducted with a view to establishing ability factors involved in

3 "Testing in Foreign Language Teaching," in A. Valdman, ed., *Trends in Language Teaching* (New York, 1966), pp. 176–77.

learning a foreign language for active use. As this type of prediction is of considerable concern to the organizers of intensive foreign-language courses for persons about to be sent overseas on business, diplomatic, military, or foreign-aid assignments some of the experimental testing has been conducted in conjunction with such training. Other testing has been carried out in universities and high schools. Since the two situations are not comparable, we shall concentrate in this discussion on appropriate tests for the normal school situation.

After extensive testing, Carroll and Sapon designed a *Modern Language Aptitude Test* (MLAT) based on the factors they considered most important in foreign-language learning: *phonetic coding* (ability to "code" auditory phonetic material in such a way that this material can be recognized, identified, and remembered over something longer than a few seconds); *ability to handle "grammar"* (being sensitive to the functions of words in a variety of contexts); *rote memorization ability;* and *ability to infer linguistic forms, rules and patterns* from new linguistic content itself with a minimum of supervision or guidance.[4] To test these abilities, they constructed the following subtests: (1) *Number Learning:* the candidate learns an artificial number system constructed of nonsense syllables, and is then asked to write the appropriate numerals for numbers dictated; (2) *Phonetic Script:* the candidate learns phonetic symbols for certain English sounds and is tested on this learning; (3) *Spelling Clues* (a type of vocabulary test with foreign words and possible English meanings); (4) *Words in Sentences:* the candidate is expected to detect the functions of words and identify in other sentences words which have the same function; (5) *Paired Associates,* the learning of a twenty-four-item foreign vocabulary list with English equivalents.[5]

4 J. B. Carroll, "The Prediction of Success in Intensive Foreign Language Training," mimeographed (Cambridge, Mass., 1960), quoted in W. Lambert, "Psychological Approaches to the Study of Language," *MLJ* 47, no. 2: 60. The Lambert article is reprinted in H. B. Allen, ed., *Teaching English as a Second Language* (New York, 1965), pp. 25–50, and J. Michel, ed., *Foreign Language Teaching* (New York, 1967), pp. 215–50.

5 J. B. Carroll and S. M. Sapon, *Modern Language Aptitude Test* (New York, 1958).

Pimsleur has developed a *Language Aptitude Battery* (LAB) with six subtests: (1) *Grade-Point Average* (a measure of achievement in a number of school subjects) ; (2) *Interest* in studying the foreign language, registered on a five-point scale; (3) *Vocabulary* (a test of knowledge of native-language vocabulary, in this case English) ; (4) *Language Analysis* (a test of ability to discern the function of language elements in a number of forms in an unknown language for which English equivalents are given) ; (5) *Sound Discrimination* (the candidate learns certain foreign words and is expected to recognize them when he hears them spoken) ; (6) *Sound-Symbol* (recognition of the graphic form of words the candidate has heard spoken).[6] Pimsleur's research in schools [7] has led him to believe that ability to handle verbal materials, important as it is, is not sufficient in itself to ensure success in foreign-language learning. He lays great stress on motivation to learn the language and auditory ability. The latter ability is obviously of great importance when the course is conducted on an aural-oral basis.

Language aptitude tests are still largely at an experimental stage. Both the tests described have been found to have predictive and diagnostic value. In the present state of research, however, it would be unwise to use them as definitive instruments for deciding which students will, or will not, be allowed to undertake the study of a foreign language, except in specialized institutions where for financial and professional reasons only those with the greatest possibilities of success can be accepted. At school level all students can profit from some experience of foreign-language learning, as part of their general educational program. Some will learn more slowly than others; some will continue the study longer than others. Aptitude tests can help the teacher to understand the particular problems which certain students are facing, and to identify students who could be learning more quickly if they were willing to study more diligently. As Pimsleur, Sundland, and McIntyre have remarked: "Future research should concern itself with the improvement of foreign language programs and

---

6 P. Pimsleur in Valdman (1960), pp. 178–79.
7 P. Pimsleur, D. Sundland, and R. McIntyre, "Under-Achievement in Foreign Language Learning," *IRAL* II/2 (1964): 135–36.

with the development of teaching techniques suitable for students of various levels of ability, including those of low auditory ability. . . . The objective is to provide for every student a rewarding foreign language experience, one which equips him with a serviceable degree of competence in the foreign language." [8]

ANNOTATED READING LIST

LADO, ROBERT. *Language Testing.* London: Longmans, 1961. A thorough study of testing principles and test construction, with suggestions for suitable types of tests for all aspects of foreign-language learning.

PIMSLEUR, PAUL. "Testing Foreign Language Learning." Chapter 11 of *Trends in Language Teaching,* edited by ALBERT VALDMAN. New York: McGraw-Hill, 1966. An examination of the problems involved in designing tests of language aptitude, listening comprehension, speaking, and reading comprehension. Useful bibliographic references.

STREVENS, P. D. *Papers in Language and Language Teaching.* London: Oxford University Press, 1965. Chapter 7, "Objective Testing," discusses the function of testing and the desirable features of objective tests for grammar, vocabulary, and pronunciation.

VALETTE, REBECCA M. *Modern Language Testing: A Handbook.* New York: Harcourt, Brace & World, 1967. Gives useful information on preparing and giving tests for the major skill areas and for knowledge of culture and literature, with many examples of possible types of tests. Examples are in English, French, German, Italian, Russian, and Spanish. Essential for close study.

8 *Ibid,* p. **137.**

13

Tape Recorders and Language Laboratories

Foreign-language teachers have been quick to seize upon the possibilities opened up by the easy availability of tape recorders and magnetic tape. Where previously it was difficult in many countries to provide opportunities for students to hear a great deal of authentic native speech, now at the press of a switch an abundance of such material is available, even in remote and isolated areas. From the tape recorder in the classroom to a special room equipped with individual listening or recording-playback facilities is an obvious development. At what moment this step can be taken in a particular school depends on the funds available. Whether the teacher is using a tape recorder in the classroom or a specially equipped language laboratory, he will be applying the same principles, although in practice each of these teaching situations will have its own problems. In this chapter, we shall discuss the use of tapes particularly in the context of the language laboratory, where all the problems associated with this type of work are accentuated. Teachers who can use only a single tape recorder to supplement their classroom teaching will, however, be able to derive from the discussion a great deal of information for their particular situation.

There is no such thing as a "language laboratory method" as many people falsely assume. The tape recorder is a tool like the textbook or the chalkboard. It can be used by a teacher accustomed to any method, but to varying degrees of effectiveness. With certain methods, any time spent in the laboratory must be considered so much time wasted.

If understanding the foreign language when spoken by a native speaker and speaking the language intelligibly are not primary objectives of the teacher's method, then time spent with the tape recorder would be better spent with books. When the desired priority in the acquisition of skills is understanding, speaking, reading, and writing, the tape recorder can help in developing all four skills, understanding and speaking providing a foundation for more rapid control of reading comprehension and the ability to write idiomatically in the language.

The use of tapes does not of itself guarantee the effective development of listening and speaking skills. With materials originally prepared with other aims, or other tools, in mind, work with tapes can be ineffectual, confusing, and frustrating. Teachers need to study carefully and critically the available materials to see that they are based on sound grammatical and pedagogical principles and are interesting to the students. They must also plan the laboratory lessons carefully to ensure full participation with a maximum of practice for each student.

THE LANGUAGE LABORATORY IS NOT A TEACHER

Just as the language laboratory is not in itself a method, neither is it a teacher. It will not do the teacher's work for him, nor even reduce the amount of work he is called upon to do. It will relieve him of the direction of a great deal of the repetitive practice which is so valuable to the student and so wearying to the teacher.

Experimental psychology demonstrates that we learn what we do. In the learning of a foreign language, mental comprehension is not enough. The student must practice the use of the complex elements of the language until they come to him freely and effortlessly. In the past, many teachers have looked only for signs of mental comprehension of each element before moving on to teach the next. The result has been that structural patterns, and even vocabulary, have had to be taught and retaught several years in succession as students have continued to make the same mistakes. In a class of thirty or more students, it has not been possible during classroom sessions to give each student all the practice he needed, and there has been no effective way of controlling the amount and accuracy of his learning practice out of school hours. With the establishment of a laboratory, much of this individual practice takes place in a situation where an accurate model and immediate correction of mistakes are available. Each student is provided with carefully graded and sequenced learning practice, and a way of verifying how he is progressing. It must be emphasized, however, that the effectiveness of the learning is dependent on the thought and care which the teacher has put into the programming of the practice tapes. The work of the students in the laboratory will be only as good as the program with which they are asked to work. This important question of the programming of tapes will be discussed at length later in this chapter.

LABORATORY WORK MUST BE AN INTEGRAL PART OF THE
LANGUAGE PROGRAM

The language laboratory cannot teach. The teaching must be done by the teacher in the classroom, in a personal interchange with the students.[1] Sessions in the laboratory will be interspersed with classroom lessons. The work in any one laboratory session must consist of practice of what has been taught in a previous class lesson, or work for which the student has been prepared in some way by the teacher. Moreover, the work done in the laboratory should be used by the teacher as a basis for developing further skill in this area during subsequent classroom lessons. If the class has not reached the stage where the work programmed for a particular laboratory session is meaningful, it is better to omit that session; otherwise, the student

---

1 In some situations the student learns with a programmed text or teaching machine (see chapter 4). Even in these situations the most experienced experimenters with programmed instruction for foreign-language learning advocate supplementary sessions with a teacher for developing communication skills.

who is forced to practice actively what he has not been taught will find the session exasperating, disappointing, and frustrating. It is for this reason that tapes programmed in individual lessons by commercial publishers are difficult to use. They presume that in widely diverse schools teachers will be teaching and students will be learning at the same regular rate.

ADVANTAGES OF A LANGUAGE LABORATORY

Since a language laboratory is such an expensive tool, it is as well to consider, before installing one, what advantages it provides which may justify this expense.

(1) For the first time in the history of foreign-language teaching, each student may have the opportunity to hear native speech clearly and distinctly.

(2) The student may hear this authentic native speech as frequently as he and his teacher desire.

(3) The taped lesson provides an unchanging and unwearying model of native speech for the student to imitate.

(4) In the laboratory the student may listen to a great variety of foreign voices, both male and female.

(5) The laboratory booth provides the student with psychological isolation which releases him from some of his inhibitions about making embarrassing foreign-language sounds in front of his fellows.

(6) Each student may hear and use the foreign language throughout the laboratory session, instead of wasting time waiting for his turn in a large group, as he does in the usual classroom situation.

(7) The laboratory frees the teacher from certain problems of class direction and classroom management, enabling him to concentrate on the problems of individual students.

With recording-playback facilities:

(8) The student is in a position to compare objectively a specimen of his own speech in the foreign language with that of a native model.

(9) Each student may practice each language element as many times as he wishes before moving on to the next.

(10) The laboratory provides means for testing oral production in the foreign language in a more detached, objective fashion. Tapes of test utterances may be compared with each other and reconsidered carefully in a way which is impossible in a series of personal interviews. The time taken for individual testing is reduced if tapes of speech production are made at the console during a class session, while other students continue with their normal practice.

(11) The laboratory provides the teacher with a ready means of improving his own articulation and intonation where this is desirable, or of keeping his skill in these areas at a high level when he is not able to meet and talk with native speakers.

(12) In certain laboratory situations, which we shall discuss later, each student can study at his own pace, concentrating on the parts of the work in which he needs most practice, rather than being forced to keep pace with his fellows.

TYPES OF LANGUAGE LABORATORIES

1. *Listen-Respond Laboratory*

The simplest form of Listen-Respond laboratory is a classroom with tape recorder in operation. There should preferably be some form of amplification if the tape recording is to be heard clearly in all areas of the classroom. Certain advantages are gained when the school establishes a special room, acoustically treated, in which groups may be brought closer to the tape recorder.

Such a room will be situated away from distracting noises, from busy roads, playing fields, workshops, or frequently used corridors. A further refinement is the addition for each student of headphones plugged into the tape recorder, or recorders, or into a single or multiple jack box attached to these. This addition enables each student to hear more clearly without being distracted by the other students around him. He finds it easier to concentrate. Listening units such as these may be installed on some kind of moveable tray or table and taken from room to room, or, for more distraction-free listening, installed permanently in an acoustically treated room.

This simple form of laboratory is not expensive to install and maintain. It enables students to hear at frequent intervals authentic native speech, with a variety of voices and accents. The teacher who is not a native speaker cannot provide such an excellent model himself, and if his language training has been deficient he finds this aid invaluable.

With this type of installation the student can practice correct articulation, intonation, and phrasing in imitation of the native model. For aural-comprehension practice he can listen to dialogues, news bulletins, simulated telephone conversations, lectures, or short stories. His appreciation of literature can be deepened by listening to poems and literary extracts read by fine readers, and scenes from plays performed by professional actors. He can learn songs from recordings by famous singers. More prosaic, but none the less essential, will be his work with structural pattern drills for which he will hear the correct response immediately following his own version of each drill item.

There is, however, room for improvement to the simple Listen-Respond system. Because of the earphones he is wearing the student is not able to hear his own voice clearly. He will be tempted, almost without realizing it, to mumble or whisper, thus developing bad speech habits in the foreign language. Later, when called upon to express himself in the language, he will experience many of the same inhibitions which bedevil the student trained in a silent, book-ridden classroom. His pronunciation cannot be corrected immediately because he cannot hear the teacher speaking to him. In this type of installation there is no possibility for a student to work at his own pace. It is as inflexible in this respect as any traditional classroom lesson.

The elementary Listen-Respond system can be recommended only where financial considerations prohibit the addition of the distinctive features of the second system, which we shall now describe.

2. Listen-Respond Laboratory with Activated Headphones

The value of the laboratory is greatly increased by the addition of a microphone and activated headphones for each student. As the student speaks into the microphone his own voice is amplified and comes to him through the earphones much as another person would hear it, and with a similar volume to that of the program to which he is listening. This gives him a surer basis for comparison of his utterances with those of the native model. With this addition, the laboratory is called "audio-active." When these facilities are installed in separate, acoustically treated booths, the students profit in several ways. They hear the program more clearly because they are freed to a greater degree from extraneous noise and the voices of their fellow students repeating aloud. It is easier for them to concentrate. Certain types of students, too, gain from the impression of isolation, and this helps them to overcome their diffidence about pronouncing foreign sounds in the presence of others. When they feel that they have achieved a fair approximation of the sounds they become more confident about taking part in oral work in class.

This type of language laboratory is completed by the addition of a console with one or more tape decks for the emission of the program. The console is wired to permit two-way communication between students and teacher. The teacher not only listens to the student's utterances but is able to make helpful comments, which are heard only by the student addressed. A further facility enables the teacher to address the whole group over the broadcast system in order to give instructions, or guidance and teaching. Some consoles are wired so that groups of students may be put in touch with each other for group discussions or for purposes of mutual evaluation. The usefulness of the laboratory is increased if the initial wiring of the console permits the broadcasting through several channels of different programs to specific groups of booths. In this way, different languages or several levels of the same language can be provided for at the same time.

If there are two tape decks at the console the teacher is usually able to record the utterances of individual students in their booths. This can be very useful for testing oral production, or for enabling students to listen more objectively to their utterances where no other playback facilities are available.

It is also useful to give students some opportunities to listen to foreign speech in less favorable conditions than through the headphones. The laboratory should therefore be wired to permit the broadcasting of parts of the program from room amplifiers. This feature is particularly useful where songs are used as a diversion from the concentration of the main program; students will join in the singing of the songs if they are broadcast to the whole room but will feel embarrassed by the sound of their own voices if the music is coming only through the headphones.

Some institutions have introduced closed booths in which the student listens to the taped program amplified to normal speech level and responds naturally, without using either headphones or microphone, thus hearing the taped voice and his own voice much as he would hear them in an ordinary speech situation. Booths of this type are used for regular practice in listening, imitation of sounds and intonation, and structure drill.

3. Listen-Respond-Compare Laboratory

The addition of individual recording facilities increases the scope of the laboratory: tape recorders are installed at each student place. The student is now able to record his utterances and compare them with those of the native model.

If single-track recording facilities are used, the system has limited usefulness. The student must listen to perhaps fifteen minutes of recording, hearing his own mistakes of pronunciation and intonation over and over again, before he is able to correct them. This becomes tedious and frustrating. He must record the master program again and his second version in full before being able to see if he has improved.

If dual-track tape recorders are used, the student is able to record the master program sent out to him from the console on one track, and his own imitation or response on a second track. Later, he is able to replay his recording for comparison. Frequently the master track is already recorded for him before the session begins. Once the master track is completely recorded, he can rewind a part of the tape each time he feels he can improve his work and rerecord a phrase or a section of work on the second track, erasing his first effort as he does so. This process does not affect the master model on the first track in any way. He therefore has the opportunity to compare his own efforts with the tape model as often as he likes. He can listen and rerecord, listen and rerecord, working at his own pace, without interrupting the work of his fellow students or being forced to wait for them to catch up with him.

Where financial considerations prohibit the installation of recording-playback facilities of this type in every booth, serious consideration should be given to the installation of such facilities in a certain number of the booths. The students in each class can then, by a system of rotation, have the opportunity to playback and rerecord at certain intervals (perhaps every third or fourth session), thus studying their oral production more objectively. In this case, they will need to be supplied with prerecorded tapes which are much shorter than those being used for the normal broadcast program for the Listen-Respond booths, so that they will have time to work through the tape several times with a view to self-improvement. The Listen-Respond-Compare facilities can be used for all the purposes listed for the Listen-Respond system, but their unique contribution is obviously in the area of improvement of pronunciation and intonation, and oral reading of prose and poetry. Because the student can stop and start the tape when he pleases, they are useful for such exercises as advanced listening comprehension, simulated conversation with a tape model, practice in taking notes of foreign-language lectures, and learning roles in foreign-language plays.

Where recorders are available in student booths it is usual to have wiring which permits the starting and stopping of all recorders from the console. This permits the making of multiple copies of tapes for individual work in the booths, which is an important time-saving consideration. Such a facility is also useful for the giving of tests for which students record answers on their individual recorders.

4. Listen-Respond-Compare Laboratory with Remote Control

A further development in language laboratory design removes the recording facilities from the student booth to a central location. The program source may also be in the same location, remote-controlled from the console. This system simplifies the purely manipulative operation of both booth and console. It also facilitates maintenance since the equipment for a number of laboratories may be in the one place. The student is still able to hear the master program, record the master and his own responses, and play back both the master and his own version. Since he has less equipment to handle in his booth the risks of his running into difficulties of a mechanical nature are reduced.

With remote control, the student moves switches in his booth for all the necessary operations of listening, recording, playback, or rerecording. In some individualized systems he has a telephone type of dial in the booth, by the operation of which he can be connected with the particular tape he requires in the central location. Under this system, student booths for practice can be established in different parts of a building, or buildings. In some institutions amplification is also installed in a certain number of classrooms from which the teacher may dial for a particular program in the central stack. In this way each teacher may interpolate illustrative or practice material into his lessons as he needs it, or teachers in different classrooms may give one test simultaneously to several classes at the same level of instruction. Improvements and refinements of this system are continually being developed, and these should be studied carefully by all who have the responsibility of advising on new equipment.

INSTALLING A LANGUAGE LABORATORY

The teacher who is called upon to advise on the installation of a language laboratory in his school should study carefully some of the excellent books available on types of installation and their purpose, and the particular features to look for in the choice of equipment. He should then visit installations of various kinds and see them in operation in a school situation before making any decision. The comments of teachers who are using these installations will soon draw his attention to the advantages and disadvantages of various features. It is only by such visits that he will be able to judge whether the type of installation he has in mind will perform the kind of function he envisages for his own school. It is also the best way of studying facility of operation and the kinds of problems a particular type of installation leaves unsolved.

If *audio-visual courses* are to be used in the school other considerations will arise. Audio-visual courses, which are discussed fully in chapter 7, require the constant use of films, filmstrips, or slides in association with classroom teaching and practice sessions with taped materials. For maximum efficiency, audio-visual equipment will need to be installed in classrooms and, for individual practice, viewing equipment in the booths which can be controlled by each student according to his requirements. If individual viewing facilities cannot be provided, the laboratory must be so constructed that the necessary slides or films associated with oral practice can be projected, without undue effort on the part of the teacher, on screens which are clearly visible to each student from his working position. The subject of proper provision for the requirements of audio-visual courses will need to be discussed very thoroughly in the laboratory planning stages.

Having carefully established the purposes for which he and his colleagues intend to use the laboratory the teacher responsible for the laboratory should plan the future installation with these purposes in mind. In this planning he would be well advised to have the help of a qualified independent consultant, familiar with foreign-language teaching aims and methods as well as with the technical aspects of the installation. Such a consultant can help him to see where the equipment proposed by commercial suppliers is adequate for his purposes and where it should be adapted or redesigned to suit the specific needs of his school.

Throughout the planning stages the teacher should keep in the forefront of his thinking the importance of the audio quality of the equipment to be installed. Discrimination of foreign-language sounds is much more difficult for the student than comprehension of the native language and requires the highest quality of reproduction available. Chrome and fine woodwork and an impressive array of gadgets will soon use up money which should be spent on the finest of microphones, headphones, and recording equipment if the essential purpose of the laboratory is to be realized.

Particular attention should also be paid to the durability of the essential parts of the equipment. The teacher should seek out companies which are making equipment specially designed for the almost continuous use they receive in the language laboratory. Standard equipment built for other purposes may appear cheaper at first, but will prove costly in maintenance and replacements.

No school should embark on the installation of a language laboratory without having carefully weighed the implications of the following observations.

1. *The initial expense of installation is only part of the financial commitment involved.* Laboratories need continual maintenance and regular overhaul, with eventual replacements of expensive parts, if a high level of efficiency and audio quality is to be maintained.

2. There should be available *a person qualified to keep a continual check on equipment,* to make minor running repairs, and to perform necessary routine maintenance: such as the cleaning of parts, the demagnetizing of tape recorder heads, the tightening of screws and knobs, and the checking of headphone and microphone cords. The company installing the laboratory should be requested to supply a schedule of such necessary operations. Without them equipment cannot be kept in fine condition, and with the passage of time frequent breakdowns and expensive repairs will be inevitable. Certain small operations, like the cleaning of the recorder heads, must be carried out very regularly if the sound quality is to be satisfactory. Some person within the school can be trained to do these things, since they do not require the competence of a technician. Emergency breakdowns are another matter. If the school does not employ a technical assistant, it is as well to have a contract with a local repairman who will undertake to come on call. Otherwise, booths will be out of order for lengthy periods—with resultant disorder for the language teacher. At intervals of six months a thorough overhaul of all equipment will be necessary. Since most companies contract to provide such a service only during the first year after installation, the cost of the regular overhaul must be included in estimates of the maintenance budget in succeeding years.

3. *The laboratory will be an unjustifiable expense if it is not*

used effectively. Before a laboratory is installed or extended, the department head should ascertain the attitude of the staff to its use.

It may be necessary to conduct an evaluation study of the effectiveness of methods and materials already in use, and of changes which must be made in the program if language laboratory work is to be fully integrated with it. Investigations should be made into the availability of well-designed tapes for the age level of the students in the particular languages being taught. Teachers should be given the opportunity of observing language laboratory work in nearby schools and discussing advantages and problems with teachers who have already had success in this area. As many as possible of the teachers who will be using the equipment should be encouraged to attend seminars, workshops, or courses on the use of the laboratory and the integration of the laboratory with classroom teaching. These teachers can then help their colleagues through a preparatory training program within the school. For the inexperienced, such training should include actual manipulation of the equipment to dispel the irrational fears of some teachers when confronted with knobs, switches, and revolving tapes.

With forethought and planning, much antagonism, frustration, and ineffectiveness on the part of the staff can be avoided, and the laboratory will be accepted and used instead of being the costly disappointment it has sometimes proved to be.

THE DIRECTOR OF THE LABORATORY

As soon as the installation of the laboratory becomes a real possibility, one teacher should be put in charge of it as director. His are the many duties of organization and administration: advising on equipment and installation, ordering of tapes, direction of in-service training, scheduling of classes, setting up and cataloguing of the library of tapes, making program tapes from available master tapes, splicing broken tapes and erasing used tapes, training students and new teachers in the use of laboratory equipment, and studying the latest developments in laboratory facilities with an eye to future improvements.

The director will find that equipment is kept in better condition if certain rules for behavior in the laboratory and some clear instructions for the orderly handling of tapes and equipment by both students and teachers are established and enforced. Suggestions for such regulations drawn up by experienced laboratory directors are provided in some of the books in the Annotated Reading List at the end of this chapter. Experience will suggest others.

Time will have to be allowed on the teaching program of the laboratory director for these duties, many of which are humble and time-consuming but essential to the smooth and effective functioning of the laboratory.

Once the laboratory is established, many visitors will wish to see it. Such visits can take up a great deal of the director's time and become very wearisome after a while, yet they are valuable for teachers from other schools where laboratories are soon to be installed. They also keep parents and public officials informed on what the school is doing. The laboratory director can save much time if he prepares an orientation tape explaining what most visitors want to know about the laboratory and giving them the opportunity to listen to and repeat some of the elementary material, as though they themselves were students. Mimeographed sheets of the script of the orientation tape can then be distributed to the visitors for future reference.

For many other more technical aspects of his work which cannot be discussed here, the director should have access to several of the standard reference books on the language laboratory recommended in the Annotated Reading List at the end of this chapter. In these he will find invaluable information on the selection, maintenance, and servicing of equipment, and suggestions for efficient organization and administration.

CHOOSING TAPED MATERIALS FOR THE LABORATORY LIBRARY

It is important not to rush ahead and buy a great quantity of taped material in order to fill the empty shelves of the laboratory storeroom. The same care in choice is required with sets of tapes as in the setting up of a new library of books. Taped materials are expensive and money must be invested wisely in those which will best serve the purposes of the courses offered or proposed.

Textbooks currently in use should be studied thoughtfully in association with the taped materials offered by their publishers or the possibilities within the school of making tapes for use with them. Most publishers will send demonstration tapes for examination. A textbook which has proved very suitable in the past when other methods have been employed may be found to be unsuitable for use in association with a laboratory. If listening and speaking skills are not primary aims of the course set out in the textbook, then a choice must be made between the textbook and the use of the laboratory. Many teachers are misled in this matter because publishers now issue tapes of lessons for nearly all available textbooks. If the texts were not originally designed with the specific conditions of laboratory study in mind, the tapes made to go with them can prove very exasperating and frustrating to the student. An exercise designed to be studied by the eye at leisure often consists of segments too long and too varied in vocabulary and structural content to be held in the student's mind long enough for repetition. Succeeding segments often require several changes at once which demand an impossible performance of mental and verbal gymnastics. The only way for the teacher to appreciate the effect of such exercises on the student in the laboratory booth, and to assess their effectiveness, is for him to play one of the lesson tapes in the laboratory and try himself to produce the responses required in a limited interval of time without the textbook before him. The difficulty he experiences will be much greater for the student, to whom the work is unfamiliar.

In the early stages of establishing a library of materials, a group of teachers experienced in teaching students of widely varying abilities at different levels of instruction should form a committee to listen to demonstration tapes and to examine accompanying text materials. A checklist should be drawn up of qualities to be noted, and each should be given a rating or comment during the listening period so that an objective comparison may be made during committee discussions. Such a checklist would include the following items:

Production

    Clarity of recording.
    Fidelity.
    Accent in the foreign language (standard native, near-native, unacceptable to native speaker, artificial).
    Speed of speech (fast native, normal native, slow but acceptable native, unnaturally slow, distorted).
    Quality of speech (distinct, slurred, high-pitched . . .).
    Intonation.
    Tone of voice (pleasant, uninteresting, bored, condescending, unintentionally humorous . . .).
    Extraneous noise in the recording.

Material Recorded

(a) *Dialogues or passages for imitation and memorization:*
    Clarity.
    Naturalness of subject matter and speech.
    Interest of material for level required.
    Standard of difficulty for level required.
    Authenticity of cultural setting.
    Value of phrases for memorization.
    Length of segments for repetition.
    Background (music, "noises off" . . .).

(b) *Exercises and Drills:*
    (See discussion on pattern drills in chapter 4.)
    Designed for laboratory use or traditional exercises originally designed to be read or written.
    Instructions unambiguous with sufficient examples as a guide to students.
    Length of segments for repetition. (Five to eight syllables is quite sufficient at an elementary level. At a more advanced level, eight to twelve syllables may be accepted if the material has sufficient inbuilt redundancy.)
    Structural content of each segment (one structure, two, three . . . ?).
    Number of examples of a similar pattern for practice before making a change.

Number of changes from one segment to the next (minimal structural change, several changes at once).

Vocabulary range. (If this is too extensive, it can prove distracting and confusing.)

Stimulus items that can elicit only one correct response.

Correct response given immediately after interval for student response.

Length of interval for student response. (This is not a vital consideration in evaluating a commercial tape, as the interval can be shortened or lengthened when copying from master to program tape. Some commercial tapes do not include an interval, but leave it to the teacher to insert one. Some types of equipment have a pause button with which the student can put in his own length of pause.)

Careful consideration should be given to the acquisition of a well-designed set of materials on basic structures of the language, prepared for use with any textbook. These can supplement textbook tapes or provide remedial exercises. They are particularly useful in situations where the teacher cannot prescribe his own textbook, but is obliged to continue using one which is unsuitable for laboratory work.

Some money should be set aside, too, for the acquisition of tapes and records of songs, poems, and scenes from plays. These will be useful for certain sections of the program tape, the designing of which will be discussed later in this chapter.

The novice laboratory director may not realize that a substantial sum will need to be allocated for blank tapes of good quality. Cheap tapes will not stand up to the wear and tear of constant use. A careful estimate of the year's requirements will be based on the number of program tapes needed for the console, and the number of record-playback tapes needed for student positions, if the laboratory has such facilities. The program tapes, if well prepared, will be kept for the following year. Unless the courses offered change radically the main expense for program tapes will be in the first year, when the quantity required will depend on the number of lessons each class has in the laboratory during the year. The record-playback tapes for individual positions, once purchased, will not need replacing for a long time, since previous recording is automatically erased by the heads as the next student records his work. A certain number of blank tapes will also be needed for some experimental programs designed by the teachers, for recording visiting native speakers or radio news bulletins, and for testing purposes (particularly if it is desired to keep tests for comparison in later years).

With the variety of carefully constructed and recorded materials now available commercially, it is inadvisable for inexperienced teachers to make their own master tapes. The designing of effective lessons for the laboratory requires thorough training in linguistics and considerable knowledge of pattern-drill techniques. One master lesson tape requires many hours of meticulous work. Teachers who have had the necessary training and have been using the laboratory for some time may wish to prepare materials for purposes for which commercial materials are unobtainable. In this case Preparation of Laboratory Materials should appear on the teacher's timetable with his class teaching assignments, preferably in blocks of several hours. He can then give time and thought to lesson tapes which will be useful to other teachers as well, and to a succession of students for several years. To complete his work he will need to have access to a properly equipped recording studio where he may put the material he has prepared onto tape without extraneous noise and distraction.

Where an inexperienced teacher is asked to prepare tapes to accompany a prescribed textbook, he should first put considerable study into the matter of the construction of effective drills and dialogues and, if possible, attend a seminar or workshop before attempting to work on his own. In this way many pitfalls will be avoided, and time will not be wasted on materials which are frustrating to the student and disappointing to their hard-working creator.

USING THE LANGUAGE LABORATORY

Once the laboratory is installed and the teachers have had some training in its operation, a great deal of thought and effort will still be necessary before it will produce results.

Added to the vagaries of the equipment, there will now be the human element, in some thirty individual segments. If this element is ignored the whole enterprise will be sabotaged.

It is important to prepare students from the beginning for the kind of work they will be doing in the laboratory. This orientation may be given in class or by means of an introductory tape. Students should realize that they will learn to understand a foreign language only by hearing it spoken frequently, and that they will not learn to speak it with ease unless they have frequent and systematic practice in repeating and varying regularly recurring combinations of language elements. They must not be led to believe that the laboratory is a short and effortless road to language mastery, but must see it as one part of an integrated learning process, demanding work and concentration on their part. Many students are at first confused on hearing authentic native speech spoken at normal speed. They must understand that this confusion will pass as their ears become more trained and as their knowledge increases.

Having been prepared for the laboratory method, the students must then be given explicit instructions for the operation of the equipment from their booth positions, and practice in performing different kinds of drills. The more familiar they are with procedures before actual lesson tapes are played the less likely it is that they will feel nervous or frustrated in the first few sessions.

Much thought has been put into the question of the length of time during which students can be expected to concentrate on practice in the laboratory. Such purely physical factors as discomfort from headphone pressure have to be taken into account, as well as span of attention at different ages and for different individuals. In the laboratory, much more than in the usual classroom lesson, each student is expected to give his full attention to active participation. This can be very fatiguing. Twenty minutes of such concentrated attention without a break is ample at high school level, with ten or fifteen minutes for younger children. In some schools where the laboratory is close to the language classrooms, classes are scheduled in the laboratory for twenty-minute periods as part of the lesson several times a week. The New York City experiment

(1959–63) [2] supports this practice of shorter, more frequent periods of laboratory practice rather than one long session once a week. With the introduction of flexible scheduling, the allocation of short laboratory sessions at regular intervals becomes more feasible for many schools.

Where dispersion of practice over several days is a scheduling impossibility, the program tape should be planned so that it allows for a distinct break after some fifteen or twenty minutes of work. After the break, there should be some variation of activity. Sessions may be lengthened as the age and maturity of the students increase, but these principles of a break and variety of programming should always be observed if fatigue, mental and physical, is to be avoided.

The master tapes of commercial materials, as well as the originals of taped material produced in the school, should not be used regularly on the tape decks in the laboratory. As will be seen in the later discussion, each lesson tape, or program tape, should be carefully planned to fit into the lesson sequence of the week. The master tapes provide source material from which the sections required are copied on to programmed lesson tapes. It is these lesson tapes which are subjected to the hard wear and tear of regular laboratory use. If the lesson tape is broken or damaged in any way, the damage is not irreparable because the original masters are still available for recopying. These original masters, carefully catalogued, are kept in the tape library where they will not be in danger of accidental erasure, either by too close proximity to a bulk eraser, or by human error. Whether in a library situation, where students are working at their own pace on a series of commercial tapes or on remedial tapes specially prepared by the teacher, or in a group situation where programmed tapes provided by the textbook company or planned by the teacher are in use, the students are provided with tape copies. If after long use the signal becomes attenuated, or more copies are required, the master tape in the library is still available for recopying in its original clarity and fidelity.

It is of the utmost importance that the program tape for a

2 The New York City experiment conducted by Sarah Lorge from 1959 to 1963 is described and discussed in the Area of Controversy "Is the Language Laboratory Effective?" at the end of this chapter.

laboratory lesson should contain that part of the material which fits into the immediate context of the teaching in progress. In this way, the student with his headphones on in the laboratory is fully prepared for what he is to hear. Except in the special case of a self-instructional programmed course, the laboratory is not the place for teaching new work. This has been done in the classroom. The student now practices what he has learned in class, repractices work which he needs to review, and has extra practice in certain skills, such as listening comprehension, for which the laboratory is most suited. Subsequently, what he has practiced in the laboratory is taken up and developed in the next class lesson. Where it seems appropriate and desirable, the laboratory work is tested in class so that the student who has worked well is rewarded with the satisfaction of achievement, and the student who has not assimilated the work realizes that he must work harder next laboratory session. In this way the work in the laboratory bcomes an integral part of the ongoing program, and not an isolated and irrelevant activity.

Some commercial companies provide programmed tapes for use in laboratory sessions. For these to be useful, the teacher must be very familiar with the contents of individual programs and be sure that the class is ready for the next programmed tape, in just the form in which it has been recorded, by the time it is broadcast from the console. This will require vigilance and foresight.

In designing his own lesson or program tapes the teacher should strive for a balance of activities, with variety to avoid monotony. The tape may be relentless and unwearying in dispensing material, but the students are all-too-human in their reaction to sameness and lack of imagination. A well-designed lesson tape will contain some practice in listening comprehension and in learning dialogues or phrases for fluency and intonation, with at times additional exercises in problems of pronunciation; some pattern practice (moving from imitation to practice with variation, and, finally, to drills requiring creative participation); and some activity of a recreational nature, such as singing. The order of these elements should not be fixed for every tape, but varied to provide an element of surprise. For each activity, instructions to the student should be explicit and unambiguous, with sufficient examples to dispel any perplexity about how to proceed. Many experienced teachers believe these instructions should be in the native language so that no student will be in doubt about what he is expected to do. This will depend on the level of experience of the student.

If the laboratory sessions are of twenty minutes or less, it may not be possible to include practice in all these areas on each tape, but even the shorter tape should be varied in content. Each of the types of exercises we have listed should still be provided for during the two or three sessions of the week. If recording-playback facilities are available, the amount of material in the lesson tape will be reduced, and time allowed at the end of the session for playing back and rerecording at least one section of the work.

As the work in the laboratory gets under way, the teacher should study carefully the reaction time of his students in response to pattern drills. Some commercial materials are based on the theory that the response should be made very smartly, and the pause allowed for response on these tapes is, consequently, rather short. In the first weeks, when students are becoming familiar with laboratory techniques, this short pause can be disconcerting and frustrating and may need to be lengthened slightly. With other prepared materials the pauses are very irregular and at times far too long, which is again disconcerting to the student who is waiting for the next cue from the voice. These situations can be rectified by the teacher when he is copying the material on to the lesson tape. Adjusting the pauses is a simple matter of the operation of the stop lever on one or the other of the recorders during the copying process. Some commercial materials do not provide any pauses on the master but leave it to the teacher to insert pauses of an appropriate length during the copying process. Where the student has full control of the equipment, but is not recording on a lower track, he may introduce the pause he requires by operation of a pause lever. As the student becomes more experienced and fluent, he should not require a long pause but be encouraged by the steady progress of the tape to respond promptly, without allowing himself a long time for reflection on the construction of the response.

As the year advances and wider discrepancies are observable

in individual achievement, the teacher with a console wired for more than one program channel should try to provide a second tape, with more difficult work for the more rapid learners or, alternatively, simpler exercises or repetition of exercises for those who are lagging.

At advanced levels teachers can experiment with all kinds of material for listening comprehension. News bulletins may be recorded from shortwave radio stations. Scenes from plays being read in class may be obtainable in recorded form. Excellent recordings are available commercially where the voices are those of leading professional actors. Poems being studied have sometimes been recorded as read by native speakers. Interesting short stories or biographies of famous men may be taped. Sometimes the sound track of a foreign film or documentary can be studied in the laboratory before or after the showing of the film.

It is difficult for the work in the laboratory to give practice in spontaneous expression in a foreign language, because stimulus questions are designed so as to extract a standard answer from all students. The system is based on providing the students with the opportunity to compare their responses with the version on the tape for immediate correction. Some conversation-type exercises have been designed with a low voice on the tape indicating to the student the basic information required in the response to be framed. This technique does permit of a model response from the tape with which the student can compare his own. Without some such safeguard the direction of the responses of the students may so diverge from the plan established for the tape as to make any continuity of interchange impossible. At more advanced levels where monitoring is less vital, the teacher may leave one section of the students to work with the tapes, while he gathers a small group around him for practice in the real give-and-take of conversation. (Teaching techniques for conversation groups are discussed in chapter 8).

DISCIPLINE IN THE LANGUAGE LABORATORY

Some teachers complain of serious discipline problems in the laboratory. One of the commonest reasons for such trouble is student boredom. It is inevitable that students will be bored if lesson tapes have not been carefully planned to retain their interest, just as they become bored with an unplanned, repetitive lesson. With headphones on they cannot even take refuge in daydreams as they do in class. Exercises may be too easy so that the students are soon weary of repetition which would be useful at a lower level. Equally disastrous is the provision of material which is too difficult or too fast-moving for the students concerned. This results in vague mumbling and the repeating of fragments of what has been asked for. In such a situation some of the students withdraw from the unequal contest with the tape and begin to play with wires, experiment in communication with other booths, or damage parts of the equipment in their exasperation.

Strong feelings of hostility and resistance can grow in students kept for long periods at one type of activity, particularly if this activity does not demand some thoughtful contribution on their part. They feel "brain-washed" and resent the obligation to participate in further sessions of this nature. Sometimes this reaction is due to sheer physical fatigue because no breaks have been introduced at reasonable intervals. At times an exercise involving writing can provide the necessary change of position and activity. This written exercise may be in the form of a multiple-choice questionnaire on a listening-comprehension passage, a short dictation, written answers to a quiz given on tape, or the identification of contrasting pairs in an aural-discrimination exercise. Above all, the teacher must study the length of practice which is useful to the students at the particular stage of learning they have reached.

Having learned to use the laboratory with reasonable efficiency, the teacher must keep in mind that it is only an aid and can be overused as much as any other aid. The laboratory is important for providing regular and frequent individual practice in the manipulation of language forms, but the free and fluent use of the language must still be practiced in face-to-face communication situations contrived in and out of the classroom. No student can feel a spontaneous desire to communicate his thoughts to a machine, except perhaps to curse it in his native tongue. The opportunity the laboratory provides for all students to practice elements of the speaking skill in isolation, with immediate correction, frees both students and teacher during the classroom lesson for the more difficult task of using the foreign language in active communication.

The preceding discussion of the special problems of a language laboratory at junior and senior high school level has highlighted the importance of complete integration of laboratory practice with classroom teaching and application. This becomes difficult if laboratory practice has to take place during arbitrarily scheduled blocks of time in a location away from the classroom. On occasions, the students may need the full half-hour or forty minutes scheduled for that particular day in order to practice exactly the material which the teacher has planned for the program tape. On other occasions teaching may not have proceeded to the precise point where this practice is most useful—some part of the work may not have been taught fully in class as yet—but the scheduled laboratory session must go on for organizational reasons. (Perhaps another class has been allotted the normal classroom space for that period, or this is the only opportunity for the week for this class to use the laboratory.)

This type of experience is not infrequent, particularly at junior high school level and the lower levels of senior high school. For these reasons some teachers prefer a laboratory installed in the classroom. Early attempts were made to keep equipment in quickly convertible desks so that, when required, the students could raise their desk tops to give them access to the equipment, perhaps insert collapsible isolating partitions at the sides, and set about their laboratory practice in their normal places in the classroom. This type of arrangement was useful up to a certain point. It was usually found, however, that equipment could not be kept in perfect condition in such cases. Dust and lint penetrated the desks, collapsible partitions sometimes ceased to function satisfactorily, the classroom-laboratory was noisy because of insufficient isolation, and students were tempted to meddle during class lessons with parts of the equipment to which they could gain access. More recently, some of these problems have been solved by the suspension above the heads of the students of audio-active equipment which may be lowered to a level accessible to the students when it is required as part of the normal lesson.

A more satisfactory type of classroom-laboratory is, possible, however. In this arrangement, fully equipped and isolated booths are set around the walls of the classroom so that students face the wall as they work and are not disturbed by other students. The console equipment is at the teacher's desk. The teacher may teach a section of work, move students rapidly to prearranged places in the laboratory for practice, then recall students just as rapidly to the classroom situation for immediate application of what they have been learning. Pedagogically, this is an ideal arrangement. The teacher prepares a program tape as before, but the students do not use it until the precise moment when they are fully prepared to profit from such practice, or they use a small part of it if this only is appropriate. If the students are not yet ready to practice the work which has been programmed, the teacher can postpone the practice session until it is appropriate. If the teacher observes that in programming the tape he has kept the students too long at some section of the work for which it is now evident they do not need so much practice, he can shorten the practice session. If it is apparent that the students need more practice than he had planned, he can lengthen the session and repeat a section of the tape. The students are now able to show immediately in the classroom situation what they have learned during the laboratory practice. If they show in application that they have not learned the work to a satisfactory degree of mastery, they can be sent back to the booths immediately for further practice. If, on the other hand, they show that they have mastered the work, they can continue to use it in communication with their classmates and teacher, or proceed to new areas of study.

In short, in a classroom-laboratory the practice with the equipment and the integration of this practice with classwork is as fully under the control of the teacher, for expansion, curtailment, or application as the needs of the group evolve, as is any other part of his teaching.

If it is not possible because of numbers of parallel classes and financial considerations to establish classroom-laboratories of this type, the laboratory should be so placed that students have direct and ready access to it from classrooms on either side. In this way, two classes can use the equipment as part of their lesson during the same class hour, it being understood, for instance, that Teacher A will always use it during the first half of the session and Teacher B during the second half. Where the laboratory is so situated, the insulation between classrooms and laboratory will need to be carefully considered so that classes on either side will not be disturbed by movements of students to and from the laboratory. Where finances permit of several types of laboratories, classroom-laboratories may be equipped, while a smaller laboratory of the more conventional type is installed for library study by the senior classes and remedial work as assigned by the teacher.

Decisions on laboratory arrangement and types of equipment must be based in the first instance on the requirements of the most efficient teaching situation. A laboratory which unnecessarily complicates the teacher's task without adding to the program anything which is not already provided by the use of a tape recorder in the classroom will eventually be used very perfunctorily, if at all, and its potential as a pedagogical instrument will not be realized.

AREAS OF CONTROVERSY

Should Laboratory Sessions be Monitored?

In many schools a feature of the laboratory work is monitoring of student responses by the teacher at the console. Most consoles are wired so that the teacher can not only listen to individual students, but also speak to them directly to give advice, help, or admonition. With full recording facilities, where students are working with individual copies of the master program, the student is asked to stop his tape recorder while the teacher is speaking to him, and his work is not disturbed.

In a group situation the teacher's communication usually cuts out the reception of the master program from the console, interfering with the continuity of the student's work. Even when the program continues at a lower level of sound the student cannot follow it and still pay careful attention to the teacher's comments. If the interruption comes at a moment when there is some change in what the program requires of him, the student may have difficulty in taking up his work again in an orderly way. The teacher's comment has usually to be rather brief because of the ongoing broadcast, and the student who is reintegrating himself into the program sequence has little time to think about the suggestions made, or to practice the correct pronunciation or grammatical form called to his attention. For these reasons, some experienced teachers question the value of monitoring.

On the other hand, some students feel that they are speaking in a void in the laboratory, and are glad to hear the teacher's voice from time to time encouraging or helping them. This gives them the impression that someone is listening and is interested in what they are saying. Other students, less industrious, need to feel that the teacher knows the degree to which they are participating. Since most students prefer to know when the teacher is listening to them, some word, even a short expression of commendation, should be spoken to each person monitored, so that the students will not have the impression that the teacher is either spying on them or ignoring them.

Students unmonitored in the laboratory may well be reinforcing their faults. It is hard for students to detect the defects of their articulation and intonation without guidance. They can continue to accent wrong syllables and slur others while still being convinced that they are repeating what was said on the tape. Even when they realize where they are wrong, they often do not know what to do about it.

In view of the inevitable interruption with monitoring, the teacher should listen carefully and analyze accurately the fault to be corrected before speaking to the student, so that the interruption may be as short and as useful as possible. He must avoid interrupting the student to correct some trivial slip of the tongue, or some minor fault which is not relevant to the main purpose of the particular exercise. If a long explanation is required, the teacher should make a note of this and discuss it with the student at the end of the session. The note may then be given to the student as a reminder for the next session. If many of the students are making the same mistake, the teacher should stop the tape, discuss the fault with the whole group, and then wind the tape back to a position preceding the general fault, so that all may profit from another repetition. As with a textbook, the tape must not become a tyrant. It is better to cover half the material on the program tape well rather than allow the class to continue making mistakes. The laboratory session is essentially a learning session.

Monitoring enables the teacher to keep a record of the achievements and particular difficulties of individual students; he should keep his class list before him and evaluate the students' work at regular intervals in order to arrive at a more objective grade for their oral production. With a large group, he may find it best to monitor carefully one half of the students each session, merely tuning in to the others briefly to see that they are not in any particular difficulty.

Group system or library system?

Ideally each student in the laboratory should be able to practice at his own pace. Under a library system this becomes possible. The student takes out the tape with the work which logically follows what he has already completed, proceeding with as much of the next section as he can assimilate. He works over the material several times if he is a slow learner, or moves on to new material after the first hearing if he is confident he can use it effectively. In some high schools this system operates with the help of student assistants who check out tapes, supervise sessions, see that tapes are returned, and keep a regular account of what each student has been doing. With such a system, and regularly scheduled sessions for individual students, it is possible to keep the laboratory in use all day for every day of the week to provide for students' needs.

This type of operation is particularly suited to more mature students and is frequent at university level. Some experienced teachers maintain that the average high school student needs considerable guidance under this system to ensure that he is using the material in the most effective way for his purposes. Some students are disorganized in their study habits; others are overcautious and spend far too much time on each section; still others are overconfident and feel that they know the work thoroughly when they have just begun to learn it. Guidance in how to approach individual study sessions should be given in the preceding class lessons, for students will not be practicing in the laboratory what they have not studied with the teacher in class. Tests which the student may take as he completes each section will provide some check on the way the student is working and indicate to the teacher which students need more individual supervision, and which students need to work again with a tape which was not thoroughly assimilated.

In many high schools, the library system is not practicable because of the numbers of students involved or because of the complicated scheduling it implies. It certainly creates difficulties in the integration of work into the classroom program if, because of the great numbers of students, some cannot practice assigned exercises on the same day as others. Where this is the case the pattern of regular laboratory sessions for class groups is usually adopted. Even within such groups, however, certain adaptations can be made to provide for differences in rate of learning. With a little more thought and work two, or even three, program tapes constructed around the week's work may be prepared, and channeled to different groups of booths. Most consoles allow for such a procedure. One of these tapes will provide the regular diet of practice material for the average learner; a second tape will concentrate, with more repetition and review material, on the needs of the slow learner; a third tape, less repetitive, will provide extra material of a more challenging nature for the fast learner. On each tape the basic material will be the same: namely, the section necessary for practice of what has been learned in class, and preparatory to the application work in the next class lesson.

Even in schools where the main laboratory facilities are of the audio-active listening type, there should be several positions with recording-playback facilities where students may make up on a library basis work they have missed or do special remedial or advanced work assigned by the teacher.

To record or not to record?

Opinions are divided on the value of complete dual channel recording-playback facilities for each student.

Where such facilities are provided, the student is supplied with a tape with the lesson recorded on the upper track. He plays this tape over on his individual recorder, recording his responses on a lower track at intervals corresponding to the pauses on the upper track. If a number of students are requiring the same tape at the same time he may record the lesson broadcast from the console on the upper track of a blank tape, recording his responses on the lower track. In either case, he then proceeds to play back his tape to compare his version with that of the native model. As he records a second version of the responses, he automatically erases his first version, but not the model. During this second attempt, he concentrates on improving those sections where he has observed weaknesses. Sometimes more than half the lesson is taken up with this process of comparing and rerecording several versions.

At first glance this appears to be an ideal arrangement. The student is able to compare his efforts objectively with the native model. He then has the opportunity by rerecording, to apply what he has observed for the improvement of his weaknesses; by playing this second effort back he can observe with a minimum of delay whether he has really improved. He can work at his own pace, playing back and rerecording a short section as often as he wishes if he feels he can still improve it.

Experience has shown, however, that it is very difficult for a student to diagnose his own errors, particularly in pronunciation. After a certain rough approximation has been reached, he is often quite pleased with his efforts, even when these would be quite unacceptable to a native speaker. On the other hand, he may be well aware of the deficiencies of his pronunciation but at a loss to know how to overcome them; he may then cease to improve because of discouragement. In either case, he goes on repeating his errors and establishing them just as firmly in his repertoire as he would in a laboratory without playback facilities. As for structure exercises, if he has already answered correctly he is wasting his time listening to the whole tape over again; if he has made mistakes, these have already been drawn to his attention by the immediate correction of the model voice and he would be better employed repeating the exercise than listening to his mistakes as he plays back the tape.

Students enjoy hearing their own voices, and this is often cited as an additional motivational incentive with recording-playback facilities. A lively interest of this type is often, however, short-lived; after some time the process of playing back becomes routine and may hold only a small part of the student's attention, particularly when the section to be played back is lengthy. Continual playing back and rerecording is very time-consuming, and such time may well be better employed in further active practice of difficulties of pronunciation or structure.

Some teachers feel that recording-playback-rerecording activities are valuable only in small well-regulated doses. According to this view ten minutes should be set aside for such activities at the end of a long session in the laboratory, or, if sessions are short, opportunities for comparison and rerecording should be provided during one session in three or four. With either system students will be recording and comparing their best efforts after a period of practice, and will be anxious to see what improvement they have made.

If comparison and rerecording is to be effective in improving pronunciation, students should be given training in the differences to listen for in the foreign sound system and in systematic detection of their own weaknesses. They need explicit instructions on how to rectify these weaknesses when observed. During the playback session, the teacher should be readily available for consultation on problems of improvement.

The area in which recording-playback facilities have an undoubted superiority over audio-active listening facilities is that of testing aural-oral skills. A test tape can be made by each student simultaneously without the delay involved in recording successive students at the console.

The question whether to record or not to record is resolved for many teachers by financial considerations. Where complete recording-playback facilities cannot be provided in all places, students are still able to have a great deal of valuable practice.

They are, however, more dependent on the active vigilance of the teacher in pointing out to them their areas of weakness in the production of sounds. The important thing for the teacher to do is to analyze the kinds of activities in which he wishes his students to participate in the laboratory, and then to use the type of equipment which enables the student to practice these activities most efficiently. Where several types of equipment are available, each will then be used fully for that for which it is most appropriate.

Is the language laboratory useful at all levels of language study?

For several reasons the laboratory has been most frequently used for elementary foreign-language classes. First of all, space has been limited and the benefits for beginners in practicing correct pronunciation and structural patterns in imitation of a native model have been obvious. Often, by the time the first-year classes were scheduled there was no time left for the others. Second, most commercial materials have been published over a period of years, starting at the elementary level. There is therefore an abundance of taped material suitable for beginners. Third, the more advanced classes are sometimes faced with regional examinations of a traditional kind and there has been a certain fear that unless students were prepared traditionally they would fail in these examinations.

This question is then an open one, requiring further study and experimentation. Many teachers believe firmly that the laboratory can be used effectively to improve reading and literary appreciation, particularly of poetry and drama, and that students at advanced levels need constant practice in listening and speaking in order to retain the level of skill which they attained through earlier laboratory practice. Laboratory work at the advanced level must be designed to demand creative effort from the student and is most useful if students work with tapes on a library basis.

The laboratory can be very valuable for developing aural comprehension of more complicated material: lectures, fast native speech with a variety of regional accents, plays recorded by professional actors, sound tracks of carefully selected films, informational radio and television programs, mock telephone conversations. It will take the teacher time to gather together sufficient material of this nature, but more and more of it is becoming available commercially, or from diplomatic and trade representatives.

The laboratory can also be used in the development of writing skills by providing opportunities, again on a library basis, for practice in advanced dictation. Notetaking and the writing of reports can be further developments from exercises in listening comprehension. Background material on authors and works being studied can be recorded on tape and the students sent to the laboratory to make notes on these as a basis for written composition. Where lectures are given in French on literary or cultural subjects, a résumé tape may be recorded to be used by the weaker students who have not been able to follow the lecture and take notes at the same time. Where native speakers are invited to the school, the talks they give can be taped for further listening practice and used again in later years. Outstanding students may like to practice simultaneous translation, comparing their recorded efforts with the original script.

The memorizing of poems with the help of a native model is not to be despised. Listening to and repeating poems and prose is a useful exercise if students of a foreign language are to develop an appreciation of the melody and rhythm of sound patterns and the importance of variations of word order.

The uses to which the laboratory can be put at advanced levels are limited only by the imagination, resourcefulness, and enthusiasm of the teacher.

Is the language laboratory effective?

The Keating *Study of the Effectiveness of Language Laboratories*, published in 1963,[3] has aroused considerable interest. The intention of this study was administrative rather than

3 Raymond F. Keating, *A Study of the Effectiveness of Language Laboratories* (New York: The Institute of Administrative Research, Teachers College, Columbia University, 1963).

methodological. Conducted by the Institute of Administrative Research of Teachers College, Columbia University, its aim was to find out whether the money invested in laboratories by the high schools, in response to an offer of matching grants from the U.S. Federal Government, was money well spent in view of the fact that it was presumably being drained away from other worthwhile areas of the curriculum.

Five thousand students in New York schools associated with the Metropolitan School Study Council were involved in the investigation during the period 1961–62. These schools are described as "relatively well favored, especially as regards expenditure," and they were therefore able to employ "superior teachers" [4] who might be presumed to know how to employ the language laboratory to its full potential. No attempt was made to find out whether the teachers had had any training in the use of a language laboratory and no record was kept of how they did in fact use it. No information is available on the kinds of materials the teachers used, except that some were commercially prepared and some were teacher-prepared. As an administration study, these elements were not important; the interest was in "results . . . with the laboratory as it was actually being used." [5]

In testing the students the study concentrated on reading comprehension (which is not an area for which advocates of the laboratory urge its use), on listening comprehension, and on speech production. Results showed the no-laboratory groups to be superior to the laboratory groups on all these measures at four levels of instruction, except in speech production at the end of the first year.

It does not surprise foreign-language teachers to find that students who spent twenty-five per cent more time with their books proved to be superior in reading comprehension. It is even less surprising when we note that the reading comprehension test used was constructed in 1940, that is, before the advent of the laboratory and of the aural-oral emphasis in language teaching. It therefore contained material much more similar in content to that in most textbooks for traditional

4 *Ibid.,* p. vii.
5 *Ibid.,* p. 37.

classroom use than to the materials commonly used with a laboratory.

The results in listening comprehension were more surprising, since this is a skill which teachers aim to develop by using the laboratory. Here again, the test used was constructed before laboratories were installed in the schools and was originally designed to test students accustomed to classroom discussion of reading-oriented texts.

The results in speech production also favored the no-laboratory group at the three upper levels, but not in the first year. This test was specially constructed for the experiment and was used in identical form at all levels. On close examination it hardly justifies its name as a test of "speech production," but may be considered, rather, as a very limited test of pronunciation (of ten simple words in isolation), followed by a test of the ability to read ten short sentences with acceptable articulation and intonation, a skill which is cultivated by superior teachers in classrooms where reading is the primary objective. This Speech Production Test is the only one of the three that attempts to test the oral facility which the laboratory aims to develop. Interestingly enough, despite its shortcomings it showed that the laboratory did develop good pronunciation and fluency in short phrases at the level at which specially prepared materials for the laboratory were available in 1961.

In every test, high IQ students recorded higher scores in the no-laboratory groups than in the laboratory groups. If inefficient materials prepared by inexperienced teachers were used in the laboratory, particularly at the higher levels for which commercial materials were not available in 1961, then high IQ students with only four-fifths of the time in class that the no-laboratory students had would be expected to perform less well.

The investigator concludes by stating: "While this study does not purport to demonstrate that the language laboratory cannot be used effectively, it does show that in schools of the Metropolitan School Study Council, a group of schools characterized by competent and well-prepared teachers, better results in certain important skill areas are being achieved in instructional situations which do not use the language laboratory."[6]

6 *Ibid.,* p. 39.

Since he had stated earlier in his conclusion that lack of accurate information on how the laboratory was used at any one time was "the inevitable outcome of improvisation with the laboratory by relatively inexperienced teachers,"[7] a justifiable interpretation of the results of the investigation would appear to be that the students of experienced and competent teachers teaching material to which they are accustomed achieve better results in tests constructed with this material in mind than do the students of inexperienced teachers experimenting with a new medium and new materials for which the tests are inappropriate.

The lack of understanding of the particular problems of foreign-language teachers and of their current aims in instruction that characterizes the report as a whole is strikingly demonstrated by the rather startling statement in W. Vincent's Foreword that, since laboratories are effective in developing speech production principally in the first year, "once a student 'has the tongue in his head' the value of the laboratory appears to have passed its peak."[8] At that stage, the student no longer needs the competent teacher in the foreign-language classroom either.

Interesting light is thrown on the results of the Keating investigation by the report of the *New York City Study 1959–1963*, under the direction of Sarah Lorge.[9] The results of this study were published soon after the Keating report. The New York City experiment consisted of two studies. *The first study* was designed "to test the extent to which the regular use of the language laboratory would lead to measurable improvement in competence in speaking French and in comprehension of spoken French" (skills for which the laboratory is considered most appropriate) "without significant loss in reading

7 *Ibid.*, p. 38.
8 *Ibid.*, p. viii.
9 *Foreign Language Laboratories in Secondary Schools,* a special report summarizing four years of research by the Bureau of Audio-Visual Instruction, Board of Education of the City of New York, for the New York State Education Department 1959/1963. The report is discussed at length by Sarah W. Lorge in "Language Laboratory Research Studies in New York City High Schools: A Discussion of the Program and the Findings," *MLJ,* 48 (November, 1964): 409–19.

comprehension and in written aspects of language study." [10] Teachers in the classes involved in the investigation were instructed in laboratory techniques recommended by experienced teachers, materials designed for the laboratory were used in teaching, and special tests were devised to evaluate the listening and speaking skills.

The tests of speaking ability required answers to questions on a sight-reading passage and scores were given for fluency, pronunciation, and intonation in sight-reading, and for appropriateness, grammatical correctness, and fluency in response to questions. This test was therefore a much more valid test of "speech production" than the Keating test described. The tests for listening comprehension were also specially designed. The no-laboratory groups were not at a disadvantage on these tests, since they were taught by an audio-lingual method with similar materials to those used by the laboratory groups.

At the first- and second-year levels, the laboratory groups showed significant gains in fluency of speech and in intonation, and at the third-year level, in listening comprehension. The laboratory groups also showed a significant increase in motivation to continue with the study of the language. In no case did the traditional skills of reading and writing suffer because of time taken for laboratory practice.

Also of interest in interpreting the Keating report is the *second study of the New York City schools.*[11] The report shows that regular daily practice for twenty minutes produces significant improvement in speaking and listening skills, whereas a laboratory session once a week does not. The schools in the Keating investigation followed, with two exceptions, the once-a-week pattern. The New York City study also shows recording-playback equipment to be more effective than audio-active listening facilities. In very few of the M.S.S.C. schools were full recording facilities available to all students.

The New York City report concludes that "the mere instal-

---

10 New York City report, p. 5. The first study was entitled: "A Comparison of Results in the Teaching of French in High School Achieved with and without the Use of the Language Laboratory."

11 The second study was entitled: "The Relative Effectiveness of Four Types of Language Laboratory Experience."

lation of a language laboratory is no guarantee that improvement in linguistic skills will occur automatically. Good results demand: equipment of good quality with potential for a variety of learning experiences: teachers skilled in handling equipment; materials prepared specifically with regard to the goals of the course and techniques of laboratory learning; and careful allotment of laboratory time." [12] These are the very things which Keating preferred to ignore in the report of his investigation.

(A full discussion of these two reports is to be found in the *Modern Language Journal*, 48, no. 4 [April, 1964]: 189–210.)

It was too early for any final judgment on the effectiveness of the language laboratory in 1963. Its effectiveness depends on the teacher's skill in using it, and this in its turn depends on the teacher's understanding of the nature of his tool and his training and experience with the laboratory. Until the majority of teachers using laboratories have such training and experience, it will be inadvisable to pass judgment. As with any teaching aid, experimentation by experienced teachers is needed to eliminate defects in the use of the laboratory, to develop more effective materials at all levels, and to guide other teachers in their work.

ANNOTATED READING LIST

HUTCHINSON, J. C. *The Language Laboratory*. In the series Modern Foreign Languages in High School. Washington, D.C.: U.S. Office of Education, 1961. A short but thorough introduction to all aspects of language laboratory work, with a glossary of terms and expressions for use in the laboratory in French, German, Italian, Russian, and Spanish.

HAYES, A. S. *Language Laboratory Facilities*. Washington, D.C.: U.S. Office of Education, 1963. A technical guide for the selection, purchase, use, and maintenance of laboratory equipment. It is essential reading for the teacher or official concerned with the installation of a language laboratory, and with its operation and maintenance. Reprint forthcoming, Oxford University Press.

12 New York City report, p. 8.

STACK, E. M. *The Language Laboratory and Modern Language Teaching.* rev. ed. New York: Oxford University Press, 1966. An important book of reference on types of installation, essential equipment, and the administration and use of the laboratory. There are excellent chapters on the construction of suitable drills and tests.

MARTY, F. *Language Laboratory Learning.* Roanoke, Va.: Audio-Visual Publications, 1960. This book sets out the principles underlying effective techniques and materials for the laboratory, and examines ways of using the laboratory in the teaching of various aspects of the language. The second half of the book gives useful technical information on tape recorders, recording, and laboratory equipment.

HOLTON, J.; KING, P.; MATHIEU, G.; and POND, K. *Sound Language Teaching.* New York: University Publishers, 1961. A thorough study of all aspects of teaching with the use of a laboratory. Practical advice on choosing equipment, recording, designing programs, testing, laboratory administration and supervision.

LÉON, P. *Laboratoire de Langues et Correction Phonétique.* Paris: Didier, 1962. This book includes a detailed history of the development of language laboratories. Special attention is given to the problems of teaching the sound system of the language.

HOCKING, E. *Language Laboratory and Language Learning.* Washington, D.C.: Department of Audiovisual Instruction of the N.E.A., 1964. An account of experimentation and research in the use of laboratories, and present-day trends in equipment and teaching practices.

14

And What Else?

Elementary school classes may seem very distant to the high school teacher. Yet it is important that the high school teacher take an interest in the teaching of foreign languages at other levels. He is in a key position: he is preparing many students for further study at undergraduate level and, in many areas, he is receiving into his classes students who have already had some instruction in the language at the pre-high-school stage. Rare is the high school teacher who does not know something about instruction in foreign languages at the higher level: he himself studied for advanced courses, many of his recent students are continuing their studies, and his present students are acutely conscious of the requirements for university or college entrance. Many high school teachers do not, on the other hand, give a great deal of thought to the rationale and operation of elementary school foreign-language instruction.

Parents and teachers often wonder at what age children can most profitably be introduced to the study of a foreign language. They look back nostalgically to the age of infancy when their native language and, in some cases, another language were acquired with little apparent effort. They realize that most children will not have the opportunity to acquire a foreign language in such an ideal situation, but they wonder if it is reasonable to defer the introduction into the curriculum of foreign-language study until the students are in their teens. Some neurophysiologists who have studied language functions in the brain set the best age for learning foreign languages in a nonnatural situation as between the ages of four and ten.[1] At

---

1 W. Penfield and L. Roberts, *Speech and Brain Mechanisms* (Princeton, N.J., 1959), p. 255.

this stage they consider the brain still sufficiently plastic for the child to acquire another language with ease, yet the native language is not firmly enough established to cause undue interference in the learning process.[2]

In many countries the traditional age for the learning of a foreign language has been eleven or twelve: in the early years of secondary education.[3] In recent times, there has been an increasing body of opinion maintaining that this is already too late. It is claimed that we are not capitalizing on the natural ability to learn languages which the younger child possesses and which is already waning as the child approaches his teens. As a result the FLES movement has spread rapidly, not only in the United States but also in the United Kingdom and some countries of Europe. Foreign languages have long been taught at this early age in many countries of Asia and Africa where much of the child's education has had to be in a national or international language, rather than in the vernacular.

When it is felt in a community that an elementary school foreign-language program should be established, it is frequently the high school teacher who is approached for advice and guidance. A number of questions must be given careful consideration if the instruction is to be effective. It behooves the high school teacher, then, to study the requirements of a good elementary school foreign-language program so that, should the need arise, he may be able to give intelligent leadership in the context of the school situation in which he finds himself.

Why a FLES program?

Elementary school foreign-language programs are often begun as a fad; those responsible for the school system want to be

2 T. Andersson, "The Optimum Age for Beginning the Study of Modern Languages," *International Review of Education*, 6, no. 3 (1960): 303–4, reprinted in S. Levenson and W. Kendrick, eds. (1967), p. 65.
3 Some countries like Sweden and Germany have a tradition of beginning foreign-language study in the elementary grades, at approximately fifth-grade level. See W. R. Parker, *The National Interest and Foreign Languages*, 3d ed. (Washington, D.C., 1962), p. 97, and T. Huebener, *Why Johnny Should Learn Foreign Languages* (Philadelphia and New York, 1961), chapter 3.

abreast of latest developments, whatever these may be and whatever their value. This is a dangerous beginning for a FLES program. It can mean that instruction is introduced in a rush, with inadequate preparation of teachers or community, and without any serious consideration of the place of foreign-language study in the educational framework. A FLES program should be introduced only if teachers, administrators, and parents are convinced that the learning of a foreign language is an important educational experience, requiring a long apprenticeship, and that it is best introduced at an age when, physiologically, children are most receptive to this type of learning.

Which language should be taught?

In the abstract, this is a very difficult problem. In many areas it is not easy to predict which language, of all the possible languages, will be of most use and interest to the pupils in later life. From the practical point of view it is less complicated. Unless there are, for reasons of geography or community composition, legitimate pressures for the introduction of the study of an uncommon language, it will be wisest to select one of the major languages of international communication, leaving it to the students to acquire languages of more limited utility at a later date. In a particular district, the area of choice will be limited even further. It will be advisable to select for elementary school study a language which the pupils may continue to learn in the local high school, and one for which suitable teachers are not only available at the time the program is established but are likely to be available for a continuing program.

In what grade will the program begin?

In their enthusiasm for a new cause, many school systems introduce the teaching of the foreign language as early as possible in the primary or elementary grades, without consideration of the practical consequences. A third-grade program this year means a third- and fourth-grade program next year, and a third-, fourth-, and fifth-grade program the year after. This is as it should be in an ideal situation. When a program is proposed, those responsible for its continuance must ask themselves the question: Will we have enough qualified teachers in the next few years to extend the program up through the school? If the answer is in the affirmative, fourth- or third-grade level is considered to be a good starting point. The pupils in these grades are at an age when their native-language habits are established and they are well settled into their elementary school program, yet they are still young enough to acquire a foreign language readily. If the answer is in the negative, then the program must be designed to fit the practical situation. It is better to establish the program at sixth-grade, or fifth-grade, level and expand downwards as circumstances permit, rather than to be forced to curtail the program after several years, leaving enthusiastic fifth graders with a hiatus of some years before they can continue with their language study at a higher level. If this system of downward expansion is adopted the teaching content for the different years will need to be redesigned as the program is extended.

To whom should the foreign language be taught?

In the past there has been among some foreign-language teachers an unfortunate conviction that theirs is a subject which should be reserved for an intellectual elite. As a result some teachers have actively discouraged students from undertaking or continuing foreign-language study. In the elementary school situation this means that foreign-language classes are sometimes regarded as an appropriate form of curriculum enrichment for the brightest of the students. The premise on which this attitude has been based is debatable. Foreign languages have often been taught in the past in a way which demanded much abstract thinking on the part of the students. When the language is taught as a skill to be acquired, many students who are considered to be of lower intelligence can profit from the study. The introduction of foreign languages in the elementary school has been proposed because it has been considered that the pupils can acquire a language in a more direct and natural fashion at this age than in the adolescent and post-adolescent years. Since the skill-training approach does not involve lengthy explanations of abstract relationships, there is no longer any need to keep foreign-language study as a special preserve for the intellectually inclined.

When the language is taught through memorization, repetition, and activity all elementary school pupils can profit from this experience to a greater or less degree, at least for the first few years. As time goes on, some will outstrip others and this will create the usual problem of providing for individual speeds of learning. This is a situation which must be faced when it arises, but it cannot be considered a valid reason for depriving the slower learners of the opportunity to find out how other people speak and act.

How should the foreign language be taught?

Elementary school children love to imitate and mimic; they are uninhibited in acting out roles, and they enjoy repetition because it gives them a sense of assurance and achievement. They are ready to accept the fact that other people do and say things differently without worrying about the reasons for the differences. They love an active situation where they can express themselves vocally and physically. They enjoy singing and playing, and doing as the teacher does. All of these characteristics of young children can find expression in an audio-lingual or direct-method approach in the foreign-language classroom.

At the elementary school level, the learning should be aural and oral. Dialogues are memorized, sentence patterns are practiced, little scenes are acted out, language games are played, and songs are sung; simple stories, with much repetition, are related with the help of flannel board, chalkboard, or pictures. The language learning does not consist of the acquisition of many words in isolation, as labels for this and that, nor is it a pretext for another social studies lesson on the way of life of a foreign people. Real language is learned in useful utterances which the child employs immediately in communication and play in the classroom. Grammatical structures are acquired without specific instruction in abstract relationships. The native language is rarely heard; it is mostly superfluous when the lessons are carefully prepared. Reading and writing are not emphasized; the pupil has enough to do to learn to read and write his own language. If he is learning the foreign language through activity he will not feel the need to write it down or to see it written for quite some time. When he is a little older and is introduced to the written form of the language, it will come as a novelty and he will be able to cope with it because he has acquired, through instruction in his native language, an understanding of what is involved in reading and writing.

It is not proposed here to set out in detail how the foreign language should be taught in the elementary school. This is a specialized study for which several references are given in the Annotated Reading List. It must be emphasized, however, that if the teaching at this level is to be effective, careful selection must be made of materials appropriate to the interests and abilities of elementary school children. Provision should be made in the timetable for instruction at frequent intervals; the foreign-language lesson must not be a special feature appearing only once or twice a week. The pupils must have the opportunity to exercise their growing skills every day, even if only for short fifteen-minute periods, if they are to retain and use with facility what they are learning.

By whom should the foreign language be taught?

The automatic and unthinking response is: by a foreign-language expert, of course. As an answer this is insufficient. The best teacher at this level is a foreign-language expert with training in the teaching of elementary school children. Such people are not numerous in most areas. If FLES instruction is to be established on an extensive scale, more trained elementary school teachers must be given the opportunity to improve their foreign-language skills and to learn appropriate methods of teaching languages to their pupils. Native speakers in the community may be willing to undertake training as FLES specialists. Some high school foreign-language teachers may be willing to undertake courses of training in elementary school teaching. "May" and "might" will not solve the problem. Opportunities must be provided in the form of specialized training courses, summer institutes, and workshops in order to increase the number of specialized FLES teachers in the community.

In some areas, attempts have been made to bridge the gap by the use of television lessons, or part-live part-television lessons. These have their usefulness in bringing a first-class teaching specialist into each classroom. Sometimes it is suggested that the class teacher learn with the students from a tape. With a specially gifted and self-assured teacher this may be possible; for most, it means a very unsatisfactory compromise which becomes a burden when the class begins to outstrip the teacher. The problem of efficient staffing must be given careful consideration and plans made to improve the situation, where necessary, before any school system embarks on an extensive foreign-language program for its elementary schools.

How should a FLES program be started?

Like any educational innovation, a FLES program should be launched with the support not only of the teachers but of parental and community opinion, and especially of the administration. Where parents are opposed to the scheme, pupils will be discouraged, and problems which arise will be magnified. Where the administration is unsympathetic the many details of scheduling, provision of materials and equipment, and smooth transition from grade to grade will be made unnecessarily difficult; small failures will be exaggerated and successes unrecognized. Where the grade teachers are unsympathetic, they will quickly communicate their attitude to their pupils.

The establishment of the FLES program should be preceded by much discussion of plans, visits to neighboring systems where successful programs are in operation, publicity of an informational character, careful examination of proposals to see if they are appropriate for the local situation, and advance training of all those who will be involved in the teaching. Consideration must naturally be given to the financial aspects of the scheme, not only for the first year of its operation but on a long-term basis. The staffing of the program should also be studied with an eye to the future. Special training for the early stages will take much of the attention of the organizers, but consideration will have to be given also to the arrangements for continuing training and guidance.

And afterwards?

The production of a large group of elementary school graduates with a degree of skill in a foreign language is an attractive proposition. What will happen to them when they go on to high school? Nothing is more disappointing and frustrating for such children than to find themselves during their first year of high school in classes with students who have never studied a foreign language. The elementary school must keep closely in touch with the high school to ensure that provision will be made for its former pupils to continue their foreign-language study from the stage they had reached on transferring to the new level. With this in mind, the elementary and high school programs should be carefully and cooperatively examined to ensure that one leads to the other and that one follows from the other.

Finally, the FLES program must be objectively reexamined after some years of operation to see whether it is working effectively and achieving the aims for which it was established. This will only be possible if these aims were clearly set out in the beginning. If it appears, after several years, that the program has provided only an opportunity for fun and games for all, that the teachers have not taken seriously the necessity for improving their own skills, or that cooperation could not be obtained at the high school level, then decisions will have to be made on the value of continuing the program for a longer period. It is preferable to have no FLES program rather than a bad one. Elementary school children learn foreign languages rapidly and thoroughly; they acquire incorrect pronunciations, prejudiced views about foreign people, and unsatisfactory attitudes toward foreign-language learning just as thoroughly as anything else. With a carefully planned program, teachers willing to work hard to acquire new skills and techniques, and full community and interschool cooperation, such a situation need not arise.

The *Second Statement of Policy on Foreign Languages in the Elementary School,* issued by the Modern Language Association of America in 1962, should be carefully studied by all who are interested in the introduction or improvement of a local elementary school program. It reads as follows:

A. *Five Years Later.* Since the publication in 1956 of the first MLA statement on FLES [4] there has been increasing awareness of the need for an early start to foreign-language learning. There is equal awareness of the dangers of inadequate attempts to meet this need. Hundreds of communities have ignored our warning against "faddish aspects of this movement" and our insistence upon "necessary preparations." Many of the resulting programs have been wasteful and disappointing, and they have misled many citizens about the nature and value of foreign-language learning.

B. *Redefinition.* We must sharpen our definition of FLES. It is not an end in itself but the elementary-school (K–6) [5] part of a language-learning program that should extend unbroken through grade 12. It has 15- or 20-minute sessions at least three times a week as an integral part of the school day. It concerns itself primarily with learning the four language skills, beginning with listening and speaking. Other values (improved understanding of language in general, intercultural understanding, broadened horizons), though important, are secondary.

C. *FLES in Sequence.* We believe that FLES, as here defined, is an essential part of the long sequence, ten years or more, needed to approach mastery of a second language in school. There is good evidence that the learning of a second language considerably quickens and eases the learning of a third language, even when there is little or no relation between the languages learned. Since children imitate skillfully and with few inhibitions in the early school years, the primary grades (K–3) are the ideal place to begin language learning, and the experience is in itself exciting and rewarding.

D. *Priority.* If a school system cannot provide both a FLES program and a six-year secondary-school foreign-language sequence (grades 7–12), it should work *first* toward establishing the grade 7–12 sequence. Unless there is a solid junior- and senior-high-school program of foreign-language learning with due stress on the

4 The first M.L.A. statement of policy on FLES may be read in S. Levenson and W. Kendrick, eds. (1967), pp. 10–11.
5 K–6 means kindergarten to sixth grade.

listening and speaking skills and fully articulated with the previous instruction, FLES learnings wither on the vine.

E. *Articulation.* It requires: 1) a foreign-language program in grades 7 and 8 for graduates of FLES, who should never be placed with beginners at *any* grade level; 2) a carefully planned coordination of the FLES and secondary-school programs; 3) a frequent interchange of visits and information among the foreign-language teachers at all levels; 4) an overall coordination by a single foreign-language supervisor or by a committee of administrators. These cooperative efforts should result in a common core of language learning that will make articulation smooth and effective.

F. *Experimental Programs.* Experimentation is desirable in education, but we now know enough about FLES methods and materials to obviate the need for "pilot" or "experimental" programs if these adjectives mean no more than "tentative" or "reluctant." If a shortage of teachers makes it impossible to offer instruction to all the pupils in a grade, a partial FLES program is an acceptable temporary expedient, but it will pose a special scheduling problem in grade 7. An "experimental" program should be a genuine experiment, not a desperate, inadequately planned program instituted by community pressure against the advice of language authorities in the field.

Experimentation in *methods* should be undertaken only after teachers and administrators are thoroughly familiar with current theories of foreign-language learning and with current practices in successful FLES programs. The development of experimental teaching *materials* should be undertaken only after teachers are thoroughly familiar with existing materials.

G. *The Teacher.* Ideally he should be an expert in the foreign language he teaches, with near-native accent and fluency, and also skillful in teaching young children. Few teachers are currently expert in both areas. If a teacher's foreign-language accent is not good, he should make every effort to improve it, and meanwhile he should rely on discs or tapes to supply authentic model voices for his pupils. But since language is communication, and a child cannot communicate with a phonograph or a tape recorder, no FLES learning can be wholly successful without the regular presence in the classroom of a live model who is also an expert teacher. The shortage of such doubly skilled teachers is the most serious obstacle to the success of FLES. To relieve this shortage every institution that trains future elementary-school teachers should offer a major in one or more foreign languages.

H. *Cautions.* A FLES program should be instituted only if: 1) it is an integral and serious part of the school day; 2) it is an integral and serious part of the total foreign-language program in the school system; 3) there is close articulation with later foreign-language learning; 4) there are available FL specialists or elementary-school teachers with an adequate command of the foreign language; 5) there is a planned syllabus and a sequence of appropriate teaching materials; 6) the program has the support of the administration; 7) the high-school teachers of the foreign language in the local school system recognize the same long-range objectives and practice some of the same teaching techniques as the FLES teachers.

THE TEXTBOOK

The textbook will determine the major part of the classroom teaching. In it decisions have already been made about what the student will learn, how he will learn it, and what sections of the work will receive most emphasis. The experienced teacher will adapt the material in the textbook, supplement it in many ways, and add emphases of his own. He will not work his way through the textbook from beginning to end, making students read every word consecutively and do every exercise. His work will, however, be greatly facilitated if he is able to use a textbook which reflects his objectives and his chosen method for achieving these objectives. It is the inexperienced teacher who needs to be most careful in the initial selection of a textbook. He will learn much about presentation of material from a well-constructed textbook, but he needs to be alert to the deficiencies of an ill-conceived and poorly written book.

A checklist for evaluation of textbooks follows. The examination in the light of this checklist of a textbook, or several textbooks, which the reader is considering for adoption will provide him with an opportunity for practical application of what he has gained from the study of this book.

Checklist for Textbook Evaluation

1. On what *method* is the book based?
   Is this method appropriate for your purposes?
   Is this method carried through well in the unit design?
2. Is the material of a kind which would *interest* junior high school or senior high school students?

Is it too juvenile? Is it too dull? Does it make too obvious an effort to amuse?

3. Does the unit design allow for *progressive development* of and practice in listening comprehension? speaking? reading? writing?

4. Is provision made for the presentation of *new work in oral form* first? Can this material be presented in oral form first in any case?

5. If there are *dialogues,* are they realistic, authentic in language and situation, with sentences which are not too long for memorization? Are the dialogues too long to be useful?

6. Is *reading* introduced early or late?
Does the reading material provide for progressive teaching of the reading skill? Is it interesting and written in language which is appropriate for the content, and for your students?

7. Is *writing* introduced early or late?
Do the writing exercises provide for progressive development of this skill?

8. What is the *proportion of working time* which is allotted to each skill in the unit design?
Is this proportion right for the objectives of your course?

9. Is the *language* in the lessons authentic (not stilted or artificial; not old-fashioned; correct for the persons and relationships for which it is used)?

10. How is *pronunciation* dealt with? Is this satisfactory? Is attention paid to distinctions between near-equivalents in the native and foreign languages, and within the foreign language? Is the sound system taught as an interdependent whole? Are stress and intonation considered?

11. Is the *grammar* presented through structures? Some other way? Does this suit your purposes?
Is the grammar summarized from time to time? Are the grammatical descriptions sound?
Do you think the number of structures (or the amount of grammar) is sufficient for this level? Too much? Are there significant omissions? Is provision made for thorough drilling before new structures are introduced? Are the structures reintroduced systematically through the different units?

Are verb forms drilled sufficiently for this level? Are there summaries of verb forms (paradigms, conjugations) somewhere in the book?

12. How much is the *native language* used in the exercises (or other sections of the book)? Could the foreign language have been used instead?

13. Is there *variety* in the types of exercises? Do they give adequate practice in what they purport to teach? Do they test instead of teaching? Are the exercises interesting? Do the grammatical exercises and drills emphasize the *contrasts* which are most likely to cause native-language interference?

Are the drills well designed (programmed)?

Are there enough (too many) exercises and (or) drills in each unit for practical use?

14. Is the *vocabulary* well presented? How much per lesson? Is the vocabulary reintroduced sufficiently within the unit and in successive units? Is it summarized in some way? At the end of the book? in a foreign-language dictionary section or in a bilingual list? Does the way it is summarized suit your teaching approach?

Is attention paid to roots, cognates, synonyms, antonyms, thematic groupings?

Is choice of vocabulary based on a frequency count? If so, is the level of the count for this book sufficient, or too advanced, for your purposes?

15. Are there indications of ways in which students can be encouraged to use what they have learned in *actual communication* (in speech and writing)?

16. Does the material give a fair, balanced *picture of life in the foreign country?* Does it bring out contrasts between the foreign culture and the culture of your students?

Are there pictures, maps, diagrams?

17. Are the *illustrations* in a style which is likely to make the book seem old-fashioned or ridiculous to your students?

18. Are indications given of *extra activities* (games, songs, poems, crossword puzzles) which would add variety to the lessons?

Does the publisher provide a teacher's manual with indi-

cations on how to use the book and suggestions for extra
activities?

19. Are *tapes, films, slides, filmstrips,* or *flashcards* available
with this book? If so, are they well constructed methodo-
logically and effectively produced? (See checklist for tapes
in chapter 13 and guidelines for evaluation of pictorial aids
in chapter 7.) Are there *practice records* for the students?
Are these aids reasonably priced?

20. Are *supplementary readers, workbooks,* or *tests* available
with this book?
Are they satisfactory for the standard of your class? Do
they correspond precisely with what is in the textbook?

21. Is the book *printed* in an interesting style?
Is the type clear?
Is the work set out so that it is easy to find what you
want?
Are the binding, cover, quality of paper, and general spac-
ing satisfactory?
Is there a detailed *index?*

22. *Would you enjoy working with this book* at this level?
Is it hard on the teacher in any way?
Could the other teachers (particularly the inexperienced
ones) work with it?

23. Is the *price* reasonable for your school situation?

24. Is the book *part of a series* which would be adequate for
the sequence of classes in your school?
Are the later books in the series satisfactory for the purposes of your higher classes?

25. Has the book been *pre-tested* in schools and revised before
being printed in its final form?

PLANNING THE LANGUAGE LESSON

Most student teachers approach their first lesson with some
trepidation. "Yes, I know a lot of things," they say, "but what
do I do when I am actually there, in front of my first class?"
The answer lies in the carefully planned lesson. In an effective
lesson given by an experienced teacher it is always possible to

detect a clear progression of activities. For the expert teacher the underlying plan may have taken only two minutes to elaborate, as he walked down the passage to meet his class, but the outline of it is clear to the student teacher taking notes in the back of the room. It will be some years before the inexperienced teacher can hope to do likewise; he may never reach this stage. In the meantime, his plan should be thoughtfully established according to certain principles, so that each lesson will contain the necessary ingredients for developing the language skills of his students. He should outline his plan in brief form on a small card which he can keep in his textbook for quick reference. He should later mark on this card what he achieved during the lesson and use it as a guide when elaborating his next plan. A file of these cards should be kept and examined from time to time, so that the young teacher can see how to improve his lessons. From a series of such cards it will become clear whether he has been expecting too much from his students too soon, or moving too slowly for his class. He will also see clearly where he has been forced to reteach work on which he did not spend enough time in the first place. For his own edification, he should also note on his cards whether the students found the lessons interesting or dull, or accepted them as part of the routine. Analysis of his performances in class will help the teacher to identify combinations of ingredients which improved the attractiveness and effectiveness of his lessons.

GENERAL PRINCIPLES

1. The teacher is *not the slave of the textbook*. He is a trained person who knows the capabilities of his class and the objectives of his course. The textbook provides him with material which he can use in innumerable ways. He must know what is in the textbook and be able to select, omit, recombine, and supplement what is supplied for him as he sees fit. He must know his textbook well enough to be able to prepare students for what is coming, to refer quickly to other parts of the book when this is desirable, and to make up for deficiencies he has discovered. Every experienced teacher will feel that the perfect textbook is the one he is yet to write. In the meantime, he will

take great care in selecting the one which most closely approximates his ideal in its objectives and in the material it provides for attaining these objectives. Unless he wishes to have an unhappy year with his class, he will examine the proposed textbook very carefully to see that it is appropriate for the age and maturity of the students he is teaching.

2. Each lesson must be based on *clearly established aims.* A lesson is not a haphazard collection of more or less interesting items, but a progression of interrelated activities which reinforce and consolidate each other in establishing the learning toward which the teacher is directing his efforts. Some of these activities test, in an unobtrusive way, what other activities have been teaching, others reteach what has not been assimilated by the students. At the end of the lesson, both students and teacher should be able to identify what has been learned thoroughly and what has still to be perfected.

3. Each lesson should *move smartly,* the teacher leading the class from one activity to another with assurance, never allowing time to be wasted while he makes up his mind. This brisk tempo will be possible only when the teacher is sure of his plan.

4. The class should *not* be kept for *too long at one type of activity,* even when the students appear to be enjoying it. The teacher should not wait until his students cease to enjoy what they are doing before calling a new tune. Too much drilling, even of difficult and essential structures, can lead to emotional fatigue, absent-mindedness, and boredom; it can also cause the student to become so fixed in the use of certain patterns that he is incapable of using them flexibly in communication. Too much reading and writing means the neglecting of classroom opportunities for practicing the communication skills; too much unsystematic oral work often means that the student has little opportunity for studying new material about which he may talk. A well-designed lesson will contain a number of different activities, with a return to certain exercises at intervals for further consolidation of learning. Frequent spaced practice is more effective than great blocks of one activity for undue lengths of time.

5. The teacher should plan to *do in class what cannot be done out of class*. This requires careful thought. It means that the student must have sufficient classroom time for practice in communication under the teacher's supervision. It does not mean that all reading and writing will be done out of class. This may be an unwise procedure, as we have seen in chapters 9 and 10. The student will do out of class only what the teacher knows he can do on his own with reasonable probability of success. Out-of-class work will consolidate learning done in class. At more advanced stages, it will include preparation for work to be done in subsequent lessons.

6. The lesson should be planned so that the class is on its toes: *never sure of what comes next*. Nothing is more tedious for the student than lessons which always follow the same pattern. Many lessons will inevitably contain very similar activities, but the ordering of the elements should be varied: some being included today, some left out, a few kept for occasional inclusion. Imagination must direct the final form of the plan.

7. The teacher should be ready to *toss aside his plan* or change it as he goes along. The mood of the class, the unexpected difficulty or simplicity of some section of the work, an interesting possibility which did not occur to the teacher when drawing up his plan—all of these things, and many others, may cause him to change his mind about the appropriate form for the next step in the progression. Although the teacher must be ready to change his plan, he must not do so on a whim; he should know why he is changing it and in what direction his new plan will take the students.

INGREDIENTS

1. After the early stages, or the prereading period, each lesson should provide *some practice in each of the four skills*, not necessarily in the same proportion. Not only does one activity consolidate the other, but a change of activity keeps the interest of the class. This does not mean that there will be practice in listening to, speaking, reading, and writing the same material during the one lesson. What has already been heard in a

previous lesson may be being repeated by the class or being used for practice in communication; what has already been heard and said may be being read; what has already been heard, said, and read may be being written; what has already been studied in oral or graphic form may be being drilled. There will be a continual interplay among new elements and familiar elements, so that what has already been learned is not allowed to fade from the memory.

2. Each lesson must have *variety and some spice.* Since there are many ways of presenting and practicing material in all the skill areas, there is no reason for the teacher to keep to certain well-worn techniques. The spice is provided by surprise items (a language game, an anecdote, some cultural information with a visual accompaniment, a culture quiz, or a competitive test of what has been learned).

3. The teacher should think up *games and competitions* which provide the same type of activity as drills and exercises. The old game of "Simon Says" can be adapted to dialogue repetition: the teacher repeats dialogue sentences with or without prefixing a foreign-language equivalent of "Simon Says." A chaining game where each student in turn must change a certain element in the sentence is very similar to a substitution drill. A game or competition which provides the same habit-forming practice is more amusing and spontaneous than a drill, and students will continue doing the same thing for a longer period without boredom.

4. A *repertoire of songs* well learned can always be called upon to bring variety to the lesson. A simple song, with uncomplicated words and some repetition, relaxes and refreshes the class. The period of singing need not be prolonged. It should not always occur at the end of the lesson, although sometimes this is where it is most appropriate. It may provide a very welcome interlude in the middle of a period of hard work.

AND SO, THE PLAN

The danger in trying to set down a plan for a language lesson is that some inexperienced persons may take it to be *the* plan, and continue to follow it unswervingly from lesson to lesson. This would violate Principle 6.

—The lesson should begin with some *review* of the work of previous lessons. This may take the form of oral practice of material set for home study or of some of the work of the previous day; it may provide an opportunity to reuse material from previous units, in questions and answers or in a contrived communication situation. For variety, this review may involve some brief writing activity. At a more advanced stage, students may have oral reports to present to the class.

—*New work* is now introduced in an interesting fashion. Some dialogue sentences may be memorized; it may be the day for reading a recombination narrative which the students will listen to before they read it. The new work will be studied and practiced until the students are very familiar with it.

—Out of the new work will emerge *some sections which must be drilled*. As they are being drilled, some short explanations may prove to be necessary. After the main point of the drill appears to be assimilated, some individual response, competition, or game will show whether the students have thoroughly mastered what they have been learning. If not, the teacher will return briefly to the drill, or reserve it for a second practice a little later in the lesson. Some teachers have found that if practice on material which has not been well assimilated is deferred till the next day student performance shows considerable improvement over the work of the previous day. Once again, teachers will vary their approach on different occasions.

—There follows a period for the *practical application* of what has been learned. The teacher may engage the students in an interchange of communication using what they have drilled; later, this work may be combined with elements from earlier lessons. The application may involve reading a passage for which previous work has prepared the class; it may necessitate some form of writing exercise; or it may take the form of a dramatization in front of the class. The teacher may initiate a game which enables the students to use what they have learned, while concentrating on the progress of the game or on the success of their team. If they are able to use material successfully during such an activity, the teacher has some evidence that they have assimilated it.

—There will now be some *preparation of the work for home study*. This will not necessarily be overt preparation. The teacher, knowing what he will later ask the students to do, will see that he has prepared all the aspects of it which could cause problems for the students. He may induce them to discuss orally what he will be assigning as a written exercise; he may give them practice in reading what they will be asked to copy or adapt at home; he may discuss with them material he will later ask them to read by themselves.

He will take care to see that the homework is assigned well before the final bell so that each student may have a clear idea of what he is being asked to do.

—The lesson will *end with a relaxing and enjoyable activity* in the foreign language: some acting out of recombination conversations, a game, a song, a short, illustrated talk on some aspect of the culture. No matter what form this activity may take, the teacher should plan his lesson so that the students will have time to relax and enjoy the use of the foreign language before the end of the lesson is signaled. The students should leave the classroom in a cheerful mood, feeling that foreign-language lessons are among the best in the day.

DISCIPLINE AND CLASSROOM MANAGEMENT

During his training, and in the early weeks of his first teaching appointment, the inexperienced teacher is bombarded with helpful hints on how to establish a satisfactory relationship with his students. Every teacher with whom he works has his favorites. The following suggestions provide nothing new, but give a short, nonexhaustive summary of what every good teacher discovers as he teaches. Attention to these hints may save the new teacher from some uncomfortable experiences.

To keep good discipline in the classroom, it is essential to *know the students' names* as soon as possible. Nothing disconcerts the erring student or arrests an incipient disturbance so quickly as calling an individual by his name. Many a young teacher has lost control of a class during an overlong initial period of anonymity.

A class which is *kept actively involved* has little time or energy for disruptive activities. Choral recitation or drill, rapid change of roles from group to group, brisk alternation of oral and written work, constant shifting of response from individual to group and from group to individual, questions asked of everyone, even the weakest, in no recognizable order so that the students do not know at any moment when they will be called upon to participate, class repetition of individual response, group practice in reading: these are all techniques for keeping the attention of students on the progress of the lesson. The teacher who constantly relies on individual responses, asking questions in order around the class, must expect a high proportion of students to be inattentive at some period during the lesson.

If the teacher feels the time has come for *a sequence of individual responses* and wants to ensure that all are finally interrogated, he should crisscross around the class in a pattern which cannot be identified by the students. This has the same effect on the students as a random choice, while enabling the teacher to verify the progress of each in turn. The teacher should always ask the question first, then name the student for individual response; this induces all the students to think about the answer while waiting to see if they will be asked the question. Name first, question afterwards, is an invitation to the rest of the students to think of other things.

When a student answers a question sincerely he should never be made to feel stupid or ignorant; the teacher should take what elements he can from the answer and use it for further teaching, or as the basis of a question to another student. When an answer is unsatisfactory, the teacher should consider carefully whether the wrong answer was an indication of laziness or inattention on the part of the student or whether it was the result of weakness in his own presentation and insufficient drilling of the point at issue. When a student has given a wrong answer, the teacher should put the same question to another student and, on receipt of the correct answer, put the question again to the student who made the mistake. An alternative to this procedure is to ask the class to repeat the correct answer in chorus, since the point where one student has made a mistake is frequently the place where other students are weak. Students should be encouraged to ask about things that puzzle them, even apparently simple things. Because what puzzles one usually puzzles others in the group, such questions often show the teacher where his explanations or presentation were deficient.

As the year progresses, *the problems of the bright, fast-working student and the dull, slow, frustrated student* will emerge. The bright student may be asked more difficult questions, invited to help lead the drills, encouraged to do extra, more demanding, work, or be set to help others in the class. The slow student must not be humiliated or embarrassed if he is working to the best of his ability. His deficiencies will not be very obvious to the other students in group work in the early stages, or in the laboratory. Later, he must be encouraged to work thoroughly on some portions of each unit, even if he cannot keep up with the class at every point. He may at times be asked simple questions he can answer without difficulty to give him a feeling of success and of participation in the work of the group.

Early in his acquaintance with the class, the teacher must be able to *detect the potential nuisances* so that he may keep them busy and involved in activities. A question aimed at the inattentive before mischief has started, or a call to participate in some activity, is a good preventive move. Sarcasm should never be used; it gives the teacher an unfair advantage over a student who, if he is nettled into replying, will be considered insolent. In dealing with problem students, the teacher must never threaten what he cannot or does not intend to put into action. An extreme threat often obliges the teacher, in a calmer moment, to retreat from his position, and the unruly student has won the day. The student will remember this on a later occasion. Restlessness and inattention on a general scale are often an indication to the teacher that he is laboring the point, or that he has kept the class for too long at the same type of activity. A sudden switch from oral work to a written exercise, or from individual work to choral drill or some other group activity, will often recall the attention of the students.

The teacher must *always keep faith* with his students. If he has asked them to prepare some work for the day's class, he must remember to check on it; if he has told them to expect a test, he must give it. The conscientious and hard-working have reason to feel resentful if the teacher is continually forgetful in these matters, while the lazy will soon learn how much work they can avoid without detection.

According to an old saying, the good teacher is born, not made. This refers to certain qualities of character and personality that enable some to gain the confidence and respect of students more quickly than others, to recognize the students' real problems and to approach these with clarity and patience. Most teachers acquire these abilities through practical experience. There are, however, many other requirements for the foreign-language teacher in this modern age. Many need to improve their own foreign-language skills, others need opportunities to keep their aural-oral skills at a high level. As priorities of objectives change, so do techniques. New technological discoveries bring new aids into the classroom; the teacher must learn to use these effectively. There may be new discoveries in linguistics or psychology which are relevant to his work. He must keep abreast of developments and achievements in the country where the language he is teaching is spoken; in some cases, he must study important changes in the language itself (a new spelling or writing system, an expanding lexis, evolution of structural variants, newly recognized simplification or complication of the phonemic system). Within his own classroom he should be alert to evaluate techniques on which he has come to rely and be ready to change and adapt them from year to year to increase their effectiveness.

In all these things the teacher is unwise to rely on his own resources. He should join professional associations, read and contribute to their journals, and participate in the professional discussion at their meetings and congresses. He should take advantage of the services put at his disposal for professional improvement: seminars, workshops, institutes, information centers. The teacher who remains alert professionally, evaluating carefully in the light of his experience what he has heard and read and contributing himself from his considered judgment, remains vital and interesting in the classroom, even after years of teaching the same subject. Each class is different; each year his approach is a little different, adapted to the new class and incorporating a little more of what he has learned from his colleagues and from his experience in the previous year. The beginning teacher should set before him this dual aim: to keep abreast of the developments in his profession and to keep growing professionally through systematic evaluation of his own experience.

QUALIFICATIONS FOR HIGH SCHOOL TEACHERS OF MODERN FOREIGN LANGUAGES

The appended statement of the Modern Language Association of America [6] will keep before the high school teacher what his objectives should be with regard to his own foreign-language skills and professional competence.

1. AURAL UNDERSTANDING

Minimal: The ability to get the sense of what an educated native says when he is enunciating carefully and speaking simply on a general subject.

Good: The ability to understand conversation at average tempo, lectures, and news broadcasts.

Superior: The ability to follow closely and with ease all types of standard speech, such as rapid or group conversation, plays, and movies.

Test: These abilities can be tested by dictations, by the Listening Comprehension Tests of the College Entrance Examination Board—thus far developed for French, German, and Spanish—or by similar tests for these and other languages, with an extension in range and difficulty for the superior level.

2. SPEAKING

Minimal: The ability to talk on prepared topics (e.g., for classroom situations), without obvious faltering, and to use the common expressions needed for getting around in the foreign country, speaking with a pronunciation readily understandable to a native.

Good: The ability to talk with a native without making glaring mistakes, and with a command of vocabulary and syntax sufficient to express one's thoughts in sustained conversation. This implies speech at normal speed with good pronunciation and intonation.

Superior: The ability to approximate native speech in vocabulary,

6 *PMLA,* 70, no. 4, pt. 2 (1955): 46–49.

intonation, and pronunciation (e.g., the ability to exchange ideas and to be at ease in social situations).

Test: For the present, this ability has to be tested by interview, or by a recorded set of questions with a blank disc or tape for recording answers.

3. READING

Minimal: The ability to grasp directly (i.e., without translating) the meaning of simple, nontechnical prose, except for an occasional word.

Good: The ability to read with immediate comprehension prose and verse of average difficulty and mature content.

Superior: The ability to read, almost as easily as in English, material of considerable difficulty, such as essays and literary criticism.

Test: These abilities can be tested by a graded series of timed reading passages, with comprehension questions and multiple-choice or free-response answers.

4. WRITING

Minimal: The ability to write correctly sentences or paragraphs such as would be developed orally for classroom situations, and the ability to write a short, simple letter.

Good: The ability to write a simple "free composition" with clarity and correctness in vocabulary, idiom, and syntax.

Superior: The ability to write on a variety of subjects with idiomatic naturalness, ease of expression, and some feeling for the style of the language.

Test: These abilities can be tested by multiple-choice syntax items, dictations, translation of English sentences or paragraphs, and a controlled letter or free composition.

5. LANGUAGE ANALYSIS

Minimal: A working command of the sound-patterns and grammar-patterns of the foreign language, and a knowledge of its main differences from English.

Good: A basic knowledge of the historical development and present characteristics of the language, and an awareness of the difference between the language as spoken and as written.

Superior: Ability to apply knowledge of descriptive, comparative, and historical linguistics to the language-teaching situation.

Test: Such information and insight can be tested for levels 1 and 2 by multiple-choice and free-response items on pronunciation, intonation patterns, and syntax; for levels 2 and 3, items on philology and descriptive linguistics.

6. CULTURE

Minimal: An awareness of language as an essential element among the learned and shared experiences that combine to form a particular culture, and a rudimentary knowledge of the geography, history, literature, art, social customs, and contemporary civilization of the foreign people.

Good: First-hand knowledge of some literary masterpieces, and understanding of the principal ways in which the foreign culture resembles and differs from our own, and possession of an organized body of information on the foreign people and their civilization.

Superior: An enlightened understanding of the foreign people and their culture, achieved through personal contact, preferably by travel and residence abroad, through study of systematic descriptions of the foreign culture, and through study of literature and the arts.

Test: Such information and insight can be tested by multiple-choice literary and cultural acquaintance tests for levels 1 and 2; for level 3, written comments on passages of prose or poetry, that discuss or reveal significant aspects of the foreign culture.

7. PROFESSIONAL PREPARATION

Minimal: Some knowledge of effective methods and techniques of language teaching.

Good: The ability to apply knowledge of methods and techniques to the teaching situation (e.g., audio-visual techniques) and to relate one's teaching of the language to other areas of the curriculum.

Superior: A mastery of recognized teaching methods, and the ability to experiment with and evaluate new methods and techniques.

Test: Such knowledge and ability can be tested by multiple-choice answers to questions on pedagogy and language-teaching methods, plus written comment on language-teaching situations.

ANNOTATED READING LIST

Foreign Languages in the Elementary School

ANDERSSON, THEODORE. "The Optimum Age for Beginning the Study of Modern Languages." *International Review of Education 6, no. 3* (1960): 298–308. Reprinted in *Readings in Foreign Languages for the Elementary School,* edited by S. LEVENSON and W. KENDRICK. Waltham, Mass.: Blaisdell, 1967. Pp. 61–69. Examines the psychological and physiological justification for early foreign-language learning. (Although many of the articles reprinted in *Readings* have little to do with FLES, others are of considerable interest to specialists in this field.)

DONOGHUE, MILDRED R. *Foreign Languages and the Elementary School Child.* Dubuque, Ia.: William Brown Co., 1968. Discusses the psychological and linguistic background of FLES and examines research in the field. Sets out appropriate classroom techniques and lesson plans, and lists instructional resources for French, German, and Spanish.

FINOCCHIARO, M. *Teaching Children Foreign Languages.* New York: McGraw-Hill, 1964. A very practical study of all aspects of foreign-language teaching in elementary schools. Examples mainly in English, French, and Spanish.

STERN, H. H., ed. *Foreign Languages in Primary Education.* Hamburg: UNESCO Institute for Education, 1963. Conference report.

The Teacher in the Classroom

NORTHEAST CONFERENCE (1968). *Foreign Language Learning: Research and Development,* edited by T. E. BIRD. Report of Working Committee II: "The Classroom Revisited" (pp. 58–72) outlines the various roles of the teacher in the classroom and discusses the planning of the foreign-language lesson.

BIBLIOGRAPHY

AGARD, F. B., and DI PIETRO, R. J., 1965. *The Grammatical Structures of English and Italian.* Contrastive Structure Series. CHARLES A. FERGUSON, General Editor. Chicago: University of Chicago Press.

————. 1965. *The Sounds of English and Italian.* Contrastive Structure Series. CHARLES A. FERGUSON, General Editor. Chicago: University of Chicago Press.

ALATIS, JAMES E., ed. 1968. *Contrastive Linguistics and its Pedagogical Implications.* Monograph Series on Languages and Linguistics, no. 21 (19th Roundtable). Washington, D.C.: Georgetown University Press.

ALLEN, HAROLD B., ed. 1965. *Teaching English as a Second Language: A Book of Readings.* New York: McGraw-Hill.

ANDERSSON, THEODORE. 1960. "The Optimum Age for Beginning the Study of Modern Languages." *International Review of Education* 6, no. 3 (1960): 298–308. Reprinted in *Readings in Foreign Languages for the Elementary School,* edited by S. LEVENSON and W. KENDRICK.

BROOKS, NELSON. 1964. *Language and Language Learning—Theory and Practice.* 2d ed. New York: Harcourt, Brace & Co. 1st ed., 1960.

————. 1968. "Teaching Culture in the Foreign Language Classroom," *FL Annals* 1, no. 3: 204–17.

BROWN, ROGER W. *et al.* 1953. "Developing Cultural Understanding through Foreign Language Study: A Report of the MLA Interdisciplinary Seminar in Language and Culture." *PMLA* 48, no. 5 (1953): 1196–1218.

CARDENAS, D. 1961. *Applied Linguistics: Spanish. A Guide for Teachers.* Boston: D. C. Heath & Co.

CARROLL, JOHN B. 1963. "A Primer of Programmed Instruction in Foreign Language Teaching." *IRAL* I/2 (1963): 115–41.

————. 1964. *Language and Thought.* Foundations of Modern Psychology Series. Englewood Cliffs, N.J.: Prentice-Hall.

————. 1953. *The Study of Language.* Cambridge, Mass.: Harvard University Press.

CHOMSKY, NOAM. 1965. *Aspects of the Theory of Syntax.* Cambridge, Mass.: M.I.T. Press.

————. 1966. "Linguistic Theory." In Northeast Conference on the Teaching of Foreign Languages, 1966, Reports of the Working Committees, edited by ROBERT G. MEAD, JR. [hereinafter referred to as Northeast Conference (1966)].

————. 1957. *Syntactic Structures.* The Hague: Mouton & Co.

DACANAY, FE R. 1963. *Techniques and Procedures in Second Language Teaching,* edited by J. DONALD BOWEN. Quezon City: Alemar-Phoenix Publishing House. Distributed in the U.S.A. by Oceana Publications, Dobbs Ferry, N.Y.

DELATTRE, PIERRE. 1951. *Principes de phonétique française à l'usage des étudiants anglo-américains.* Middlebury, Vt.: Middlebury College.

DODSON, C. J. 1967. *Language Teaching and the Bilingual Method.* London: Sir Isaac Pitman & Sons Ltd.

DONOGHUE, MILDRED R. 1968. *Foreign Languages and the Elementary School Child.* Dubuque, Ia.: William Brown Co.

DONOGHUE, MILDRED R., ed. 1967. *Foreign Languages and the Schools: A Book of Readings.* Dubuque, Ia.: William Brown Co.

FEIGENBAUM, I. 1965. "The Cultural Setting of Language Teaching." *English Teaching Forum,* 3, no. 4 (Winter, 1965): 11–13.

FINOCCHIARO, MARY. 1964. *Teaching Children Foreign Languages.* New York: McGraw-Hill.

FODOR, JERRY A., and KATZ, JERROLD J., eds. 1964. *The Structure of Language: Readings in the Philosophy of Language.* Englewood Cliffs, N.J.: Prentice-Hall.

FOTITCH, T., ed. 1961. *Teaching Foreign Languages in the Modern World*. Washington, D.C.: Catholic University of America Press.

FRIES, CHARLES C. 1963. *Linguistics and Reading*. New York: Holt, Rinehart & Winston.

————. 1945. *Teaching and Learning English as a Foreign Language*. Ann Arbor, Mich.: University of Michigan Press.

GEORGETOWN UNIVERSITY INSTITUTE OF LANGUAGES AND LINGUISTICS. 1961. *The Meaning and Role of Culture in Foreign Language Teaching*. Report of Conference, March, 1961. Mimeographed.

GLEASON, H. A., JR. 1961. *An Introduction to Descriptive Linguistics*. Rev. ed. New York: Holt, Rinehart & Winston.

————. 1965. *Linguistics and English Grammar*. New York: Holt, Rinehart & Winston.

GRAVIT, FRANCIS W., and VALDMAN, ALBERT, eds. 1963. *Structural Drill and the Language Laboratory*. INTERNATIONAL JOURNAL OF AMERICAN LINGUISTICS, vol. 29, no. 2. Publication 27 of the Indiana University Research Center in Anthropology, Folklore, and Linguistics.) The Hague: Mouton & Co.

GRAZIA, ALFRED DE, and SOHN, DAVID A., eds. 1964. *Programs, Teachers and Machines*. New York: Bantam Books.

GRITTNER, FRANK M. *Foreign Language Teaching in America's Schools*. New York: Harper & Row (forthcoming).

HALL, ROBERT A. 1961. *Applied Linguistics: Italian—A Guide for Teachers*. Boston: D. C. Heath & Co.

HALL, ROBERT A. 1966. *New Ways to Learn a Foreign Language*. New York: Bantam Books.

HALLIDAY, M.; MCINTOSH, A.; and STREVENS, P. 1964. *The Linguistic Sciences and Language Teaching*. London: Longmans.

HAYES, ALFRED S. 1963. *Language Laboratory Facilities*. Washington, D.C.: U.S. Office of Education. Reprint forthcoming, Oxford University Press.

HOCKING, ELTON. 1964. *Language Laboratory and Language Learning*. Washington, D.C.: Department of Audio-Visual Instruction of the N.E.A.

HOLTON, J.; KING, P.; MATHIEU, G.; and POND, K. 1961. *Sound Language Teaching*. New York: University Publishers.

HUEBENER, THEODORE. 1961. *Why Johnny Should Learn Foreign Languages*. Philadelphia and New York: Chilton Co.

HUGHES, JOHN P. 1968. *Linguistics and Language Teaching*. New York: Random House.

HUTCHINSON, JOSEPH C. 1961. *Modern Foreign Languages in High School: The Language Laboratory*. Washington, D.C.: U.S. Department of Health, Education, and Welfare, OE 27013. Bulletin 1961, no. 23.

JERMAN, J.; VAN ABBÉ, D.; and DUTTON, B. 1965. *A Guide to Modern Language Teaching Methods*. London: Cassell & Co. Ltd.

JESPERSEN, OTTO. 1904. *How to Teach a Foreign Language*. London: George Allen & Unwin Ltd. Reissued, 1961.

KUFNER, H. 1962. *The Grammatical Structures of English and German*. Contrastive Structure Series. CHARLES A. FERGUSON, General Editor. Chicago: University of Chicago Press.

LADO, ROBERT. 1964. *Language Teaching: A Scientific Approach*. New York: McGraw-Hill.

———. 1961. *Language Testing*. London: Longmans.

LAMBERT, WALLACE E., and KLINEBERG, OTTO. 1967. *Children's Views of Foreign Peoples*. New York: Appleton-Century-Crofts.

LEAVITT, STURGIS E. 1962. "The Teaching of Spanish in the United States." In *Reports of Surveys and Studies in the Teaching of Modern Foreign Languages*, edited by J. W. CHILDERS, DONALD D. WALSH, and G. WINCHESTER STONE, JR. New York: Modern Language Association of America.

Le français dans le monde 41 (June, 1966). Numéro Spécial sur les Exercices Structuraux.

LÉON, PIERRE R. 1962. *Laboratoire de Langues et Correction Phonétique.* Paris: Didier.

LEVENSON, STANLEY, and KENDRICK, WILLIAM, eds. 1967. *Readings in Foreign Languages for the Elementary School.* Waltham, Mass.: Blaisdell Publishing Co.

LUMSDAINE, A. A., and GLASER, R., eds. 1960. *Teaching Machines and Programmed Learning.* Washington, D.C.: Department of Audio-Visual Instruction of the N.E.A.

MACKEY, WILLIAM F. 1965. *Language Teaching Analysis.* London: Longmans.

MAGNER, T. 1961. *Applied Linguistics: Russian—A Guide for Teachers.* Boston: D. C. Heath & Co.

MARCHAND, J. 1960. *Applied Linguistics: German—A Guide for Teachers.* Boston: D. C. Heath & Co.

MARCKWARDT, ALBERT H. 1967. "Teaching English as a Foreign Language: A Survey of the Past Decade." *Linguistic Reporter,* Supplement 19 (October, 1967): 1–8.

MARTY, FERNAND. 1960. *Language Laboratory Learning.* Wellesley, Mass.: Audio-Visual Publications.

———. 1962. *Programing a Basic Foreign Language Course.* Hollins College, Va.

MATHIEU, G., ed. 1966. *Advances in the Teaching of Modern Languages.* Vol. 2. London: Pergamon Press.

MICHEL, JOSEPH, ed. 1967. *Foreign Language Teaching.* New York: MacMillan Co.

MILLER, GEORGE A. 1951. *Language and Communication.* New York: McGraw-Hill.

MODERN LANGUAGE ASSOCIATION OF AMERICA. 1956. "FL Program Policy." *PMLA* 71, pt. 2 (September, 1956): xiii–xxiv. Reprinted in *Foreign Language Teaching,* edited by JOSEPH MICHEL. New York: MacMillan Co., 1967.

———. 1962. *MLA Selective List of Materials for Use by Teachers of Modern Foreign Languages,* edited by MARY J. OLLMAN. New York: Modern Language Association of America. (1964 Supplement for French and Italian; 1964 Supplement for Spanish and Portuguese; 1964 Supplement for German, Norwegian, Polish, Russian, and Swedish.)

———. 1962. *Reports of Surveys and Studies in the Teaching of Modern Foreign Languages, 1959–1961,* edited by J. W. CHILDERS, DONALD D. WALSH, and G. WINCHESTER STONE, JR. New York: Modern Language Association of America.

MOULTON, WILLIAM G. 1966. *A Linguistic Guide to Language Learning.* New York: Modern Language Association of America.

———. 1961. "Linguistics and Language Teaching in the United States 1940–1960," in C. MOHRMANN, A. SOMMERFELT, and J. WHATMOUGH, eds. *Trends in European and American Linguistics, 1930–1960.* Utrecht: Spectrum Publishers.

———. 1962. *The Sounds of English and German.* Contrastive Structure Series. CHARLES A. FERGUSON, General Editor. Chicago: University of Chicago Press.

NEWMARK, MAXIM, ed. 1948. *Twentieth Century Modern Language Teaching: Sources and Readings.* New York: Philosophical Library.

NIDA, EUGENE A. 1957. *Learning a Foreign Language.* Rev. ed. Ann Arbor, Mich.: Friendship Press.

———. 1964. *Toward a Science of Translating.* Leiden: E. J. Brill.

Northeast Conference (1959): FREDERICK D. EDDY, ed. *The Language Learner.* Containing: Modern Foreign Language Learning: Assumptions and Implications; A Six-Year Sequence; Elementary and Junior High School Curricula; Definition of Language Competences through Testing.

Northeast Conference (1960): G. REGINALD BISHOP, ed. *Culture in Language Learning.* Containing: An Anthropological Concept of Culture; Language as Culture; Teaching of Western European Cultures; Teaching of Classical Cultures; Teaching of Slavic Cultures.

Northeast Conference (1961): SEYMOUR L. FLAXMAN, ed. *Modern Language Teaching in School and College.* Containing: The Training of Teachers for Secondary Schools; The Preparation of College and University Teachers; The Transition to the Classroom; Coordination between Classroom and Laboratory.

Northeast Conference (1962): WILLIAM F. BOTTIGLIA, ed. *Current Issues in Language Teaching.* Containing: Linguistics and Language Teaching; Programmed Learning; A Survey of FLES Practices; Televised Teaching.

Northeast Conference (1963): WILLIAM F. BOTTIGLIA, ed. *Language Learning: The Intermediate Phase.* Containing: The Continuum: Listening and Speaking; Reading for Meaning; Writing as Expression.

Northeast Conference (1964): GEORGE FENWICK JONES, ed. *Foreign Language Teaching: Ideals and Practices.* Containing: Foreign Languages in the Elementary School; Foreign Languages in the Secondary School; Foreign Languages in Colleges and Universities.

Northeast Conference (1965): G. REGINALD BISHOP, ed. *Foreign Language Teaching: Challenges to the Profession.* Containing: The Case for Latin; Study Abroad; The Challenge of Bilingualism; From School to College.

Northeast Conference (1966): ROBERT G. MEAD, JR., ed. *Language Teaching: Broader Contexts.* Containing: Research and Language Learning; Content and Crossroads: Wider Uses for Foreign Languages; The Coordination of Foreign-Language Teaching.

Northeast Conference (1967): THOMAS E. BIRD, ed. *Foreign Languages: Reading, Literature, and Requirements.* Containing: The Teaching of Reading; The Times and Places for Literature; Trends in FL Requirements and Placement.

NORTHEAST CONFERENCE (1968): THOMAS E. BIRD, ed. *Foreign Language Learning: Research and Development.* Containing: Innovative FL Programs; The Classroom Revisited; Liberated Expression.

NOSTRAND, HOWARD L. 1965. *Research on Language Teaching: An Annotated International Bibliography, 1945–64.* Seattle: University of Washington Press.

O'CONNOR, PATRICIA. 1960. *Modern Foreign Languages in High School: Pre-Reading Instruction.* Washington, D.C.: U.S. Office of Education, OE 27000.

OHANNESSIAN S. *et al.,* eds. 1964. *Reference List of Materials for English as a Second Language.* Washington, D.C.: Center for Applied Linguistics.

PALMER, H. E. 1921. *The Principles of Language-Study.* London: Harrap. Reprinted, 1964. London: Oxford University Press.

PARKER, W. R. 1962. *The National Interest and Foreign Languages.* 3d ed. Washington, D.C.: National Commission for UNESCO, Department of State.

PARRY, ALBERT. 1967. *America Learns Russian.* Syracuse, N.Y.: Syracuse University Press.

PIMSLEUR, PAUL. 1964. "Under-Achievement in Foreign Language Learning." *IRAL* II/2 (1964): 113–50.

POLITZER, ROBERT L. 1965. *Foreign Language Learning: A Linguistic Introduction.* Englewood Cliffs, N.J.: Prentice-Hall.

———. 1965. *Teaching French: An Introduction to Applied Linguistics.* 2d ed. New York: Blaisdell Publishing Co. 1st ed., Boston: Ginn & Co., 1961.

———. 1968. *Teaching German: A Linguistic Orientation.* Waltham, Mass.: Blaisdell Publishing Co.

POLITZER, ROBERT L., and STAUBACH, C. 1961. *Teaching Spanish: A Linguistic Orientation.* Boston: Ginn & Co.

PRATOR, JR., C. H. 1957. *A Manual of American English Pronunciation.* Rev. ed. New York: Holt, Rinehart & Winston.

RIVERS, WILGA M. 1964. *The Psychologist and the Foreign-Language Teacher.* Chicago: University of Chicago Press.

SAUSSURE, FERDINAND DE. 1959. *Course in General Linguistics,* edited by C. BALLY and A. SECHEHAYE; translated by WADE BASKIN. New York: Philosophical Library.

SCHERER, GEORGE A. C. 1964. "Programming Second Language Reading." In *Teacher's Notebook,* Spring 1964. New York: Harcourt, Brace & World. Reprinted in *Advances in the Teaching of Modern Languages,* vol. 2, edited by G. MATHIEU.

————., and WERTHEIMER, MICHAEL. 1964. *A Psycholinguistic Experiment in Foreign-language Teaching.* New York: McGraw-Hill.

SHANNON, CLAUDE E., and WEAVER, WARREN. 1959. *The Mathematical Theory of Communication.* Urbana, Ill.: University of Illinois Press.

STACK, EDWARD M. 1966. *The Language Laboratory and Modern Language Teaching.* Rev. ed. New York: Oxford University Press.

STERN, H. H. 1963. *Foreign Languages in Primary Education.* Hamburg: UNESCO Institute for Education.

STEVICK, E. W. 1963. *A Workbook in Language Teaching with Special Reference to English as a Foreign Language.* New York: Abingdon Press.

STOCKWELL, R. P. and BOWEN, J. D. 1965. *The Sounds of English and Spanish.* Contrastive Structure Series. CHARLES A. FERGUSON, General Editor. Chicago: University of Chicago Press.

STOCKWELL, R. P.; BOWEN, J. D.; and MARTIN, JOHN W. 1965. *The Grammatical Structures of English and Spanish.* Contrastive Structure Series. CHARLES A. FERGUSON, General Editor. Chicago: University of Chicago Press.

STREVENS, P. D. 1965. *Papers in Language and Language Teaching.* London: Oxford University Press.

SWEET, H. 1899. *The Practical Study of Languages.* London: Dent. Reprinted 1964. London: Oxford University Press.

THOMPSON, MARY P. 1965. "Writing in an Audio-Lingual Modern Foreign Language Program." In *Teacher's Notebook,* Spring 1965. New York: Harcourt, Brace & World. Reprinted in *Foreign Languages and the Schools,* edited by M. R. DONOGHUE, and in *Readings in Foreign Languages for the Elementary School,* edited by S. LEVENSON and W. KENDRICK.

TITONE, RENZO. 1968. *Teaching Foreign Languages: An Historical Sketch.* Washington, D.C.: Georgetown University Press.

VALDMAN, ALBERT. 1961. *Applied Linguistics: French—A Guide to Teachers.* Boston: D.C. Heath & Co., 1961.

————, ed. 1966. *Trends in Language Teaching.* New York: McGraw-Hill.

VALETTE, REBECCA M. 1967. *Modern Language Testing: A Handbook.* New York: Harcourt, Brace & World.

WATTS, GEORGE B. 1963. "The Teaching of French in the United States: a History." *French Review* 37, no. 1 (1963): 9–165.

WEST, MICHAEL. 1941. *Learning to Read a Foreign Language.* London: Longmans.

WYLIE, L.; FLEISSNER, E. M.; MARICHAL, J.; PITKIN, D.; and SIMMONS, E. S. 1962. "Six Cultures (French, German, Hispanic, Italian, Luso-Brazilian, Russian): Selective and Annotated Bibliographies." In *Reports of Surveys and Studies in the Teaching of Modern Foreign Languages,* edited by J. W. CHILDERS, DONALD D. WALSH, and G. WINCHESTER STONE, JR. New York: Modern Language Association of America.

ZEYDEL, EDWIN H. 1962. "The Teaching of German in the United States from Colonial Times to the Present." In *Reports of Surveys and Studies in the Teaching of Modern Foreign Languages,* edited by J. W. CHILDERS, DONALD D. WALSH, and G. WINCHESTER STONE, JR. New York: Modern Language Association of America.

Index

Variations in pitch. *See* Intonation

Vincent, W., 354

Vocabulary: and speaking, 208–10; tests of, 300–301

Weaver, W., 137

Webster's Third New International Dictionary, 33–34

Whorf, Benjamin, 284; *Language, Thought, and Reality*, 282–83

Word groups, reading in, 224–25

Writing: accuracy in, 258–60; and audio-lingual method, 52–54; as composition, 243, 252–55; and copying (transcription), 245–46; correction of, 255–57; and dictation, 247, 249–50; and dictionaries, 252, 253; guided, 250–52; as notation (spelling), 242–43; as practice, 243; and reading, 52–54, 244, 254–55; and recombination, 247–50; and reproduction, 246–47; and speaking, 202, 207–8

Wylie, Laurence, 280